DUMBARTON OAKS TEXTS

XIII

NICETAS DAVID

THE LIFE

OF

PATRIARCH IGNATIUS

CORPUS FONTIUM
HISTORIAE BYZANTINAE

CONSILIO SOCIETATIS INTERNATIONALIS
STUDIIS BYZANTINIS PROVEHENDIS
DESTINATAE EDITUM

VOLUMEN LI

NICETAE DAVIDIS

VITA
IGNATII PATRIARCHAE

EDIDIT, ANGLICE VERTIT
ANDREW SMITHIES

ADNOTAVIT
JOHN M. DUFFY

SERIES WASHINGTONIENSIS,
EDIDIT JOHN M. DUFFY

In aedibus Dumbarton Oaks
Washingtoniae, D.C.
MMXIII

NICETAS DAVID

THE LIFE OF PATRIARCH IGNATIUS

TEXT AND TRANSLATION

by

ANDREW SMITHIES

with notes by

JOHN M. DUFFY

DUMBARTON OAKS

RESEARCH LIBRARY AND COLLECTION

WASHINGTON, D.C.

2013

LIBRARY OF CONGRESS CATALOGING-IN-PUBLICATION DATA

Nicetas, the Paphlagonian, 10th century.
The life of Patriarch Ignatius = Vita Ignatii Patriarchae / Nicetas David;
Greek text and translation by Andrew Smithies ; with notes by John M. Duffy.
    p.   cm.
(Dumbarton Oaks texts ; 13) (Corpus Fontium Historiae Byzantinae ; 51)
Title on page preceding title page: Vita Ignatii Patriarchae
In Greek; with English translation.
Includes bibliographical references and index.
ISBN 978-0-88402-381-4 (hardcover)
1. Ignatius, Patriarch of Constantinople, 797-877.
2. Photius I, Saint, Patriarch of Constantinople, approximately 820-891.
3. Orthodox Eastern Church—Biography.
4. Constantinople (Ecumenical patriarchate)—History.
5. Church history—9th century.
I. Smithies, Andrew. II. Duffy, John M.
III. Nicetas, the Paphlagonian, 10th century. Vita Ignatii Patriarchae.
IV. Nicetas, the Paphlagonian, 10th century. Vita Ignatii Patriarchae. English.
V. Title. VI. Title: Vita Ignatii Patriarchae.
BX395.I453N53   2013
270.3092—dc23
[B]
                                            2012047642

+

In accordance with the rules adopted by the
International Commission
for the Edition of Sources of Byzantine History,
the text and translation of this volume have been verified
by John Duffy and Nigel Wilson.

In memoriam

magistri eruditi et serenissimi

L. G. Westerink

CONTENTS

PREFACE

In 1987 Andrew Smithies submitted a critical edition of the text of the *Vita Ignatii*, along with an English translation, as a doctoral dissertation to the State University of New York at Buffalo, where his research was directed by the late L. G. Westerink. Subsequently Dr. Smithies, an Englishman by birth, took up residence in Australia, where he became a professional librarian in a field far removed from Byzantine studies. He has had a very successful career in libraries and until his recent retirement was in charge of the Australian Antarctic Division Library near Hobart on the island of Tasmania. In the intervening years his dissertation has been cited with some frequency, but has not been easily reachable for consultation. In view of the importance of the *Vita Ignatii* as a historical and cultural document and given the excellent quality of Dr. Smithies' edition and translation, there has long been a desire to see the work fully published in the *CFHB* series. In 2003, during a term spent at Dumbarton Oaks, I had the opportunity, kindly granted by the then Director of Byzantine Studies, Alice-Mary Talbot, to make the Smithies work the focus of a "reading group" for resident fellows and other scholars. The scholars participating were—in addition to Dr. Talbot—Denis Sullivan, Sofia Kotzabassi, Emmanuel Papoutsakis, Paul Stephenson, Aaron Johnson, and Conrad Leyser. The results of this productive exercise were a short list of minor improvements for text and translation and a longer list of additions to the apparatus of sources, the latter greatly facilitated by the *Thesaurus Linguae Graecae,* a resource not yet readily available in the 1980s.

In more recent times I was able to engage the services of a talented Harvard undergraduate, Michael Zellmann-Rohrer, who did an expert job of converting the original typescript of Introduction,

Greek text, and apparatus to electronic documents. Dr. Smithies did the same for the translation. For my part, I have contributed the set of notes to the text, and the Greek indices.

It remains for us to thank Nigel Wilson for verifying the quality of the text and translation, and to acknowledge the expertise and skillful help of the Dumbarton Oaks Publications Department, in particular Joel Kalvesmaki, Lionel Yaceczko, Noah Mlotek, and Kathleen Sparkes.

—John M. Duffy

INTRODUCTION

AUTHOR AND WORK

The *Vita Ignatii* attributed to Nicetas David the Paphlagonian is closely linked with the so-called Anti-Photian Collection, the greater part of which was probably compiled in the last decade of the ninth century.[1] That collection is presented as additional material in some manuscripts of the Greek acts of the anti-Photian eighth synod of Constantinople (869–870), and in most cases it is accompanied by the *Vita Ignatii*.[2] That fact led Assemanus to conjecture that Nicetas was also responsible for compiling the Anti-Photian Collection and in this he is followed by Dvornik, who admits, however, that some material must have been added after 899, probably by another copyist.[3] This assumes that Nicetas died in the 890s, which is close to the older accepted date of ca. 890.[4]

Using internal evidence from the *Vita Ignatii* itself, however, Jenkins has shown that a much more likely time for its composition is the period following the tetragamy scandal of 906–907.[5] Jenkins argues that Nicetas found in the situation faced by Ignatius over Bardas's sexual laxity a close parallel with that of Leo VI's fourth marriage and he sees a reference to the latter in a passage of the *Vita Ignatii* (PG 105:505D–508D = 28.29–32.2 in this edition), which he believes to have been inspired by a letter of Arethas on the same subject written in 906.[6] He is less convincing, however, as Westerink has pointed out,[7] when he tries to equate this passage with the hostile tract (mentioned in the *Vita Euthymii*)[8] which Nicetas wrote against patriarch Euthymius and emperor Leo in 907. That tract must have been a separate and highly libellous pamphlet. Nevertheless, Jenkins's thesis seems essentially correct and has the advantage of explaining Nicetas's motives in writing the *Vita Ignatii*: to castigate the conduct of patriarch Euthymius in the tetragamy scandal and to calumniate Photius, master of his own former master, Arethas, who had betrayed Nicetas with his change of mind on the same tetragamy issue.

Following the discovery of the hostile tract mentioned in the *Vita Euthymii* Nicetas was brought to trial and saved only by Euthymius himself, who interceded with the emperor on his behalf. Nicetas was then allowed to retire to (or was perhaps confined in) the Euthymian monastery of Agathou, where he remained for two years (908–910). It would seem, then, that the most likely date for Nicetas's composition of the *Vita Ignatii* would be between 910 and 920, the year in which all previous dissensions were closed by the reunion synod held in Constantinople, at which whatever had been written or said against Ignatius and Photius was declared forever anathema.[9]

Whether Nicetas alone was responsible for the content of the *Vita Ignatii* is not known. Karlin-Hayter thinks it unlikely that the narrative of events prior to 878 was the result of Nicetas's personal research and suggests that Nicetas simply reedited and added material to an already existing anti-Photian document.[10] In view of the fact that the *Vita Ignatii* is the only one of Nicetas's numerous panegyrics to contain anything of historical value,[11] this interpretation may well be correct. Whatever the case, it is quite natural that it should have been appended to the earlier body of material known as the Anti-Photian Collection.

Further biographical details on Nicetas the Paphlagonian are provided by Jenkins, who suggests that he was born not earlier than ca. 885 on the basis that "if Nicetas was still Arethas's pupil in 906, he is not unlikely to have been much over 20; but if he was already setting up as a teacher himself, he will not, however brilliant, have been less."[12] There is no indication of how long Nicetas lived, but Jenkins accepts Vogt's statement that he was still writing as late as 963.[13] Jenkins also reviews the many accretions which appear with Nicetas's name in various combinations in the different manuscripts, which have resulted in some modern scholars distinguishing up to three different people.[14] He rightly dismisses the title "bishop of Dadybra" either as a misinterpretation of Δᾱδ (sc. David) or as confusion with an earlier Nicetas, bishop of Dadybra, who signed the acts of the Seventh Council in 787, and concludes that there is no need to assume any more than a single individual. Westerink adds information on two of these accretions, pointing out, in relation to the term *rhetor*, that in the addresses of Arethas's letters Nicetas is called a *scholastikos*, which usually means a lawyer; and that the designation "Nicetas, also called David," in which David is supposed to be the monastic name, is comparatively rare in the manuscripts, which may indicate that he took vows only later in life.[15] In connection with this latter point it is interesting to note that in the oldest surviving manuscript of the *Vita Ignatii* (Venice Marcianus gr. 167 = **B**) the work is attributed to "Nicetas, servant of Jesus Christ," and the words "who is also David, the Paphlagonian" are added in the margin by another hand.

TRANSMISSION OF THE TEXT

The verdict of the reunion synod of 920, which had declared everything written or said against Photius and Ignatius forever anathema, was still being felt more than five hundred years later, at the time of the Council of Ferrara-Florence (1438–1439). At the opening of the fourth session at Ferrara, Cardinal Cesarini repeated an earlier request for the Greeks to lend him the book containing the Acts of the Eighth Synod (against Photius) and provoked a strongly worded response from Mark, metropolitan of Ephesus, who pointed out that the acts of that synod had been annulled and reiterated the declaration of anathema. It was only when the Cardinal quickly added that he wished to consult only the Acts of the Sixth and Seventh Synods (also contained in the book) that the metropolitan agreed to provide a copy for him.[16] Mark's unionist opponent, Gregory Mammas, patriarch of Constantinople, also writes in his refutation of Mark's profession of faith[17] that a book containing the same synod material was held by Μονὴ τοῦ Προδρόμου (ἐν τῇ

Πέτρᾳ)[18] and, furthermore, that a book containing the *Vita Ignatii* was held by Μονὴ (τῆς Θεοτόκου) τῆς Περιβλέπτου.[19]

It was another figure who played a prominent role in the Council of Florence, Cardinal Bessarion, who was ultimately responsible for the transfer of the text of the Anti-Photian Collection from East to West. An enthusiastic scholar and patron of scholars, he determined after the fall of Constantinople to collect as much as he could of extant Greek literature and in 1468 he bequeathed over thirty cases of manuscripts to St. Mark's in Venice. Two of these manuscripts, numbers 193 and 194 in the inventory published by Omont,[20] correspond to Venice Marcianus gr. 167 (**B**) and Munich gr. 436 (= **C**), the two oldest surviving manuscripts which contain the *Vita Ignatii* and the Anti-Photian Collection.

After Bessarion's death the manuscripts given to Venice were poorly protected and part of the collection found its way into private libraries. Despite an apostolic brief which excommunicated all who unlawfully kept volumes in their possession, the manuscripts were only partly restored.[21] One of the casualties was Munich gr. 436 (**C**), which is already noted as missing from the library in the catalogue compiled in 1545.[22] It does, however, appear to have remained in Venice, where it was used as a source for at least two other copies and eventually came into the possession of Manuel Glynzounios, a copyist and seller of books and manuscripts who was active in Venice from about 1570 until his death in 1596.[23] Although Glynzounios bequeathed all his manuscripts to the king of Spain, there is no trace of them going to Madrid or the Escurial, and Sicherl makes a strong case for believing that the fifty or so Greek codices put up for sale in Venice in 1602 and bought for the Augsburg library by Marcus Welser were in fact the manuscripts of Glynzounios.[24] They subsequently passed from Augsburg to Munich in 1806.[25]

The rediscovery of the *Vita Ignatii* and the Anti-Photian Collection in the West is closely associated with the Council of Trent (1545–1563) and no fewer than seven of the extant manuscripts were copied around this time (**EFGHJMP**). A key figure in that activity was Don Diego Hurtado de Mendoza,[26] Charles V's ambassador to Venice from the year 1538 or earlier and one of the Spanish emperor's representatives at the opening of the Council of Trent. A learned scholar and patron of the arts, he built up a magnificent library during his stay in Venice, employing scribes whom he sometimes sent to other parts of Italy or even outside the country in order to acquire or copy manuscripts. Escurial gr. X-I-5 (= **E**) was copied for Mendoza from the Venice codex (**B**) by Andronic Nuccius, probably in 1545, and corresponds to numbers 151, 152, and 153 of Mendoza's library.[27] It was in summer 1545 that his library was transferred from Venice to Trent and was thus made generally available to those attending the Council.[28]

From 1538 to 1546, the most active period in the creation of Mendoza's library, his librarian was Arnold Arlenius,[29] a copyist and editor skilled in both Latin and Greek, and he was constantly rendering services to travelers such as copying or acquiring books and manuscripts. He may well have been instrumental in acquiring a copy of the Venice codex (**B**) for the well-known Basle printer Henricus Petri, to whom Basle gr. O.II.25 (= **F**) is known to have belonged. This codex is made up of two manuscripts, the first of which contains the same material as the Venice codex, and it is at the head of the second manuscript that a later note makes the attribution to Arlenius.[30]

Of the remaining manuscripts of this group, Madrid gr. O.29 (= **G**) was copied in Venice in 1557 by Cornelius of Nauplion (from the colophon). The latter is known to have copied at least fourteen other codices in Venice between 1551 and 1565,[31] a number of them for Francisco de Mendoza y Bobadilla, the great literary patron and collector of manuscripts, who later became Cardinal of Coria, then of Burgos. The manuscript under discussion does not seem to have belonged to the Burgos collection, but strangely enough it did closely follow the movements of the Cardinal's library after his death.[32] Amsterdam University 68 (= **H**) belonged to Cardinal Granvelle, another of Charles V's representatives at the Council of Trent. Ottobonianus gr. 27 (= **J**) and Vatican gr. 1452 (= **P**) both belonged to Cardinal Sirleto, who was scriptor and (from 1554) custodian of the Vatican library and provided patristic texts from the manuscripts of the Vatican for the Council of Trent.[33] After Sirleto's death his manuscripts were sold to Cardinal Colonna in 1588[34] and it was in Colonna's library that Cardinal Baronius discovered the manuscripts of the *Vita Ignatii* (**P**) and the Anti-Photian Collection (**J**), of which he made extensive use in his *Annales ecclesiastici*, written between 1588 and 1601.[35] After Colonna's death the library was eventually sold to the Duc d'Altemps in 1611, but in the following year Paul V bought back thirty-six of Sirleto's Greek manuscripts for the Vatican. Altemps had copies of these manuscripts made for himself in 1619–20 and Ottobonianus gr. 138 (= **Q**) is the Altempsian copy of Vatican gr. 1452 (**P**). Finally, the other manuscript belonging to this group, Munich gr. 27 (= **M**), provided the exemplar from which **P** was copied.

All the manuscripts so far mentioned derive directly or indirectly from Venice Marcianus gr. 167 (**B**). However, one seventeenth-century manuscript, Metochion Panagiou Taphou 361 (= **X**), seems to represent a branch of the text independent from **B**. Interestingly enough, this version of the text of the *Vita Ignatii* also appears to be represented by one of the manuscripts used by M. Raderus,[36] who produced the first printed edition of the Anti-Photian Collection (including the *Vita Ignatii*) in 1604.

Two other sixteenth-century manuscripts survive which contain the text of the Anti-Photian Collection (incomplete at the end) but do not include the *Vita Ignatii*. Both manuscripts belonged to the great humanist and scholar Antonio Agustin, another figure who played a prominent part at the Council of Trent.[37] Vatican gr. 1183 was copied by Manuel Glynzounios[38] (perhaps using as his exemplar Munich gr. 436 = **C**)[39] and was then offered for sale to Agustin in an extant letter dated 6 April 1581.[40] Escurial gr. X-II-8 (= de Andrés no. 368)[41] contains exactly the same material as Vatican gr. 1183, was numbered next to it in Agustin's library and may well prove to be a copy of it. In 1587, the year following Agustin's death, his library was acquired by the Escurial, except for certain items (including Vatican gr. 1183) which were appropriated by the Vatican.[42]

INDIVIDUAL MANUSCRIPTS

All surviving manuscripts of the *Vita Ignatii* except for Metochion Panagiou Taphou 361 (**X**) derive from Venice Marcianus gr. 167 (**B**), and the paramount importance of this manuscript was long ago recognized by K. Schweinburg.[43] Unfortunately, the copyists of Basle O.II.25 (**F**), Madrid O.29 (**G**) and Ottobonianus gr. 27 (**J**) appear to have complicated the picture somewhat by consulting a second exemplar in addition to **B**. The evidence suggests that **F** and **G** both made extensive use of Munich gr. 436 (**C**), while **J** seems to have closely followed **G** for some sections. Another branch of the tradition is represented by Metochion Panagiou Taphou 361 (**X**) and by the unknown manuscript used by Raderus for his edition (= [**d**]). Again the situation appears to be somewhat complicated, as **X** also has clear links with Escurial gr. X-I-5 (**E**). The overall relationship of the surviving manuscripts is illustrated by the following stemma:

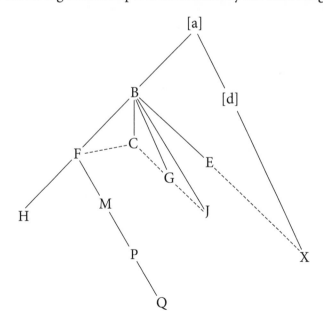

B   Venice Marcianus gr. 167, 14th century, folios 174.[44] The manuscript once belonged to Cardinal Bessarion, as a note of possession written in Greek and Latin indicates (folio 1ᵛ), and it can be identified as no. 193 in the inventory of Bessarion's manuscripts (see n. 20). Damage suffered from water and insects has made the codex difficult to read in places, but most of the doubtful readings can be verified by agreement among the derivative manuscripts and are consequently not mentioned in the apparatus criticus. Mioni identifies two scribes, the first writing folios 1–36, the second folios 117–73. Another hand has made a marginal addition at folio 1ʳ and a comment at folio 23ʳ.[45] The codex contains the following material:

    I.   Acta Concilii Constantinopolitani IV vel Oecumenici VIII (869–870) et additamenta cum illis connexa.

        1. Nicetas David Paphlago, *Vita Ignatii patr. CP.* (ff. 1–36).

        2. Michael Syncellus, *Laudationis Ignatii patr. CP. fragmentum* (ff. 37–39).

        3. *Libellus de causa Ignatii*, missus ad Nicolaum papam Romae a Theognosto monacho (ff. 39–43v).

        4. Nicolaus I, episcopus Romae, *Epistolae duae* (ff. 43ᵛ–46).

        5. Epiphanius archiep. Cipri, *Epistola ad Ignatium patr. CP.* (f. 47ʳ⁻ᵛ).

        6. Acta Concilii (ff. 47ᵛ–116).

    II. *Acta synodi Photii Constantinopoli habitae* pro unione ecclesiarum ann. 879–880 (ff. 117–163).

    III. Photius patr. CP., *Excerptum ex encyclica epistola ad archiepiscopales thronos Orientis* (ff. 163ᵛ–164ᵛ); *De Spiritus Sancti mystagogia* (ff. 164ᵛ–173ᵛ).

The last item is imperfect and breaks off in mid-sentence with the words καὶ φθοροποιῶν ἑαυτοὺς ἀπολαύνουσιν εἰ . . . (= PG 102.345B11).

A detailed examination of the text of the *Vita Ignatii* in manuscripts **CEFGJ** shows that their copyists all used **B** as exemplar. The mistakes and omissions in **B**, as compared with Raderus's edition (= **v**, for vulgata), are usually taken over by the rest, as these sample readings illustrate:

14.11	ἐξέτρεφε v: ἐξέστρεφε **BEFGJ** (**C** deficit)
30.28	ἀθεσμίαις v: ἀθεσίαις **BEFGJ** (**C** deficit)
40.3	καὶ πᾶσαν βάσανον v: om. **BEFGJ** (**C** deficit)
68.30	φυγαὶ v: φημὶ **BEFGJ** (om. **C**)
74.9	ἵν᾽ v: om. **BCEFGJ**
82.3	ἦν v: om. **BCEFGJ**
84.9	κατέστεψε v: καταστέψας **BCEFGJ**
86.9	δείλαιος v: δίκαιος **BEFGJ**
96.11	σπουδῆς v: παντὸς **BEFGJ**
106.1	ὁ ὁμολογητὴς v: om. **BEFGJ**
124.21	τὴν αὐτοῦ κοινωνίαν v: τὴν ἀξίαν τῆς αὐτοῦ κοινωνίας **BEFGJ**

C Munich gr. 436, 14th century, folios 104.[46] The manuscript once belonged to Cardinal Bessarion, as a note of possession in Latin and Greek indicates (folio 1ʳ), and it can be identified as no. 194 in the inventory of Bessarion's manuscripts (see n. 20). The codex contains the same material as **B** but is damaged at the end and breaks off in actio VI of the Photian synod (= **B** item II). A long section is also missing from the text of the *Vita Ignatii* (8.6 τέκνων . . . 56.6 σπηλαίοις καὶ), which otherwise follows **B** very closely. In several places the copyist has corrected the exemplar, e.g.,

62.29	παρὰ **B**: περὶ **C**
72.29	πρὸς **B**: πρὸ **C**
76.22	ἀλόγως **B**: ἄλογος **C**
114.20	περίεστι **B**: περιέστη **C**
116.15	προσφευγότων **B**: προσφευγόντων **C**

There are a number of small omissions (e.g., τε at 4.9; φημὶ καὶ at 68.30–31; ἐν at 70.16; ἀλλ᾽ at 74.6; πᾶν at 94.17; θεὸν at 102.12) and a longer one at 114.3–4 (αἱ θαυματουργίαι τοῦ ἱεράρχου προσπελάζουσιν) caused by the copyist's eye wandering from the immediately preceding word πελάζουσιν to the later προσπελάζουσιν. Sample mistakes and misinterpretations:

56.26	ταύτας **B**: πάντας **C**
58.14	χριστὸς **B**: κύριος **C**

68.6	πορθοῦντες **B**: ποθοῦντες **C**
76.30	κεχειροτόνητο **B**: κεχειροτόνητε **C**
80.1	ἰδιόχ(ει)ρα **B**: ἰδιότερα **C**
92.7	ἀπροσπαθῶς **B**: ἀπροπαθῶς **C**
94.13	ἀνίστασθαι **B**: ἐνίστασθαι **C**
106.13	ἐπύθετο **B**: ἐπίθετον **C**

E Escurial gr. X-I-5 (de Andrés no. 347), 16th century, folios 245.[47] The manuscript was copied by Andronic Nuccius for Diego Hurtado de Mendoza, who is recorded in a surviving part of the Marciana loan register as having borrowed the Venice codex (**B**) on 29 March 1545, and as having returned it on 26 September of the same year.[48] Nuccius is known to have copied at least four other codices in Venice for Mendoza between 1541 and 1543 and it seems highly likely that his copy of the Venice codex was made in 1545.[49] The manuscript contains the same material as **B**, breaking off in mid-sentence at the same point, but the whole is preceded by Hierocles' commentary on the Pythagorean *Carmen aureum* (ff. 1–47). De Andrés mentions two watermarks, which he compares with Briquet no. 761 (Udine 1533; var. ident. Laibach 1534) and no. 493 (Udine 1524–30; var. simil. Arnoldstein 1529). The copyist follows **B**'s text of the *Vita Ignatii* very closely but has also corrected the exemplar in many places, e.g.,

20.11	τέρας **B**: κέρας **E**
52.12	πλεῖα **B**: πλείω **E**
60.28	τού<τω> **B**: τούτω **E**
62.29	παρὰ **B**: περὶ **E**
66.12	νότον **B**: νῶτον **E**
72.29	πρὸς **B**: πρὸ **E**
102.13	παράφυσιν **B**: παρὰ φύσιν **E**
118.22	τί γὰρ εἰ **B**: τί γὰρ ἢ **E**

There are a number of small omissions (e.g., καὶ at 6.2; φασὶ at 6.26; καὶ at 10.22; δὲ at 22.15; οὓς at 24.16; τὴν πονηρὰν at 24.27; etc.) and two longer ones at 52.5–6 (καὶ τήξεως . . . σταυροῦντες αὐτὸν) and at 126.28–29 (κατεδεῖτο . . . ἠσφαλίζετο), which were apparently caused by the copyist's eye wandering down to another occurrence of the same word (in the first case) or word ending (in the second case) in the line below. Sample mistakes and misinterpretations:

10.2	ἐπανηρημένος **B**: ἀνηρημένος **E**
16.21	ἀντείχοντο **B**: ἀντείχοντες **E**
22.6	πνεύματος **B**: πεύματος **E**
26.22	μετεωριζόμενον **B**: –ομένη **E**
30.5	καὶ τῷ **B**: καὶ τὸ **E**
74.3	θαμβούμενος **B**: θορυβούμενος **E**
122.24	λόγον **B**: λόγου **E**
124.24	ἀνατεθεματισμένῳ **B**: ἀναθεματισμένῳ **E**

F Basle gr. O.II.25 (Bibliothèque de l'Université 28), 16th century, folios 172 and 130.[50] The codex comprises two manuscripts, the first containing the same material as **B** and breaking off at the same point, the second containing Hermias's commentaries on Plato's *Phaedrus*. It once belonged to the well-known Basle printer Henricus Petri, as a note at the head of the first manuscript indicates: "Hic liber est D. Henricopetri quem ab eo Car. Utenhovius commodato accepit." Nothing is known about Car(olus?) Utenhovius, but the loan of the codex to him may have had something to do with one of the copies made from it (see **H** and **M** below). At the beginning of the second manuscript is a note by R. Faesch dated 1632: "Huncce codicem a. circiter 1530, una cum aliis comment. graecis in Platonem accepit Henricus Petri typographus celebris Basiliensis ab Arnoldo Paraxylo Arlenio, qui in contubernio vixit Don Diego Hurtadi a Mendozza, Caroli V. imp. ad Venetos legati." Faesch's source was apparently Marcus Hopperus in the dedicatory letter to his edited works of Plato in Greek printed by Henricus Petri in 1556, but the approximate date 1530 can hardly be right, as Arlenius was Mendoza's librarian from 1538 to 1546.[51] The attribution to Arlenius may well be correct, but it is not clear whether the first manuscript as well as the second is covered by the statement. The codex has a watermark which closely resembles Briquet no. 3086 (Laibach 1543).[52]

For his text of the *Vita Ignatii* the copyist appears to have consulted **B** and **C** simultaneously, since the peculiarities of each are exhibited throughout. **F** repeats **B**'s marginal addition at 2.4–5, takes over the mistakes of **B** at 62.29 (παρὰ) and 72.29 (πρὸς), and follows **B** in all places mentioned above where words have been omitted in **C**. On the other hand, **F** frequently takes over the idiosyncrasies of **C**, e.g.,

56.10	θήρας **B**: θύρας, et η supra υ, **CF**
58.14	χριστὸς **B**: κύριος **CF**
80.1	ἰδιόχ(ει)ρα **B**: ἰδιότερα **CF**
82.27	φραγγίας **B**: σφραγγίας **C** σφαγίας **F**
88.4–5	πάντες λιβέλλους μετανοίας **B**: πάντες [space] μετανοίας **C** πάντες [space] καὶ μετ. **F**
92.7	ἀπροσπαθῶς **B**: ἀπροπαθῶς **CF**
94.13	ἀνίστασθαι **B**: ἐνίστασθαι **CF**
118.25	παιδίων **B**: παίδων **CF**

Finally, **F** also exhibits some mistakes and misinterpretations of its own, which are generally also found in the derivative manuscripts **HMP**, e.g.,

6.10	εἰρήνην **BC**: εἰρημένην **FHMP**
8.1	παντέφορον **BC**: παντάφορον **FHMP**
56.24	ἐξωνεῖτο **BC**: ἐξανεῖτο **FHMP**
60.8	ἐκείνας **BC**: ἐκεῖνον **FHMP**
66.6	μετατεθεὶς **BC**: μετατιθεὶς **FHMP**
72.12	σολέας **B**: [space]λέας **C** πολέας **FHM**, **P** a. corr.
80.17	ἐνεγέγραπτο **BC**: ἐνεδέγναπισι **FHMP**
116.8	νεφρικῶ **B**: νεφριτικῶ **C** νεφ[space]κᾶν **FHMP**

At the end of the *Vita Ignatii* manuscripts **FMP** add the phrase: τέλος τῆς πρώτης ὁμιλίας.

G Madrid gr. O.29, 16th century, folios 300.[53] The manuscript was copied by Cornelius of Nauplion in Venice in 1557, as the colophon indicates, and it contains the same material as **B**, breaking off at the same point. As with **F**, the copyist appears to have consulted **B** and **C** simultaneously for his text of the *Vita Ignatii*. In addition to taking over the mistakes of **B** mentioned above (under **B**), **G** also follows **B** in many of the places where words have been omitted in

C (e.g., τε at 4.9; φημὶ καὶ at 68.30–31; ἐν at 70.16; ἀλλ’ at 74.6; πᾶν at 94.17), and the idiosyncrasies at 70.19 (ἐγγγάγγραις) and at 114.8 (συμβαλλεῖν) appear in **BG** alone. On the other hand, a number of C’s idiosyncrasies appear only in **CG**, e.g.,

70.1	σαυτὸν **B**: αὐτὸν **CG**
76.30	κεχειροτόνητο **B**: κεχειροτόνητε **CG**
88.21	ἀπολογίαν **B**: ἀπολογία **CG**
94.11	πεσὸν **B**: πεσὼν **C**, a. corr. **G**
102.12	θεὸν **B**: om. **CG**

Furthermore, in the long section missing from **C** (8.6–56.6), **G** often follows the **F** group against **B**, which suggests that at the time of copying the section was present in **C**, e.g.,

8.9	καταπιέζων **B**: καὶ ἀπιέζων **FGHMP**
12.15	φιλοπ(ό)νως **B**: φιλόπυρος **FGHMP**
18.10	καταγχομένων **B**: καταυχομένων **FGHMP**
24.6	προῆγε **B**: προῆδε **FG**
26.12	ὑπεποιεῖτο **B**: ἐπεποιεῖτο **FGHMP**

There are a number of small omissions in **G** (e.g., ὦν at 6.23, καὶ καταπαυθεῖσαν at 8.17, etc.) and a longer one from 40.15 (αὐτοῖς[1]) to 42.33 (μυτιλήνη). The copyist has also introduced a whole host of his own mistakes (samples under **J**, below).

H Amsterdam University 68, 16th century, folios 319.[54] The codex has the distinctive Turkish leather binding of Cardinal Granvelle and includes an ex-libris of Nicolaus Joseph Foucault (d. 1721). It contains the same material as **B**, breaking off at the same point (ff. 1–189), but this is followed by another work of Photius (*Diatriba de voluntatibus in Christo gnomicis*) and letters of Clement of Rome and Basil the Great. Da Costa distinguishes three separate hands, two of which were involved in copying folios 1–189.[55] For the text of the *Vita Ignatii* the copyist follows **F** very closely (sample conjunctive errors under **F** above) except that additions above the line and corrections found in **F** are generally ignored by **H**. There are a number of small omissions (e.g., ἀρετῆς at 42.10; ἦν ὁρᾶν . . .

θαυματουργίαν at 108.18; ἔνστασιν at 126.4) and the copyist has introduced some peculiarities of his own, e.g.,

8.29	μετεσχηκότα F:	μεσχηκότα H
16.15	προσηγάγετο F:	προσηγάτε H
40.10	αὐτοῦ τοῖς F:	αὐτοῖς H
58.18–19	κατατακέντες F:	κατακέντες H
76.15	ψευδοσύλλογον F:	ψευδοσύλλον H

J Ottobonianus gr. 27, 16th century, folios 402.[56] The codex belonged to Cardinal Sirleto and can be identified as number 41 among his Greek theological manuscripts.[57] In addition to the anti-Photian material, the manuscript also contains the *Acts of the Second Synod of Nicaea* (ff. 1–219). Folios 221 to 401 contain the same material as **B**, breaking off at the same point, except that the *Vita Ignatii* (ff. 292–315ᵛ) appears out of order, following **B** item I.6 and preceding **B** item II. Canart distinguishes a number of copyists and correctors, one of whom was responsible only for copying the *Vita Ignatii*. Folios 292 to 315 have a distinctive watermark, but Canart can find no parallel in Briquet.

For his text of the *Vita Ignatii* the copyist appears to have followed **B** for the most part (sample conjunctive errors under **B** above), but also to have made occasional use of **G**. The errors of **G** are found scattered throughout **J**, but in at least one small section (on page 64) **J** appears to have been using **G** exclusively. Sample conjunctive errors:

24.9	σκληρότατα **B**:	κληρότητος **G** σκληρότητος **J**
64.16	ἐξέτασις **B**:	ἐξέτασε **GJ**
64.20	ἐχειροδότησεν **B**:	ἐχειροδότεᵉᵛ **G** ἐχειροδότε **J**
64.22	τιν' ἄλλον **B**:	τ' ἤελλον **GJ**
64.30	γίνεται **B**:	γίαν **GJ**
66.1	τις **B**:	τε **GJ**
78.13	μάμαντος **B**:	μάμαρτος **GJ**
80.26	δεσμούμενον **B**:	θεσμούμενον **GJ**
92.18	καταδοχῆς **B**:	καταδοκῆς **GJ**
120.5	σύγγραμμα **B**:	σύγγραμα **GJ**

The copyist has also corrected **B** in several places, e.g.,

2.17	διεστὼς **B**: διεστὸς **J**
20.11	τέρας **B**: κέρας **J** (following **G**)
62.29	παρὰ **B**: περὶ **J** (following **G**)
78.12	τῷ **B**: τὸ **J**
94.7	μόλιβον **B**: μόλιβδον **J**

There are a number of small omissions (e.g., τὸν τῶν at 10.30; οὖν at 18.22; χαλεπὸν at 56.14; καὶ τοῦ τῆς ἁμαρτίας at 100.3; καὶ προφητικώτατον at 122.7) and a longer one at 104.14–15 (ὁ θεῖος ἰγνάτιος τοιαύταις νουθεσίαις καὶ διδασκαλίαις). The copyist has also introduced some peculiar errors of his own, e.g.,

4.24	ὑπῆρχε **B**: ὑπῆσχε **J**
8.2	φυγάδων **B**: φυγάδα **J**
8.11	ἐντεῦθεν **B**: ἠταθεν (*sic*) **J**
10.2	ἐπανηρημένος **B**: ἀνηρημένος **J**, etc.

M Munich gr. 27, 15th and 16th centuries, various hands, folios 499.[58] In addition to the anti-Photian material, the codex contains writings of Bessarion and others on the procession of the Holy Spirit, material relating to the synod of Ephesus and a treatise on the heretical writings of Acindinus and Barlaam (incomplete at the end, where the manuscript is damaged). Folios 284 to 463 contain the same material as **B**, breaking off at the same point. The copyist follows **F**'s text of the *Vita Ignatii* very closely (sample conjunctive errors under **F** above), but a whole series of marginal corrections have been added by what looks like a different hand. Almost all of these have been faithfully repeated by **P**, which clearly used **M** as exemplar. Sample marginal corrections:

8.9	καὶ ἀπιέζων **FMP**: ἴσως καταπιέζων add. mg. **MP**
12.26	παιδοτριβούνιος **FMP**: ἴσ. παιδοτριβούμενος add. mg. **MP**
26.9	ἐναποθέμεθα **FMP**: ἴσ. ἐναποθέμενος add. mg. **MP**
34.29	τὰ **FMP**: ἴσως τε add. mg. **MP**
40.23	παρεδίδου **FMP**: ἴσως παρεδίδουν add. mg. **MP**
60.28	καυχασμὸν **FMP**: ἴσως καγχασμὸν add. mg. **MP**

78.9   φιλία **FMP**: ἴσως φιλίαν add. mg. **MP**

94.7   μόλιβον **FMP**: ἴσως μόλιβδον add. mg. **MP**

There are a number of small omissions (e.g., τε at 4.9; δὲ at 8.23; καὶ¹ at 36.16; δὲ at 38.10, etc.) and the copyist has introduced some peculiar errors of his own, which are generally also found in **P**, e.g.,

4.9   ἀγνοοῦσιν **F**: ἀγνοῦσιν **MP**

4.24   ἄνω μεταχωρήσαντος **F**: ἄνωθεν χωρήσαντος **MP**

10.21   οὔτε **F**: ὅτε **MP**

18.11   ἄφθονον **F**: ἄφονον **MP**

32.8   ἐπιδαψιλεύεται **F**: ἐπιδαψιλεύετε **MP**

46.23–24 ἐνδυσάμενος **F**: ἐνδησάμενος **MP**

48.10   χειροτονηθεὶς **F**: χειροτονησθεὶς **MP**

54.19   ἀνειλημμένος **F**: ἀνειλημένος **MP**, etc.

P   Vatican gr. 1452, 16th century, folios 62.⁵⁹ The codex belonged to Cardinal Sirleto and can be identified as number 128 among his Greek theological manuscripts.⁶⁰ It has a watermark which closely resembles Briquet no. 518 (Verona 1545). The manuscript contains only the *Vita Ignatii* and is clearly a copy of **M** (sample conjunctive errors and identical marginal corrections under **M** above). The copyist has also introduced some peculiar errors of his own, e.g.,

12.7   νικήτας **M**: νικήσας **P**

34.29   προσεπέλασε **M**: προσέλασε **P**

38.31   ἔρευναν **M**: εὔρευναν **P**

56.7   ἀποστολικῶς **M**: ἀποστολιστῶς **P**, etc.

Q   Ottobonianus gr. 138, 17th century, folios 100.⁶¹ As mentioned above, this codex is the copy of **P** made for the Duc d'Altemps in 1619–20 after Paul V had bought back thirty-six of Sirleto's Greek manuscripts (including Vatican gr. 1452) for the Vatican.⁶²

X   Metochion Panagiou Taphou 361, 17th century, folios 132.⁶³ The codex contains six miscellaneous items followed by an acephalous text of the *Vita Ignatii* (ff. 92–132). The colophon has a note of possession written in Greek by a certain Gregory of Crete, but unfortunately it is not possible to decipher what appears to be a family name. In addition to the section missing at the beginning (2.1–24.15), the text of the *Vita Ignatii* has several lacunas (92.28–94.11; 98.1–104.15; 106.7–114.7; 114.15–116.7) and another section (44.17 τῶν γνωσιωτέρων . . . 52.28 εἰσελθεῖν), omitted in its proper place, has been included at a later point (after ἐβλασφημεῖτο at 60.30). The large number of instances in which **X** and the text of Raderus's edition are in agreement against the other manuscripts indicates that the version in **X** derives, at least in part, from **[d]** (the unknown manuscript used by Raderus), and corresponding readings have been reported in the apparatus criticus (**Xv**). Elsewhere, however, **X** joins the tradition found in **B** and its derivatives against the edition, and it has not been thought necessary to report these readings in the apparatus, e.g.,

24.31	ἀποτρίψασθαι **BX**: ἀπορρύψασθαι **v**
26.3	κρίνει **BX**: κρίνων **v**
26.24	προσχωρεῖ **BX**: προχωρεῖ **v**
26.27	ἀποκείρας **BX**: ἀπόκειραι **v**
26.30	κατὰ **BX**: om. **v**, etc.

Furthermore, in a number of places **X** follows the peculiar errors of **E**, which seems to indicate that the latter or one of its derivatives provided the **B** group exemplar for **X**'s version. Sample conjunctive errors:

26.22	μετεωριζόμενον **v**: μετεωριζομένη **EX**
30.5	καὶ τῷ **v**: καὶ τὸ **EX**
52.5–6	καὶ πήξεως . . . σταυροῦντες **v**: om. **EX**
122.24	λόγον **v**: λόγου **EX**
124.24	ἀνατεθεματισμένῳ **v**: ἀναθεματισμένω **EX**
126.28–29	κατεδεῖτο . . . ἠσφαλίζετο **v**: om. **EX**

X provides few worthwhile readings in its own right and only the following corrections (made by **X** or its exemplar?) have been retained:

56.12	ἐξεσπασμένον **X**: ἐξηπτασμένον **Bv**
56.14	δρόμωσι **X**: δρομεῦσιν **B** δρομεῦσι **v**
82.15	προφερόμενα **X**: προσφερόμενα **Bv**

In general, the copyist displays an indifference to textual accuracy and is frequently responsible for arbitrary rewriting, tendentious changes, and transpositions of the text, e.g.,

24.21–22 οὐκ ἀγαθὸς δέ, ἀλλὰ καὶ λίαν πικρὸς **Bv**: οὐκ ἀγαθὸς μέν, μᾶλλον δὲ καὶ λίαν πονηρὸς καὶ πικρὸς **X**

58.25 ἐπισυστάσεως ληστρικῆς **Bv**: ληστ. ἐπιστάσεως **X**

70.15–16 οὐδὲ τοῦ μεγάλου βασιλείου τῶν λόγων κατακούων ηὐλαβήθης **Bv**: οὐδὲ τῶν λόγων τοῦ ἁγίου βασιλείου ηὐλαβήθη ἀκούων **X**

78.16 κεκρατηκὼς **Bv**: βεβασιλευκὼς **X**

84.21–22 τῇ εἰσόδῳ συμπεσοῦσαν **Bv**: εἰσόδοις ἐμπεσοῦσαν **X**

104.23 θεοῦ νόμον **Bv**: θεοῦ φόβον **X**

116.14 ἁλύσεως πᾶσαν **Bv**: ἁλύσεως ἧς τοὺς ἱεροὺς πόδας πρῶτον ἄνδρες κατέκλεισαν ἀσεβεῖς πᾶσαν **X**

124.17 τις αὐτῶν αὐτῷ μετὰ ταῦτα κοινωνεῖν ἀνωμολόγησεν **Bv**: τινα αὐτῶν κοινωνεῖν αὐτῷ εὗρεν ἀνομολογοῦντα μετὰ ταῦτα **X**

All such idiosyncracies and inaccuracies have been left out of the apparatus.

The copyist has also added numerous marginal comments, sometimes to make brief mention of some of Nicetas's main points, sometimes to indulge in anti-Photian exclamations. "Just look at Photius's virtue!" appears several times, always sarcastically, and ὥραιον is found more than once in praise of anti-Photian rhetoric. Furthermore, at the point where Nicetas mentions Photius excommunicating the Pope (76.15–16), the copyist exclaims: "Just see what the new devil is perpetrating!"

Editions, translations

1. Editio princeps of the *Vita Ignatii* by M. Raderus, *Acta sacrosancti concilii octavi* (Ingolstadt, 1604), 78–193. Raderus edited the whole of the Anti-Photian Collection, but it is not clear which manuscripts he used. Assemanus states that he collated the Munich manuscripts (**CM**) with codices of the Vatican and Antonio Agustin (**J** and Vatican gr.

1183).[64] However, this cannot be the full picture, as it does not account for the unknown manuscript (= [**d**]) used by Raderus. The readings of the edition are recorded in the apparatus as **v** (= vulgata) and where Raderus mentioned a variant, the readings are recorded as **v**¹ and **v**² (e.g., at 24.20 etc.) Raderus also provided a translation into Latin, which was published with the text.

2. Raderus's text and translation were then republished with additional annotations in the various collections of church councils:

> *Concilia generalia ecclesiae catholicae* (Rome, 1608–1612), 3.2:302–47.

> P. Labbe and G. Cossart, *Sacrosancta concilia* (Paris, 1671–1672), 8:1179–1260.

> I. Hardouin, *Acta conciliorum* (Paris, 1715), 5:943–1009.

> I.D. Mansi, *Sacrorum conciliorum nova et amplissima collectio* (Venice, 1769–1798), 16:209–92.

Their final republication was in PG 105:488–574. PG column numbers are given in the inner margin of the text in this edition.

3. The *Vita Ignatii* was translated into vernacular Greek in 1640 by Neophytus Rhodinus and presented to the Congregation for the Propagation of the Faith. It survives today in the Vatican library as Borgianus gr. 17.[65]

Editorial conventions

In establishing the text the readings of **B** have been preferred except where an alternative in the edition seems obviously correct or where words appear to have been omitted from **B** (e.g., καὶ πᾶσαν βάσανον at 40.3; ἵν᾽ at 74.9). Whenever **B** and **v** are at variance, the difference is highlighted in a positive apparatus, in which all readings that make any kind of sense by themselves are recorded. The readings of all manuscripts deriving from **B** have been eliminated, except for the small number of cases where they have corrected the text by a successful conjecture (e.g., 20.11 κέρας **EGJ**: τέρας **B** πέρας v). This also applies to **X**, which otherwise appears in the apparatus only when it has readings in common with **v**, in order to illustrate what might have been the reading of [**d**].

Spelling errors in **B** and **v** have generally been corrected silently unless they are of some special interest. Cases such as the following have not been mentioned:

2.25	ἀπηλλαγμένοις **B**: ἀπηλαγμένοις **v**
4.6	παρακολουθήσασαν **B**: παρακαλουθήσασαν **v**
8.17	μυσαρὸς **v**: μισαρὸς **B**
10.11	συνωμοτῶν **v**: συνομωτῶν **B**
24.16	παρρησιάσαιτο **v**: παρρησιάσετο **B**
28.17	ἀμυνεῖσθαι **Xv**: ἀμηνῦσθαι **B**
40.21	μιτυλήνην **Xv**: μυτιλήνην **B**
62.16	συνετέτατο **Xv**: συνετέταττο **B**
70.19	ἐν γάγγραις **Xv**: ἐγγγάγγραις **B**
114.8	συμβαλεῖν **Xv**: συμβαλλεῖν **B**

B seems to prefer -γγ- to -γκ- (see also 114.17 ἐγκυμονοῦσα **v**: ἐγγυμονοῦσα **B**, etc.).

Numerous cases of iotacism, particularly in **B**, have also been passed over in silence, e.g.,

6.3	διιθύνας **v**: διηθύνας **B**
6.11	πριγκιπίους **B**: Πριγκιπείους **v**
8.6	ἀπηνῆ **v**: ἀπεινῆ **B**
20.9	λεκανομάντιν **v**: λεκανομάντην **B**
20.14	ὑπομεμενηκὼς **v**: ὑπομεμενικὼς **B**

With regard to movable nu the text follows **B**'s practice, which is generally correct in using it only before vowels (though it often applies the same principle at the end of sentences too). There are, however, a few exceptions in **B** to the general rule (e.g., ἐξέκοψεν at 28.16; δρομεῦσιν at 56.14; πάθεσιν at 98.32; πίστεσιν at 100.14).

In matters of elision too the text follows **B**'s practice, which again seems reasonably consistent. Prepositions with final vowels are generally elided before a following vowel (exceptions with ὑπὸ at 8.8; 28.8; 124.23), as are ἀλλὰ and other commonly elided words. The particles δέ and τε are generally not elided, except when combined with the negative (i.e. οὐδ᾽, μητ᾽). There are a few exceptions to this, however (e.g., δ᾽ ἂν at 2.20; τ᾽ ἐγεγόνει at 38.9; δ᾽ ἄρ᾽ ἦν at 76.5; δ᾽ ἀληθὲς at 116.26). Crasis is used by **B** when appropriate.

Notes to the Introduction

1   For a detailed account of this material see F. Dvornik, *The Photian Schism: History and Legend* (Cambridge, 1948), 216–78.

2   Two known exceptions are Vatican gr. 1183 and Escurial gr. X-II-8, which are discussed in more detail on p. xvi.

3   G. S. Assemanus, *Bibliotheca iuris orientalis canonici et civilis*, vol. 1, *Codex canonum ecclesiae Graecae* (Rome, 1762), 322–25. Dvornik, *Photian Schism*, 274–75.

4   K. Krumbacher, *Geschichte der byzantinischen Litteratur* (Munich, 1897), 167.

5   R. J. H. Jenkins, "A Note on Nicetas David Paphlago and the *Vita Ignatii*," *DOP* 19 (1965): 244–47.

6   R. J. H. Jenkins and B. Laourdas, "Eight Letters of Arethas on the Fourth Marriage of Leo the Wise," *Hellenika* 14 (1956): 298–303.

7   L. G. Westerink, "Nicetas the Paphlagonian on the End of the World," in *Essays in Memory of Basil Laourdas* (Thessalonike, 1975), 181.

8   P. Karlin-Hayter, *Vita Euthymii* (Brussels, 1970), 106, 9–10. For a detailed reconstruction of Nicetas's part in the tetragamy affair based on the evidence of *Vita Euthymii*, Arethas's letters to Nicetas, and Nicetas's letters to Arethas and others, see Westerink, "Nicetas the Paphlagonian," 178–82.

9   [The date at which the *VI* was written has long been the subject of scholarly debate and disagreement, mainly due to the lack of indisputable data either within the Life itself or available from other sources. In modern times the issue seemed to have been more or less settled by an important short article that Romilly Jenkins published under the title, "A Note on Nicetas David Paphlago and the *Vita Ignatii*" (above, n. 5). Jenkins argued that the document reflected Nicetas David's emotional preoccupation with the Tetragamy struggle of 906–907, was partly composed in that period, and probably completed in the years 908–910. That timeframe has generally been accepted and A. Smithies, as we see, went a step further and posited the reasonable *terminus ante quem* of 920, based on the promulgation of the Tome of Union in that year. In recent times, however, a Russian scholar, Irina Tamarkina, has reopened the discussion. Her careful study, "The Date of the Life of the Patriarch Ignatius Reconsidered," *BZ* 99, no. 2 (2006): 615–30, not only subjects each of the traditional arguments to minute scrutiny, but also brings into the picture some passages from lesser-known writings of Nicetas David and other relevant texts. She does succeed in highlighting the precariousness of the evidence cited

by Jenkins and makes a plausible case for distancing the composition of the *VI* from the context of the Tetragamy affair. Her own suggested time frame is between 886 (after the death of Emperor Basil I) and 901–902 (the beginning of the patriarchate of Nicolaus Mysticus, the third successor of Photius).

It seems to me that, after everything has been taken into account, the most secure estimate of the time of composition would be the first or second decade of the tenth century. JMD.]

10   Karlin-Hayter, *Vita Euthymii*, 218.

11   As Krumbacher, *Geschichte*, 168, points out.

12   "Note on Nicetas David Paphlago" (see n. 5), 243–44. The quoted text is on 243, n. 18; the passage that refers to him setting up as a teacher is in *Vita Euthymii* (see n. 8), 104, 19.

13   A. Vogt, "Deux discours inédits de Nicétas de Paphlagonie," *Orientalia Christiana* 23 (1931): 6.

14   "Note on Nicetas David Paphlago," 241–43.

15   Westerink, "Nicetas the Paphlagonian," 178, 182.

16   J. Gill, *Quae supersunt Actorum Graecorum Concilii Florentini*, pt. 1, *Res Ferrariae gestae*, Concilium Florentinum: documenta et scriptores, series B (Rome, 1953), 5:89–91.

17   *Apologia contra Ephesii confessionem*, PG 160:89B–C.

18   On this monastery see R. Janin, *La géographie ecclésiastique de l'empire byzantin, Première partie: Le siège de Constantinople et le patriarcat oecuménique*, vol. 3, *Les églises et les monastères*, 2nd ed. (Paris, 1969), 421–29 (no. 26).

19   On this monastery see ibid., 218–22 (no. 96).

20   H. Omont, "Inventaire des manuscrits grecs et latins donnés à Saint-Marc de Venise par le Cardinal Bessarion (1468)," *Revue des bibliothèques* (1894): 156.

21   C. Graux, *Essai sur les origines du fonds grec de l'Escurial* (Paris, 1880), 183.

22   C. Castellani, "Il prestito dei codici manoscritti della Biblioteca di San Marco in Venezia ne' suoi primi tempi e le conseguenti perdite de' codici stessi," *Atti del Istituto Veneto di Scienze, Lettere ed Arti* 55 (1896–97): 321, n. 3.

23   On Glynzounios see M. Sicherl, "Manuel Glynzounios als Schreiber griechischer Handschriften," *BZ* 49 (1956): 34–54; P. Canart, "Nouveaux manuscrits copiés par Emmanuel Glynzounios," Ἐπετηρὶς Ἑταιρείας Βυζαντινῶν Σπουδῶν 39–40 (1972–73): 527–44. Sicherl discusses Munich gr. 436 in 51 n. 90.

24   Sicherl, "Manuel Glynzounios," 43ff. See also n. 46 below under manuscript **C**.

25   W. Hörmann, "Das Supplement der griechischen Handschriften der Bayerischen Stadtbibliothek" in ΧΑΛΙΚΕΣ: *Festgabe für die Teilnehmer am XI. Internationalen Byzantinistenkongress, München, 15–20 September 1958* (Freising, 1958), 42.

26   On Mendoza see H. Jedin, *A History of the Council of Trent* (London, 1961), 2:280–82, etc.; Graux, *Essai sur les origines*, 165ff.

27   Graux, *Essai sur les origines*, 372 n. 1. For the date see discussion below under manuscript **E**.

28   Jedin, *History*, 474.

29   On Arlenius see Graux, *Essai sur les origines*, 185–89.

30   Discussed in more detail below under manuscript **F**.

31   M. Vogel and V. Gardthausen, *Die griechischen Schreiber des Mittelalters und der Renaissance* (Leipzig, 1909), 233–34.

32   See Graux, *Essai sur les origines*, 47–56, 71, 78 n. 1.

33   Jedin, *History*, 471, etc.

34   Canart, "Nouveaux manuscrits," 530, n. 2, describes what happened to Sirleto's manuscripts from the time of his death down to their acquisition by the Vatican.

35   C. Baronius, *Annales ecclesiastici, una cum critica historico-chronologica P. Antonii Pagi* (Lucca, 1738–59). On Baronius see Dvornik, *Photian Schism*, 371–75, etc.

36   I have been unable to identify this manuscript or to locate a copy of Raderus's original edition. See discussion at p. xxvii.

37   On Agustin see Graux, *Essai sur les origines*, 280ff.

38   Canart, "Nouveaux manuscrits," 530–31. He also gives a detailed description of this manuscript (no. 161 of Agustin's library), 534–35.

39   Suggested by Sicherl, "Manuel Glynzounios," 51 n. 90. This can be ascertained only by a full collation of all the manuscripts containing the text of the Anti-Photian Collection.

40   Quoted by Graux, *Essai sur les origines*, appendix no. 17, and discussed at 297–98. Also discussed by Canart and Sicherl (see nn. 38–39 above).

41   G. de Andrés, *Catálogo de los códices griegos de la Real Biblioteca de El Escurial* (Madrid, 1965), 2:273. It was no. 162 of Agustin's library.

42   Canart, "Nouveaux manuscrits," 531 and n. 3.

43   See *Monumenta Germaniae Historica: Epistolarum tomus VII (Karolini aevi V)* (Berlin, 1928), 371. [N. G. Wilson has raised the possibility that **X** may in fact be derived from Rader's edition; due to the loss of the Smithies collation materials in a fire, the testing of this hypothesis has not been feasible. JMD.]

44   See E. Mioni, *Bibliothecae Divi Marci Venetiarum codices graeci manuscripti: Thesaurus antiquus*, vol. 1 (Rome, 1981).

45   [N. G. Wilson, who has examined the manuscript, thinks that there might be three scribes at work, although he would not be completely confident about this, because of the considerable variation in the script. JMD.]

46   See I. Hardt, *Catalogus codicum manuscriptorum graecorum Bibliothecae Regiae Bavaricae* (Munich, 1810), 4:352–54. Prior to 1806 the manuscript was in Augsburg and is recorded as "Inferioris Bibliothecae,

armario primo, num. 13" in the catalogues of E. Ehinger (*Catalogus biblio-thecae amplissimae rei publicae Augustanae*, Augsburg, 1633) and A. Reiserus (*Index manuscriptorum bibliothecae Augustanae*, Augsburg, 1675). It is not found in the earlier catalogues of M. Mangerus (1575), D. Hoeschelius (1595), and V. Schonigk (1600).

47   See E. Miller, *Catalogue des manuscrits grecs de la Bibliothèque de l'Escurial* (Paris, 1848), 293; de Andrés, *Catálogo de los codices*, 245–46.

48   Castellani, "Il prestito dei codici," 327–28. See also Graux, *Essai sur les origines*, 372 n. 1.

49   See Vogel and Gardthausen, *Die griechischen Schreiber*, 31.

50   See H. Omont, *Catalogue des manuscrits grecs des bibliothèques de Suisse* (Leipzig, 1886), 15.

51   On Arlenius see above, p. xv and n. 29.

52   For this information I am grateful to Dr. Martin Steinman, Assistant Keeper of Manuscripts, Öffentliche Bibliothek der Universität Basel (letter dated 29 May 1975).

53   See E. Miller, "Bibliothèque royale de Madrid: Catalogue des manuscrits grecs," *Notices et extraits des manuscrits de la Bibliothèque nationale et autres bibliothèques*, 31, no. 2 (1886): 75.

54   See H. Omont, *Catalogue des manuscrits grecs des bibliothèques des Pays-Bas* (Leipzig, 1887), 12–13 (Amsterdam, Bibliothèque de l'Université, 5[14]); M. B. Mendes da Costa, *Bibliotheek der Universiteit van Amsterdam: Catalogus der Handschriften*, vol. 2, *De Handschriften der Stedelijke Bibliotheek* (Amsterdam, 1902), 14.

55   It is interesting to speculate that Georgios Tryphon, who copied Amsterdam University 69 (containing the *Bibliotheca* of Photius and dated May 1548) for Cardinal Granvelle, may have been connected with the copy-ing of this codex. According to a surviving part of the Marciana loan register he borrowed a manuscript containing letters of Gregory of Nazianzus and of Basil on 21 August 1547 and returned it on 26 October of the same year (Castellani, "Il prestito dei codici," 338). On the latter date he borrowed (among others) Venice gr. 167 (**B**) and a codex containing *Bibliotheca Photii* (ibid., 340). For this line of inquiry to fit what is already known about the manuscripts of the *Vita Ignatii*, we would have to assume that this was the occasion for the copying of **F** and that the latter was then used (by Tryphon and associates?) as exemplar for copying the first part of **H**.

56   See A. Capecelatro, *Codices manuscripti graeci Ottoboniani Bibliothecae Vaticanae descripti*, rev. E. Feron and F. Battaglini (Rome, 1893), 25.

57   The inventory drawn up on the Cardinal's death is preserved in Vatican lat. 6163. For this identification and other details about the manuscript I am indebted to P. Canart (letter dated 9 July 1975).

58   See I. Hardt, *Catalogus codicum manuscriptorum*, vol. 1 (Munich, 1806), 140–56. The manuscript was recorded as no. 115 in the catalogue of 1602 (A. Sartorius, *Catalogus graecorum manuscriptorum codicum qui asservantur in inclyta serenissimi utriusque Bavariae Ducis . . . bibliotheca*, Ingolstadt, 1602, 45–48).

59   See *Catalogus codicum hagiographicorum graecorum Bibliothecae Vaticanae*, ed. Hagiographi Bollandiani and P. F. de' Cavalieri, Subsidia hagiographica 7 (Brussels, 1899), 126.

60   For this identification and other details about the manuscript I am indebted to P. Canart (letters dated 27 January and 9 July 1975).

61   See Capecelatro, *Codices manuscripti graeci*, 78.

62   See G. Mercati, *Codici latini Pico Grimani Pio e di altra biblioteca ignota del secolo XVI esistenti nell' Ottoboniana*, vol. 4, *I codici Altempsiani acquistati da Paolo V* (Vatican City, 1938), 121.

63   See A. Papadopoulos-Kerameus, "Κατάλογος κωδίκων εὑρισκομένων ἐν τῇ βιβλιοθήκῃ τοῦ ἐν Κωνσταντινουπόλει Μετοχίου τοῦ Παναγίου Τάφου," Ἱεροσολυμιτικὴ βιβλιοθήκη ἤτοι κατάλογος τῶν ἐν ταῖς βιβλιοθήκαις τοῦ ἁγιωτάτου ἀποστολικοῦ τε καὶ καθολικοῦ ὀρθοδόξου πατριαρχικοῦ θρόνου τῶν Ἱεροσολύμων καὶ πάσης Παλαιστίνης ἀποκειμένων ἑλληνικῶν κωδίκων, vol. 4 (St. Petersburg, 1899), 335.

64   Assemanus, *Bibliotheca iuris orientalis*, 259.

65   See P. F. de' Cavalieri, *Codices graeci Chisiani et Borgiani Bibliothecae Apostolicae Vaticanae* (Rome, 1927), 130.

ABBREVIATIONS

BZ	*Byzantinische Zeitschrift*
DACL	*Dictionnaire d'archéologie chrétienne et de liturgie*
DOP	*Dumbarton Oaks Papers*
JÖB	*Jahrbuch der Österreichischen Byzantinistik*
Mansi	J. D. Mansi, *Sacrorum conciliorum nova et amplissima collectio* (Paris–Leipzig, 1901–27)
ODB	*The Oxford Dictionary of Byzantium*, ed. A. Kazhdan et al. (New York–Oxford, 1991)
PG	Patrologiae cursus completus, Series graeca, ed. J.-P. Migne (Paris, 1857–66)
PmbZ	*Prosopographie der mittelbyzantinischen Zeit* (Berlin, 1998–), compiled by R.-J. Lilie, C. Ludwig, T. Pratsch, I. Rochow, et al., based on preliminary work by F. Winkelmann
SV	*Synodicon Vetus*

SIGLA

B*	Venice Marcianus gr. 167, s. XIV
C	Munich gr. 436, s. XIV
E	Escurial gr. X-I-5, s. XVI
G	Madrid gr. O.29, s. XVI
J	Ottobonianus gr. 27, s. XVI
X	Metochion Panagiou Taphou 361, s. XVII
v	Editio M. Raderi, Ingolstadii, 1604
Westerink	L. G. Westerink
< >	addenda
[ ]	supplenda in lacuna codicis
( )	compendia soluta
††	corrupta

*The folio divisions of **B** are given in the inner margins of the text.

The Life

of

Patriarch Ignatius

ΒΙΟΣ ΗΤΟΙ ΑΘΛΗΣΙΣ ΤΟΥ ΕΝ ΑΓΙΟΙΣ ΠΑΤΡΟΣ
ΗΜΩΝ ΙΓΝΑΤΙΟΥ ΑΡΧΙΕΠΙΣΚΟΠΟΥ
ΚΩΝΣΤΑΝΤΙΝΟΥΠΟΛΕΩΣ

συγγραφεὶς παρὰ Νικήτα δούλου Ἰησοῦ Χριστοῦ τοῦ καὶ
5   Δαυὶδ τοῦ Παφλαγόνος

1. Πάντων μὲν τῶν ἁγίων τοὺς βίους ἀνατάττεσθαι καὶ διηγεῖσθαι παίδευμά τε πρὸς ἀρετὴν καὶ παράκλησιν ταῖς ἐπιούσαις τῷ
βίῳ παραδιδόναι γενεαῖς, κάλλιστον ὁμοῦ καὶ σωτήριον· μάλιστα
δὲ τῶν ἱεραρχίᾳ σεπτῇ κεκοσμημένων καὶ διὰ τῆς οἰκείας λαμπρό-
10 τητος τοῦ βίου εἰς ζῆλον ἀκάθεκτον τὸν πικρὸν διώκτην ἀνερεθι-
σάντων καὶ δυσμενῆ καὶ διὰ τῆς ἀνενδότου τῶν πόνων ὑπομονῆς
καὶ γενναιότητος λαμπρὰν ἐπιδεδειγμένων τὴν ἀριστείαν κατ’
αὐτοῦ. Εἰ δὲ καὶ πρὸς τοῖς ἐσχάτοις καὶ τοῖς καθ’ ἡμᾶς τούτοις
ἐγγίζοντες τύχοιεν καιροῖς, πολλῷ μᾶλλον ἀξιομνημονευτότατοι
15 ἂν εἶεν ἁπάντων καὶ ἀξιεπαίνετοι ὡς πολὺ πλέον οἰκοδομεῖν τῇ
ἐγγύτητι δυνάμενοι τὴν Ἐκκλησίαν. Τὸ γὰρ ἀρχαῖον καὶ πάμπολυ
κατὰ χρόνον διεστός, εἰ καὶ πιστεύεται τῇ ἀξιοπιστίᾳ τῆς γραφῆς,
ἀλλὰ καὶ θᾶττον ἂν τοῖς πολλοῖς πρὸς τὴν μίμησιν ἀπογινώσκοιτο,
λογιζομένοις ὡς κρεῖττον | ἢ κατὰ τὴν παροῦσαν τῶν πρεσβυτέρων 1ᵛ
20 | ἐκείνων δυναμένων κατορθοῦν γενεῶν. Ὅσα δ’ ἂν τοῖς καθ’ ἡμᾶς 489
κατορθοῦσθαι πιστεύοιτο καιροῖς, μᾶλλον ἂν οἶμαι ταῦτα παρακνίζειν τοὺς εὐσεβεστέρους καὶ πρὸς τὸν ἴσον τῆς ἀρετῆς διερεθίζειν
ζῆλον. Διὰ ταῦτά μοι τοῦτον ἐνστήσασθαι νῦν τῷ λόγῳ τὸν ἀγῶνα
καί μοι σφοδρὸς πόθος κατακάρδιος ἀληθινοῖς διηγήμασι καὶ
25 πάσης προλήψεως ἀπηλλαγμένοις ψεύδους τὸν μέγαν ἱεράρχην καὶ
ποιμένα τῆς βασιλίδος Ἰγνάτιον, ὑπό γε Θεῷ Πνεύματι τῆς Ἀλη-

6-7 cf. Luc. 1.1   10 cf. Greg. Naz. Ad Julianum, PG 35, 1049A; In laud. Cypr., ibid., 1192B

---

1 ΒΙΟΣ…ΑΘΛΗΣΙΣ B: post ΚΩΝΣΤΑΝΤΙΝΟΥΠΟΛΕΩΣ trsp. v   1-24.15 ΒΙΟΣ…πᾶσαν
deest X   4 συγγραφεὶς B: συνεγράφη δὲ v   4-5 τοῦ…Παφλαγόνος v: add. mg. al. m. B
7 τε v: τι B   8 βίῳ B: om. v   17 διεστός v: διεστώς B   20 γενεῶν B: γενεάν v
23 post νῦν coni. σκοπὸς Rader   25 ψεύδους B: ψευδοῦς v

THE LIFE OR STRUGGLE OF OUR HOLY FATHER IGNATIUS, ARCHBISHOP OF CONSTANTINOPLE,

by Nicetas, servant of Jesus Christ, who is also called David, the Paphlagonian.[1]

1. To write biographies of all the saints and thereby pass on instruction and encouragement in virtue to subsequent generations is a very fine and salutary thing to do; especially when those concerned are men invested with the holy priesthood who by the shining example of their lives provoked the bitter and inimical persecutor[2] to uncontrollable jealousy and by steadfast perseverance in their labors and noble-mindedness showed splendid bravery in opposing him. And if besides they should be close in time to the most recent past or even to this present age in which we live, they would deserve much more than anyone else to be mentioned and praised, because they would be far more capable of edifying the Church on account of their proximity to the present day.[3] For in fact most people would be all too ready to despair of imitating anything that is very old and removed from them by a long interval of time, even though it is believed on the authority of the report; they would think that the potential of those ancestors to lead a good life was greater than that of the present generation. But as for all the good acts which are believed to have been performed in our time, I think that they would rather spur on the more pious and incite them to an equal emulation of virtue. That is why it is my present aim[4] to put this man's struggle into words and why I have such a strong desire in my heart to give a true account, free of all suspicion of falsehood, of Ignatius, the great bishop and shepherd of our imperial capital, and (with God, Spirit of Truth, as my guide

θείας ὑφηγητῇ καὶ συλλήπτορι, τοῖς ἀγνοοῦσιν ὁποῖός τις ἦν ἐκ τῆς
κατ' αὐτὸν πολιτείας ἀποδεῖξαι· Ἰγνάτιόν φημι τοῦτον τὸν ὕστερον
μὲν τῷ χρόνῳ καὶ πρὸ τῆς καθ' ἡμᾶς ταύτης ἀναδειχθέντα γενεᾶς,
οὐδενὸς δὲ τῶν πρὸ αὐτοῦ τιμίων ἱεραρχῶν τὴν πίστιν τὴν ὁμολο-
5 γίαν τὴν ὑπὲρ τῆς δικαιοσύνης ἄθλησιν καὶ πρὸς τὸν Θεὸν εὐδοκί-
μησιν ἀπολειπόμενον. Τούτῳ τὴν παρακολουθήσασαν ἐξ ἀρχῆς
ἄχρι τέλους βίωσιν μετὰ πλείονος ὑφηγούμενος τῆς ἀκριβείας καὶ
πᾶσαν τὴν περὶ αὐτὸν ἀλήθειαν ἐκ τῶν ἐγγράφως τε καὶ ἀγράφως
πεπληροφορημένων ἐν ἡμῖν πραγμάτων ἀπροσπαθῶς τε καὶ ἀν-
10 υποστόλως διηγούμενος, πέποιθα πρῶτον μὲν ἐνώπιον τῆς ἐνυπο-
στάτου καὶ ζώσης δίκαια γράφειν Ἀληθείας· δεύτερον δὲ τὸ χρόνοις ἱκανοῖς ἤδη καταπυκνωθὲν τῆς ἀγνωσίας νέφος καὶ τὰς τῶν
πολλῶν ἀμαυρῶσαν διανοίας λεπτῦναί τε καὶ σκεδάσαι· ὥστε τοὺς
ἐθέλοντας πρὸς τὴν τῶν πραγμάτων ἀλήθειαν εἰλικρινῶς ὁρᾶν τὸν
15 ἐργάτην μὲν ἀληθῶς τῆς δικαιοσύνης καὶ τῆς ἀρετῆς εἰδέναι καὶ
ὑμνεῖν καὶ ζηλοῦν· τὸν αὐτουργὸν δὲ τῆς κακίας καὶ τῆς ἀδικίας
ἐνδίκως ἀπωθεῖσθαι. Ἀρκτέον δὲ ἐντεῦθεν.

2. Ἰγνάτιος οὗτος ὁ μακαριώτατος καὶ θεῖος ἱεράρχης πατρίδα 2
μὲν ἔσχεν ἐπὶ τῆς γῆς Κωνσταντινούπολιν, ταύτην δὴ λέγω τὴν
20 πάσης χώρας καὶ πόλεως περιφανεστάτην βασιλίδα· πατέρας δὲ
Μιχαὴλ καὶ Προκοπίαν τοὺς εὐγενεστάτους καὶ πιστοτάτους
βασιλεῖς. Ὧν ὁ Μιχαὴλ μὲν Θεοφυλάκτου πατρικίου μεγαλοπρε-
ποῦς υἱὸς ἦν, Προκοπία δὲ Νικηφόρου θυγάτηρ τοῦ εὐσεβοῦς
ὑπῆρχε βασιλέως. Τούτου δὲ πρὸς τὰ ἄνω μεταχωρήσαντος βασί-
25 λεια καὶ τοῦ υἱοῦ δὲ Σταυρακίου ὀλίγιστον χρόνον ἐπιβιώσαντος τῇ
βασιλείᾳ καὶ αὐτοῦ μεταναστεύσαντος, Μιχαὴλ ὁ προρρηθεὶς
οὗτος ἅτε γαμβρὸς ὢν ἐπὶ θυγατρὶ τοῦ τετελευτηκότος Νικηφόρου
καὶ τὰ πρῶτα τῶν ἐν τῷ παλατίῳ τιμωμένων ἀποφερόμενος (κουροπαλάτης γὰρ ἦν), ψήφῳ μὲν Θεοῦ, ψήφῳ δὲ τῆς συγκλήτου
30 πάσης τὰ σκῆπτρα τῆς βασιλείας ἐγχειρίζεται. Τούτου τὴν περὶ τὸ
Θεῖον εὐσεβῆ γνώμην καὶ τὴν ἄλλην πᾶσαν ἀρετὴν καὶ δικαιοσύνην τοῖς ἱστορεῖν κατὰ μέρος ἐθέλουσι παρήσομεν· ἡμῖν δὲ ἀρκέ-

---

9 τε Β: om. ν   20 πόλεως Β: πόλεων ν   24 ἄνω μεταχωρήσαντος Β: ἄνωθεν χωρήσαντος
ν   26 μεταναστεύσαντος Β: μεταναστάντος ν   28–29 κουροπαλάτης ν: κοροπαλάτης Β

and helper) to demonstrate from his way of life what sort of man he was to those who are unaware of it. Let me tell you that although this Ignatius lived at a later date, indeed in the generation preceding ours,[5] he did not fall short of any of the venerable bishops before him in his faith and its profession, in his struggle for justice and in his good standing in the eyes of God. And so by giving a more precise account of the course of his life from beginning to end and by relating dispassionately and frankly the whole truth about him from what has been ascertained among us in written and unwritten reports,[6] I believe that I shall in the first place be setting down what is right in the presence of the Substantiated and Living Truth; and that, second, I shall dissolve and disperse the cloud of ignorance which has already grown thick from the passage of years and has dimmed the perceptions of the majority of people. As a result, those who are willing to look purely and simply at the true facts will truly recognize the practitioner of justice and virtue, and they will praise and emulate him; whereas they will rightly spurn the author of wickedness and injustice.[7] Let me now begin my account.

2. Our Ignatius, most blessed and holy bishop, had for his native land on earth Constantinople, this most renowned capital of all cities and regions in the empire, and his parents were Michael and Procopia, most noble and devout imperial sovereigns.[8] Michael was the son of the distinguished patrician Theophylact, Procopia the daughter of the pious emperor Nicephorus;[9] and when Nicephorus left this life for the kingdom above, and his son Stauracius survived him as emperor for only a very short time before dying himself, then Michael (the one I just mentioned)—since he was the son-in-law of the late Nicephorus and held the position of highest honor at the palace (*curopalates*)[10]—was chosen by God and by vote of all the senators to be entrusted with the sceptre of imperial office. As for Michael's piousness in matters divine and all his virtue and righteousness in general, I leave that to those who wish to make a detailed investigation;[11] let it suffice for me to praise the

6

σει πρὸς ἔπαινον ἡ τοῦ ἤθους πραΰτης τε καὶ ἐπιείκεια ἦν ἔργοις
ἐκεῖνος καὶ οὐ πλάσματι μόνον ἐπεδείξατο· διετῆ γὰρ ὀλίγου δεῖν
χρόνον εὐσεβέστατα τὴν βασιλείαν διϊθύνας ἑκουσίως αὐτῆς
ἐξέστη καὶ τῷ τυραννικῶς ἐπιθεμένῳ (Λέοντι δὴ τῷ Ἀρμενίῳ φημὶ)
5 στρατηγῷ μὲν πρῶτον ὑπ᾿ αὐτοῦ τῶν Ἀνατολικῶν προχειρισθέντι,
κατὰ Βουλγάρων δὲ στρατευσαμένῳ κἀκεῖθεν τὴν ἐπανάστασιν
βουλευσαμένῳ ὑποχωρεῖ τῆς ἀρχῆς ὁ μακάριος ἑκὼν καὶ τῆς κοσμι-
κῆς ἀλαζονείας καὶ τῶν ἐμφυλίων πολέμων καὶ | φόνων· πολλῷ   492
κρείττω καὶ λυσιτελεστέραν ἑαυτῷ τε καὶ τῷ κοινῷ τὴν ἑκούσιον
10 ὑποχώρησιν καὶ τὴν εἰρήνην ὡς υἱὸς τῆς ἀληθοῦς εἰρήνης ἡγησά-
μενος. Ἀπαίρει μὲν τῆς πόλεως πανοικί, | πρὸς τὰς Πριγκιπίους δὲ   2ᵛ
νήσους μετακεχωρηκὼς καὶ τὸν μονήρη βίον ἅμα γυναικὶ καὶ
τέκνοις οὐ τῷ σχήματι μόνον, ἀλλὰ καὶ τῷ πράγματι καταδεξάμενος, τῷ παμβασιλεῖ Θεῷ τὴν αὐτοῦ κρίσιν καὶ δίκην ἀνέθετο.
15   3. Τούτῳ δὴ τῷ μακαρίῳ Μιχαὴλ τῷ θαυμαστῶς τὴν ἐπίγειον
τῆς οὐρανίας ἀντικαταλλαξαμένῳ βασιλείας παῖδες οἱ πάντες
πέντε λέγονται γενέσθαι· ὧν θήλειαι δύο, πρώτη μὲν ἡ καλουμένη
Γεωργώ, πάντων δὲ ὑστάτη Θεοφανώ· αἵ καὶ παρθενικῶς τὸν ὅλον
βίον καὶ μοναχικῶς διαβιώσασαι μακαρίως ἐκοιμήθησαν. Ἄρρενες
20 δὲ τρεῖς, Θεοφύλακτος Σταυράκιος Νικήτας· τούτων Θεοφύλακτος
μὲν ὁ πάντων πρωτότοκος καὶ ὁ Σταυράκιος ἀμφότεροι τῷ διαδή-
ματι πρῶτον τῆς βασιλείας ἐστεφάνωντο· εἶτα ὁ μὲν κομιδῇ νέος
ὢν ἔτι ὁ Σταυράκιος πρὸ τῆς καταβάσεως τελευτᾷ· Θεοφύλακτος
δὲ ἅμα τοῖς πατράσιν αὐτοῦ καὶ βασιλεῦσι τότε κειράμενος εἰς
25 Εὐστράτιον μετωνομάσθη. Νικήταν δὲ πρῶτον μὲν δεκαέτη τυγχάνοντα τῶν λεγομένων ἱκανάτων δομέστικον παρὰ Νικηφόρου φασὶ
τοῦ πάππου προβεβλῆσθαι, δι᾿ ὃν ἐκεῖνο τὸ τάγμα πρῶτον κατα-
στῆναι· τεσσαρεσκαιδεκαέτης δὲ γεγονὼς καὶ τὰ ἐπὶ γῆς ἅμα τοῖς
ἀγαθοῖς τοκεῦσι βασίλεια καταλιμπάνων ἀποκείρεται μὲν καὶ
30 αὐτός, Ἰγνάτιος δὲ μετονομάζεται.
     4. Ὁ τοίνυν Λέων ἐκεῖνος ὁ δυσώνυμος θὴρ ἣν ὠδίνησεν
ἀδικίαν ἐκτετοκὼς καὶ τῆς βασιλείας τυραννικῇ περιδεδραγμένος

---

1 cf. 2 Cor. 10.1   10 cf. Luc. 10.6   31–32 cf. Ps. 7.15

8 φόνων Β: φθόνων v   17 λέγονται Wilson: λέγουσι Βv   22 ἐστεφάνωντο Β: -ωνται v
26 δομέστικον Β: om. v   27 τάγμα Β: πρᾶγμα v   28 δὲ v: om. Β

mildness of his disposition and the gentleness which he displayed in his actions—and not just for the sake of appearances. For when he had directed the empire most piously for not quite two years, he voluntarily stepped down; faced with the man who attacked him as a usurper, that is, Leo the Armenian[12] (the one who first was appointed by the emperor to be military governor of the Anatolikon theme, then campaigned against the Bulgars, and from there plotted his insurrection)—faced with this, Michael the blessed willingly withdrew from office, from the arrogance of the world and from internecine wars and bloodshed, judging, like a son of true peace, that his voluntary retirement and peace were much better and more advantageous for both himself and the state. So he left the capital with all his household and moved to the Princes' Islands,[13] where along with his wife and children he took up the monastic life (not just superficially donning the habit but in actual fact) and referred judgment in his case to Almighty God.

3. Well now, Michael the blessed, who so admirably exchanged his earthly kingdom for the Kingdom of Heaven, is said to have had five children in all:[14] two girls, the elder called Georgo and the youngest of them all Theophano, who spent their whole lives as virgins and under religious vows and passed away in a state of blessedness; and three boys, Theophylact, Stauracius, and Nicetas. Theophylact, the eldest of all, and Stauracius were both originally crowned with the diadem of the empire. Then Stauracius died while still quite young, before his father's abdication, and Theophylact was tonsured at the same time as his parents, the emperor and empress, and took the name Eustratius. As for Nicetas, he is said first to have been appointed chief of the emperor's ceremonial bodyguard (the so-called *hicanati*) at the age of ten by his grandfather Nicephorus, on whose account that office was first created.[15] Then at the age of fourteen, in the company of his good parents, he left behind the royal palace of this world and he also was himself tonsured and took the name Ignatius.

4. So then, when Leo, that wild beast with a name of bad omen, had given birth to the injustice which he had conceived, when he had seized the empire in his usurper's grasp, he paid no

8

χειρί, οὐ πρὸς τὸν παντέφορον ἀπέβλεπεν ὀφθαλμόν, οὐ τὴν
ἐπιείκειαν τῶν μακαρίων ηὐλαβήθη φυγάδων, οὐδὲ τὸ μέγεθος τῆς
εὐεργεσίας ἧς αὐτὸν οἱ μακάριοι παρ' ἀξίαν κατηξίωσαν, ἐπὶ τοσοῦτον τῷ δολερῷ τῆς κακοτρόπου δελεασθέντες γνώμης, ὥστε καὶ
5 ἀνάδοχον αὐτὸν ἀπὸ τῆς πνευματικῆς κολυμβήθρας τῶν | τῆς   3
βασιλείας ἀναδεῖξαι τέκνων. Οὐδὲν τούτων τὴν ἀπηνῆ καὶ θηριώδη
κατεδυσώπησε ψυχήν· ἀποστείλας δέ, διείργει μὲν αὐτοὺς ἀπ'
ἀλλήλων ἰδίᾳ κατὰ τὰς νήσους ἕκαστον περιορίζων καὶ ὑπὸ ἀσφαλεῖ καταπιέζων φρουρᾷ· ἀφαιρεῖται δὲ τοὺς παῖδας καὶ τῶν γεννη-
10 τικῶν ὁ καταδικάσας ἀμείλικτος μελῶν εὐνουχίᾳ.
    5. Ἐντεῦθεν αὐτὸς μὲν πονηρὰν τῇ αὐτοῦ βασιλείᾳ κατα-
βαλλόμενος ἀρχὴν καὶ τέλος ἄξιον ἀπηνέγκατο τῆς ἀρχῆς. Τὴν γὰρ
πάλαι κακῶς μὲν καὶ θεοστυγῶς μελετηθεῖσαν τῶν Εἰκονομάχων
αἵρεσιν ὑπὸ Λέοντος ἐκείνου τοῦ δυσσεβοῦς καὶ Κωνσταντίνου τοῦ
15 δυσσεβεστέρου κραταιωθεῖσαν υἱοῦ, καλῶς δὲ καὶ εὐσεβῶς διὰ
προνοίας Θεοῦ καὶ τῆς ἁγίας ἑβδόμης συνόδου καθαιρεθεῖσαν καὶ
καταπαυθεῖσαν ὁ μυσαρὸς οὗτος ὄφις καὶ τῆς ἀληθείας παραλογι-
στὴς ἀνανεοῦν αὖθις ἐπιχειρεῖ· καὶ τῷ πύργῳ τῆς ὀρθοδοξίας εὐθὺς
ἐρραγεὶς (Νικηφόρος δὲ οὗτος ἦν ὁ τῆς εὐσεβείας προστάτης καὶ
20 τῆς βασιλίδος ἱεράρχης), τούτῳ προσβαλὼν θωπείαις καὶ ἀπειλαῖς,
ἐπειδὴ στερροτέρῳ μᾶλλον ἢ κατὰ τὴν αὐτοῦ περιέπιπτε βουλήν,
ἐξελαύνει μὲν τυραννικῇ τοῦ θρόνου χειρὶ ἐννέα ἔτεσιν ἤδη ἀποστολικῶς ἰθύναντα τὴν Ἐκκλησίαν, πρὸς τοῖς δεξιοῖς δὲ τοῦ Στενοῦ
μέρεσι κατά τι | σεμνεῖον αὐτὸν ὁ ἀπηνὴς ὑπερορίζει· ὅπου δὴ   493
25 χρόνον ἑπτακαιδέκατον ὁ μακάριος ἐκεῖνος ἐν τῇ καλῇ διαβεβιω-
κὼς ὁμολογίᾳ πρὸς τὸν Θεὸν μετέστη.
    6. Θεόδοτον δέ τινα τῶν ἐν πολιτικοῖς φενακιζομένων ἀξιώ-
μασιν ἄνδρα κοσμικοῖς ἤθεσί τε καὶ πράγμασιν ἐντεθραμμένον,
οὐδεμιᾶς δὲ παιδείας οὐ γνώσεως ἀγαθῆς μετεσχηκότα, μόνον δὲ
30 τῆς Χριστιανοκατηγορικῆς τῶν Εἰκονομαχούντων αἱρέσεως ζηλω-
τὴν νομιζόμενον, κληρικὸν ἀποκείρας ὁ παμβέβηλος τῷ τῆς βασι-

25-26 cf. 1 Tim. 6.12

6 ἀναδεῖξαι v: ἀναδείξ( ) B   8-9 ἀσφαλεῖ v: ἀσφαλῆ B   10 ὁ καταδικάσας B: trsp. v
11-12 καταβαλλόμενος B: καταβαλόμενος v   18 εὐθὺς B: om. v   19 ἐρραγεὶς B:
ἐκραγεὶς v   23 ἰθύναντα B: ἰθύναντι v | τοῖς δεξιοῖς δὲ B: δὲ τοῖς δεξ. v   27 τῶν v: τὸν B

attention to the eye of God, which superintends all things, nor did he respect the virtue of the blessed exiles or the magnitude of the benefaction which the blessed pair had thought him worthy to receive, unworthy though he was. To such an extent had they been deceived by the treachery of Leo's malicious heart that at the holy baptismal font they had actually made him godfather of the imperial children. None of these things, however, brought his cruel and savage heart to shame. Instead, he separated them from one another and banished each of them to a different island, where they were also confined under strict guard. Furthermore, he cruelly condemned the sons to be castrated and had them deprived of their genitals.[16]

5. Then, after founding his reign upon such a wicked beginning, he won for himself an end also worthy of the beginning.[17] For this loathsome serpent and distorter of the truth attempted to revive the wicked heresy, hateful in the eyes of God, of the Iconoclasts, which had been devised long before by that impious emperor Leo and had been strengthened by his even more impious son Constantine, before being piously overthrown and brought to an end by Divine Providence and by the sacred Seventh Synod.[18] He quickly directed his attack against "the tower of orthodoxy" (this was Nicephorus, patriarch of Constantinople and the champion of piety), and using both flattery and threats against him and finding him too obstinate for his liking, he drove him arbitrarily from his patriarchal throne, after he had guided the Church like an apostle for nine years, and harshly banished him to a monastery on the east bank of the Bosphorus.[19] And indeed blessed Nicephorus lived there and splendidly professed his faith for seventeen years before departing to meet his Maker.

6. And that monster of profanity tonsured as a cleric Theodotus, one of those cheats enmeshed in a political career, a man brought up amid the values and affairs of the secular world, who had had no training and possessed no sound knowledge and whose only qualification was that he was considered to be a zealous proponent of the iconoclastic heresy which traduces orthodox Christians—and this was the man whom he set upon the patriar-

λίδος ἐνιδρύει θρόνῳ. Ἐντεῦθεν διωγμὸν πικρὸν | καὶ ἀπάνθρωπον 3ᵛ
κατὰ τῶν εὐσεβεῖν βουλομένων ἐπανῃρημένος εὗρε δὴ κατὰ πόδας
καὶ τὰ τῆς ἁμαρτίας ὀψώνια τὸν θάνατον, ἐν ἑπτὰ μὲν ἔτεσι καὶ
μικρόν τι πρὸς τῆς ἀρχικῆς ἐξουσίας συντετμημένης αὐτῷ, ἐν
5 μέσοις δὲ τοῖς ἀδύτοις τοῦ ναοῦ τῆς Θεομήτορος ὃν δὴ Φάρον ἐν
τῷ παλατίῳ φασὶ κυνὸς τρόπον τοῖς ξίφεσιν ὁ δυστυχὴς κατακο-
πεὶς καὶ καταθανών. Ὁ μὲν οὖν οὕτω φιλοτίμως τὰ τῆς ἀσεβείας
σπέρματα καταβαλόμενος ἀναλόγως τῶν αὐτοῦ πόνων ἐτρύγησε
καὶ τὰς ἐπικαρπίας. Μιχαὴλ γὰρ ὃν καὶ Ψελλὸν εἶναί φασι δομέστι-
10 κος τῶν ἐκσκουβίτων ὢν τότε καὶ ὡς τυραννίδα μελετῶν διαβλη-
θεὶς καὶ κατακλεισθείς, διὰ τῶν αὐτοῦ δὲ συνωμοτῶν καὶ συνασπι-
στῶν λεληθότως τοῖς βασιλείοις ἐν σχήματι κληρικῶν ἐπεισελ-
θόντων ὄρθρου καὶ τὸν τύραννον ἀνῃρηκότων αὐτὸς εὐθὺς ἀναγο-
ρευθείς, τὸν μὲν ἐν σάκκῳ συγκεκομμένον βαλὼν εἰς τὴν Πρώτην
15 καλουμένην νῆσον ἀτίμως προσέταξε ταφῆναι, τοὺς αὐτοῦ δὲ
υἱοὺς εὐνουχισθῆναι καὶ καρῆναι· ὡς "ἐπιστρέψαι τὸν πόνον αὐτοῦ
ἐπὶ τὴν κεφαλὴν αὐτοῦ" κατὰ τὴν Γραφὴν "καὶ ἐπὶ τὴν κορυφὴν
αὐτοῦ τὴν αὐτοῦ ἀδικίαν καταβῆναι."

7. Αὐτὸς δὲ Μιχαὴλ Ἀμοριανὸς καὶ τὴν αἵρεσιν Σαββατιανὸς
20 ὢν ἐπὶ ἐννέα μὲν χρόνους καὶ ἥμισυ τὰ σκῆπτρα διεῖπε τῆς ἀρχῆς,
οὐδεμίαν δὲ τῆς ὀρθοδοξίας φροντίδα ἐποιεῖτο, ἀλλ' οὔτε δὲ βίαν
τοῖς εὐσεβεῖν ἐθέλουσιν ἐπῆγεν. Θεοδότου δὲ τοῦ καὶ Κασσιτερᾶ
λεγομένου τεθνηκότος τὸν Βυρσοδέψην καλούμενον Ἀντώνιον
μητροπολίτην μὲν ἤδη Πέργης γενόμενον καὶ τῆς αἱρέσεως κοινω-
25 νόν, σχολάζοντα δὲ ὁ αὐτὸς Μιχαὴλ ἀναλαβὼν ἀρχιερέα Κωνσταντινουπόλεως ἀποδείκνυσι.

8. Μετὰ τὸν Μιχαὴλ δὲ Θεόφιλος ὁ υἱὸς ἐπὶ δέκα καὶ τρεῖς
χρόνους ἐγκρατὴς γίνεται τῆς βασιλείας. Καὶ ἦν τἆλλα μέν, ὥς
φασιν, οὐ κακὸς καὶ δικαιοκρισίας ἀντεχόμενος· τὴν ἀθέτησιν δὲ | 4
30 τῶν ἱερῶν εἰκόνων καὶ τὸν τῶν ὀρθοδόξων διωγμὸν οὐδενός, ὡς
εἰπεῖν, τῶν πρὸ αὐτοῦ διωκτῶν ἐνομίζετο κουφότερος· καὶ τοῦτο

---

3 Rom. 6.23   16–18 Ps. 7.16

6–7 ὁ...καταθανών B: om. v   9 εἶναί B: om. v   10 ἐκσκουβίτων B: ἐξκουβίτων v
15 αὐτοῦ δὲ B: τε αὐτοῦ v   17 τὴν³ B: om. v   19 Σαββατιανὸς v: σαβατιανὸς B
21 ἀλλ' οὔτε δὲ B: ἀλλὰ καὶ v   22 καὶ B: om. v   23 Βυρσοδέψην v: βυρσοδέψιν B
27 τὸν...δὲ B: δὲ τὸν Μιχαὴλ v   30 εἰκόνων B: om. v

chal throne of Constantinople.[20] But then, after undertaking a bitter and inhuman persecution of those who wished to remain devout Christians, Leo found death, the wages of his sin, close upon his heels; for within the space of a little more than seven years his ruling power was brought to an abrupt end when the wretch was cut down by swords and slaughtered like a dog inside the inner sanctuary of the Church of the Mother of God (the one at the imperial court which they call "Pharos").[21] And so, after sowing the seeds of impiety with such eagerness, he also reaped the fruit of his labors in like proportion. For Michael, who is also known as "Stutterer," was at that time chief of the palace guard and had been imprisoned after being accused of pursuing absolute power for himself; but his soldiers and fellow conspirators entered the palace secretly at dawn disguised as clerics and did away with the tyrant and Michael was immediately proclaimed emperor.[22] He then had Leo cut up into pieces and thrown into a sack and he gave orders for him to be buried ignominiously on the island of Prote[23] and for his sons to be castrated and tonsured. And so, in the words of the Holy Scriptures, "his mischief returned upon his own head and his violent dealing came down on his own pate."

7. Michael, who was from Amorium and was a follower of the heresy of Sabbatius,[24] held the sceptre of imperial office for nine and a half years, and although he showed no concern for orthodoxy, neither did he use force against those who wished to remain devout Christians. And when Theodotus (also known as "Tinker") died, Michael recalled Antony (nicknamed "Tanner"), a follower of the heresy of Sabbatius, who had already been made metropolitan of Perge but had no diocese, and appointed him patriarch of Constantinople.[25]

8. After Michael, his son Theophilus ruled the empire for thirteen years;[26] and although it is said that he was in other respects not a wicked man but in fact an upholder of fair judgments, nevertheless in his rejection of the sacred images and his persecution of orthodox Christians he was held to be no less oppressive than any of the persecutors before him. This was believed to have been done

ἐπιστεύετο εἶναι καὶ γίνεσθαι ἐξ ὑποβολῆς μάλιστα τοῦ Ἰωάννου ὃν
μετὰ τὸν Ἀντώνιον ἐκεῖνος ἐπὶ τὸν πατριαρχικὸν ὕψωσε θρόνον.

    9. Ἐν τούτοις τῶν τε πολιτικῶν καὶ τῶν ἐκκλησιαστικῶν πραγ-
μάτων ὁρωμένων καὶ ἐπὶ τριακονταέτη χρόνον τῆς ὀρθοτομούσης
5 μὲν Ἐκκλησίας μυρίοις ὅσοις κινδύνοις καὶ θανάτοις καὶ θλίψεσι
προσομιλούσης, τῶν ἀσεβῶν δὲ τὰ ἅγια καταπατούντων βεβήλοις
ποσὶ καὶ ἀκαθάρτοις τὰ θεῖα μεταχειριζομένων χερσί, Νικήτας ὁ καὶ
Ἰγνάτιος οἷά τις εὐγενέστατος ὄρπηξ ἐν τῷ οἴκῳ τοῦ Θεοῦ φυτευ-
θεὶς καὶ ἐν ταῖς αὐλαῖς τῆς μοναδικῆς πολιτείας ἐξηνθηκὼς οὐκ
10 ἔμελλεν ἄκαρπος ἐνώπιον τοῦ φυτεύσαντος αὐτὸν ὁρᾶσθαι, οὐδὲ
φύλλοις μόνον εἴτ' οὖν ἀπειροκάλοις | ἐνδύμασι κομᾶν καὶ στολαῖς,   496
κατὰ τὴν κατηραμένην ἐκείνην συκῆν· παρ' ὕδασι δὲ θείοις καὶ
ἀφθονωτάταις τοῦ Πνεύματος μέναν ἐπιρροαῖς καὶ πᾶσαν μὲν
Παλαιὰν Διαθήκην, πᾶσαν δὲ Νέαν ἐκμελετῶν, πᾶσι δὲ λόγοις τῶν
15 ἱερῶν Πατέρων φιλοπόνως ἐσχολακὼς καὶ τούτων τήν τε πρᾶξιν
μιμούμενος καὶ τὴν θεωρίαν ἀναλεγόμενος καὶ τὸν ἐντὸς ἄνθρωπον ὅλως πιαινόμενος ἐν τούτοις καὶ κραταιούμενος καρποφορεῖ τὸν ἥδιστον τῆς ἀρετῆς καρπὸν τῷ Θεῷ. Καρποφορεῖ
πρῶτον μὲν νηστείαν ἀγρυπνίαν ψαλμῳδίαν ἐπιτεταμένην καὶ
20 προσευχὰς τύλους γονάτων δάκρυα στηθῶν ἐπιτίμησιν γλώσσης
ἐγκράτειαν ὑπομονὴν πρὸς πάσας αἰκίας τοῦ καθηγεμόνος σκλη-
ροῦ τε τὴν γνώμην ὄντος καὶ τῷ τοῖς Εἰκονομάχοις χαρίζεσθαι
σκληρῶς πάνυ παιδαγωγοῦντος αὐτόν· πρὸς τούτοις πρᾷτητα καὶ
ταπείνωσιν καὶ ὑπακοὴν πᾶσαν πρὸς πᾶσαν τὴν κατὰ Κύριον ἀδελ-
25 φότητα. Πρῶτον μὲν ταῦτα διὰ πράξεως | ὁ μακάριος μετιὼν καὶ   4ᵛ
τούτοις παιδοτριβούμενος καὶ κάλλιστα προτελούμενος ἀκολού-
θως τῇ αὐξήσει τοῦ σώματος καὶ τὴν πνευματικὴν ἡλικίαν προκόπ-
των κατωρθοῦτο. Ἔπειτα καρποφορεῖ τῷ Θεῷ τὰ τελεώτερα, πίστιν
δὴ λέγω καὶ ἐλπίδα καὶ ἀγάπην· πίστιν τελείαν ἐκ τελείας καὶ ὁλο-
30 κλήρου διανοίας τῷ τελείῳ προσαγομένην Θεῷ· πίστιν ἀνυπό-
κριτον, ἐλπίδα ἀκαταίσχυντον, ἀγάπην εἰλικρινῆ ἐξ εἰλικρινοῦς
καρδίας πρὸς τὸν Θεὸν καὶ τὸν πλησίον κατὰ τὴν ἐντολὴν κατορ-

9–12 cf. Matth. 21.19; Marc. 11.13–14; 21   28–29 1 Cor. 13.13   30–32 cf. 1 Tim. 1.5
32 ἐντολὴν] Matth. 19.19

13 ἀφθονωτάταις B: -τάτοις v   15 φιλοπόνως B: φιλοπείρως v   19 ἐπιτεταμένην B:
ἐπιτεταγμένην v   27 πνευματικὴν B: παιδικὴν v   28 τελεώτερα B: τελειότερα v

mostly at the instigation of John, whom he had elevated to the patriarchal throne to succeed Antony.[27]

9. While matters of Church and state found themselves in this condition and while the orthodox Church for a period of thirty years[28] underwent countless dangers, deaths, and afflictions, as the impious trampled what is sacred beneath profane feet and handled what is holy with impure hands, Nicetas, who took the name Ignatius, like a noble sapling planted in the House of the Lord and brought to full bloom amid the cloisters of monastic life, was not destined to appear unfruitful beneath the planter's gaze or to have merely an abundance of leaves (garments and clothing that know nothing of goodness) like the fig tree which Jesus cursed. By remaining instead beside the sacred waters and abundant streams of the Holy Spirit, by closely studying the whole of both Old and New Testaments, by devoting himself zealously to all the writings of the Holy Fathers, imitating their actions and taking up their spiritual contemplations, he was altogether enriched and strengthened in his inner self and he brought forth for God the sweetest fruits of virtue.[29] These were, in the first place, fasting, vigils, intense singing of psalms and praying; calluses on his knees, tears, beating his breast, moderation of language, and patient endurance of all physical abuse of his teacher who was not only harsh in his views but also used considerable severity in training him to favor the Iconoclasts; and, in addition, gentleness and humility and complete obedience to all the brotherhood of the Lord.[30] So blessed Ignatius first of all pursued these goals in his actions and was educated in these matters, thereby receiving a very fine initiation, while at the same time, in conjunction with the growth of his body, he also succeeded in advancing his spiritual growth.[31] Then he brought forth for the Lord fruits of greater perfection—faith and hope and charity.[32] He offered perfect faith, from a perfect and complete understanding, to God, Who is perfect; and he attained to faith that is free of pretence, hope that can not be put to shame, charity that is pure, from a pure heart, towards God and towards his neighbor, in accordance with God's commandments. By bring-

14

θουμένην. Ταῦτα καρποφορῶν ὁ θεῖος Ἰγνάτιος κἂν τούτοις ἐκ
νεαρᾶς ἡλικίας τοῖς κατορθώμασι συζῶν πάντα τὸν χρόνον ᾧ τὸν
Θεὸν οἱ ἀσεβοῦντες παρεπίκραινον αὐτὸς πρὸς τὴν κατ' εὐσέβειαν κατωρθοῦτο τελειότητα.

5   10. Καὶ γὰρ τοῦ πατρὸς αὐτῷ καὶ [τοῦ] καθηγητοῦ τὸν ἀνθρώπινον μετηλλαχότος βίον, πάσης δὲ τῆς τῶν ἀδελφῶν ἐπιμελείας
καὶ τῆς τῶν ψυχῶν ἐπιστασίας ὡς ποιμένα καλὸν καὶ τῶν λογικῶν
προβάτων καθηγητὴν περιϊσταμένης εἰς αὐτόν, ἔδειξεν ἐν πρώτοις
εὐθὺς τὴν ἐσύστερον ἐν αὐτῷ τοῦ Πνεύματος δύναμιν ἀναφανησο-
10 μένην. Οὕτω γὰρ ταῖς συνεχέσι τῶν λόγων ὁμιλίαις καὶ ταῖς σοφαῖς
παραινέσεσι τὰς αὐτῶν ἐξέτρεφε ψυχὰς καὶ ἐπὶ τὰς ἀειθαλεῖς
ὡδήγει τοῦ Θεοῦ μονὰς ὡς πολλαπλασιασθῆναι μὲν αὐτῷ τὸ τῆς
χάριτος τάλαντον καὶ τῆς πνευματικῆς διδασκαλίας, πολλαπλασιασθῆναι δὲ καὶ τὸ ποίμνιον ἐπὶ τοσοῦτον ὡς μηκέτι τούτους ἑνὶ
15 τόπῳ μηδὲ μιᾷ μονῇ δύνασθαι χωρεῖσθαι, τέσσαρα δὲ τὰ πάντα διὰ
τῆς αὐτοῦ σπουδῆς ἀναστῆναι καὶ καταστῆναι μοναστήρια· ἑκά-
στου τὰς ἁρμοζούσας οἰκοδομὰς καὶ τῶν ἱερῶν σκευῶν καὶ τῶν
ἀναγκαίων χρειῶν τὴν περιποίησιν καὶ πᾶσαν τὴν αὐτοῖς πρέπου-
σαν κατασκευήν τε καὶ διάταξιν διὰ τῆς τοῦ μεγάλου λαμβάνοντος
20 ἐπιμελείας· | καὶ πάντων ὑπ' ἐκείνῳ καθηγεμόνι καὶ πατρὶ διδασκο-   5
μένων ἔργον μὲν ποιεῖσθαι τὴν τοῦ Θεοῦ δοξολογίαν καὶ προσευ-
χήν, ἐν παρέργῳ δὲ καὶ τῆς κατ' αὐτοὺς ἕκαστον ἀντιλαμβάνεσθαι
διακονίας καὶ πάντα ποιεῖν εἰς δόξαν καὶ ἔπαινον Θεοῦ.

11. Πλάτη μὲν οὖν καὶ Ὑάτρος τότε καὶ Τερέβινθος αἱ Πριγκί-
25 πιοι νῆσοι προσαγορευόμεναι ταῖς ἐκείνου προνοίαις οἰκιζόμεναι
καὶ ἀνοικοδομούμεναι εἰς ἐκκλησίας Κυρίῳ καὶ εὐαγεῖς μοναχῶν
καθίσταντο μονάς. Καὶ γὰρ τὴν ἀντικρὺ τούτων κατὰ τὴν ἤπειρον
πρὸς τῇ ἀκτῇ κει|μένην, ταύτην δὴ λέγω τὴν προκαθημένην τοῦ   497
μεγάλου ταξιάρχου μονήν, ἐπὶ τῷ τέλει τῆς αὐτοῦ ζωῆς ὁ μακάριος
30 τελευταίαν ἀνεστήσατο καὶ καθηγίασε τῷ Θεῷ· ἧς τὴν ἐπισημό-
τητα καὶ περιφάνειαν τοῦ τε ναοῦ τὴν ὑπέρκαλον ἀγλαΐαν καὶ

3 κατ' Β: om. v   4 τελειότητα Β: τελειότατα v   5 αὐτῷ Β: αὐτοῦ v | τοῦ² Bv: del.
Karlin-Hayter   6 μετηλλαχότος Karlin-Hayter: -ότων Bv: v. annot. 34 | τῶν Β: om. v
7 τῶν¹ Β: om. v   11 ἐξέτρεφε v: ἐξέστρεφε Β   20 ὑπ' Β: ἐπ' v   26 καὶ ἀνοικοδομ. Β:
om. v | κ(υρί)ῳ Β: Κυρίου v   30 τὴν Β: om. v

ing forth such fruits and associating himself with these virtues from an early age and throughout the whole period when the impious were inciting God to anger, holy Ignatius thus succeeded in attaining perfection in piety.[33]

10. And indeed when his father and teacher left this life, and the charge of his brethren and care of their souls devolved entirely upon him as a good shepherd and guide of the spiritual flock, right from the first he showed the force of the Holy Spirit in him that would appear clearly thereafter.[34] In fact, to such an extent did he nourish their souls with continual sermons and wise admonitions and guide them towards the evergreen Kingdom of God, that his talent of grace and spiritual teaching multiplied,[35] and his flock too multiplied so greatly that they could no longer be contained in a single place or a single abode, and four monasteries in all were set up and established as a result of his zeal.[36] Each one received suitable buildings, provision of its sacred implements and of the necessities of life, and all appropriate equipment and dispositions thanks to the diligence of this great man; and everyone was taught by him, their illustrious teacher and parent, to concern themselves primarily with praying to God and celebrating His glory and that, as a secondary consideration, they should each take up in turn their own ministries and do all things for the glory and praise of the Lord.

11. So then, Plate and Hyatrus and Terebinthus, the so-called Princes' Islands, were at this time reoccupied and settled as a result of his care and attention and turned into churches of the Lord and holy monasteries; and the one situated on the coast of the mainland opposite, that is the preeminent monastery of the Great Archangel Michael, was last to be established and was consecrated to God by blessed Ignatius at the end of his life. The nobility and splendor of this monastery, the exceeding beauty and magnificence of the

μεγαλοπρέπειαν καὶ τὴν ὅλην ἁγιοπρέπειαν καὶ δόξαν, ὡς λόγου κρείττω, ταῖς ὄψεσι παραχωροῦντες ἐπὶ τὰ ἑξῆς τοῦ βίου προΐωμεν.

12. Ἐν τούτοις τοίνυν ὁ ὅσιος ἐνώπιον εὐαρεστῶν Κυρίου ψήφῳ μὲν Θεοῦ Πνεύματος, ψήφῳ δὲ τῶν ὑπὲρ εὐσεβείας ἀγωνιζο-
5 μένων καὶ δεδιωγμένων θεοφόρων ἱεραρχῶν τῆς ἁγίας ἱερωσύνης ἀξιοῦται· καὶ χειρὶ μὲν Βασιλείου (τῆς κατὰ τὸ Πάρεον δὲ οὗτος ἱερᾶς ἐκκλησίας ἀρχιερεὺς ὢν πλείσταις ὅσαις ὑπὲρ τῶν ἱερῶν εἰκόνων θλίψεσι τότε προσωμίλει καὶ διωγμοῖς), τούτου χειρὶ τὸ φαινόμενον, αὐτουργίᾳ δὲ τοῦ παναγίου Πνεύματος τὸ νοούμενον
10 πρῶτον μὲν ἀναγνώστης ἤτοι τῶν θείων ἱεροκῆρυξ Γραφῶν εἶτα ὑποδιάκονος εἶτα διάκονος καὶ ἱερεὺς μετὰ ταῦτα τάξει καὶ νόμῳ πνευματικῆς καθίσταται ἀκολουθίας. Ἠγωνίζετο δὲ ἀεὶ πολλαπλά-σιον τῷ εὐεργέτῃ τὸ τῆς χάριτος τάλαντον ἀποδιδόναι καὶ μὴ τῇ ὀκνηρίᾳ καταχῶσαι, ἀλλὰ τῇ προθυμίᾳ περισσεῦσαι· ὥσπερ δὲ τῷ
15 μοναδικῷ | βίῳ πολλοὺς διὰ τῆς οἰκείας ἀσκήσεως προσηγάγετο 5ᵛ καὶ σπουδῆς, οὕτω διὰ τῆς ἱερατικῆς πάλιν ἀναρίθμητα πλήθη παίδων βαπτίζων ἐσφράγιζε Θεῷ.

13. Ἐπὶ πολὺ γὰρ τῆς αἱρετικῆς ἀχλύος οἷα νυκτὸς χαλεπῆς ἐπικρατούσης καὶ τῆς τυραννίδος δὲ τῶν ἀνιέρων ἐπικειμένης
20 μισθωτῶν, πάντες ὀλίγου δεῖν ἄνθρωποι ὅσοι κατὰ τὸ Βυζάντιον τῆς ὀρθοδόξου πίστεως ἀντείχοντο καὶ ὅσοι δὲ Βιθυνίας καὶ τὰς ἐχομένας κατῴκουν κωμοπόλεις ἄλλος ἄλλον ταῖς ὑπὲρ τοῦ Ἰγνα-τίου διανιστῶντες εὐφημίαις τὰ οἰκεῖα τέκνα προσῆγον καὶ δι' αὐτοῦ βαπτίζεσθαι ταῦτα καὶ ἁγιάζεσθαι κατελίπαρον. Καὶ ἦν
25 ὁρᾶν τοῦτον ὥσπερ ἕνα τῶν πρότερον Χριστοῦ μαθητῶν ἔργον τοῦτο ποιούμενον, τοὺς πρὸς αὐτὸν ἰόντας ὡς ὑπὸ Χριστοῦ πεμπο-μένους προθύμως καταδέχεσθαι, διδάσκειν τε καὶ νουθετεῖν πάντα ἄνθρωπον ἀντέχεσθαι μὲν τῆς ὀρθοδόξου πίστεως, ἀπέχεσθαι δὲ τῆς τῶν αἱρετικῶν δυστροπίας καὶ φρενοβλαβείας, καὶ πάσης μὲν
30 ἑαυτοὺς ῥυπαρίας καὶ παντὸς ἀνακαθαίρειν πνεύματος μολυσμοῦ καὶ σαρκός, πάσης δὲ ἀρετῆς ἐπιμελεῖσθαι καὶ κοσμιότητος καὶ σωφροσύνης· ταῦτα καὶ τὰ τούτοις ὅμοια τοὺς πατέρας παιδεύων

---

3 cf. Ps. 55.14; Gen. 17.1   **12–14** cf. Matth. 25.14–30   **30–31** 2 Cor. 7.1

---

4 θ(εο)ῦ B: θείου v   **21** βιθυνίας B: Βιθυνίου v   **30** παντὸς v: πάντας B

church and all its sanctity and majesty, I must leave for the eyes to see, since no words can describe it, and move on to the rest of Ignatius's life.

12. During this period pious Ignatius pleased the Lord well, and by decree of God the Holy Spirit and the vote of those inspired church leaders who were fighting and suffering persecution on behalf of piety, he was deemed worthy of the sacred priesthood.[37] Through the agency of Basil (he was bishop of the holy church of Parium and was at that time being afflicted by the heaviest possible oppression and persecution for the cause of the holy images)— through the agency of Basil, as it appeared, but in actual fact, from the spiritual point of view, through the unaided activity of the All-Holy Spirit, he was appointed first of all reader, or proclaimer of the Holy Scriptures, next subdeacon, then deacon, and after that priest, according to the canonical order of spiritual precedence.[38] He was forever striving to pay back the talent of grace many times over to his Benefactor, to make it abound through his zeal rather than bury it through sluggishness on his part; and just as he used to attract many to the monastic life by his own devoutness and zealous efforts, so again by his energies as a priest did he baptize countless numbers of children and set God's seal on them.

13. For during the long period when the mist of heresy prevailed like an oppressive darkness and the tyranny of the godless mercenaries was imposed, almost everyone who adhered to the orthodox faith in (the city of) Byzantium, and those too who inhabited the neighboring village-towns of Bithynia, stimulating one another with praise of Ignatius, would bring their children to him and earnestly entreat that they might be baptized and consecrated by him. And like one of the original disciples of Christ, he was to be seen making this his task: eagerly receiving those who came to him as if sent by Christ, teaching and admonishing everyone to adhere to the orthodox faith, to reject the perversity and folly of the heretics, to purge themselves of all foulness, of every defilement of the soul and of the flesh, and to cultivate all virtue, propriety and moderation. And by training the parents in these and similar ways, blessed Ignatius gave their youngsters preliminary

καὶ νουθετῶν τὰ τούτων βρέφη προκατηχῶν ὁ μακάριος δι᾽ ὕδατος
καὶ Πνεύματος ἡγίαζε τῷ Θεῷ.

14. Ὁ μὲν οὖν κατὰ τῆς Ἐκκλησίας τότε χειμὼν βαρὺς καὶ ἡ
κατὰ τῶν ἱερέων δίωξις χαλεπή, ὅσοι Χριστοῦ τῆς εἰκόνος διὰ τὸ
5 πρωτότυπον προκινδυνεύειν εἵλαντο δεῖν· εὔδιος δὲ πᾶσι καὶ γαλή-
νιος ὅρμος τοῖς χειμαζομένοις ὁ ἱερὸς Ἰγνάτιος καὶ ὅλος αὐτοῦ ὁ
οἶκος παρὰ τῆς τοῦ Ὑψίστου προητοίμαστο δεξιᾶς. Τίς γὰρ τῶν
ὑπὲρ εὐσεβείας θλιβομένων οὐχ εὕρισκεν ἐκεῖθεν αὐτάρκη τῶν
θλίψεων ἀναψυχήν; τίς τῶν ἐν φυλακαῖς, | τίς τῶν ἐν ὑπερορίαις καὶ 6
10 δεσμοῖς κατεχομένων καὶ λιμοῖς καταγχομένων οὐ τῆς δεούσης
ἐτύγχανε παρηγορίας καὶ ἄφθονον εἶχε τῶν ἀναγκαίων τὴν ἐπιχο-
ρηγίαν παρ᾽ αὐτοῦ; Οἱ δὲ τὰς τῶν τυράννων φεύγοντες χεῖρας καὶ
τῶν οἰκείων στερούμενοι καὶ τῶν ἰδίων ὑπάρξεων στερούμενοι καὶ
ἐκπί|πτοντες καὶ ἐσχάτῃ πενίᾳ περιπίπτοντες ὅσοι τε τῆς ἱερατικῆς 500
15 μάλιστα καὶ ὅσοι τῆς μοναδικῆς ἐτύγχανον ὄντες τάξεως οὐδὲν
ἄλλο τοῦ βίου παραμύθιον καὶ τῶν λυπηρῶν εἶχον ἀπαλλαγὴν ἢ
τὸν μέγαν Ἰγνάτιον καὶ Προκοπίαν, τὴν αὐτοῦ λέγω μητέρα, καὶ
τὴν ἀδελφὴν ἐπιπολὺ τῷ βίῳ παρατεταμένας καὶ οὕτως ἀφειδῶς τε
καὶ ἱλαρῶς τὸν πλοῦτον ἐκκενούσας καὶ τὸν ἔλεον μιμουμένας τοῦ
20 Θεοῦ, ὡς ἐπ᾽ αὐτοῖς ἀληθῶς τὸ ἱερὸν ἐκεῖνο πληροῦσθαι λόγιον.
Ὅλην γάρ, ὡς εἰπεῖν, τὴν ἡμέραν ἠλέουν καὶ ἐδάνειζον καὶ τὸ
σπέρμα αὐτῶν εἰς εὐλογίαν ἦν. Ὁ μὲν οὖν οὕτω τοῖς ἀγωνισταῖς
συνηγωνίζετο τοῖς κακοπαθοῦσι συνεπάθει τοῖς δεομένοις ἐπήρκει
καὶ τῇ θλίψει μὲν τοῖς θλιβομένοις ὑπέμενε συλλυπούμενος· τῇ
25 προσευχῇ δὲ προσκαρτερῶν ἀδιαλείπτως καὶ τῇ εὐχαριστίᾳ καὶ τῇ
κοινωνίᾳ τοῦ ἄρτου καὶ ταῖς τῶν ἁγίων χρείαις, κατὰ τὸν ἀπόστολον, κοινωνῶν οὕτω πρὸς τοὺς μείζους ὑπὲρ τῆς ἀρετῆς ἀγῶνας
ἡτοιμάζετο. Οὕτω δὲ τὴν μέλλουσαν ἐπ᾽ αὐτὸν ἐμφανήσεσθαι χάριν
τῆς ἱεραρχίας ὁ θαυμάσιος τοῖς ὁρῶσιν ἐπεδείκνυεν ὥστε καὶ
30 Θεοφάνην ἐκεῖνον τὸν μέγαν ἐν τοῖς ὑπὲρ εὐσεβείας ἀγῶσι καὶ
πολὺν ἐν σημείοις καὶ θαύμασι, τὸν τῆς καλουμένης Σιγριανῆς
λέγω μονῆς οἰκιστήν, ἐπιδεδημηκότι πότε πρὸς αὐτὸν τῷ μακαρίῳ

1–2 cf. Ioann. 3.5   6–7 cf. Ps. 76.11   18–19 cf. 2 Cor. 9.6–7   21–22 Ps. 36.26   24–26
Rom. 12.12–13

---

4 τῶν B: om. v   5 εἵλαντο B: εἵλοντο v   9 ἐν φυλακαῖς τίς τῶν B: om. v   12 φεύγοντες
B: φέροντες v   12–13 καὶ…στερούμενοι[1] B: om. v   14 τε B: δὲ v

instruction and consecrated them to God with water and the Holy Spirit.

14. This then was a time of heavy weather for the Church and of harsh persecution for all those priests who felt obliged to brave danger on behalf of Christ's image for the sake of its archetype. But the right hand of the Almighty had prepared in advance a calm and tranquil haven for all those tossed by the storm in the form of holy Ignatius and his whole household. For which of those who were oppressed for their piety did not find there an adequate respite from their afflictions? Which of those held in check by confinement, banishment or imprisonment, or hard pressed by starvation, did not find proper consolation, or have a plentiful supply of the necessities of life from him?[39] Those who fled the clutches of the tyrants and were deprived of their friends and of their personal property, who were banished and fell into a state of utter poverty, and priests and monks in particular, had no other comfort in life or relief from their distress beyond great Ignatius, his mother Procopia, and his sister, who were far advanced in years and yet so generous and gracious in pouring forth their wealth in imitation of God's mercy, that the word of the Psalms was truly fulfilled in them.[40] For close on twenty-four hours a day were they merciful and lending, and their seed was blessed. This then was the way he shared the fight of the champions of Christ, joined in the suffering of those in distress, helped the needy, and patiently offered condolence to the afflicted; and by devoting himself unceasingly to prayer, the eucharist and the communion and "distributing to the necessity of saints," as Paul says, he prepared himself for greater struggles in the interests of virtue. Such signs of the grace which he was to exhibit later as patriarch did our excellent one display to onlookers, that once, while still a young man, when he was visiting the famous Theophanes (a man mighty in his struggles on behalf of piety and strong on signs and miracles, the one who founded the so-called Sigrian monastery), even the latter, so the story goes, laid

νέῳ ἔτι τυγχάνοντι τὴν δεξιάν, ὡς λόγος, ἐπιβαλεῖν καὶ ὡς πατριάρχην αὐτὸν εὐλογεῖν.

15. Ἐν τούτοις τοίνυν αὐτοῦ διαπρέποντος τοῖς κατορθώμασι
τελευτᾷ μὲν ὁ Θεόφιλος, εἰς Θεοδώραν δὲ τὴν εὐσεβεστάτην
5 βασιλίδα | τὴν τιμιωτάτην τῶν γυναικῶν καὶ πιστοτάτην περιέστη 6ʳ
τὰ τῆς ἀρχῆς· ἔτι δὲ νήπιος κομιδῇ τότε Μιχαὴλ ὁ υἱὸς ἦν. Ἐντεῦθεν
ἡ μὲν κατὰ τῶν ἁγίων εἰκόνων αἵρεσις ἐκλείπει, τὸ ἁγίασμα δὲ τῆς
ἱερᾶς Ἐκκλησίας ἐξανθεῖ. Ἐντεῦθεν καὶ Ἰωάννης εὐθὺς ὁ δυσώνυ-
μος Ἰαννῆς (ὃν καὶ λεκανομάντιν ἔλεγον καὶ τῆς Θεοφίλου πλάνης
10 ὑπαίτιον) τοῦ πατριαρχικοῦ θρόνου καὶ τῆς ἱερωσύνης ἐνδίκως
καθαιρεῖται, ἀνίσταται δὲ κέρας σωτηρίας τῷ λαῷ τοῦ Θεοῦ Μεθό-
διος ὁ καλὸς ὄντως τοῦ Χριστοῦ προβάτων ποιμὴν καὶ τῶν ὀρθῶν
τῆς Ἐκκλησίας δογμάτων ὀρθοτόμος ὑφηγητής· ὃς πολλοὺς ὅτι
μάλιστα πόνους καὶ κινδύνους ὑπὲρ τῶν ἁγίων πρότερον ὑπομεμε-
15 νηκὼς εἰκόνων ἀνίσταται μὲν Θεοῦ ψήφῳ καὶ τῆς βασιλίδος συνεργίᾳ πρόεδρος τῆς Ἐκκλησίας Κωνσταντινουπόλεως· καθαιρεῖ δὲ
πάντας καὶ κατασπᾷ τῶν ἐκκλησιῶν ὅσοι τῷ μύσει τῆς αἱρέσεως
ὑπήχθησαν· ἀνίστησι δὲ Ἐκκλησίαν καινὴν ἱερεῖς τε καὶ ἀρχιερεῖς
ἐπὶ τῷ θεμελίῳ τῆς κατ᾽ αὐτὸν ὀρθοδόξου πίστεως προεχειρίσατο.
20 Καὶ γὰρ τῶν αἱρεσιωτῶν ὡς ἤδη καὶ πρότερον ἐπὶ Ταρασίου τοῦ θείου καὶ
ἱεροῦ ποιμένος καὶ τῆς εὐσεβοῦς Εἰρήνης ἀνατεθεματικότων μὲν τὴν
αἵρεσιν καὶ οὕτω συγκεχωρημένων, παλινδρομησάντων δὲ καὶ πρὸς
τὴν αὐτὴν αὖθις λύμην ὑπενηνεγμένων· τούτων μὲν οὖν τελείαν
καθαίρεσιν καὶ διηνεκῆ Νικηφόρος τε ἔτι τῷ βίῳ περιὼν ὁ μέγας
25 καὶ αὐτὸς οὗτος θεοβουλεύτως ὁ ἱερὸς καταψηφισάμενος Μεθό-
διος καὶ τοῦ θεοφόρου ταῖς ὑποθήκαις Ἰωαννικίου κατὰ πάντων
τῶν | αἱρεσιωτῶν ἀποφηνάμενος εὔθετον τοῖς ὀρθοτομεῖν ἐθέλουσι 501
τὴν τῆς ὀρθοδοξίας ὑπέδειξεν ὁδόν· ἐπὶ τέσσαρας δὲ χρόνους
κάλλιστά τε καὶ ἄμεμπτα τὴν τοῦ Κυρίου ποιμάνας Ἐκκλησίαν ἐν
30 εἰρήνῃ πρὸς αὐτὸν μετέστη.

16. Πολλῶν τοιγαροῦν εἰς προστασίαν τῆς Ἐκκλησίας προχει-
ριζομένων καὶ ἄλλων δι᾽ ἄλλας αἰτίας διαμαρτανόντων τοῦ
σκοποῦ, ἵνα ἡ προορισθεῖσα τοῦ Θεοῦ βουλὴ μείνῃ, | Ἰγνάτιος ὁ 7

---

9 cf. 2 Tim. 3.8   11 Luc. 1.69   12 Ioann. 10.11; 14

11 κέρας EGJ: τέρας B πέρας v   12 τοῦ B: τῶν v   27 εὔθετον B: εὐθεῖαν ἔτι v

his hand upon blessed Ignatius and gave him his blessing as future patriarch.[41]

15. While Ignatius was distinguishing himself amid these virtuous pursuits, Theophilus died and control of the empire passed to Theodora, most pious empress and most honorable and trustworthy of women, since their son Michael was at that time still a minor.[42] From then on the sect opposed to the holy images began to wane and the sanctity of the sacred Church blossomed forth. Then too was John rightly deposed from the patriarchal throne and from the priesthood—he earned himself the bad name of Jamnes and people said he was a dish-diviner and responsible for Theophilus's going astray.[43] And a horn of salvation was raised up for God's people in the person of Methodius, who was in truth the good shepherd of Christ's flock and orthodox exponent of the true teachings of the Church.[44] He had in the past endured the greatest number of tribulations and dangers for the sake of the holy images and now by God's decree and with the help of the empress he was raised to the position of head of the Church in Constantinople.[45] He deposed and drove out from the churches all those who had been brought under the taint of the heresy, established the Church anew, and appointed priests and bishops based upon the foundations of his own orthodox faith.[46] For just as happened earlier in the time of Tarasius, sacred and holy shepherd, and of pious Irene, the heretics condemned their sect and were forgiven, but then reverted and slipped back into the same old corrupt ways.[47] So Nicephorus the mighty, while still alive, and this same holy Methodius condemned them to total and permanent deposition in accordance with God's will, and following the opinion of divinely inspired Joannicius decreed the same against all heretics, while indicating the suitability of the path of orthodoxy to those willing to follow it.[48] For four years Methodius shepherded the Church of the Lord in a most excellent and irreproachable manner and then departed in peace to meet his Maker.

16. Many were then put forward for the office of leader of the Church, but for one reason or another all fell short of the mark, until Ignatius, the most holy presbyter, was appointed, so that God's

ὁσιώτατος πρεσβύτερος πλείστοις ἔτεσιν ἤδη τοῖς τῆς ἱερωσύνης
χαρίσμασιν ἐνευδοκιμηκὼς καὶ βαθμὸν ἑαυτῷ καλὸν ἐν πολλῇ
παρρησίᾳ καὶ τῇ ἐν Χριστῷ Ἰησοῦ πίστει περιποιησάμενος καὶ ἐν
τοῖς ἁπάντων διὰ τοῦτο στόμασιν ᾀδόμενος, καίτοι γε πλεῖστα
5 παραιτούμενος καὶ τὸν ὄγκον τοῦ ἀξιώματος ἀποδιδράσκων πανευλαβῶς, ὅμως ἐνεργείᾳ μὲν Θεοῦ Πνεύματος, συνεργίᾳ δὲ καὶ
ψήφῳ ἀρχιερέων Θεοῦ τῆς θείας ἱεραρχίας ἀξιοῦται καὶ τῷ θρόνῳ
τῆς βασιλίδος ἐνίδρυται καὶ τῇ λυχνίᾳ ὁ λύχνος ἐπιτίθεται. Πρὸ
πάντων δὲ τῶν ἀρχιερέων καὶ τῶν λαῶν τῆς βασιλίδος ἀποστειλά-
10 σης καὶ ἀξιωσάσης διὰ Κυρίου γνωρίσαι τὸν ἄξιον προφητικῶς ὁ
μέγας τοῦτον Ἰωαννίκιος ψηφίζεται· καὶ οὕτως διὰ τῆς θύρας ὁ
ποιμὴν ὁ καλὸς εἰς τὴν αὐλὴν τῶν προβάτων εἰσελθὼν τὰ ἴδια
πρόβατα ἐκάλει κατ' ὄνομα· καὶ πάσης μὲν νομῆς θανασίμου καὶ
βλαβερᾶς, πάσης δὲ λύμης καὶ ἀπωλείας ἐξῆγεν αἱρετικῆς πρὸς τὰς
15 ἀειζώους δὲ καὶ ἀειθαλεῖς τῆς ὀρθοδόξου πίστεως καὶ δικαιοσύνης
ὡδήγει καὶ εἰσῆγε νομάς· καὶ αὐτὸς μὲν κακίας ἁπάσης τοσοῦτον
ἀπείχετο ὅσῳ πάσης ἀντείχετο δικαιοσύνης· ἐξαιρέτως δὲ πρὸς τὰς
τῶν ἀρετῶν κατορθούμενος γενικὰς τῆς κατ' εὐσέβειαν τελειό-
τητος ἐπεμελεῖτο. Φρόνησις μὲν γὰρ αὐτῷ διεσπούδαστο οὐχ ὥστε
20 πλοῦτον ἑαυτῷ καὶ δόξαν πορίζεσθαι κοσμικὴν καὶ ποικίλας σώματος ἡδονάς, ἀλλ' ὥστε τὸ θέλημα τοῦ Θεοῦ τὸ ἀγαθὸν καὶ εὐάρεστον καὶ τέλειον ἐν διακρίσεως πνεύματι καλῶς συνιέναι καὶ ποιεῖν.
Ἀνδρία δὲ αὐτῷ τὸ μὴ ἡττᾶσθαί ποτε τῆς ἁμαρτίας, ἀλλ' ἐλεύθερον
εἶναι καὶ δεσπόζειν τῶν παθῶν καὶ μὴ κατὰ τοὺς πολλοὺς πρόσωπα
25 κρυφῇ θαυμάζειν τῶν δυναστῶν· ἀποτόμως δὲ τὸν ἁμαρτάνοντα
κατὰ τὸν ἀποστολικὸν νόμον διελέγχειν καὶ τοῦτο πολλάκις ἐνώπιον πάντων καὶ μὴ καθυφίεσθαι δουλοπρεπῶς, ἵνα καὶ οἱ λοιποί,
φησί, φόβον ἔχωσι. Σωφροσύνη δὲ οὐ τοῦ οἰκείου σώματος μόνον
ἡ ἁγνότης τε καὶ καθαρότης, ἣν ἐκ νεαρᾶς ἡλικίας οὕτω πόνοις
30 συχνοῖς | καὶ ἱδρῶσι κατωρθώσατο ὡς εἰς ἄκραν αὐτὸν ἀπάθειαν   7ᵛ
ἤτοι παντελῆ νέκρωσιν τοῦ σαρκίνου φρονήματος ἐλθεῖν. Οὐ ταύτῃ
γοῦν μόνον τὸ τῆς σωφροσύνης ὡρίζετο καλόν, πάσῃ δὲ σπουδῇ

2-3 1 Tim. 3.13 8 Matth. 5.15; Marc. 4.21; Luc. 8.16; 11.33 11-13 Ioann. 10.2-3
21-22 Rom. 12.2 24-25 cf. Iob 13.10 25-28 1 Tim. 5.20 29-30 cf. Greg. Naz. Or. II,
PG 35, 461B; Bas. Hom. in pr. prov., PG 31, 421A

6 θ(εο)ῦ Β: θείου v 24-25 τῶν...θαυμάζειν Β: om. v 25 κρυφῇ LXX: κρυφῆ Β

predetermined design might be fulfilled.[49] He had gained glory already by his tenure of the holy office of the priesthood over a period of very many years and acquired high standing for himself by frequent outspokenness and his faith in Jesus Christ. For these qualities his praises were sung by everyone, and though he refused most emphatically and reverently shunned the weighty dignity of office,[50] nevertheless by the agency of the Holy Spirit and through the cooperation and decree of God's high ministers he was judged worthy of the holy office and was established in the patriarchal see of the capital, like a lamp placed on its stand. The empress had sent off to ask Joannicius ahead of all the bishops and the people to discover with the Lord's help who was worthy of the position, and the great man prophetically cast his vote for Ignatius.[51] Thus did the good shepherd enter through the gate into the fold of his flock and call his own individual sheep by name. He led them out of all harmful and deadly pastures, away from all the corruption and depravity of the heretics, and guided them to the eternal evergreen pastures of justice and the orthodox faith. His strict abstinence from every vice was rivaled by his equally strict adherence to every form of justice, and by attaining in particular to the principal virtues he cultivated perfection in piety. Prudence was a quality he zealously pursued, not with the idea of gaining riches for himself or worldly glory or manifold pleasures of the flesh, but for the purpose of knowing well and carrying out in a spirit of right discernment the will of God—what is good and well pleasing and perfect in His eyes. Fortitude meant to him never to be overpowered by sin, but to be free and keep the upper hand over his emotions and not, like the majority, secretly admire the characteristics of those in power; to expose sinners relentlessly in accordance with the precepts of the Apostle—and to do this often before the eyes of everyone rather than give in to them in subservient fashion, in order that the rest of them, so he says, might be filled with fear. Temperance too he pursued, and not only in terms of his own body's chastity and purity, which he had cultivated from an early age with such hard work and sweat of his brow that he had arrived at a state of absolute mastery over his passions and of complete mortification of his

καὶ τὴν κατ᾽ αὐτὸν Ἐκκλησίαν ἐπὶ τοσοῦτον ἥγνιζε καὶ τῷ ἐμβριθεῖ
τε καὶ συνεχεῖ τῆς τοῦ Πνεύματος διδασκαλίας ἐσωφρόνιζεν ὡς
μηδ᾽ ὄνομα πορνείας ἤ τινος ἄλλης ἀκαθαρσίας ἐν τοῖς αὐτῷ πλη-
σιάζουσιν ἀκούεσθαι· ἀλλ᾽ ὥσπερ αὐτὸς τὴν ἄμωμον ὁδὸν τοῦ
5 Κυρίου ἀμώμως ἐπορεύετο, οὕτω καὶ τὴν ἐκείνου νύμφην ὡς
ἀγαθὸς νυμφοστόλος ἐν ἀμώμῳ προῆγε πολιτείᾳ. Περὶ δικαιοσύνης δὲ τί χρὴ καὶ λέγειν; ἣν οὕτω στερρῶς καὶ μεγαλοπρεπῶς ὁ
μακάριος ἐνδέδυτο ὥστε καὶ μέμψιν δι᾽ αὐτὴν ὑπέχειν πολλάκις
παρὰ τοῖς ἀδίκοις τοῦ δικαίου | διαιτηταῖς καὶ σκληρότατα κατα- 504
10 γινώσκεσθαι τὸν ὡς ἀληθῶς πρᾶον ποιμένα καὶ Θεοῦ μιμούμενον
δικαιοσύνην· καὶ γὰρ οὐκ ἐν τοῖς ἀνθρωπίνοις πράγμασι μόνον,
ἀλλὰ καὶ ἐν ταῖς ἐκκλησιαστικαῖς πολὺ μᾶλλον ἀμφισβητήσεσι καὶ
κρίσεσι τὸ πρὸς ἀλήθειαν μὲν καὶ δικαιοσύνην ἐπιρρεπές, ὑπερ-
οπτικὸν δὲ αὐτοῦ καὶ ἀπότομον πρός τε τὸ ψεῦδος καὶ ἀδικίαν
15 πᾶσαν ἐγνωρίζετο· καὶ οὐ πρὸς τοὺς πολλοὺς μόνον καὶ χυδαιο-
τέρους πρὸς οὓς ἀδικοῦντας τάχα καὶ ἄλλος ἂν παρρησιάσαιτο,
ἤδη δὲ καὶ πρὸς τοὺς τὰς πρώτας περιβεβλημένους δυναστείας καὶ
πρὸς τοὺς βασιλέας αὐτοὺς ὁ τοῦ ἀρχιερέως ζῆλος καὶ ἡ ἔνθεος
παρρησία διεδείκνυτο· δηλώσει δὲ νῦν ὁ λόγος.
20   17. Τὸν Βάρδαν ἐκεῖνον οἶδ᾽ ὅτι πάντες ἀκούετε ὃς Θεοδώρας
μὲν τῆς ἀγαθῆς βασιλίδος ἀδελφὸς ἦν, οὐκ ἀγαθὸς δέ, ἀλλὰ καὶ
λίαν πικρὸς καὶ ἀπάνθρωπος· ὃν σπουδαῖον μὲν εἶναι καὶ δραστή-
ριον περὶ τὴν τῶν πολιτικῶν πραγμάτων μεταχείρισιν, οὐδεὶς δὲ
περὶ τὴν Ἐκκλησίαν χρηστὸν ἔφησε γενέσθαι· τοῦτον τῇ ἰδίᾳ φασὶν
25 οὕτως ἐπιμανῆναι νύμφῃ ὡς ἀνὰ πᾶσαν τοῦτο τὴν πόλιν περιβομ-
βηθῆναι· καὶ οὐκ ἄχρι τῶν πολλῶν μόνων, ἀλλὰ καὶ μέχρις αὐτοῦ
τοῦ ἀρχιερέως τὴν πονηρὰν φήμην ἐλθεῖν. Τί οὖν ἐκεῖνος; Οὐ τὸ
μέγεθος ἠυλαβήθη τοῦ προσώπου οὐδὲ συνεσκίασε τὸ ἀμπλάκημα
τῇ σιωπῇ, | ἀλλὰ καὶ ἤλεγξε κατὰ τὴν ἐντολήν, ἀλλὰ καὶ ἐπετίμη- 8
30 σεν, ἀλλὰ καὶ παρεκάλεσε φείσασθαί τε τῆς ἰδίας ψυχῆς καὶ τὸ
φρικτὸν τουτὶ μῦσος ἀποτρίψασθαι· ὁ δὲ οὐ μόνον οὐκ ἀπέσχετο
τοῦ κακοῦ, ἀλλὰ καὶ ἐπὶ τῆς ἐκκλησίας (ἑορτὴ δὲ τῶν ἁγίων Θεο-

---

3 cf. Ephes. 5.3   4 Ps. 100.6; 118.1   6–8 cf. Ephes. 6.14; Ps. 131.9   29–30 2 Tim. 4.2

6 προῆγε B: προσῆγε v   8 ἐνδέδυτο B: ἐνεδέδυτο v   15 ab ἐγνωρίζετο incipit X   18 ἡ
B: om. v   20 ὃς BXv²: ὡς v¹   23 περὶ Xv: παρὰ B   26 μόνων B: μόνον Xv   31 μῦσος
v: μῖσος B | ἀποτρίψασθαι B: ἀπορρύψασθαι v

desires of the flesh. Not only, then, was the splendor of his temperance defined in this manner, but so thoroughly and zealously did he purify his Church and make it chaste by the austerity and perseverance of his spiritual teaching, that not even a mention of sexual impurity or of any other uncleanness was heard among his familiars. And in just the same way as the man himself walked blamelessly along the blameless paths of the Lord, so he also, like a good guardian and escort, guided the bride of the Lord in blameless conduct of life. What need is there to speak of his sense of justice (a quality which blessed Ignatius so firmly and magnificently assumed that he often met with censure on account of it from unjust arbiters of what is just and was condemned in the harshest terms, though he was in truth the gentle shepherd and imitator of God's justice)?[52] Not only in the affairs of men, but much more so in ecclesiastical disputes and judgments was his leaning towards truth and justice well known, as was his contempt for and abruptness with lies and every form of injustice; and the zeal of the patriarch and his God-given boldness of speech was displayed, as the account will now show, not only with the common and ordinary folk, against whose injustices others might perhaps be tempted to speak out, but also with those in the positions of the highest power, even the emperors themselves.

17. I know that you've all heard of the famous Bardas, brother of the good empress Theodora, but not a good man himself—he was too cruel and inhumane.[53] He was zealous and energetic in his handling of the affairs of state, but nobody could call him good for the Church. They say he was so infatuated with his own daughter-in-law that it was openly talked about throughout the city and his bad reputation reached the ears not only of the ordinary people but also of the patriarch himself.[54] What then did Ignatius do? He paid no heed to the man's importance, nor did he gloss over the sin by remaining silent, but reproached him in accordance with God's commandment and censured him, entreating him to spare his own soul and cleanse himself of this awful defilement. However, not only did he not desist from his evil ways, but on the feast of the Epiphany he actually had the gall to enter the church in person

φανίων ἦν) καὶ αὐτὸς ἀναιδῶς προσῆλθε τῶν θείων μεθέξων μυστηρίων. Τί δὲ ὁ ἀρχιερεύς; Ἀποβάλλεται τῆς κοινωνίας, ἀνάξιον
τοῦτον τῆς τοῦ Δεσποτικοῦ σώματος κρίνει μεταλήψεως. Ὁ δὲ μαί-
νεται μανίᾳ πικρᾷ καὶ κατὰ τῆς ἰδίας ὁπλίζεται ψυχῆς· ἀπειλεῖ τὸ
5 οἰκεῖον ξίφος τοῖς σπλάγχνοις τοῦ ἱεράρχου καταχῶσαι· ὁ δὲ ἀντ-
απειλεῖ τὸν δυνάμενον ἐκκαλούμενος ἐπιστρέψειν τὴν ῥομφαίαν
αὐτοῦ ἐπ᾽ αὐτόν. Αὕτη γίνεται σκανδάλων ἀρχή· αὕτη πρώτη τῆς
ἐκκλησιαστικῆς ἀκαταστασίας ἀφορμή. Ἐντεῦθεν βαρὺν ἑαυτῷ
χόλον καὶ μῆνιν ὁ Βάρδας ἐκεῖνος ἐναποθέμενος κατὰ τοῦ Ἰγνατίου
10 πάντα κάλων ἐκίνει, τὸ δὴ λεγόμενον, τῷ βασιλεῖ τοῦτον διαβαλεῖν.
Πατρίκιος δὲ τότε καὶ τῶν σχολῶν δομέστικος ὢν ὅλην τοῦ Μιχαὴλ
ἅτε δὴ θεῖος εἰς ἑαυτὸν τὴν ἀρχὴν ὑπεποιεῖτο. Καί ποτε προσεληλυ-
θὼς τῷ μειρακίῳ καὶ λόγοις καταγοητεύων ἀπατηλοῖς· "Ἵνα τί"
ἔλεγεν "ὦ δέσποτα, παραχωρεῖς τὴν βασιλείαν τῇ μητρὶ καὶ ταῖς
15 ἀδελφαῖς; μὴ γὰρ ἔτι νήπιος εἶ; μὴ τὴν ἡλικίαν ἀτελής; Ἀλλ᾽ ἰδού"
φησὶν "ἐζεύχθης καὶ γυναικὶ καὶ ἤδη εἰς ἄνδρας τελεῖς· ὀφείλεις καὶ
φρόνημα λοιπὸν ἀναλαβεῖν ἀνδρός· τὴν μητέρα δὲ καὶ τὰς ἀδελφὰς
τὸν πατριάρχην μετακαλεσάμενος ἀποκεῖραι πρόσταξον. Σὲ γὰρ
βασιλεύειν μόνον λοιπὸν καὶ τοὺς ἐκ σοῦ τεχθησομένους καὶ Θεῷ
20 καὶ πᾶσιν ἡμῖν ἀρεστόν." Αὐτίκα τοίνυν ἐκεῖνος τὸν τίμιον ἱεράρχην
μεταπέμπεται· εὐρίπιστον γὰρ ἡ νεότης καὶ ῥᾳδίως ταῖς κεναῖς τῶν
ἐλπίδων μετεωριζόμενον. Εἰ δὲ καὶ ἐξουσίας ὑπεροχὴ προσείη,
μείζων μὲν ἡ κουφότης, εἰς μείζω δὲ ἄνοιαν καὶ πτῶσιν ὡς τὰ πολλὰ
προσχωρεῖ. Τότε τοίνυν ἀρχὴν ταῖς κατ᾽ αὐτὸν ἀταξίαις καὶ ἀπαι-
25 δευσίαις, μᾶλλον δὲ ἀσεβείαις, ὁ Μιχαὴλ καταβαλλόμενος, "ταχὺ
τὴν ἐμὴν μητέρα καὶ τὰς ἀδελφάς" | πρὸς τὸν δίκαιον | ἔφη "λαβὼν   8ᵛ|505
καὶ ἀποκείρας τῷ μοναχικῷ σχήματι ταύτας καταδίκασον." Ὁ δὲ
παρρησιασάμενος "Ἀδύνατόν μοι τοῦτο ποιεῖν" εἶπεν ὑπολαβών·
"τῆς γὰρ Ἐκκλησίας τοὺς οἴακας τὴν ἀρχὴν ἐγχειριζόμενος ἔγγρα-
30 φον ὅρκον ἐθέμην μηδεμίαν κατὰ τῆς βασιλείας ὑμῶν ἐπιβουλὴν ἢ
οἱανοῦν ἐπήρειαν πώποτε διαλογίσασθαι. Καὶ νῦν τί τὸ ἀδίκημα
τῶν βασιλίδων; Καὶ τίς ἡ κατ᾽ αὐτῶν αἰτία, ὅτι τὸ ὑμέτερον κράτος ταῦτα

---

10 CPG II 201

3 κρίνει B: κρίνων v   23 μείζων Xv: μεῖζον B   24 προσχωρεῖ B: προχωρεῖ v   27 καὶ B:
om. v | ἀποκείρας B: ἀπόκειραι v   30 κατὰ B: om. v   31 πώποτε B: ποτε v

with the intention of partaking of the holy sacrament.[55] And what did the patriarch do? He rejected him from communion and judged him to be unworthy of partaking of the Lord's body. Bardas was filled with bitter rage and took up arms against his own salvation by threatening to bury his sword in the patriarch's heart, while the latter made a counter-threat, invoking Him Who had the power to do so to turn his sword against Bardas. This was the start of the disturbances, the origin of the disorder in the Church. From this point on Bardas harbored in his heart a deep resentment and anger against Ignatius and left no stone unturned, as the saying goes, in bringing him into discredit with the emperor. He was a patrician and *domesticus scholarum*[56] and because he was Michael's uncle, he had at this time assumed complete control of the empire. And on one occasion he went to the young man and beguiled him with deceitful talk, saying: "Why, my lord, do you yield control of the empire to your mother and sisters? You're not still a child, are you? Are you not a full-grown man? Why, you have even taken a wife and have already entered the world of men. So for the future you should also adopt a man's self confidence. Summon the patriarch and order him to tonsure your mother and sisters, since it pleases God and all of us to see you and your line as sole rulers for the future." So Michael immediately sent for the venerable patriarch. Youth is so inflammable and easily buoyed up by empty hopes, but whenever preeminence in power is an added ingredient, greater is its levity and greater the folly and calamity to which it generally proceeds. So it was that Michael embarked upon his unbridled, undisciplined (I should say impious) course and said to the righteous patriarch: "Seize my mother and sisters, tonsure them and condemn them to don the monastic habit." But the patriarch spoke his mind in reply and said: "That is impossible for me to do. When I was first entrusted with the office of helmsman of the Church, I took an oath in writing that I would never countenance a plot or any kind of attack against your imperial power. So now what wrong have the empresses done, what are they accused of that makes your Majesty form such designs against them?"[57] When the patriarch

κατ' αὐτῶν διενοήθη;" Οὕτως εἰπόντος τοῦ ἀρχιερέως καθοσιώσεως τοῦτον ὁ Βάρδας ἐγράψατο γραφὴν Γηβοβασίλευτον ἔναντι τοῦ βασιλέως διαλοιδορούμενος. (Ἦν δὲ ὁ Γήβων οὗτος ἐπίληπτος ἄνθρωπος καὶ τὰς φρένας οὐ πάνυ καθεστηκὼς ὃς πρὸ τῶν ὀλίγων
5 ἐκείνων ἡμερῶν ἀπὸ τοῦ Δυρραχίου παρεγένετο, σχῆμα μὲν περικείμενος κληρικοῦ, παῖδα δὲ ἑαυτὸν τῆς βασιλίδος Θεοδώρας ἐξ ἀνδρὸς ἑτέρου ληρῶν· ᾧ οἱ πολλοὶ τοῦ δήμου ὡς βασιλεύειν μέλλοντι προσεῖχον· τότε δὲ ἐν Ὀξείᾳ τῇ νήσῳ ὑπὸ ἀσφαλεῖ συνείχετο φρουρᾷ.) Ὁ μὲν οὖν πατριάρχης ἐν ὑπονοίᾳ διὰ ταῦτα τῷ Μιχαὴλ
10 καταστὰς εὐθὺς ὑπενόστει πρὸς τὴν ἐκκλησίαν. Ὁ δὲ παραχρῆμα τὴν μητέρα καὶ τὰς ἀδελφὰς καταγαγὼν ἐν τοῖς Καριανοῦ λεγομένοις ἀπενεχθῆναι κελεύει καὶ καρῆναι. Μετὰ μικρὸν δὲ καὶ αὐτὸν ἀπελαύνει τοῦ πατριαρχείου τὸν Ἰγνάτιον καὶ πρὸς τὴν νῆσον Τερέβινθον αὐτὸν ὑπερορίζει· κατ' αὐτὴν δὲ τὴν ἡμέραν καὶ Γήβονα
15 ἐκεῖνον ἀπὸ τῆς Ὀξείας εἰς Πρίγκιπον μετενεγκὼν τά τε σκέλη καὶ τοὺς βραχίονας ἐξέκοψεν, καὶ τοὺς ὀφθαλμοὺς ἐξορύξας ἀπέκτεινεν αὐτὸν οἰόμενος ταύτῃ τὸν πατριάρχην ἀμυνεῖσθαι.

18. Οὔπω τρεῖς μετὰ τὴν κατάβασιν διεληλύθεισαν ἡμέραι καὶ παρῆσαν τῶν ἐπισκόπων οἱ νομιζόμενοι λογάδες λίβελλον ἀποτα-
20 γῆς ἤτοι παραίτησιν διὰ τὴν ἐνεστῶσαν τοῦ καιροῦ κακίαν ἀξιοῦντες λαβεῖν παρ' αὐτοῦ. | Καὶ ταῦτα τίνες; Οἱ ἐγγράφως αὐτῷ πρό- 9
τερον ὀμωμοκότες καὶ αὐτῆς ἐκπεσεῖν τῆς ὑπερουσίου Τριάδος εὐξάμενοι, εἴγε τὸν οἰκεῖον ποιμένα ἄνευ καταγνώσεως ἀθετήσαιεν κανονικῆς. Ἀλλ' αὐτοὶ μὲν ὑπέστρεφον ἀνήνυτα πεπονηκότες.
25 Μετ' ὀλίγας δὲ αὖθις ἡμέρας πατρίκιοι καὶ τῶν κριτῶν οἱ ἐπιφανέστατοι σὺν τοῖς προλαβοῦσιν ἐπισκόποις ἐξιόντες πάσαις μηχαναῖς ὑποσχέσεσί τε καὶ ἀπειλαῖς τὸν θρόνον ἐγγράφως παραιτήσασθαι κατεβιάζοντο, εἴγε μὴ μέλλοι εἰς προφανῆ καθεῖναι κίνδυνον ἑαυτόν. Ἔμενε δὲ ἀμετάθετος οὐδὲν ἧττον ἢ πέτρα παράλιος εἰς
30 βάθος γῆς ἐρριζωμένη καὶ πάσαις ἀνένδοτος κυμάτων ἐπιφοραῖς. Ἐπειδὴ οὖν οὐκ εἶχον εὐλόγως παρανομεῖν οὐδεμιᾶς αὐτοῖς ἀπὸ τοῦ ἀνευθύνου προφάσεως ἐνδιδομένης, γυμνῇ λοιπὸν τῇ κεφαλῇ

---

32 CPG I 392

2 ὁ B: om. v   4 καθεστηκὼς Xv: καθεστικὸς B | τῶν B: om. v   8 προσεῖχον B: προσέσχον v | ἀσφαλεῖ v: ἀσφαλῆ B

said this, Bardas indicted him on a charge of high treason, berating him in the presence of the emperor as sympathetic to Gebo's cause.[58] This man Gebo was an epileptic and not quite right in the head, who had arrived from Dyrrhachium a few days earlier. He wore the garb of a cleric and made the foolish claim that he was the son of the empress Theodora by another man. The majority of the commons paid court to him as a future emperor, but by this time he was confined under secure guard on the island of Oxia.[59] Well then, since he had come under Michael's suspicion in this matter, Ignatius immediately retired to his church. And Michael forthwith brought in his mother and sisters and ordered them to be taken off to Carianou, as it is called, and be tonsured.[60] A little later he actually expelled Ignatius too from the patriarchal palace and banished him to the island of Terebinthus; and on the same day he also transferred Gebo from Oxia to Prinkipo Island, cut off his arms and legs, put out his eyes and killed him, thinking that by so doing he would avenge himself on the patriarch.[61]

18. Not three days after the latter's exile he was visited by a deputation of those considered to be the leading bishops, who thought fit because of the prevailing wickedness of the times to obtain from him an act of renunciation—in other words, his abdication. And who were the men who did this? The same ones who had earlier taken an oath in writing and vowed to him that they would be separated from the Supra-Essential Holy Trinity Itself, if ever they should reject the shepherd of their flock without a canonical condemnation. But they went home without having accomplished their purpose. Then again a few days later a group of patricians and the most distinguished judges went out with the bishops who had previously gone there and tried with every kind of scheme, promise and threat to make him renounce in writing his claim to the patriarchal throne, if indeed he was not to put himself into open danger. But he remained as steadfast as a rock on the shore that is firmly fixed deep into the ground and stands firm against every onslaught of the waves. And so since they did not have good reason to do him wrong (for they were offered no

καὶ ἀναιδεῖ προσώπῳ, κατὰ τὸ ᾀδόμενον, πρὸς πᾶσαν ἐχώρουν
ἀδικίαν καὶ παρανομίαν. Ὁ μὲν οὖν Κύριος ἡμῶν Ἰησοῦς Χριστὸς
ἅτε Θεὸς ἀληθινὸς καὶ ἀληθινοῦ Πατρὸς ὢν οὐ τῷ Θεὸς εἶναι
μόνον προαιώνιος τὰ πάντα πρὸ τῆς αὐτῶν γενέσεως οἶδεν, ἀλλὰ
5 καὶ τῷ ἄνθρωπος ὑπὲρ ἡμῶν γενέσθαι τῷ τεθεωμένῳ νοῖ τὰ πάντα
προκατανοῶν, "Ἀνάγκη" | φησὶν "ἐλθεῖν τὰ σκάνδαλα· οὐαὶ δὲ δι' 508
οὗ ἔρχεται." Καθ' ὅλας μὲν οὖν τὰς ἀπὸ τῆς θεανδρικῆς αὐτοῦ
παρουσίας μέχρι τοῦ δεῦρο παρεισφθαρείσας αἱρέσεις ἐν ταῖς
Ἐκκλησίαις οἱ τῶν αἱρέσεων ἔξαρχοι ὡς τῶν σκανδάλων ἐξηγού-
10 μενοι πρῶτοι ἂν ἀξίως αὐτοὶ μετέχοιεν καὶ τοῦ ταλανισμοῦ· οὐχ
ἧττον δέ, οἶμαι, τῶν πάλαι θρυλλουμένων αἱρετικῶν καὶ οἱ κατὰ
ταύτην πονηρευσάμενοι τὴν γενεὰν ὡς αἴτιοι σκανδάλων μυρίων
τῷ κόσμῳ γενόμενοι τῆς ἄνωθεν πεῖραν λήψονται ὀργῆς. Οὐ γὰρ
ὅτι δόγμασιν ὀρθοῖς δῆθεν καὶ συγγραφαῖς ἀμέτροις Θεὸν δο-
15 κοῦσιν ὁμολογεῖν, διὰ τοῦτο μόνον δικαιωθήσονται· ἀλλ' ὅτι τοῖς
ἔργοις, κατὰ τὸν ἱερὸν λόγον, ἠρνήσαντο αὐτὸν βδελυκτοὶ γενόμε-
νοι | καὶ ἀπειθεῖς καὶ πρὸς πᾶν ἔργον ἀγαθὸν ἀδόκιμοι, τούτου γε 9ᵛ
εἵνεκεν κατακριθήσονται. Οὐδ' ὅτι μόρφωσιν εὐσεβείας καὶ σχῆμα
γοῦν τι καὶ πλάσμα κενὸν εὐλαβείας περιθέμενοι πάντα δρῶσι καὶ
20 πραγματεύονται ὥστε δικαιωθῆναι παρὰ τοῖς ἀνθρώποις, διὰ τοῦτο
δίκαιοι καὶ παρὰ τῷ τῶν κρυφίων ἐπόπτῃ καὶ ἐξεταστῇ· ἀλλ' ὅτι
τῆς εὐσεβείας τὴν δύναμιν καὶ τὴν κατὰ τὸ Εὐαγγέλιον ἀπηνή-
ναντο ζωὴν πάσαις μὲν φιλαυτίαις καὶ φιλαργυρίαις, φιληδονίαις τε
πάσαις καὶ φιλαρχίαις ἑαυτοὺς ἀπεμπολήσαντες, πάσαις δὲ ἀδικίαις
25 ἐπιορκίαις σταυροπατίαις καὶ κακουργίαις δὲ κατὰ τῶν ἀθώων καὶ
ἐπηρείαις χρώμενοι πάσαις, τὴν ἐκκλησιαστικὴν εὐνομίαν διέλυσαν
καὶ συνέχεαν· τὸ θεῖον δὲ τῆς ἱερᾶς Ἐκκλησίας πρᾶγμα καὶ ὄνομα
οὕτω ταῖς ποικίλαις αὐτῶν ἀθεσμίαις καὶ παρανομίαις ἐβεβήλωσαν
ὥστε κινδυνεύειν ὀλίγου δεῖν ἐν ψιλοῖς ἡμῖν λόγοις, ἀλλ' οὐκ ἐν

---

1 Prov. 7.13   6–7 Matth. 18.7   14–17 Tit. 1.16   18–25 cf. 2 Tim. 3.2–5

7 οὗ ἔρχεται B: οὐ τὸ σκάνδαλον ἔρχεται v   18 εἵνεκεν B: ἕνεκεν v   26 πάσαις B: πᾶσαν
v   28 ἀθεσμίαις v: ἀθεσίαις B   29 ἡμῖν B: ἡμῶν v

pretext by his irreproachable behavior), they turned thereafter shamelessly and barefacedly, as they say, to every kind of lawlessness and wrongdoing. And indeed our Lord Jesus Christ, insofar as He is the true God born from the true Father, not only knows all things before they come to be by virtue of the fact that He is God eternal, but also, insofar as He was made man on our behalf, He observed all things beforehand with His deified mind and said: "It must needs be that offences come; but woe to that man by whom they come!" And so it is the case with all the heresies which have crept in to harm the Church from the time of Christ's presence on earth until the present day that the initiators, since they were the leading lights in the offences, should rightly be the first themselves to share also in the woe. And no less, I think, than those heretics who have long been notorious will those responsible for similar wickedness in the present age experience the wrath of the Lord, in that they are guilty of countless offences in the world. For although they appear to profess faith in God by beliefs supposedly orthodox and theological writings beyond measure, they will not justify themselves on these grounds alone. On the contrary, they will be condemned, according to Paul's holy word, for denying Him by their deeds, for being abominable, disobedient and discredited in regard to all good works. And whereas they put on a semblance of piety, an appearance, at least, and empty image of reverence in all they do and undertake, so as to justify themselves in the eyes of men, they are not on this account also righteous in the eyes of Him Who examines and judges that which remains hidden. But because they have rejected the power of piety and a life that follows the precepts of the Holy Gospel, selling themselves instead to all kinds of selfishness, avarice, hedonism and ambition and using against the innocent every kind of injustice, perjury, blasphemy, wickedness and insulting behavior, they have thereby destroyed and confounded the well-ordered state of the Church. And they have defiled the holy essence and name of the sacred Church with so many godless acts and transgressions that there is almost the risk of the mystery of piety being supposed to exist merely in our words

ἀληθείᾳ καὶ πράγματι τὸ τῆς εὐσεβείας μυστήριον ὑπονοεῖσθαι· διὰ
ταῦτα δικαιοτάτης τεύξονται πρὸς Θεοῦ τῆς κατακρίσεως.

19. Τούτων δὲ τῶν κακῶν ἁπάντων αἰτία προκαταρκτικὴ καὶ
ῥίζα ὁ ἀπ᾽ ἀρχῆς ἀνθρωποκτόνος καθέστηκε δηλαδή· ὃς τῷ ἀπο-
5 στῆναι τοῦ ἀγαθοῦ πάσης κακίας γενόμενος δημιουργὸς οὐ παύε-
ται μέχρι καὶ νῦν τὸν οἰκεῖον ἰὸν τοῖς πρὸς ὑποδοχὴν ἑτοίμοις κατὰ
πᾶσαν ἐναπερευγόμενος γενεάν· καὶ τοσούτῳ μᾶλλον τὴν παρ᾽
ἑαυτοῦ κακίαν ἐπιδαψιλεύεται, καθ᾽ ὅσον ἂν καὶ ἐπιτηδειοτέροις
πρὸς τὸν οἰκεῖον περιτύχοι σκοπόν. Συγχωροῦνται δὲ πολλάκις
10 κρατεῖν καὶ κοσμικαῖς δυναστείαις οἱ τοιοῦτοι μεγαλύνεσθαι, ὡς ἂν
ἐκ πολλῶν καρδιῶν, κατὰ τὸ θεῖον λόγιον, ἐκφανῶσι διαλογισμοί·
καὶ ὥστε τὸν σῖτον διακριθῆναι τοῦ ἀχύρου καὶ πυρωθῆναι μὲν ταῖς
ἐπηρείαις τὸν δίκαιον ὥσπερ ἐν χωνευτηρίῳ χρυσὸν καὶ τοῖς οὐρα-
νίοις ταμιευθῆναι βασιλείοις, ἀποποιηθῆναι δὲ καθάπερ | σκωρίαν 10
15 ὅσον ἀδόκιμον καὶ ἀνάξιον τῆς βασιλείας τοῦ Θεοῦ. Πρὸς οὖν
ταῦτα οὐκ οἶμαί τινα τῶν εὐσεβούντων ἀντερεῖν.

20. Ἴδωμεν δὲ καὶ τὰ κατὰ τὸν ἱερὸν Ἰγνάτιον παρηκολουθη-
κότα καὶ ὅσα κατὰ τῆς ἐν αὐτῷ κεκρυμμένης ἀληθείας καὶ ἀρετῆς ὁ
τῶν ἁγίων ἐχθρὸς καὶ ἐπίβουλος διὰ τῶν ὑπηρετουμένων αὐτοῦ τῇ
20 κακίᾳ κατεπράξατο· ἀλλὰ πάντα μὲν κατὰ μέρος ἐπεξιέναι ἀμήχανον εἰδὼς καὶ κρεῖττον ἢ κατ᾽ ἰσχὺν ἐμήν, τοῖς κυριωτέροις δὲ τὸν
λόγον ἐπαφιεὶς πειράσομαι | καθ᾽ ὅσον οἷόν τε πανταχοῦ τῆς ἀλη- 509
θείας πεφροντικὼς μηδὲν τῶν ἀξίων μνήμης παραλιπεῖν.

21. Ἐπειδὴ τοίνυν οἱ παρὰ τοῦ βασιλέως τότε πολλὰ πειρά-
25 σαντες τὸ πρὸς παρανομίαν ἐνδόσιμον οὐχ οἷοί τε ἐγεγόνεισαν
παρὰ τοῦ Ἰγνατίου λαβεῖν γενναίαις ἐνστάσεσι παραιτήσασθαι μὴ
καταδεξαμένου, παρ᾽ ἑαυτῶν ἔλαβον τοῦτο λοιπόν· καὶ πλεῖστα
καθ᾽ ἑαυτοὺς συσκεψάμενοι καὶ πᾶσαν κεκινηκότες βουλὴν Φώτιον
πρωτοσπαθάριόν τε ὄντα καὶ πρωτασηκρῆτις εἰς ἀρχιερέα τῆς
30 βασιλίδος προχειρίζονται. Ἦν δὲ οὗτος ὁ Φώτιος οὐ τῶν ἀγενῶν τε
καὶ ἀνωνύμων, ἀλλὰ καὶ τῶν εὐγενῶν κατὰ σάρκα καὶ περιφανῶν
σοφίᾳ τε κοσμικῇ καὶ συνέσει τῶν ἐν τῇ πολιτείᾳ στρεφομένων

---

4 cf. Ioann. 8.44   11 λόγιον] Luc. 2.35   13 Sap. 3.6   30–31 Greg. Naz. Orat. fun. in Bas.,
cap. 15

---

14 σκωρίαν v: σκορίαν B   29 πρωτασηκρῆτις B: πρωτοασηκρῆτιν v   30 ἀγενῶν B:
ἀγεννῶν v

and not in truth and reality. And so for these reasons they will meet with a most just condemnation at God's hands.

19. The initial cause and origin of all these troubles is clearly the one who has been the murderer of men from the beginning and who, by rebelling from the Good, has become the creator of every kind of wickedness and has not ceased right up to the present day spewing forth his venom upon those ready to receive it in every generation.[62] And the more he meets with men who are more suited to his own ends, the more he dispenses his particular type of wickedness. Such men are often allowed to rule and be exalted by powers in this world, so that the opinions of many hearts, as the Holy Scriptures say, might be laid bare. And so the grain is separated from the chaff and the man of righteousness is put to the test (like gold proved in the furnace) by abuses and insults before being stored in the treasure house of the Lord, while those who fail to gain approval and are unworthy of the Kingdom of Heaven are rejected like dross. I don't think that would be contradicted by anyone of those who are numbered among the pious.

20. Let us now look at the sequel of what happened to holy Ignatius and the things which that enemy and adversary of men of God perpetrated through those ministering to his wickedness against the hidden truth and virtue of Ignatius. I know that it would not be possible for me to go through everything in detail (a task which is quite beyond me) and so I shall deal with the more important points and try, as far as lies in my power, to concern myself with the absolute truth and leave out nothing worth mentioning.

21. So then, when the deputation from the emperor had tried many times over to tempt Ignatius but had been unable to get from him authorization for their lawless behavior (for he offered courageous resistance and refused to abdicate), they finally took matters into their own hands.[63] After a great deal of deliberation among themselves in which every kind of plan was aired, they appointed Photius, who was *protospatharius* and chief secretary, to the position of patriarch of the imperial city.[64] This man Photius was not from an ignoble or unknown background but came from a

34

εὐδοκιμώτατος πάντων ἐνομίζετο. Γραμματικῆς μὲν γὰρ καὶ ποιή-
σεως ῥητορικῆς τε καὶ φιλοσοφίας ναὶ δὴ καὶ ἰατρικῆς καὶ πάσης
ὀλίγου δεῖν ἐπιστήμης τῶν θύραθεν τοσοῦτον αὐτῷ τὸ περιὸν ὡς
μὴ μόνον σχεδὸν φάναι τῶν κατὰ τὴν αὐτοῦ γενεὰν πάντων δι-
5 ενεγκεῖν, ἤδη δὲ καὶ πρὸς τοὺς παλαιοὺς αὐτὸν διαμιλλᾶσθαι.
Πάντα γὰρ συνέτρεχεν ἐπ' αὐτῷ, ἡ ἐπιτηδειότης τῆς φύσεως ἡ
σπουδὴ ὁ πλοῦτος δι' ὃν καὶ βίβλος ἐπ' αὐτὸν ἔρρει πᾶσα· πλέον δὲ
πάντων ὁ τῆς δόξης ἔρως δι' ὃν αὐτῷ καὶ νύκτες ἄϋπνοι περὶ τὴν
ἀνάγνωσιν ἐμμελῶς ἐσχολακότι. Ἐπεὶ δὲ καὶ πρὸς τὴν Ἐκκλησίαν
10 αὐτήν (ὡς μὴ ὤφελεν) ἐπεισελθεῖν ἔδει, καὶ τῶν ἐκκλησιαστικῶν
διὰ τοῦτο | βιβλίων τῆς ἀναγνώσεως οὐ κατὰ πάρεργον ἐπεμελήθη·   10ᵛ
ἀγνόημα δὲ ἠγνόησεν, ἵν' εἴπω θεολογικῶς, σφόδρα τῆς αὐτοῦ
σοφίας ἀνάξιον. Οὐ γὰρ ἠθέλησε προσέξειν τὸν νοῦν ὅτι· "Εἴ τις
θέλει σοφὸς γενέσθαι ἐν τῷ αἰῶνι τούτῳ, μωρὸς γενέσθω ἵνα γένη-
15 ται σοφός." Οὐδὲ τὴν ὁδὸν εἵλατο τῆς ταπεινοφροσύνης δι' ἧς ἡ
μεγάλη τοῦ Θεοῦ χάρις καὶ ἡ ἀληθὴς σοφία δίδοται καὶ κατορθοῦ-
ται· οὐδὲ στραφῆναι καὶ γενέσθαι ὡς τὸ παιδίον διὰ τὴν τοῦ Θεοῦ
βασιλείαν, ὡς ἡ τοῦ Κυρίου διαμαρτυρία, κατεδέξατο· ἀλλ' οὐδὲ
σκάψαι τὴν αὐτοῦ ψυχὴν καὶ βαθῦναι τὴν διάνοιαν διὰ πάσης ὑπο-
20 ταγῆς, κατὰ Κύριον, καὶ ἀτιμοτέρας ἀγωγῆς καὶ ταπεινόφρονος καὶ
δι' ἀπαθείας οὕτω τῇ πέτρᾳ προσεγγίσαι Χριστῷ καὶ ἐπ' αὐτῷ
θεῖναι θεμέλιον πίστεως ἀρραγῆ καὶ δι' ἀγαθῶν πράξεων οὕτω τῆς
σοφίας ἑαυτὸν οἰκοδομεῖν· οὐ ταῦτα διανενόηται ὁ σοφός· πολλοῦ
γε δεῖ· καὶ οὐδὲν τούτων ἐπὶ νοῦν ἦλθεν αὐτῷ, ἀλλ' ἐπὶ σαθρῷ
25 θεμελίῳ καὶ ἀμμώδει τῇ κοσμικῇ σοφίᾳ καὶ τῇ ἀλαζονείᾳ τοῦ μὴ
κατὰ Χριστὸν πεπαιδευμένου λόγου τὴν ἑαυτοῦ καρδίαν στηρίξας
καὶ τὸν νοῦν καὶ τοῖς κενοῖς τῶν ἀνθρώπων ἐπαίνοις καὶ κρότοις
φυσιούμενος καὶ ἐπὶ πολὺ τῇ κενοδοξίᾳ μετεωριζόμενος δι' αὐτῆς
τῇ ἐχθρᾷ τοῦ Θεοῦ ὑπερηφανίᾳ προσεπέλασε, δι' ἧς κακουργίαν τε
30 πᾶσαν καὶ πᾶσαν σκανδάλων ὑπόθεσιν μυσταγωγεῖται. Ὅθεν ἀδό-

---

12-13 Greg. Naz. *Contra Jul.* I, PG 35, 533A   **13-15** 1 Cor. 3.18   **17-18** Matth. 18.3
19-23 cf. Luc. 6.48   **20** cf. Greg. Naz. *Or.* XL, PG 36, 369A; *Or.* XXXII, ibid. 209A

10 ἐκκλησιαστικῶν B: om. v   **13** προσέξειν B: προσέχειν v   **15** εἵλατο B: εἵλετο v
24 δεῖ B: δεῖν v   **29** Θεοῦ ὑπ. Χv: θ(εο)ῦ τῇ ὑπερηφανίᾳ B

highborn and illustrious family and was considered to have the best reputation of anyone in worldly wisdom and political acumen. In fact, so great was his mastery of literary criticism, poetry, rhetoric, philosophy, even medicine, and almost every kind of knowledge in the secular realm that he not only surpassed all his own generation, but, one might almost say, he even rivaled the ancients. Everything was combined in the one man: natural aptitude, enthusiasm, riches (the means by which every book found its way into his possession); and above all, desire for glory, in pursuit of which he spent sleepless nights devoting his time diligently to reading. And so when he was also required to assume the leadership of the Church (and I only wish it had never happened), he consequently gave his full and undivided attention to reading ecclesiastical books too.[65] But there was a deficiency in his knowledge, to use the words of the theologian, which was most unworthy of his wisdom. For he refused to pay attention to these words, that "if any man seemeth to be wise in this world, let him become a fool, that he may be wise." He did not choose the path of humility, through which God's boundless grace and true wisdom is granted and realized. He did not allow himself to be converted and become like a little child for the sake of the Kingdom of Heaven, as the Lord admonishes. He did not cultivate his soul and deepen his understanding by every kind of subjection, as the Lord recommends, and by a way of life more ignominious and humble. He did not by achieving a state of contemplative peace draw near Christ the Rock and upon Him set an unshakeable foundation of faith and through good works build himself into an edifice of wisdom. No; far from it. Our "wise" man thought of none of these things; they didn't enter his head. Instead, he established his heart and mind upon an unsound and sandy foundation—his worldly wisdom and the imposture of a doctrine taught not in accordance with Christ's precepts. Puffed up by men's empty praises and plaudits and very much elated by vainglory, he resorted as a result to a pride hostile to God, which led to his initiation[66] in every kind of villainy and every excuse for causing disturbances. Hence it was a spurious foundation stone which he laid for his priesthood and the completion to which it was brought suited such a begin-

κιμον αὐτοῦ τὴν τῆς ἱεραρχίας καταβαλλόμενος ἀρχὴν ἀκόλουθον
ἔσχε τῇ ἀρχῇ τὸ τέλος. Οὐ γὰρ παρητήσατο τὴν ὡς παρὰ | κοσμι- 512
κῶν ἀρχόντων ἀκόσμως αὐτῷ καὶ ἀθέσμως ἐνδιδομένην Ἐκκλησίαν, οὐδ᾿ ὡς ἑτέρῳ ἀνδρὶ καθηρμοσμένην μοιχικῶς ἑαυτῷ κατεγ-
5 γυᾶσθαι ηὐλαβήθη· τοὐναντίον μὲν οὖν καὶ περιχαρῶς, ἢ ἀναιδῶς
μᾶλλον, κατησπάζετο καὶ ὡς ἰδίας τῆς ἀλλοτρίας σαφῶς ἀντεποι-
εῖτο· καὶ ἐν τῇ αἰσχύνῃ αὐτοῦ ἐγαυρία δοξαζόμενος καὶ ἐν τῇ
ἀδικίᾳ αὐτοῦ ἐνευλογεῖτο καὶ ἐν ἓξ ταῖς ὅλαις ἡμέραις χερσὶν ἀνθρώπων τελειούμενος τῆς ἐπιθυμουμένης ἐπελαμβάνετο καθέδρας·
10 καὶ ἦν ἀληθῶς ἐκεῖνον ὁρᾶν | αὐθήμερον ἅγιον πλαττόμενον, κατὰ 11
τὴν παροιμίαν. Πρώτη γὰρ ἡμέρα μοναχὸς ἀντὶ λαϊκοῦ, τῇ δευτέρᾳ
δὲ ἀναγνώστης καὶ ὑποδιάκονος, τῇ ἑξῆς εἶτα διάκονος εἶτα πρεσ-
βύτερος· ἔπειτα τῇ ἕκτῃ (Χριστοῦ δὲ ἦν τὰ γενέθλια) καὶ αὐτὸς τῷ
ἱεραρχικῷ προσβὰς θρόνῳ τὴν εἰρήνην τῷ λαῷ προσεφώνει μηδὲν
15 τῆς ἀληθινῆς εἰρήνης ἄξιον ἐννοούμενος.

22. Ἦν δὲ αὐτῷ καὶ καθηγητὴς καὶ ἱεροτελεστὴς τὰ πάντα
Γρηγόριος ἐκεῖνος ὁ καλούμενος Ἀσβεστᾶς ὅν ποτε καὶ Συρακού-
σης μὲν ἐπίσκοπον ἔφασαν γενέσθαι, ἐπ᾿ ἐγκλήμασι δέ τισιν εἰς τὸ
Βυζάντιον κατηγορούμενον, ἤδη δὲ καὶ ὑπὸ τῆς τῶν Ῥωμαίων
20 Ἐκκλησίας ὡς παρὰ κανόνα πράξαντα καθηρημένον. Ἰγνάτιος ἄρτι
πρῶτον χειροτονεῖσθαι μέλλων μὴ παρεῖναι τοῦτον τῇ χειροτονίᾳ
διεπέμψατο, ἄχρις οὗ τὰ κατ᾿ αὐτόν, φησίν, ἐπὶ σχολῆς ἀκριβέ-
στερον διαγνωσθῇ. Τοῦτο ὁ πατριάρχης ἐν πρώτοις οὐ καλῶς μὲν
ὥς γε δοκοῦν τοῖς πολλοῖς, πέπραχε δ᾿ οὖν ὅμως ἐν δικαιοσύνῃ.

25 23. Ἐντεῦθεν ὦ τίς ἂν ἐξείποι τὴν ταραχὴν καὶ τὴν σκοτόμαι-
ναν; τίς τὴν ἀπὸ τοῦ μικροῦ ῥήματος τούτου φιλονεικίαν καὶ ἔριν
καὶ μνησικακίαν τοῦ δεινοῦ ἐκείνου Σικελοῦ παραστῆσαι; Εὐθὺς
γὰρ ἀκούσας οὐκ ἐφιλοσόφησε πρὸς τὴν ἀγγελίαν, οὐ τὴν ἰδίαν ὡς
φρόνιμος συνεκάλυψεν αἰσχύνην, τοὺς ἐπὶ χειροτονίᾳ δὲ κηροὺς

7-8 cf. Ps. 9.24   10-11 Greg. Naz. *Or. fun. in Bas.*, cap. 26

---

1 ἱεραρχίας καταβαλλόμενος B: ἱερουργίας καταβαλόμενος v   6 ἰδίας τῆς Xv: ἴδια τὰ τῆς B
14 ἱεραρχικῷ B: ἱερατικῷ v   16 καὶ¹ B: om. v   20 κανόνα B: κανόνας v   26 τούτου B:
om. v

ning. For he did not refuse his appointment to the Church on the grounds that it was handed over to him in a lawless and unbecoming manner by the secular authorities,[67] nor did he feel any qualms about the fact that after being united with another man it was now being betrothed to him in an adulterous union. Quite the opposite in fact. He embraced it most joyously (most impudently, I should say) and openly claimed for his own what belonged to another.[68] He exulted in the fact that shame brought him honor and injustice brought him praise, and within six full days he was initiated at the hands of men and took possession of the patriarchal seat which he desired. And it was truly possible to see him being fabricated into a man of God overnight, as the saying goes. For on the first day he was made a monk instead of a layman, on the second day a reader, the next day a subdeacon, after that a deacon, then a presbyter. And finally on the sixth day, which was Christ's birthday, he himself ascended the patriarchal throne and proclaimed peace to the people, though he was intending nothing that was worthy of true peace.[69]

22. He had as his teacher and initiator in all the sacred rites the well-known Gregory Asbestas, a man whom they said had once been bishop of Syracuse, but was accused on certain criminal charges at Constantinople and had already been deposed too by the Church of Rome for acting contrary to canon law.[70] When Ignatius was about to be ordained for the first time, he had sent a message to prevent this Gregory from being admitted to the ordination until such time, he said, as his case might be more accurately determined at leisure. This was one of his first acts as patriarch and it was not well received by the majority, but nevertheless he acted with justice.[71]

23. Who could recount the tale of chaos and spiritual ignorance that followed? Who could describe the contentiousness that resulted from this trifling remark and the wrangling and malicious behavior of that clever Sicilian? For as soon as he heard the message, he did not remain indifferent and conceal his own shame, like a prudent man would. Instead, he threw down the wax tapers used for the ordination from his hands and, in his impu-

τῶν αὐτοῦ χειρῶν ἀπορρίψας καὶ καταναιδευσάμενος πάσης ἐνώπιον τῆς ἐκκλησίας ἐσχάτως διελοιδορεῖτο τὸν ἀναίτιον καὶ λύκον
ἀντὶ ποιμένος ἐπεισιέναι τῇ ἐκκλησίᾳ μανιωδῶς διϊσχυρίζετο· ὃ καὶ
Πέτρος ὁ Σάρδεων ὁ λεγόμενος Δείλαιος, πρὸς δὲ καὶ ὁ Ἀπαμείας
5 Εὐλάμπιος καὶ ἄλλοι τινὲς τῶν ἀσημοτέρων εἵποντο κληρικῶν
ἀλόγως τῆς Ἐκκλησίας ἀπορρηγνύμενοι.

24. Ἐν ὅλοις μὲν οὖν ἕνδεκα χρόνοις τῆς πρώτης αὐτοῦ ἱεραρχίας ὁ Ἰγνάτιος ἀποπειρώμενος καὶ πᾶσαν μὲν λόγων, πᾶσαν δὲ
δωρεῶν προτεινόμενος φιλοτιμίαν οὐχ οἷός τ᾽ ἐγεγόνει τὴν τοῦ
10 Ἀσβεστᾶ κακίαν κατασβέσαι. Διήρχετο δὲ πάσας οἰκίας τῶν δυνα-
στῶν μάτην διαλοιδορούμενος καὶ διασύρων πικρῶς καὶ μηδὲ
Χριστιανὸν ὀνομάζειν τὸν ἅγιον ὁ ἐναγὴς ἀξιῶν, μάλιστα δὲ
πάντων παρὰ Φωτίῳ καὶ τοῖς αὐτοῦ συγγενεῦσι τιμώμενος μέγας
τις ἄνθρωπος τοῦ Θεοῦ χρη|ματίζειν ἐπιστεύετο· ὅθεν καὶ παρ᾽   11ᵛ
15 αὐτοῦ πρώτου χειροτονηθεὶς ὁ Φώτιος ἐκ τῆς εἰς αὐτὸν πίστεως
ὅλην τοῦ ἀνδρὸς τὴν κατὰ τοῦ ἀναιτίου μανίαν ἐπεσπάσατο.

25. Καὶ ὥσπερ εἰς αὐτὸ τοῦτο πατριάρχης προχειρισθεὶς ἵνα
πάσαις ἐπινοίαις καὶ τρόποις πᾶσι τὸν ἀθῷον τιμωρήσηται, οὕτως
ἠγωνίζετο οὐ τῆς ἱερω|σύνης μόνον, ἀλλὰ καὶ αὐτῆς αὐτὸν ἀπαλ-   513
20 λάξαι, εἰ δυνατόν, τῆς ζωῆς· καίτοι γε χειρόγραφα παρὰ τῶν κατα-
δεχομένων αὐτὸν πρότερον ἀπαιτηθεὶς μητροπολιτῶν ὥστε πατρι-
κὴν ἀπονέμειν τῷ Ἰγνατίῳ τιμὴν καὶ πάντα κατὰ βούλησιν αὐτοῦ
δρᾶν καὶ ἐν μηδενὶ τοῦτον παραλυπεῖν. Οὔπω δὲ μετὰ τὴν χειροτο-
νίαν δύο μῆνες παρῆλθον καὶ αὐτὸς τοὺς ὅρκους ἠθετηκώς,
25 πρῶτον μὲν τοὺς ἐπὶ τῆς ἐκκλησίας τεταγμένους ὅσους οἰκειοτέ-
ρους εὕρισκε τοῦ πατριάρχου κατακλείων καὶ αἰκισμοῖς βιαίοις καὶ
μάστιξι καταικιζόμενος· καὶ κολακεύων δὲ πάλιν καὶ δῶρα προτεί-
νων καὶ προκοπὰς καὶ χειρόγραφα ἀπαιτῶν καὶ πᾶσι τρόποις ἐπι-
κείμενος πρόφασιν ἀπωλείας ἐζήτει κατ᾽ αὐτοῦ· ὡς δὲ οὐδὲν
30 εὕρισκε δι᾽ ἑαυτοῦ τοιοῦτον οἷον ἐπεθύμει, ὑποβάλλει τῷ κακῷ
Βάρδᾳ καὶ δι᾽ αὐτοῦ τῷ κούφῳ Μιχαὴλ ὥστε πέμψαι καὶ ἔρευναν
ἀκριβῆ ποιήσασθαι κατὰ τοῦ Ἰγνατίου ὡς αὐτοῦ λάθρα τυρεύοντος

2–3 cf. Acta 20.28–29

---

3 ὃ B: ᾧ Xv   10 δὲ B: om. v   13 συγγενεῦσι B: συγγενέσι v   16 τὴν B: om. v
17 Καὶ B: om. v   19–20 ἀπαλλάξαι B: ἀπαλλάξειν v   28–31 τρόποις...31 μιχαὴλ B: om.
v

dence, reviled to the utmost the innocent patriarch in the presence of the whole Church, maintaining in his mad fashion that a wolf, not a shepherd, was being introduced into the fold of the Church. And he was joined in this by Peter of Sardis, who was also known as "the Pitiful," Eulampius of Apameia and some other clerics who were lesser known, all of whom broke away from the Church without good reason.[72]

24. Despite every effort during the full eleven years of his first patriarchate, when he offered a rich array of arguments and every kind of reward, Ignatius was unable to quench the wickedness of Asbestas.[73] The latter went around all the houses of the influential, vainly reviling and bitterly disparaging him, not even deigning to call the holy patriarch a Christian—unholy fellow! But above all, he was held in honor by Photius and his followers and was credited with the name of a great man of God. As a result, he was the first one to ordain Photius and it was out of loyalty to him that the latter absorbed all the man's rage against innocent Ignatius.

25. And as if he had been appointed patriarch for the sole purpose of avenging himself by every design and in every way upon guiltless Ignatius, he strove to deprive him not only of his priesthood, but also, if he could, of life itself.[74] And yet written guarantees had been demanded of him by those metropolitans who previously accepted him for ordination, to the effect that he would assign Ignatius the honor due to a spiritual father, do everything in accordance with his will and not trouble him in any way. But it was less than two months after his ordination when he himself broke his oaths. To begin with he locked up all the church appointees whom he found to be close familiars of the patriarch and ill-treated them with violent torture and floggings. Then again by use of flattery and by offering gifts and preferment he demanded written undertakings and pressured people in every way as he sought a pretext for putting Ignatius to death. And when he did not find what he wanted through his own efforts, he suggested to the wicked Bardas, and through him to shallow Michael, that men be sent to undertake an exacting inquiry against Ignatius on the grounds that he was secretly intriguing against the empire. And so harsh

κατὰ τῆς βασιλείας. Εὐθὺς οὖν ἄρχοντες ἀπηνεῖς καὶ στρατιῶται
θρασεῖς τὴν Τερέβινθον καταλαβόντες καὶ πᾶσαν ποιήσαντες ἐξέ-
τασιν καὶ πᾶσαν βάσανον τοὺς ὑπ’ ἐκεῖνον ἀνθρώπους βασανί-
σαντες, ἐπειδὴ ἐξέλειπον ἐξερευνῶντες ἐξερευνήσεις καὶ λοιπὸν
5 οὐδὲν εἶχον ὥστε δικαίως τιμωρήσασθαι, τῇ ἀδικίᾳ καθαρᾷ χρῶν-
ται. Λαβόντες γὰρ τὸν ἱερὸν ἄνδρα μετὰ τῶν σὺν αὐτῷ καὶ πρὸς
τὴν λεγομένην Ἱέρειαν περάσαντες δέσμιον τοῦτον εἰς μάνδραν
αἰγῶν κατέκλεισαν· ἐκεῖθεν πρὸς τὰ Προμότου λεγόμενα διαπερῶ-
σιν ὅπου δὴ Λέων ἐκεῖνος ὁ Λαλάκων ἐπονομαζόμενος τῶν Νουμέ-
10 ρων δομέστικος ὢν ἐπὶ τοσοῦτον αὐτοῦ τοῖς ῥαπίσμασι κατέκοψε
τὰς σιαγόνας ὡς δύο μύλας ἐκεῖ τοῦ ἱερωτάτου γέροντος ἐκπεσεῖν·
εἶτα δύο μοχλοῖς σιδηροῖς, ἀνδροφόνων τρόπον, τοὺς αὐτοῦ πόδας
κατασφαλισάμενοι | καὶ μικρᾷ φρουρᾷ κατακλείσαντες ἀπήεσαν   12
δύο παῖδας καὶ μόνον πρὸς ὑπηρεσίαν αὐτῷ καταλιπόντες. Ὅλος δὲ
15 αὐτοῖς ὁ ἀγὼν καὶ ἡ ἔπειξις ἦν ὥστε λίβελλον αὐτοῖς ἀποταγῆς
δοῦναι καὶ ἑκουσίως τοῦ θρόνου παραχωρεῖν. Ὁ δὲ τὸν λύκον κατὰ
τῆς ποίμνης δεινῶς ἐπεισφρήσαντα θεασάμενος ὅσον ἦν ἐπ’ αὐτῷ
τὴν ἔφοδον ἐξεῖργεν. Ἡμερῶν δὲ παρελθουσῶν ὀλίγων εἰς τὰ
Νούμερα τοῦτον περάσαντες σιδηροδέσμιον ἐγκλείουσιν· εἶτα
20 Αὔγουστος ἐνίστατο μὴν καὶ εἰς πλοῖον αὐτὸν ἐμβαλόντες εἰς
Μιτυλήνην ἐξορίζουσι. Πάντας δὲ τοὺς ὑπονοουμένους οἰκείους
εἶναι καὶ φίλους αὐτοῦ, οὓς μὲν δαρμοῖς ἀφορήτοις καὶ θανατηφό-
ροις παρεδίδουν πληγαῖς· οὓς δέ, τὸ φιλανθρωπότατον, ὑπερώριζον
τῆς πόλεως. Ὅτε δὴ καὶ τὸν χαρτοφύλακα Βλάσιον διὰ τὴν ὑπὲρ
25 τῆς ἀληθείας παρρησίαν ἐγλωσσοτόμησαν.

26. Ἐν Μιτυλήνῃ δὲ διατρίβοντος ὁ Φώτιος τὴν κατ’ αὐτὸν
ἐκκλησίαν τῶν πονηρευομένων συναγαγὼν καὶ πρὸς τῷ ἱερῷ
τεμένει τῶν πανενδόξων Ἀποστόλων γενόμενος καθαίρεσιν ἀπο-
φαίνεται κατὰ τοῦ μὴ παρόντος Ἰγνατίου· οὐ μόνον δέ, ἀλλὰ καὶ
30 ἀναθεματίζει καὶ ἀποκηρύττει αὐτὸς κατήγορος γινόμενος καὶ
κριτής. Καὶ ὅσους μὲν ἑώρα τῷ αὐτοῦ σκοπῷ καὶ τῇ παραλόγῳ
πράξει ταύτῃ συνάδοντας καὶ τοῖς τελουμένοις ὑπογράφοντας ἐν

---

27 cf. Ps. 25.5

---

3 καὶ…βάσανον Xv: om. B   4 ἐξέλειπον B: ἐξέλιπον v   8 ἐκεῖθεν πρὸς B: ἐκεῖθέν τε πρὸς
v | προμότου B: προμήτου Xv   16 τοῦ θρόνου v: τὸν θρόνον B   23 παρεδίδουν v:
παρεδίδου B

commanders and reckless soldiers soon arrived at Terebinthus and carried out every kind of investigation, subjecting the household of Ignatius to all kinds of torture.[75] And when they left off their examination and there was no means left to them by which they could exact a just vengeance upon Ignatius, they resorted to pure and simple injustice. For they took the holy man and his retinue and transferred him to the place called Hieria, where they shut him up as a prisoner in a goat pen.[76] And from there they took him over to the place called the region of Promotus, where the well-known Leo, known also as Lalaco, who was chief of the independent cohorts, so badly beat his jaw with blows that the most reverent old man lost two molars in the process.[77] Then they bound his feet to two iron poles, as if he were a murderer, shut him up in a tiny prison and departed, leaving behind only two boys to serve his needs. The whole reason behind their anxiety and urgency was to make Ignatius sign a statement renouncing his office and so retire voluntarily from the patriarchal throne. But when the latter saw that the wolf had cleverly moved in upon his flock, he tried as far as possible to hold off the attack. After a few days they took him across to the Noumera prison and put him in irons;[78] then, at the beginning of August, they put him on board ship and banished him to Mitylene. As for all those who were thought to be his familiars and friends, some they afflicted with unendurable beatings and death-bringing blows, while others they banished from the capital as the most humane measure. In this connection they also cut out the tongue of Blasius, Keeper of the Archives, for speaking out too freely in the interests of truth.[79]

26. While Ignatius was in Mitylene, Photius convened his church of wicked elements and at a meeting in the holy temple of the all-glorious Apostles he proclaimed a sentence of deposition against Ignatius in his absence.[80] Not only that, but he anathematized and excommunicated him, acting himself as both accuser and judge. And all those whom he saw to be in accord with his goals and with this irregular act of his and to subscribe to the matter in

τοῖς πρώτοις τῶν φίλων καὶ γνησιωτάτων εἶχε συλλειτουργῶν·
ὅσοι δὲ τῇ ἀκρίτῳ κρίσει προσοχθήσαντες συναινέσαι ταῖς ἀλογι-
στίαις ταύταις οὐκ ἠβούλοντο, τούτους τῷ πραιτωρίῳ καὶ φυλακαῖς
πολυτρόποις κολασθησομένους παρεδίδου. Πολλῶν οὖν διαγογγυ-
5 ζόντων καὶ ἐπὶ ταῖς ἀκρισίαις | ταύταις Φωτίου καταγινωσκόντων   516
ὑπό τε τῶν οἰκείων ἔργων ἐκεῖνος καὶ τῆς συνειδήσεως διελεγχόμε-
νος βουλὴν βουλεύεται πονηρὰν μᾶλλον ἢ συνετήν. Οὐ γὰρ
ἀγαθῷ, ἀλλὰ κακῷ τὸ κακὸν ἰάσασθαι διανοεῖται, μᾶλλον δὲ τῷ
ἥττονι τὸ μεῖζον ἐπενεγκεῖν. Ὥσπερ γὰρ οἱ τὴν ὁδὸν ἀνιόντες τῆς
10 ἀρετῆς διὰ τῶν ἀγαθῶν ἔργων ὡς διὰ κλίμακος ἀναβαίνουσι πρὸς
τὸν Θεόν, οὕτως οἱ τὴν εὐθεῖαν ἀφιέντες διὰ τῶν πονηρῶν πρά-
ξεων τῷ τῆς | πονηρίας προσοικειοῦνται πατρί· καὶ κακῷ κακὸν   12ᵛ
ἐπιπλέκοντες οὐ διαλείπουσιν ἕως ἂν εἰς τὸν τῶν οἰκείων ἔργων
ἐρραγῶσι βόθρον.
15   27. Διανοεῖται τοίνυν κἀκεῖνος πρεσβευτὰς εἰς τὴν πρεσβυτέ-
ραν ἐξαποστεῖλαι Ῥώμην καὶ παρὰ Νικολάου τοῦ πάπα τοποτηρητὰς αἰτῆσαι, πρόφασιν μὲν εἰς διόρθωσιν τῆς Ἐκκλησίας εἴτουν
ἐκτομὴν τελείαν τῶν ἔτι τῆς Χριστιανοκατηγορικῆς τῶν Εἰκονομάχων αἱρέσεως ἀντεχομένων· τὸ δὲ ἀληθὲς ὡς ἂν μετὰ τῆς τῶν
20 Ῥωμαίων χειρὸς περιφανεστέραν τοῦ Ἰγνατίου ποιήσηται καθαίρεσιν. Ἀποστέλλει τοίνυν Θεόφιλον ἐπίσκοπον τοῦ Ἀμορίου καὶ
Σαμουὴλ ἐπίσκοπον ἄχρις ἐκείνου τῶν Χωνῶν ὑπὸ Λαοδίκειαν
τυγχάνοντα ἀρχιεπίσκοπον τετιμηκώς· δι' ὧν καὶ τὰ ψευδῆ πρὸς
τὸν πάπαν γράφειν ὁ γεννάδας οὐκ ὀκνεῖ· γράφει γὰρ ὡς Ἰγνάτιος
25 διὰ γῆρας καὶ νόσον καὶ σώματος ἀδυναμίαν παραιτησάμενος
ὑπεχώρησε τῆς Ἐκκλησίας καὶ ἐν τῇ κατ' αὐτὸν νήσῳ καὶ τῷ μοναστηρίῳ μένων πάσης τιμῆς καὶ θεραπείας ὑπό τε τῶν βασιλευόντων
ὑπό τε πάσης τῆς πόλεως καὶ τῆς κατ' αὐτὸν Ἐκκλησίας ἀξιοῦται.
Τούτους ὁ πάπας δεξάμενος καὶ τὴν τῶν πραγμάτων ἀλήθειαν
30 ἀγνοῶν δύο τοποτηρητὰς Ζαχαρίαν καὶ Ῥοδόαλδον ἐπισκόπους
ἀποστέλλει.
    28. Ἐν δὲ τῷ μεταξὺ ἐπάνεισι μὲν τῆς ἐξορίας ὁ ἀθλητὴς ἓξ
μῆνας ἐν Μιτυλήνῃ πεποιηκώς· ἐπάνεισι δὲ διὰ τῆς τῶν κρατούν-

---

hand, were regarded by Photius as his foremost friends and the truest colleagues in his ministry; whereas those who were vexed at his reckless decision and refused to agree with this piece of irrationality were handed over for punishment to the Praetorian Eparch and to many and various forms of custody. This set many people murmuring and condemning Photius for these perverted judgments, and since he was clearly convicted by the evidence of his own deeds and by his complicity, he now devised a plan that was wicked rather than ingenious. For he thought to counteract his evil not by good deeds but by further evil, adding, in fact, a greater evil to the lesser one. And just as those who climb the path of virtue ascend to meet God on the ladder of their own good deeds,[81] so also do those who depart from the straight and narrow become associated by their wicked acts with the father of wickedness and do not cease weaving evil upon evil until they fall headlong into the pit of their own misdeeds.

27. And so he decided to send an embassy to Old Rome and to request a delegation in return from Pope Nicolaus, on the pretext of setting in order the affairs of the Church, that is, completely eliminating the remaining adherents of the iconoclastic heresy that denounced true Christians.[82] But his real purpose was to use Rome's assistance in effecting a more obvious deposing of Ignatius. And so he sent Theophilus, bishop of Amorium, and Samuel, who had until this time been bishop of Chonae, under the jurisdiction of Laodicea, but was now promoted to archbishop by Photius.[83] And through them our fine outstanding fellow did not hesitate to convey lies to the pope, writing that Ignatius had begged to be excused on grounds of old age, sickness and debility and had retired from the Church;[84] and that he was staying in the monastery on his island and was deemed worthy of all honor and care by the imperial family, by the whole city and by his Church. The pope received these ambassadors and, being unaware of the truth of the matter, he sent two legates in return, the bishops Zacharias and Rodoaldus.[85]

28. Meanwhile, the champion of Christ returned from his exile after spending six months on Mitylene. However, the ruling powers

44

των προνοίας πρὸς τὴν Τερέβινθον ἀποκαθιστάμενος οὐ πρὸς
τιμὴν μᾶλλον ἢ ἀτιμίαν, οὐδὲ πρὸς ἀνάπαυσιν καὶ παραμυθίαν,
ἀλλὰ πρὸς θλῖψιν καὶ κάκωσιν περισσοτέραν. Ὅσα γὰρ ὁ ἐχθρὸς ἐν
αὐτῷ ἐπονηρεύσατο, καὶ ὅσας αὐτῷ Νικήτας ὁ τοῦ βασιλικοῦ
5 στόλου δρουγγάριος ὁ Ὠορύφας λεγόμενος θλίψεις ἐπήνεγκε καὶ
ἐπηρείας Φωτίῳ καὶ τοῖς κρατοῦσι χαριζόμενος, τίς λόγος παραστῆσαι δύναται; τίς καθ’ ἓν ἀπαγγεῖλαι τὰς ἐπαγωγὰς τὰς ὕβρεις
τὰς ζημίας καὶ τοὺς δαρμοὺς ὅσα χειρὶ μιαιφόνῳ κατὰ τῶν τοῦ
μακαρίου | οἰκείων ἐκεῖνος ἐτεκτήνατο; Ἐπεγένετο δὲ καὶ ἄλλη τῷ   13
10 ἁγίῳ συμφορά. Κατ’ ἐκεῖνον γὰρ τὸν καιρὸν τὸ μιαιφονώτατον τῶν
Σκυθῶν ἔθνος οἱ λεγόμενοι Ῥὼς διὰ τοῦ Εὐξείνου πόντου προσκε-
χωρηκότες τῷ Στενῷ καὶ πάντα μὲν χωρία, πάντα δὲ μοναστήρια
διηρπακότες ἔτι δὴ καὶ τῶν τοῦ Βυζαντίου περιοικίδων κατέδραμον
νησίων, σκεύη μὲν πάντα ληϊζόμενοι καὶ χρήματα, ἀνθρώπους δὲ
15 τοὺς ἁλόντας πάντας ἀποκτείνοντες· πρὸς οἷς καὶ τῶν τοῦ πατριάρχου μοναστηρίων βαρβαρικῷ καταδραμόντες ὁρμήματι καὶ θυμῷ
πᾶσαν μὲν τὴν εὑρεθεῖσαν κτῆσιν ἀφείλαντο, εἴκοσι δὲ καὶ δύο τῶν
γνησιωτέρων αὐτοῦ κεκρατηκότες οἰκετῶν ἐφ’ ἑνὶ τροχαντῆρι
πλοίου τοὺς | πάντας ἀξίναις κατεμέλισαν.   517
20   29. Τούτων δὲ τῶν συμφορῶν ἐκεῖνος ἐπακούων μίαν ἀεὶ
ταύτην ἐπὶ στόματος εἶχε φωνήν· “Ὁ Κύριος ἔδωκεν, ὁ Κύριος
ἀφείλατο· ὡς τῷ Κυρίῳ ἔδοξεν, οὕτως καὶ ἐγένετο,” καὶ τὰ ἑξῆς·
οὕτως εὐχαριστῶν καὶ ταῖς προσευχαῖς ἀδιαλείπτως πρὸς τὸν Θεὸν
ἀνατεινόμενος τὴν παρ’ αὐτοῦ κρίσιν καὶ βοήθειαν ἐπεκαλεῖτο,
25 ματαίαν δὲ πᾶσαν τὴν ἀπὸ τῶν κρατεῖν δοκούντων ἡγεῖτο σωτη-
ρίαν· οἵγε καὶ ἡνίκα τοῦτον τηλικαύταις περιπεσεῖν ἀνίαις ἤκουσαν
καὶ θλίψεσι, τοσοῦτον ἀπέσχον τοῦ συμπαθῆσαι καὶ παραμυθή-
σασθαι ὥστε καὶ λύπης πρόφασιν ἡγήσασθαι ὅτι μὴ καὶ αὐτὸς τῇ
βαρβαρικῇ ἑάλω χειρὶ καὶ τοῖς οἰκείοις συνανῃρέθη παισίν· οὐ
30 μᾶλλον εὐθυμοῦντες ἐπὶ τοῖς ἀνῃρημένοις ἢ ἀνιώμενοι ἐπὶ τῇ
σωτηρίᾳ τοῦ δικαίου. Καὶ οὐ θαυμαστόν. Ψυχὴ γὰρ πᾶσα τῆς
ἀγάπης μὲν ἀλλοτριωθεῖσα, τοῦ δὲ μίσους ἀναπλησθεῖσα καὶ ὡς

21–22 Iob 1.21

5 δρουγγάριος Xv: δρογγάριος B | ὠορύφας B: Ὠρύφας v   15 ἀποκτείνοντες v:
ἀποκτένοντες B   17 ἀφείλαντο B: ἀφείλοντο v   22 ἀφείλατο B: ἀφείλετο Xv | καὶ¹ B:
om. v   30 leg. ἀθυμοῦντες?

saw to it that he was merely reinstated on Terebinthus, to meet with ignominy instead of honor, with affliction and more abundant oppression rather than rest and consolation. For what words could describe all the wicked tricks that his enemy played on him and all the oppressive and spiteful treatment that Nicetas, also called Ooryphas, the commander of the imperial fleet, imposed on him to gratify Photius and the ruling powers?[86] Who could tell in a single report all the attacks, violent acts, punishments and beatings which that fellow devised with murderous hand against the friends of blessed Ignatius? Furthermore, an additional disaster now befell the holy man. For at that time the bloodthirsty Scythian race called Russians advanced across the Black Sea to the Bosphorus plundering every region and all the monasteries, and they also overran the small island dependencies of Byzantium, carrying off all the chattels and money and slaying all the people they captured.[87] In addition, they attacked with barbaric spirit and impulse the monasteries of the patriarch and removed every possession that they found; and they seized twenty-two of his most loyal household servants and cut them all to pieces with axes in the stern of one of their boats.

29. When Ignatius heard about these disastrous events, this one phrase was ever coming to his lips: "The Lord gave, and the Lord hath taken away; it so pleased the Lord and so it came to pass," etc. By giving thanks in this way and reaching out to God with unceasing prayers he invoked His judgment and help, since he considered any guarantee of safety from those who appeared to be the ruling powers to be quite useless. And in fact when they heard that he had fallen foul of such troubles and afflictions, they were so far from expressing sympathy and consoling him that they actually considered it an occasion for grief that he himself had not fallen into the hands of the barbarians and been put to death along with his household servants. They were not so much heartened by the casualties as distressed that the man of righteousness was still safe. And it was no wonder. For a soul that has become a complete stranger to charity and has been filled with hatred—consumed by it

46

ὑπὸ πυρὸς ὑπ' αὐτοῦ δαπανωμένη μίαν ταύτην ἡγεῖται τοῦ πάθους ἀναψυχήν, τὴν ἀπώλειαν τοῦ μισουμένου.

30. Οὐ πολὺ τὸ ἐν μέσῳ καὶ πάλιν συνέδρια, πάλιν ἀρχόντων καὶ ἀρχιερέων κατὰ τοῦ ἀθῴου βουλευτήρια. Ὁ μὲν οὖν εἰς τὰ
5 Ποσέως ἐκάθητο τὴν κατ' αὐτοῦ σκευωρίαν ὑφορώμενος· | Φώτιος 13ᵛ δὲ τὴν κατ' αὐτὸν ἐκκλησίαν καὶ τοὺς ἀπὸ τῆς Ῥώμης ἥκοντας λαβὼν τοποτηρητὰς τὸν ἱερὸν τῶν Ἀποστόλων κατειλήφει ναόν. Παρῆσαν καὶ οἱ βασιλεῖς, παρῆσαν καὶ πάντες ἄρχοντες καὶ πᾶσα σχεδὸν ἡ πόλις παρῆσαν ἐκεῖ. Ἐπειδὴ οὖν συνεληλύθεισαν, πρῶτον
10 μὲν Βαάνην πραιπόσιτον τὸν Ἀγγούρην ἐπικαλούμενον καὶ ἄλλους δέ τινας ἐξουθενημένους Ῥωμαίους πρὸς Ἰγνάτιον ἀποκρισιαρίους προχειρίζονται.

31. Οἳ καὶ παραγενόμενοι· "Ἡ μεγάλη" φασὶ "καὶ ἱερὰ σύνοδος καλεῖ σε πρὸς ἑαυτήν· ἐλθὲ τὸ τάχος ἀπολογησόμενος πρὸς τὰ
15 δικαίως ἢ ἀδίκως θρυλλούμενα κατὰ σοῦ." Ὁ δὲ μακάριος· "Εἴπατε," φησὶν "ἀξιῶ, πῶς ἐλεύσομαι; ὡς ἐπίσκοπος ἢ ἱερεὺς ἢ θεραπευτής;" Οἱ δὲ μὴ εἰδέναι τί πρὸς ταῦτα ἀποκριθῶσιν εἶπον· "Ἀλλὰ νῦν ἀπιόντες πρὸς τοὺς ἀποστείλαντας βεβαίαν ἀπόκρισιν αὖθις ἰόντες κομιοῦμεν." Τῇ οὖν ἐπαύριον οἱ αὐτοὶ παραγενόμενοι·
20 "Οἱ τοποτηρηταὶ τῆς πρεσβυτέρας" ἔφασαν "Ῥώμης Ῥοδόαλδος καὶ Ζαχαρίας δι' ἡμῶν τῶν ἀναξίων δηλοῦσι τάδε· Εἰς τὴν ἁγίαν καὶ οἰκουμενικὴν σύνοδον ἀνυπερθέτως ἀπάντησον ὡς ἔχει σου ἡ συνείδησις." Εὐθὺς οὖν τὴν ἀρχιερατικὴν στολὴν ἐκεῖνος ἐνδυσάμενος σὺν ἐπισκόποις καὶ πρεσβυτέροις καὶ πλήθει πολλῷ μοναχῶν
25 τε καὶ λαϊκῶν ἀπήει πεζοπορῶν. Πλησίον δὲ τοῦ ναοῦ Γρηγορίου τοῦ Θεολόγου ὅπου σταυρὸς ἐν μαρμαρίνῳ κίονι κατὰ μέσον ἀνεστήλωται τῆς λεωφόρου γενομένῳ Ἰωάννης πατρίκιος ὁ Κόξης λεγόμενος ἀπήντησεν αὐτῷ, λέγων ἀπὸ τοῦ βασιλέως ἀπεστάλθαι καὶ ἀπειλῶν ὡς εἰ μὴ παγανεύων ἐν μοναχικῷ τῷ συνήθει σχήματι
30 προέλθοι, θάνατον ἐπηρτῆσθαι τὴν ζημίαν. Ὁ καὶ πεποιηκότα τὸν ἀοίδιμον τῷ συνεδρίῳ παρεστήσαντο. Καὶ δὴ παριστάνουσιν ἑβδομήκοντα καὶ δύο ψευδομάρτυρας οὓς ἐκ πολλοῦ προητοιμάσαντο,

---

1 ὑπὸ B: om. v | ταύτην B: ταύτης v   8 ἄρχοντες B: οἱ ἄρχοντες v   10 ἀγγούρην B: Ἀγγορήν v   14 τὸ τάχος B: τάχιον v   17 εἶπον Xv: εἶπαν B   24 πλήθει πολλῷ v: πλήθ( ) πολλὰ B   25 ἀπήει Xv: ἀπείη B   26 κίονι Xv: κίωνι B

as if by fire—considers the one relief from its suffering to be the death of the man it hates.

30. Not long after, further meetings were convened, further councils of the ruling powers and chief priests against guiltless Ignatius.[88] The latter remained in the district of Poseus,[89] viewing with suspicion the intrigues being made against him, while Photius called his church and the legation which had come from Rome to meet at the holy temple of the Apostles.[90] The imperial family was present, as also were all the other ruling powers and almost all the population of the capital. And when they had convened, they first of all chose Baanes Angoures, *praepositus*, and some others who were nonentities among the Romans to go as legates to Ignatius.[91]

31. When these legates came into the presence of Ignatius, they said: "The mighty and sacred synod summons you before it. Come with all speed to defend yourself against the charges which justly or unjustly are being repeated against you." And blessed Ignatius replied: "Tell me, I beg of you, how shall I come? As bishop, or priest, or monk?" And they said that they did not know what to reply to this, (remarking) "But we will go back to those who sent us and will return bringing a firm answer." And so on the following day the same men arrived back and said: "The ambassadors of Old Rome, Rodoaldus and Zacharias, send this communication through us unworthy ones. Present yourself immediately at the sacred and ecumenical council in whatever manner your conscience dictates." And so Ignatius immediately donned his patriarchal robes and set off on foot, accompanied by bishops and presbyters and a large crowd of monks and laymen. And when he was near the church of Gregorius Nazianzenus, where a cross has been set up on a marble column in the middle of the thoroughfare, he was met by John the patrician, also called Coxes, who told him that he had been sent by the emperor and threatened that if he did not proceed as a private citizen in the common garb of a monk, he would risk the death penalty.[92] Noble Ignatius did as the man suggested and was then brought before the council. And they produced seventy-two false witnesses whom they had suborned long before—all of them impious, vulgar, and of senatorial rank,

48

ἀνθρώπους ἀσεβεῖς πάντας | ἀγελαίους καὶ συγκλητικούς, ὧν 14
ἡγεῖτο Λέων πατρίκιος ἐκεῖνος ὁ καὶ Κρητικὸς ὀνομαζόμενος καὶ
Θεοδοτάκιος πα|τρίκιος μετ' αὐτόν, ᾧ καὶ τῆς ἐπιορκίας μισθὸν τὴν 520
ἀξίαν μαγίστρου προετείνατο. Ἐφ' οἷς καὶ τοὺς λοιποὺς ἀφ' ἑκά-
5 στου βαθμοῦ καὶ τοῦ καταδεεστάτου πάντων συλλεξάμενοι, οὐ
μόνον δέ, ἀλλὰ καὶ ἀπὸ τῶν λεγομένων διβαπτιστῶν καὶ ἀπὸ
παντός, ὡς εἰπεῖν, τάγματος τοὺς αἰσχίστους καὶ μιαρωτάτους τῶν
ἀνθρώπων χρυσοῦ τε καὶ ἀξιωμάτων ἐξαγορασάμενοι ἕνα καθ' ἕνα
προσῆγον ὀμνύοντας ὡς· "Ὁ δωδεκαετῆ μικροῦ δεῖν χρόνον
10 ἀρχιερατεύσας Ἰγνάτιος ἀψηφίστως χειροτονηθεὶς ἐκράτησε τῆς
ἐκκλησίας." Τί οὖν οἱ μάταιοι τῶν τοιούτων κριταί, "ὧν ἐν χερσὶν αἱ
ἀνομίαι, ὧν ἡ δεξιὰ αὐτῶν ἐπλήσθη δώρων;" Τί οὗτοι πρὸς τὴν
ψευδορκίαν ταύτην ἀνθυπήνεγκαν; Τὸν τριακοστὸν εὐθὺς ὑπανα-
γινώσκουσι κανόνα· "Εἴ τις ἐπίσκοπος" λέγοντα "κοσμικοῖς ἄρ-
15 χουσι χρησάμενος δι' αὐτῶν ἐγκρατὴς ἐκκλησίας γένηται, καθ-
αιρείσθω." Τὸ ἑξῆς δὲ τοῦ κεφαλαίου ὅτι· "Καὶ οἱ κοινωνοῦντες
αὐτῷ πάντες" κακούργως οἱ δόλιοι παρεσιώπησαν· ἔδει δὲ πάντως,
εἴπερ ἀποστολικὸν νόμον ἠγωνίζοντο τηρεῖν, οὐκ ἐκ μέρους, ἀλλὰ
τελείως ἔδει τηρεῖν· καὶ εἰ ἀληθῶς εἶχεν ἡ κατηγορία, ὥσπερ
20 ἐκεῖνον οὕτω καὶ τοὺς ὑπ' ἐκείνου χειροτονηθέντας καὶ αὐτῷ
κοινωνήσαντας καθαιρεῖν· καὶ οὕτως ἂν ἐν τοῖς ἔργοις τῶν χειρῶν
αὐτῶν οἱ ἁμαρτωλοὶ σαφῶς συνελαμβάνοντο. Ἀδικώτατα δὲ δια-
νοούμενοι ὅσον μὲν αὐτοῖς πρὸς βλάβην τοῦ παρ' αὐτῶν ἐπηρεαζο-
μένου συνετέλει τοῦτο ἐξεφώνησαν, τὸ ἑξῆς δὲ ὡς καὶ αὐτοὺς τῇ
25 αὐτῇ ὑποβάλλον ἐπιτιμίᾳ κατεκρύψαντο· ὃ δὴ καὶ ὁ πατριάρχης
αὐτοῖς τότε παρασιωπήσασιν εὐστόχως ἐπιφωνεῖ.

32. Ὦ τῆς κακουργίας,| ὦ τῆς σκαιότητος! Τίς γὰρ οὐκ οἶδεν 14ᵛ
ὡς Ἰγνάτιος μὲν ψήφῳ πάντων ὁμοῦ τῶν ἀρχιερέων καὶ τῆς Ἐκκλησίας ὅλης συναινέσει κανονικῶς καὶ ἐνθέσμως προκεχείρισται,
30 αὐτὸς δὲ ὁ Φώτιος μᾶλλον τῷ τε δεινῷ Βάρδᾳ καὶ τοῖς κοσμικοῖς
ἄρχουσι χρησάμενος συνεργοῖς ἀκανονίστως καὶ τυραννικῶς

11–12 Ps. 25.10   14–17 Can. apost. 29   21–22 Ps. 9.17

---

2 καὶ¹ B: om. v   9 δεῖν v: om. B   17 ἔδει B: om. v   30 τε Xv: om. B

led by Leo Creticus the patrician and Theodotacius the patrician, his second in command, to whom Photius had actually offered the office of *magistros* as reward for his perjury.[93] To make up the rest, they brought together men from every order, even the lowest, and bribed with money and preferment the most foul and disgusting men of just about every class, even the so-called dibaptist heretics.[94] They brought these men forward individually to state on oath that "Ignatius, who had been patriarch for almost twelve years, had taken control of the Church without being properly elected." And what of the foolish judges of these matters "in whose hands lies lawlessness, and their right hands are filled with gifts?" What reply did they make to these false oaths? They immediately read out the thirtieth canon, which says: "If any bishop makes use of the ruling powers of the secular world and through them gains control of the Church, let him be deposed." But as for the next part of the same chapter, which adds: "and all those also who make common cause with him," they wickedly and treacherously passed over that in silence.[95] But it was altogether necessary, if they were striving to observe an apostolic canon, that they should do so in full, not in part; and that if there was any truth in the charge, those who had been ordained by him and had made common cause with him should also, like Ignatius, be deposed. And in this way the sinners would have been clearly caught in the works of their own devising. But as it was, with the most unjust of intentions they pronounced only those things which served to harm the man whom they were treating so despitefully, while they concealed the next part of the canon, since it would subject them too to the same censure. And indeed, after they had passed over it on this occasion, the patriarch scored a point by completing the quotation.

32. What a piece of wickedness and perversity on their part! For everyone knew that Ignatius had been lawfully appointed in accordance with ecclesiastical canons by vote of all the bishops and with the consent of the whole Church, whereas it was Photius himself who had used the clever Bardas and the ruling powers of the secular world as accomplices and was taking possession of the patriarchal throne not in accordance with the principles of the

μᾶλλον ἢ ἐκκλησιαστικῶς τοῦ θρόνου καταδράττεται; Ἀλλ᾽ οὐκ
ἔγνωσαν, οὐδὲ συνῆκαν οἱ τῷ τῆς φιλαργυρίας καὶ δοξομανίας
σκότει διαπορευόμενοι ὡς ἐν οἷς διαλογίζονται διαβουλίοις συλ-
λαμβάνονται.

5   33. Μετὰ πολλὴν οὖν τὴν ἐν τοῖς λόγοις ἅμιλλαν καὶ σπουδὴν
καὶ τριβὴν κατ᾽ οὐδένα δικαιοσύνης νόμον, μόνῃ δὲ τῇ ἐξουσίᾳ
μανικῶς χρώμενοι ἐνδύουσι τοῦτον ἱμάτια διερρωγότα καὶ ῥυ-
πῶντα καὶ τὴν ἱεραρχικὴν στολὴν περιβαλόντες ἐκ τῶν ὄπισθεν
ἀπαμφιάζουσιν. Ἦν δέ τις ἐκκήρυκτος ὑποδιάκονος Προκόπιος
10 τοὔνομα, τὸν λόγον ἄλογος τὸν βίον βέβηλος, ὃν ὁ πατριάρχης
πρώην διὰ τοῦτο ἔρριψε τοῦ βαθμοῦ. Οὗτος πρῶτος ἀναιρούμενος
τὸ ὠμοφόριον καὶ τὴν λοιπὴν ἐσθῆτα ἐβόα τό· "Ἀνάξιος." Ζαχαρίας
τε καὶ Ῥοδόαλδος καί τινες ἄλλοι μιαροὶ τὰ ἴσα κραυγάζοντες τῇ
ἀνοσίᾳ ψήφῳ συνεπεψηφίζοντο· οὓς πάντας οὐ μετὰ πολὺ μετῆλ-
15 θεν ἡ δίκη καὶ τὸ τοῦ Ζαχαρίου τοῦ θείου δρέπανον ἐνδικώτατα
κατακτεῖναν συνετέλεσε. Φώτιος μὲν οὖν τὴν ἐνδομυχοῦσαν ἐν
αὐτῷ κατὰ τοῦ ἀνεγκλήτου μῆνιν πῶς ἂν ἄλλως τῇ οἰκουμένῃ
πάσῃ κατεστήσατο φανερὰν καὶ πῶς ἂν ἑαυτὸν ὡς πορρωτάτω τοῦ
εἰρηνικοῦ καὶ πράου ποιμένος ἀπέφηνεν Ἰησοῦ ἢ τοιαῦτα διανοη-
20 θεὶς καὶ οὕτως ἀδικώτατα τῷ δικαίῳ ἐπιθέμενος; Ταύτην τὴν κρίσιν
οὐκ ἦν ὅστις οὐκ ἐμέμψατο καὶ τῆς ἀλογιστίας, μᾶλλον δὲ μισαν-
θρωπίας τὸ ὑπερ|βάλλον ἀπεστράφη. Οὐδὲ γὰρ οἱ τῷ μέρει μόνον 521
τοῦ ὀρθοῦ λόγου | τιθέμενοι, ἀλλὰ καὶ αὐτοὶ Φωτίου οἱ συγγενεῖς 15
καὶ οἰκεῖοι κατεστέναξαν τῶν γενομένων καὶ εἰς κακὸν ταῦτα
25 προβήσεσθαι τῷ τῆς ἀδικίας οἰωνίσαντο κριτῇ.

     34. Τί δὲ ἐκεῖνος; ἆρ᾽ ἠδέσθη τοὺς ἀνθρώπους ἢ τὸν δικαιοσύ-
νην ἀγαπῶντα καὶ κρίσιν Θεὸν φοβηθεὶς ἐξ ἐκείνου κατέσπασε τὴν
ὀργήν; Οὐδαμῶς· ἀεὶ δὲ φθόνον φθόνῳ καὶ κακίαν ἐπισυνάπτων τῇ
κακίᾳ ἠγωνίζετο σπουδῇ πάσῃ καὶ μηχανῇ οὐ θανατῶσαι μόνον,
30 ἀλλὰ (τὸ τούτου χεῖρον) καὶ ὡς θανάτου ἄξιον αὐτὸν ἀνελεῖν.

1–3 Ps. 81.5   3–4 Ps. 9.23   **14–15** 4 Macc. 18.22   **15** Zach. 5.1–4

3 σκότει Β: σκότῳ v | διαλογίζονται Β: om. v   **8** ἱεραρχικὴν Β: ἱερατικὴν v
15 ἐνδικώτατα Β: ἐκδικώτατα v   **16** κατακτεῖναν Β: κατακτεῖναι Xv   **27** κατέσπασε Β:
κατέπαυσε Xv

Church, but in an uncanonical and tyrannical fashion. However, what those who were traveling along in the shadow of avarice and crazed ambition did not know or realize was that they were being ensnared in the very plans that they were devising.[96]

33. And so after much altercation, effort, rancor and procrastination, proceeding according to no law of justice but madly employing raw power alone, they put on him torn and filthy clothing and then dressed him in his patriarchal robes only to tear them from his back. And there was among them an excommunicated subdeacon, Procopius by name, a witless man and impure in his manner of life, whom the patriarch Ignatius had for this reason recently cast out of the ministry.[97] He was the first now to lift up the pallium and the rest of the holy vestments and cry out: "Unworthy!" And Zacharias and Rodoaldus and some other blackguards shouted out the same thing and joined in ratifying it by impious vote (all of whom were soon after punished by divine justice when the scythe of the divine prophet Zacharias served to cut them down most justly).[98] As for Photius, however, how better could he have made clear to the whole world the rage which he harbored within against blameless Ignatius? How better could he have shown himself to be at the furthest possible remove from Jesus, the peaceful and gentle shepherd, than by intending such things as these and attacking the man of righteousness in this most unjust manner? There was not a man who did not censure this judgment and turn his back on its excessive irrationality, or rather its excessive inhumanity. For not only those who were counted among the followers of orthodoxy, but even Photius's own familiars and associates bemoaned these events and prognosticated that they would lead to misfortune for that unjust judge.

34. And what of Photius? Did he show any sense of shame before mankind or, fearing God and God's love of justice and judgment, did he from that time on subdue his rancor? Not at all. On the contrary, he was forever heaping ill will upon ill will, wickedness on top of wickedness, and striving by every effort and device not only to put Ignatius to death, but (what is worse) to make away with him as a man who deserved the death penalty.[99]

35. Τότε μὲν οὖν, ὡς ὑπέλαβον, καθαιρήσαντες καὶ ἐκκηρύξαντες ἀνθρώποις αὐτὸν ὠμοτάτοις καὶ ἀσεβεστάτοις τιμωρεῖσθαι
πικρῶς παραδεδώκασιν, ἄχρις ἂν ἰδίᾳ χειρὶ εἰς τὴν ἰδίαν καθαίρεσιν
ὑποσημήνηται. Ἦσαν δὲ οἱ κολαφίζοντες καὶ ταλαιπωροῦντες
5 αὐτὸν καὶ πήξεως οὔσης δριμείας ἑνὶ χιτωνίσκῳ πιέζοντες καὶ
σταυροῦντες αὐτὸν καὶ πυρπολοῦντες καὶ ἐν δυσὶν ἑβδομάσιν
ἐμφρούριον συνέχοντες καὶ ἀσιτίᾳ τελείᾳ κατατήκοντες· οὐ μόνον
δέ, ἀλλὰ καὶ ἐπ᾽ αὐτῆς αὐτὸν τοῦ Κοπρωνύμου τῆς λάρνακος ἐκά-
θιζον ἀναβιβάζοντες καὶ τῶν ποδῶν αὐτοῦ κάτωθεν λίθους ἐξαρ-
10 τῶντες βαρεῖς καὶ ἐπὶ πλεῖον τῇ τοῦ μαρμάρου τὴν ἕδραν ὀξύτητι
πικρῶς ἄγαν πλήσσοντες ἐπέτριβον. Οἱ οὖν ταῦτά τε καὶ ἄλλα
πλείω ἐνυβρίζοντες εἰς τὸν μακαριώτατον καὶ λόγοις καὶ ἔργοις
ἐμπαροινοῦντες εἰς αὐτὸν σπέρμα πονηρόν, ὡς εἰπεῖν, υἱοὶ ἄνομοι,
ὁ Μωροθεόδωρος ἐκεῖνος καὶ ὁ Γοργονίτης Ἰωάννης καὶ ὁ Θεοδού-
15 λου Νικόλαος ὁ Σκουτελόψις ἦν.
36. Μετὰ γοῦν τὰς κολάσεις ἃς οὗτοι προσήγαγον τῷ ὁμολο-
γητῇ τοῦ Χριστοῦ, μετὰ τὰς ἀπειλάς, μετὰ τὰς ἀλύσεις ἃς κατὰ τῶν
τιμίων ἐπέβαλον ποδῶν, μετὰ τὰ ῥαπίσματα, μετὰ τὸ σταυροειδῶς
ἐπὶ πρόσωπον κατὰ τῶν μαρμάρων ἐφαπλῶσαι καὶ ὅλην τὴν νύκτα
20 δεδεμένον τιμωρήσασθαι, μετὰ τὸ ἐπιβιβάσαι τῇ λάρνακι εἰς τὴν
ἑξῆς νύκτα πᾶσαν, εἶθ᾽ οὕτως | ἀπολῦσαι τῶν δεσμῶν καὶ κατὰ τοῦ   15ᵛ
ἐδάφους αὐτὸν ἀκοντίσαι καὶ συντρίψαι καὶ τῷ αἵματι φοινίξαι τὴν
γῆν· μετὰ ταῦτα πάντα μικρὸν τοῦτον ἐμπνέοντα (συνεῖχε γὰρ
μάλιστα λελυμένη καὶ ἡ γαστήρ) βίᾳ τῆς τοῦ ἁγίου χειρὸς ὁ Μωρο-
25 θεόδωρος κρατήσας καὶ χάρτην λαβὼν ἔπηξεν ὡς δι᾽ αὐτοῦ σταυ-
ρόν, ὃν καὶ ἀναγαγὼν ἐπιδέδωκε Φωτίῳ. Ὁ δὲ τὸν σταυρὸν λαβὼν
ἐξ ἑαυτοῦ ὑπέγραψεν οὕτως· "Ἰγνάτιος ἀνάξιος Κωνσταντινουπόλεως ὁμολογῶ ἀψηφίστως εἰσελθεῖν καὶ τὰ ἔτη ταῦτα οὐχ
ἡγίαζον, ἀλλ᾽ ἐτυράννουν." Ταύτης τῆς ὑπογραφῆς τῷ βασιλεῖ
30 πεμφθείσης ἀφίεται μὲν ὁ μακάριος ἐκείνης τῆς ἐνοχῆς, τὸν μητρι-

---

13 Is. 1.4

3 ἰδίᾳ B: οἰκείᾳ v: οἰκίᾳ X | εἰς B: om. Xv   5 πήξεως v: τήξεως B   12 πλείω Xv: πλεῖα B
15 Σκουτελόψις Xv: σκουτελλόψις B   18 σταυροειδῶς B: σταυρωδῶς v

35. And so then they deposed and excommunicated him (or so they thought) and vindictively handed him over for punishment to the cruellest and most impious men, until such time as he might put his signature to his own deposition. They had people punching him and making him miserable, giving him a hard time in freezing cold conditions by making him wear one scanty tunic; crucifying him and burning him with fire; keeping him confined in prison for two weeks and sapping his strength by giving him no food at all.[100] And not only that, but they also made him go up and sit upon the very tomb of Copronymus; they suspended heavy stones from his feet and furthermore kept striking the place where he was sitting most harshly on the sharp edges of the marble in an attempt to destroy it.[101] Those who mocked at the blessed patriarch in these and other ways and acted offensively towards him in word and deed were the lawless sons (or Devil's offspring, one might call them) Theodorus the Foolish, John Gorgonites and Nicolaus Scutelopsis, son of Theodulus.[102]

36. And so after the tortures which they had brought to bear upon this confessor of Christ, after the threats, after the chains which they fixed upon his venerable feet, after the punches in his face, after laying him face down in the form of a cross on blocks of marble and tormenting him as he lay bound there all night long, after putting him upon the tomb of Copronymus for the whole of the next night, then freeing him from his fetters only to dash him to the ground and bruise him all over, staining the earth with his blood—when after all this there was still a little life in him (for his loose bowels were also giving him particular trouble), Theodorus the Foolish seized him forcibly by his holy hand and taking a sheet of vellum put a cross upon it as if by Ignatius's hand. He then took it away with him and handed it over to Photius, who received the mark and wrote under it in his own hand: "I Ignatius, unworthy of Constantinople, confess that I entered office without being properly elected and for these years past I have not been officiating as patriarch but acting as a usurper." When this signed confession had been sent to the emperor, blessed Ignatius was released from custody and he went to the district of Poseus, his mother's family

κὸν δὲ οἶκον τὰ Ποσέως καταλαβὼν μικρὸν τέως ἀπὸ τῶν πολλῶν πόνων ἀνέψυχεν ἐκεῖ. Ὁ ἐχθρὸς δὲ οὐκ ἐπαύετο δόλους ἐν καρδίᾳ τεκταινόμενος καὶ πονηρὰ κατὰ τοῦ ἀθώου διαλογιζόμενος. Τοίνυν ὑποβάλλει τοῖς κρατοῦσιν ἐπὶ τὸν τῶν Ἀποστόλων αὖθις αὐτὸν
5 ἀναγαγεῖν ναὸν καὶ βιάζεσθαι πρῶτον μὲν τὴν οἰκείαν καθαίρεσιν ἀνεγνωκότα ἐπὶ τοῦ ἄμβωνος ἀναθεματίζειν ἑαυτόν· μετὰ ταῦτα δέ (ὢ τῆς μιαιφόνου βουλῆς! ὢ τῆς δεινότητος!) τούς τε ὀφθαλμοὺς ἐκκόψαι καὶ τὴν χεῖρα | μανιωδῶς ἐβυσσοδόμευον. Οὕτως αὐτῶν 524 εἰς βάθος τὸ μῖσος καθήψατο καὶ τῆς τοῦ Θεοῦ δικαιοσύνης λόγος
10 παρ' αὐτοῖς οὐδεὶς καὶ ὁ τοῦ Θεοῦ φόβος ἀπῆν καὶ ὁ τοῦ διαβόλου ζῆλος ἐσπουδάζετο.

37. Αὐτὴ συνεπληροῦτο ἡ τῆς ἁγίας Πεντηκοστῆς ἡμέρα καὶ ἰδοὺ πλῆθος στρατιωτῶν ὁπλοφόρων τὸν οἶκον ἐξαίφνης ἐν ᾧ κατήγετο περιεκύκλου. Ἰδὼν οὖν ὁ ἅγιος ἐκεῖνος τὰ ἐρχόμενα ἐπ'
15 αὐτὸν καὶ τὴν ἀδελφοκτόνον μανίαν αἰσθόμενος Ἠσαῦ βουλὴν βουλεύεται ἀντίρροπον μὲν τῆς τοῦ καιροῦ κακίας, τῆς αὐτοῦ δὲ συνέσεως καὶ τοῦ ὁδηγοῦντος αὐτὸν | θείου Πνεύματος ἐπάξιον. 16 Τίς δὲ ἡ βουλή; Ἄλλην μὲν ἑαυτῷ οἰκτρὰν καὶ λαϊκὴν παρὰ τῶν οἰκετῶν ἀνειλημμένος στολήν, δύο δὲ σπυρίδας ἐφ' ἑνὸς ξύλου τῶν
20 ἰδίων ἀπαιωρήσας ὤμων ἀχθοφόρου τινὸς τρόπον ἀπέδρα τοὺς φύλακας κατὰ μέσας νύκτας λαθών. Ἔσπευδε δὲ ἅμα τῷ μαθητῇ Κυπριανῷ τὴν ἐπὶ τὸ Συκαΐτικον διὰ τοῦ ἐμβόλου ποιούμενος πορείαν. Τὴν ψυχὴν δὲ συντριβόμενος καὶ τοῖς δάκρυσι περιρραινόμενος καὶ σφόδρα κατάπικρος τὴν καρδίαν καὶ κατώδυνος ὢν ἔτρεχεν
25 ὥσπερ Δαυὶδ ἐκεῖνος ἀπὸ προσώπου διαδρᾶναι Σαούλ. Κρείττονι δὲ προνοίᾳ συναντᾷ τούτῳ διὰ τῆς νυκτὸς ἰόντι ἀνήρ τις πάνυ τὴν πρόσοψιν εὐπρεπὴς τόν τε πώγωνα καὶ τὴν κόμην εὐσταλῶς καθειμένος τῆς κεφαλῆς· καὶ αὐτὸς στολὴν λευκὴν ἐσταλμένος καὶ ἵππῳ ἐπιβαίνων λευκῷ τὴν ὡς ἐπὶ Βλαχέρνας ἐβάδιζεν ὁδόν. Ἀγνὼς δὲ ὁ
30 ἀνὴρ ὅτι πυρσὸς οὐδαμοῦ καὶ τρανῶς ἐκεῖ τοῦτον ἰδεῖν οὐκ ἦν· πλὴν ὅστις ποτὲ ἦν Πνεύματι θείῳ κινηθεὶς ἔφη· ''Ὁ Θεὸς καὶ ἡ ὑπεραγία'' λέγων ''Θεοτόκος ἀκίνδυνόν σε, πανίερε δέσποτα, καὶ

---

12 cf. Acta 2.1   15 Gen. 27.41   25 1 Reg. 21.11

---

8 ἐβυσσοδόμευον B: ἐβυσσοδόμευεν v   18 ἄλλην μὲν ἑαυτῷ B: ἀλλοιοῖ μὲν ἑαυτὸν v: ἀλλιοῖ μὲν ἑαυτῷ X   22 συκαΐτικον B: συβαίτικον Xv   27 κόμην B: κώμην v   28–29 ἵππῳ…λευκῷ Xv: ἵππον ἐπιβ. λευκὸν B

home, where he recuperated for a little while from his many tribulations.[103] But his enemy did not cease devising treachery in his heart and planning acts of wickedness against blameless Ignatius. And so it was that he came to suggest to the ruling powers that they bring him back again to the temple of the Apostles and compel him to read aloud in the pulpit his own deposition and to declare himself anathematized. And in their mad delusion they actually considered the possibility (what a murderous plan! What a monstrous thing!) of putting out his eyes after that and cutting off his hand. Such were the depths plumbed by their hatred and they took no account of the justice of the Lord nor did they have any fear of God, but instead they zealously pursued emulation of the Devil.

37. The day of the Holy Pentecost arrived, and sure enough, a band of armed soldiers suddenly surrounded the house in which Ignatius was staying.[104] When holy Ignatius saw what he was up against and recognized the fury that had made Esau want to slay his brother, he formed a plan that was equal to the wickedness of the moment and at the same time worthy of his own intelligence and of the Holy Spirit, Who was his guide. And what was his plan? He changed into squalid civilian clothes that belonged to his servants, and slinging two large baskets from a wooden pole across his shoulders, like a porter, he ran off, slipping past the guards in the middle of the night. Accompanied in his flight by his disciple, Cyprianus, he made his way across the neck of land towards Sycaiticum.[105] Distressed in his soul, his eyes streaming with tears and with great bitterness and anguish in his heart, he ran like David fleeing from the presence of Saul. And as he traveled through the night, by divine Providence he met a man of most distinguished appearance with well-groomed hair and beard, who was dressed in white, riding a white horse and proceeding along the road in the direction of Blachernai.[106] Ignatius could not recognize the man because there was not a torch anywhere around and it was impossible to see him clearly; but whoever he was, he was moved by the Holy Spirit and said: "All-holy lord, may God and the Holy Mother keep you and your companions free from danger." Blessed Ignatius accepted

56

τοὺς μετὰ σοῦ διαφυλάξαι." Τοῦτο τὸ ῥῆμα οἷάπερ ἐφόδιον ἀγαθὸν
ἄνωθεν ἧκον ἐπ᾽ αὐτὸν ὁ μακάριος ὑποδεξάμενος προθυμότερον
ἐβάδιζε· καὶ τῷ δουλικῷ καὶ πενιχρῷ σχήματι πάντας λαθὼν καὶ εἰς
πλοῖον ἐμβὰς καὶ τὰς Πριγκιπίους καὶ Προκονησίους οὐ μόνον δέ,
5 ἀλλὰ καὶ τὰς Προποντίους νήσους ἄλλην ἐξ ἄλλης ἀμείβων καὶ ἐν
ἐρημίαις πλανώμενος ὄρεσί τε καὶ σπηλαίοις καὶ ταῖς τῆς γῆς,
ἀποστολικῶς φάναι, κατακρυπτόμενος ὀπαῖς ὑστερούμενος θλιβό-
μενος κακουχούμενος τὰς πρὸς τὸ ζῆν ἀφορμὰς ἐπαίτου τρόπον
διὰ τῶν φιλοχρίστων ἠρανίζετο.
10 38. Φώτιος δὲ τῆς θήρας διαμαρτὼν πάντα μὲν μοναστήρια,
πᾶσαν δὲ τὴν πόλιν καὶ τὰ περὶ αὐτὴν ἀνηρευνᾶτο, εἴ που ἄρα
καταλάβοι τὸν ὥσπερ δαλὸν ἐξεσπασμένον ἐκ προσώπου πυρός.
Μηδὲν οὖν ἀνύειν δυνάμενος ὧν ἐβούλετο παρασκευάζει | προσ-   16ᵛ
τάγματι βασιλικῷ τὸν χαλεπὸν ἐκεῖνον Ὡρύφαν σὺν ἓξ δρόμωσι
15 πάσας τὰς νήσους καὶ τὴν παράλιον ἀνερευνᾶσθαι καὶ εἴ που συμ-
βαίη ληφθῆναι τὸν Ἰγνάτιον εὐθὺς ἀναιρεῖσθαι τοῦτον ὡς ὅλην
ἀνατρέποντα τὴν βασιλείαν. Πολλάκις οὖν καὶ κατὰ πλείους
τόπους αὐτῷ περιπίπτοντες οἱ θηραταὶ διὰ τὴν δουλικὴν οὐκ
ἐπέγνωσαν στολήν. Καὶ ἄλλοτε πάλιν διὰ μέσου αὐτὸν παρερχόμε-
20 νον ἀορασίᾳ ληφθέντες, ὡς οἱ περὶ τὸν Ἐλισσαιὲ Ἀσσύριοι, τοῦτον
οὐκ ἠδυνήθησαν ἰδεῖν. Καὶ αὐτοὶ μὲν ὡς λύκοι μάτην κεχηνότες
ἀπῄεσαν, κατὰ τὴν παροιμίαν. Ὁ δὲ τὰς εὐχαριστηρίους εὐχὰς
ἀναπέμπων τῷ Σωτῆρι διὰ πολλῶν θλίψεων τὴν τοῦ Θεοῦ βασιλείαν ἐξωνεῖτο. Οἱ μὲν οὖν ἐν τούτοις ἦσαν. Τί δὲ ὁ μακρόθυμος
25 Κύριος ὁ δίκαιος ὁ ἰσχυρὸς ὁ μὴ τὴν ὀργὴν ἐπάγων καθ᾽ ἑκάστην
ἡμέραν; Ἆρ᾽ ἐπὶ πολὺ τὰς ὑπερβολὰς τῶν κακῶν ταύτας ἠνέσχετο
καθορᾶν; Οὐδαμῶς. |
525
39. Αὔγουστος ἐνίστατο μὴν καὶ σεισμοῖς ἐξαισίοις ἡ βασιλεύ-
ουσα κατεδονεῖτο· καὶ πᾶς οἶκος ἐκλονεῖτο καὶ πᾶσα καρδία τῷ
30 φόβῳ κατεσείετο· καὶ πᾶς ἄνθρωπος τῷ τοῦ θανάτου δέει συνεχό-

6-8 Hebr. 11.37–38   12 Amos 4.11; Zach. 3.2   20 4 Reg. 6.18   21 CPG II 121   23-24 cf.
Acta 14.22   25-26 Ps. 7.12

4 προκονησίους Β: Προικονησίους v   5 τὰς Β: om. v   12 ἐξεσπασμένον Χ: ἐξηπτασμένον
Βv   14 ὡρύφαν Β: Ὡρύφαν Χv | δρόμωσι Χ: δρομεῦσιν Β: δρομεῦσι v   15 πάσας...
ἀνερευνᾶσθαι Χv: ἀνερευνᾶσθαι τὴν παράλιον πᾶσαν καὶ πᾶσαν νῆσον Β   18 τὴν Β: om. v
20 ἐλισσαιὲ Β: Ἐλισσαῖον v   24 οὖν Β: om. v

these words as an omen sent from above for a propitious start to his journey and he went on his way with renewed zeal. Nobody recognized him in his beggarly servant's garb, and going on board ship he moved from one island to the next, visiting the Propontid Islands as well as the Princes' Islands and the Proconnesus.[107] He wandered in desolate places and hid himself in the mountains, in caverns and in holes in the ground, to use the words of the holy apostle; and suffering dire need, affliction and distress, he relied, like a beggar, on the alms of good Christians to provide what he needed to keep himself alive.

38. When Photius failed to capture his quarry, he searched every monastery and all the city and its surroundings in the hope that he might somewhere find Ignatius, who had been snatched from the face of the fire like a piece of blazing wood. And when he was unable to accomplish what he desired, he arranged by imperial command for evil Ooryphas, accompanied by six *dromons*,[108] to search the seaboard and all the islands with instructions to put Ignatius to death immediately, if he should happen to be captured, on the grounds that he was subverting the whole empire. However, even though the hunters encountered Ignatius often in a number of different places, they did not recognize him on account of his servant's garb; and just like the Assyrians with Elisha, they were struck by blindness and unable to see him even when he occasionally passed right through their midst. And so they departed without achieving their purpose, like wolves baying at the empty air, as the proverb says, while Ignatius sent up prayers of thanksgiving to the Savior and earned his place in the Kingdom of Heaven through his many tribulations. So much for them; but what about the long-suffering Almighty, the just and strong, Who does not vent His rage each and every day?[109] Could He bear to watch this excessive wrongdoing for long? Certainly not!

39. At the beginning of August the capital was shaken by violent earthquakes.[110] Every house was jolted, every heart trembled with fright, and gripped by fear of dying everyone cried out that the

μενος ἐβόα μίαν αἰτίαν εἶναι τοῦ σεισμοῦ, μίαν τὴν εἰς τὸν πατριάρχην Ἰγνάτιον ἀδικίαν καὶ παρανομίαν. Ἐν ἡμέραις δὲ τεσσαράκοντα μηκυνόμενος ὁ σεισμὸς ἐπὶ τοσοῦτον αὐτῶν τὴν ὠμότητα καὶ ἰταμότητα κατέκαμψεν ὡς καὶ τοὺς κρατοῦντας αὐτοὺς ὅρκον προ-
5 θεῖναι δημοσίᾳ μήτ᾿ αὐτὸν ἐκεῖνον τὸν ἱερὸν φυγάδα μήτε παρ᾿ ᾧ κρύπτεται φανερούμενον ὑπεύθυνον καθεστάναι λοιπόν, ἀθῳούμενον δὲ εἰς τὴν οἰκείαν ἀνενοχλήτως ἀποκαθίστασθαι μονήν. Τοίνυν οὕτως ἀκούσας ὁ ἀθλητὴς καταδηλοῖ ἑαυτὸν αὐτίκα τῷ πατρικίῳ Πετρωνᾷ· ὃς τοῦ αὐτοκράτορος θεῖος πρὸς μητρὸς ὢν καὶ τὸ τοῦ
10 βασιλέως ἄρας ἐγκόλπιον εἰς ἐνέχυρον φέρων δίδωσι τῷ πατριάρχῃ. Ὁ δὲ τοῦτο τοῦ τραχήλου ἀπαιωρήσας καὶ πρὸς τὸν Βάρδαν ἀναχθεὶς | ἔστη· πρὸς ὃν ἐκεῖνος· "Ἵνα τί" φησὶ "τρόπον δραπέτου   17
μιμησάμενος ἄλλην ἐξ ἄλλης χώραν ἀμείβων περινοστεῖς;" Ὁ δέ· "Χριστὸς" ἔφη "ὁ ἡμέτερος βασιλεὺς καὶ σωτὴρ ἐνετείλατο. Ἐὰν
15 διώκωσιν ὑμᾶς ἐκ τῆς πόλεως ταύτης, φεύγετε εἰς τὴν ἄλλην." Ἡττηθεὶς οὖν τῆς τοῦ ἀνδρὸς ἀρετῆς ἐκεῖνος ἀνεύθυνον τοῦτον καὶ ἄνετον εἰς τὴν αὐτοῦ καταστῆναι κελεύει μονήν. Εὐθὺς οὖν καὶ ὁ σεισμὸς ἔστη. Καὶ Βούλγαροι δὲ τότε προνοίαις Θεοῦ βιαίῳ κατατακέντες λιμῷ, ἅμα δὲ καὶ τοῖς δώροις τοῦ αὐτοκράτορος θελχθέν-
20 τες τὰ ὅπλα καταθέμενοι τῷ ἁγίῳ προσήεσαν βαπτίσματι.

40. Τότε καὶ οἱ προλεχθέντες τοποτηρηταὶ Ῥώμης φιλοφρόνως ὑπὸ Φωτίου δωροδοκηθέντες τὴν Ῥώμην παλινοστήσαντες κατέλαβον. Οὓς ὁ πάπας ἀνακρίνας Νικόλαος καὶ τὰ κατὰ τὸν πατριάρχην Ἰγνάτιον ἠκριβωκὼς καὶ ἐκ τοῦ στόματος αὐτῶν ὑποδίκους
25 αὐτοὺς πεφωρακὼς ὡς ἐπισυστάσεως ληστρικῆς, ἀλλ᾿ οὐ κανονικῆς συνόδου κατάρξαντας διηνεκεῖ καθαιρέσει καὶ ἀναθεματισμῷ καθυποβάλλει· καὶ οὐ μόνους αὐτούς, ἀλλὰ καὶ αὐτὸν Φώτιον ὡς ἐπιβήτορα καὶ μοιχὸν ἀποκηρύττει καὶ ὑπὸ συνόδῳ κανονικῇ καὶ ψήφῳ πάσης τῆς ὑπ᾿ αὐτὸν Ἐκκλησίας ἀναθεματίζει καὶ καθαιρεῖ
30 οὐδὲν αὐτὸν διαφέρειν Μαξίμου τοῦ Κυνικοῦ τοῦ τῷ Θεολόγῳ Γρηγορίῳ ἐπιφυέντος καὶ τὴν Ἐκκλησίαν συγχέαντος ἀποφηνάμε-

---

14–15 Matth. 10.23

6–7 ἀθῳούμενον Xv: ἀθῳσόμενον B   7 ἀποκαθίστασθαι Xv: καθίστασθαι B   9 τὸ B: om.
v   14 σωτὴρ B: πατὴρ v   15 διώκωσιν B: διώκουσιν v

reason for the tremors was nothing other than the injustice and lawlessness practiced against the patriarch Ignatius. The earthquake lasted for forty whole days and curbed their cruelty and effrontery to such an extent that even the ruling powers made a public oath that neither the holy fugitive himself nor anyone found to be harboring him would be held responsible in the future and that Ignatius would be absolved from guilt and be allowed to settle down undisturbed in his own monastery. And so when the champion of Christ heard this, he immediately made himself known to Petronas the patrician, the emperor's uncle on his mother's side; and the latter took the emperor's *encolpion* and handed it over as a pledge of security to the patriarch.[111] Ignatius hung it around his neck and sailed off to see Bardas, and when he stood before him, Bardas asked: "Why do you wander about from one place to another like a fugitive?" And he replied: "Christ, our Lord and Savior, commanded us, saying: if they persecute you in this city, flee to another." And Bardas was overcome by the man's virtue and gave orders that he be allowed to settle, guiltless and free, in his monastery. And immediately the earthquake subsided, and it was at this time too that by God's providential care the Bulgarians, wasting away from severe famine and charmed by the emperor's bribes, laid down their arms and underwent the sacrament of baptism.[112]

40. At the same time, the aforementioned ambassadors from Rome returned home after being bribed by Photius's friendly gifts.[113] Pope Nicolaus interrogated them and accurately investigated what had befallen the patriarch Ignatius; and when he discovered from the evidence of their own mouths that they were guilty of having taken the lead in a riotous meeting of bandits rather than a legitimate synod, he subjected them to the sentence of perpetual deposition and anathematization.[114] And they were not the only ones. The pope also excommunicated Photius himself for being a usurper and adulterer and anathematized and deposed him before a legitimate synod[115] and by vote of all the Roman Church, declaring that his case was no different from that of Maximus the Cynic, who had oppressed Gregorius Nazianzenus and thrown the Church

νος. Ὅθεν αὐτόν τε ὡς τῶν σκανδάλων αἴτιον καὶ τοὺς ὑπ' αὐτοῦ
κεχειροτονημένους ὡς ὁμόφρονας τούτῳ δηλονότι καθεστῶτας
ἀποστολικῇ κρίσει τῇ αὐτῇ ὑποβάλλει καταδίκῃ. Οὐ τοῦτο δὲ ποιεῖ
μόνον, ἀλλὰ καὶ τοὺς κοινωνοῦντας Φωτίῳ αὐτόν τε τὸν βασιλέα
5 καὶ τὴν ὑπ' αὐτὸν πολιτείαν πᾶσαν δι' ἐπιστολῶν ἀφορίζει. Ταῦτα
δὲ ζήλῳ θείῳ ὁ Νικόλαος καταπραξάμενος καὶ τοῖς τῆς Ἀνατολῆς
πατριάρχαις τὴν ἔνθεσμον κρίσιν ταύτην διεπέμψατο.
41. Κατ' ἐκείνας δὲ τὰς ἡμέρας καὶ ἐμπρησμὸς μέγας σφόδρα
εἰς τὰ Σοφίας γενόμενος ἀμύθητον ὅσην καταφθορὰν καὶ λύμην
10 τοῖς προσοικοῦσιν ἐνειργάσατο. | Οὐδὲν δὲ τούτων εἰς μετάμελον 17ᵛ
ἦγε τοὺς ἀνομεῖν διεγνωκότας· μᾶλλον μὲν οὖν, κατὰ τὴν ἀπο|στο- 528
λικὴν πρόρρησιν· "Ἐπὶ τὸ χεῖρον προέκοπτον πλανῶντες καὶ πλα-
νώμενοι."
42. Βάρδας μὲν γὰρ ἐφ' ἑαυτὸν τὴν Ῥωμαϊκὴν ἀρχὴν ὑποποι-
15 ούμενος πρῶτον μὲν κουροπαλάτης, μετὰ μικρὸν δὲ καῖσαρ ἀναγο-
ρευθεὶς τῆς τοῦ ἀνεψιοῦ εὐηθείας κατετρύφα αὐτὸς ἀκρασίας τε
πάσης καὶ πάσης ἡδονῆς ἀσελγοῦς ἀνδράποδον ἀποδεικνύμενος· ὁ
Μιχαὴλ δὲ νεωτερικαῖς ἐπιθυμίαις ὅλος κατεφθαρμένος τὸν νοῦν
παίγνιον ἔθετο τὰ θεῖα, παίγνιον αὐτὸς ἀκρασίας τε πάσης καὶ
20 ἁμαρτίας καὶ τοῦ τῆς ἁμαρτίας γεγενημένου πατρός· καὶ δὴ μιαρωτάτους τινὰς ἀνθρωπίσκους καὶ βεβηλοτάτους καὶ εὐτραπέλους
ἐκλεξάμενος ἀμοίρους μὲν ἁγίου παντάπασι Πνεύματος, τοῦ ἐν-
αντίου δὲ πνεύματος τῆς ἐνεργείας πεπλησμένους ἀνευλαβῶς τε
καὶ ἀπηρυθριακότως ἱερεῖς καὶ ἀρχιερεῖς κατὰ τὴν τῆς Ἐκκλησίας
25 ἐναγῆ μίμησιν ὁ ἀνούστατος ἐχειροτόνει· καὶ ἐν αὐτοῖς Θεόφιλόν
τινα πρωτοσπαθάριον ἄνδρα γελωτοποιὸν καὶ μῖμον καὶ πάντων
ἐναγῶν ἐναγέστατον πατριάρχην ἐπ' ἐκείνοις προχειριζόμενος
ὠνόμαζεν, γέλωτα ἑαυτῷ καὶ καγχασμὸν ἀσελγῆ τούτῳ ὁ κατάπτυ-
στος κατασκευαζόμενος καὶ καταγέλαστος· δι' ὧν ὑβρίζετο μὲν ἡ
30 ἁγία προσφορά, ὑβρίζετο δὲ καὶ ἐβλασφημεῖτο τοῖς ἔθνεσι τὸ
ὄνομα τοῦ Θεοῦ.

12–13 2 Tim. 3.13   30–31 Is. 52.5; Rom. 2.24

---

1 αὐτοῦ Xv: αὐτὸν B   6 Ἀνατολῆς Xv: ἀνατολικῆς B   9 τὰ B: τὰς Xv
15 κουροπαλάτης Xv: κοροπαλάτης B   20 leg. γεγενημένος?   23 τε v: δὲ B   28 ἑαυτῷ
Xv: ἑαυτὸν B | τούτῳ E: τού(τω) B: om. Xv

into confusion.[116] Hence, in a judgment inspired by the teachings of the apostles, Nicolaus subjected Photius himself, as the cause of the offences, and those who had been ordained by him, as being clearly in agreement with him, to the same condemnation. And not only that, but he also excommunicated by letter those who took part in the affair with Photius, including the emperor himself and all his government. Nicolaus carried out these things with a holy zeal and transmitted this canonical judgment to the patriarchs of the East.

41. At about this time there was also an enormous fire in the quarter of Saint Sophia which resulted in untold death and destruction for those living nearby. But none of this brought repentance from those who had decided on acts of lawlessness; instead, in the prophetic words of the apostle, they waxed worse and worse, deceiving and being deceived.

42. For Bardas assumed for himself the rule of the Roman Empire and was first proclaimed *curopalates*, then caesar shortly afterwards.[117] He delighted in his nephew's simplemindedness, while showing himself to be the slave of all incontinence and every wanton pleasure. Michael's senses, on the other hand, were completely corrupted by his youthful desires; he regarded sacred matters as a joke and was himself the plaything of all incontinence and sin—the plaything, in fact, of the true father of sin. In his supreme witlessness he picked out some of the most loathsome, profane and coarse creatures, completely bereft of the Holy Spirit and possessed by the opposite spirit of evil, and in sinful imitation of the true Church he shamelessly and irreverently appointed them as his bishops and archbishops. Among them was Theophilus, *protospatharius*, a man who was a buffoon and actor and the worst sinner of them all;[118] and he was the one whom that abominable and ridiculous man now appointed and named as his patriarch, thus providing himself with the occasion for laughter and vulgar cackling. It was through these actions that the sacred oblation was insulted and the name of God was likewise insulted and blasphemed among the pagans.

43. Ἐπὶ τοσοῦτον δὲ τῇ ἀλογιστίᾳ ἐνετρύφα ταύτῃ καὶ ἐνεκαλ-
λωπίζετο ὥστε μηδὲ τοῦτο παρρησίᾳ λέγειν αἰσχύνεσθαι, ὅτι·
"Ἐμοὶ μὲν πατριάρχης ὁ Θεόφιλος, ὁ Φώτιος δὲ τῷ καίσαρι καὶ τοῖς
Χριστιανοῖς ὁ Ἰγνάτιος καθέστηκεν·" εἰς τηλικοῦτον αὐτὸν ἀφρο-
5 σύνης μᾶλλον ἢ ἀσεβείας κατενεχθῆναι βόθρον. Ὁ μὲν οὖν εἰρημέ-
νος βωμολόχος ἐκεῖνος Θεόφιλος οὕτω παρρησίᾳ ταῖς βασιλείοις
κωμάζων αὐλαῖς ἀρρητοποιΐαις τε πάσαις καὶ ἀσελγείαις καὶ εὐτρα-
πελίαις δι' αἰσχίστης μιμήσεως τῶν ἱερῶν μυστηρίων κατωρχεῖτο
καὶ κατέπαιζε· πρᾶγμα μηδὲ τοῖς ἀσεβεστάτοις τῶν Ἑλλήνων | 18
10 πώποτε τολμηθέν. Ὁ Φώτιος δὲ τούτων τολμωμένων καὶ κατ'
ὀφθαλμοὺς αὐτοῦ πραττομένων οὐκ ἤλεγξε τὸ τοῦ ἐπιτηδεύματος
ἄτοπον, οὐκ ἀντέστη τῇ παρανομίᾳ, οὐ μικράν, οὐ μεγάλην ὑπὲρ
τῶν ὑβριζομένων θείων ὀργίων ἀφῆκε φωνήν. Καὶ οὐ θαυμαστόν·
ἦν γὰρ μισθωτὸς καὶ οὐ ποιμήν· διὸ οὐδεμία τούτῳ περὶ τῶν ἀπολ-
15 λυμένων προβάτων ἐγίνετο φροντίς. Πρὸς δύο δὲ μόνον ὅλως
αὐτῷ συνετέτατο τῆς ψυχῆς ὁ σκοπός· ἓν μὲν ὅπως τὰ πάντα χαριζόμενος τοῖς κρατεῖν δοκοῦσι τὸ τῆς πατριαρχίας κράτος μόνιμον
ἑαυτῷ διατηρῇ· δεύτερον δὲ ὅπως καὶ αὐτῆς ἀποστερῆσαι τὸν
Ἰγνάτιον, εἰ δυνατόν, τῆς ζωῆς.
20 44. Καὶ ὅτι ἀληθῆ ταῦτα καὶ οὐ λόγοι κενοὶ αὐτὰ βοᾷ τὰ πράγματα. Τίς γὰρ ἀκούσας ἐκεῖνο τὸ σκευώρημα οὐ τὴν φονικὴν παρ-
ευθὺ τοῦ ἀνδρὸς ἐπέγνω προαίρεσιν; Καὶ γὰρ ἐν μιᾷ τῶν ἡμερῶν
ξένος τις ἄνθρωπος ἄχρις ἐκείνου πρὸς πάντων ἀγνοούμενος,
σχῆμα δὲ μοναχοῦ περικείμενος, Εὐστράτιος δὲ καλούμενος τὸν
25 πατριαρχικὸν ἐξαπίνης οἶκον ἐπιβὰς καὶ εἰσελθὼν δύο πλασματο-
γραφίας ἐνώπιον πάντων ἀποκαλύψας ἐπεδίδου (ἃς αὐτὸς ὁ | 529
σοφώτατος Φώτιος, ὡς σαφὲς ὕστερον ἐγένετο, δολιευόμενος
κατεσκευάσατο)· μίαν μὲν ἐκ προσώπου τοῦ Ἰγνατίου πρὸς Νικό-
λαον τὸν πάπαν ἐπιστολὴν τὴν περὶ αὐτὸν γενομένην καινοτομίαν
30 καὶ ἀδικίαν τοῦ βασιλέως σαφῶς διαγορεύουσαν· ἥν, ὡς ἔλεγε, τοῦ
πάπα μηδὲ προσβλέψαι καταδεξαμένου ἐκεῖθεν αὐτὴν αὖθις ἀνεν-
εγκεῖν· μίαν δὲ πρὸς τὸν Φώτιον αὐτὸν τοῦτον, ὡς ἀπὸ τοῦ Νικο-

---

14-15 cf. Luc. 15.4-6   20-21 cf. Demosth. *De fals. leg.* 81.4; Dion. Hal. *Ant. Rom.* X 13.4

---

9 καὶ B: [καὶ] ν   13 ὑβριζομένων Xν: ὀργιζομένων B   25 ἐπιβὰς Xν: ἀναβὰς B
28 κατεσκευάσατο B: κατεσκεύαστο ν   29 περὶ Xν: παρὰ B   31 αὐτὴν B: αὐτὸν ν

43. To such an extent did Michael revel in and boast of this piece of foolishness that he was not even ashamed to say openly: "Theophilus is my patriarch, Photius is the caesar's, and the Christians have Ignatius." To such depths of folly, not to mention impiety, is he said to have sunk. Meanwhile, this vulgar lout Theophilus held revels quite openly in the imperial palace, practicing every kind of unmentionable vice amid his licentious and coarse behavior and prancing and sporting in most shameful imitation of the sacred mysteries—something which not even the most impious of the Greeks had ever dared. And Photius did not condemn this monstrous practice, even though it was being done before his eyes; he did not oppose the transgression by raising even a small voice in defence of the holy rites of the Church which were being outraged. And no wonder, since he was a mercenary, not a shepherd, and consequently cared nothing for the loss of his flock. On two things alone were the aims of his heart completely set: one was to secure the patriarchate permanently for himself by currying favor in all things with those who appeared to be the ruling powers; the other was to deprive Ignatius, if possible, of life itself.

44. And the facts themselves cry out and attest that these things are true and not just empty words. For what man was there who did not recognize Photius's murderous temperament as soon as he heard of that fraud which he perpetrated? For one day there suddenly arrived at the patriarchal residence a stranger who was not known to anyone before that time. Eustratius was his name and he was dressed as a monk, and when he went inside, he revealed and handed over in the presence of everyone two forged letters (which that man of great wisdom, Photius himself, had treacherously prepared, as was made clear later).[119] One letter was from Ignatius to pope Nicolaus and clearly recounted the innovation and injustice perpetrated by the emperor in his case; this letter he was now bringing back again, since, as Eustratius said, the pope did not deign even to look at it. The other letter was actually addressed to Photius, ostensibly from Nicolaus himself, and served the purpose

64

λάου αὐτοῦ διεκομίζετο, δύναμιν ἔχουσαν ἀπολογίας ὑπὲρ τοῦ
μεταξὺ αὐτῶν πρώην παρακολουθήσαντος παροξυσμοῦ, ἀγάπης δὲ
τοῦ λοιποῦ καὶ κοινωνίας δῆθεν ἀρρήκτου κυρωτικήν. Ταύτας ὁ
ταραχοποιὸς ἐκεῖνος δεξάμενος ἀνὴρ εὐθὺς τῷ τε βασιλεῖ | καὶ τῷ   18ᵛ
5 καίσαρι κατὰ τοῦ ἀναιτίου ἐμφανίζει καὶ παροξύνει κατ' αὐτοῦ·
"Πονηρεύεται" λέγων "κατὰ τῆς ὑμετέρας βασιλείας Ἰγνάτιος καὶ
διαβάλλει πρὸς τοὺς ἔξω καὶ κατηγορεῖ καὶ τὸ τῆς ὑμετέρας ἐξουσίας κράτος ἀδικώτατα συκοφαντεῖ· καὶ εἰ πρὸς δίκαιον εἶχεν, οὐδ'
ἂν ζῆν συνεχωρεῖτο τοιαῦτα κατὰ τῆς ὑμῶν διανοούμενος γαληνό-
10 τητος· καὶ ἡ τῆς κακουργίας" φησὶν "ἀπόδειξις ἰδοὺ καὶ αὐτὰ μαρ-
τυροῦσι τὰ γράμματα ἅπερ ἡμᾶς μὲν ἔβλαψεν οὐδέν, ὠφέλησε δὲ
μᾶλλον πληροφορηθέντος τοῦ πάπα τἀληθῆ καὶ ἀγάπην κεκυρω-
κότος εἰς ἡμᾶς. Οὐχ ἡγοῦμαι δὲ δίκαιον εἶναι τὴν ὑμῶν βασιλείαν
οὕτως ἐξουθενεῖσθαι παρ' αὐτοῦ." Ταῦτα μὲν ὁ συκοφάντης· φύλα-
15 κες δὲ παρ' αὐτὰ καὶ φρουρὰ περὶ τὸν ἀναιτίως κατηγορούμενον
ἀσφαλὴς ἔρευνά τε πολλὴ σφόδρα καὶ ἐξέτασις εἰ ταῦτα τοῦτον
γέγονε τὸν τρόπον. Παρήγετο τοίνυν εἰς μέσον ὁ γραμματηφόρος
ἐκεῖνος καὶ ἀπῃτεῖτο δεῖξαι πρὸς τίνος εἴληφει τὴν πρὸς τὸν πάπαν
ἐπιστολήν. Ὁ δὲ πρότερον εἰρηκὼς ὡς Κυπριανὸς ἐκεῖνος ὁ τοῦ
20 Ἰγνατίου τά τε γράμματα ταῦτα καὶ ἐφόδια ἐχειροδότησεν ἱκανὰ
οὗτος ἐπὶ μῆνα σχεδὸν ὅλον ἀπαιτούμενος τοῦτον ἐπιδεῖξαι ἠλέγ-
χετο μήτ' αὐτὸν εἰδὼς τὸν Κυπριανὸν μήτε τιν' ἄλλον τῶν ἀνθρώπων Ἰγνατίου. Οὕτω δὲ τῆς σκευωρίας φωραθείσης μάστιξιν ὑπὸ
τοῦ καίσαρος πικροτάταις ἐκεῖνος κατηκίσθη. Ὃν καὶ πολλὰ
25 Φώτιος λυτρώσασθαι διεσπουδακὼς οὐκ ἠδυνήθη· εἰς παραμυθίαν
δὲ μετὰ ταῦτα διωγμητῶν τοῦτον ἄρχοντα καθίστησι πλῆθος ῥαβ-
δούχων ὑποτάξας αὐτῷ. Ταύτης καταφανοῦς γενομένης τῆς κακο-
τροπίας οὐκ ἦν ὅστις οὐ προσώχθισε τῷ κατασκευαστῇ τῶν κακῶν.
45. Μετὰ ταῦτα τῆς Χριστοῦ μὲν Ἀναλήψεως ἐτελεῖτο μνημό-
30 συνον, πρὸς ἑσπέραν δὲ σεισμὸς γίνεται τῶν πώποτε γενομένων ὁ
φρικωδέστατος. Δι' ὅλης δὲ τῆς ἐπιούσης ἐπεκράτει νυκτός· βοὴ δέ

---

3 ταύτας Β: ταῦτα ν   8 ἀδικώτατα Β: om. ν | συκοφαντεῖ Χν: συκοφαντῶν Β   14 ἐξου-
θενεῖσθαι Β: ἐξουδενεῖσθαι ν   16 εἰ Β: εἰς ν   17 γραμματηφόρος Β: γραμματοφόρος Χν
29–30 μνημόσυνον Χν: μνημοσύνη Β

of vindicating the violent dispute that had of late prevailed between them and of establishing for the future a spirit of charity and unbroken fellowship. As soon as that troublemaker had received these items, he revealed them to the emperor and to the caesar; and he inflamed them against guiltless Ignatius, saying: "Ignatius is making mischief against your sovereignty, slandering and denouncing you to outsiders and carping most unjustly at the power of your Imperial Majesty. And if he were dealing with a fair man, he would not be allowed to live for contemplating such things against your serene Highness. See the proof of his wickedness, the evidence of these very letters, which instead of harming us in any way turned out to be quite beneficial, since the pope has been fully assured of the true situation and has guaranteed us his brotherly love. But I do not think it fair for your Majesty to be mocked by him in this way." As soon as the slanderer had spoken these words, the watch was called and a close guard put on the wrongly accused, while a most thorough inquiry was made to examine the truth of the matter. And so the bearer of the letters was brought forward and was required to indicate from whom he had received the letter to the pope. And although he had previously stated that Cyprianus from Ignatius's household had handed him this letter and supplies sufficient for the journey, nevertheless when he was now required to point out the man during almost a whole month of investigation, he was exposed as knowing neither Cyprianus himself nor any other member of Ignatius's household.[120] And so the fraud was detected and Eustratius was punished with a most severe lashing by the caesar. Although Photius tried his very best to save him from condemnation, he did not succeed, but at a later date, by way of consolation, he appointed him chief of police with a band of constables under his command.[121] And when Photius's treachery became known, there was not a single person who did not feel bitter resentment against the deviser of such evils.[122]

45. Soon after, remembrance of Christ's Ascension was celebrated, and towards evening on that day the most awful earthquake yet experienced broke out and continued right through the following night. Its roar and incomprehensible din burst forth

66

τις καὶ ἄσημος θροῦς | ἔκ τε γῆς ἔκ τε θαλάσσης σφοδρῶς ἀναδιδό- 19
μενος πάντων ἀνθρώπων ταῖς καρδίαις παράλυσιν ἐνεποίει καὶ
θραυσμόν. Ὅτε δὴ καὶ ἡ στήλη Ἰουστίνου ἐκ τῶν γονάτων κοπεῖσα
κατερράγη, τότε καὶ Βασίλειος ἐκεῖνος ὁ πρότερον μὲν Κρήτης
5 ἐπίσκοπος γενόμενος, διὰ δὲ τὴν τῶν Ἀγαρηνῶν ἔφοδον εἰς Θεσ-
σαλονίκην μετατεθεὶς (εἰς αἰσχύνην καὶ τοῦτο τοῦ τῆς βασιλίδος
προκαθεζομένου) τολμήσας αὐτὸς πρόσεισι τῷ Μιχαὴλ παραινετι-
κῶς ἅμα καὶ διδακτικῶς ἀποσχέσθαι τῆς τῶν ἱερατικῶν ἔργων
αἰσχρᾶς καὶ ἀνοσίου μιμήσεως παρακαλῶν· ἐντεῦθεν γὰρ τὴν
10 ὀργὴν τοῦ Θεοῦ ἀνακαίεσθαι διϊσχυρίζετο. Ὁ δὲ τοῖς ἐλέγχοις
ὑπερβαλλόντως πληγεὶς ῥαπίσμασι μὲν ἰσχυροῖς τοῦ τιμίου γέρον-
τος τοὺς ὀδόν|τας ἐξερρίζωσεν, οὕτω δὲ καὶ τὸν νῶτον κατηκίσατο 532
ὡς ὀλίγου δεῖν αὐτὸν ταῖς βασάνοις ἐναποθανεῖν.

46. Τούτων δὲ οὐδὲν ἔμελε τῷ μισθωτῷ· ἠρέμα γὰρ καὶ αὐτὸς
15 συνήδετο τοῖς τελουμένοις καὶ ἅμα τοῖς μιαροῖς μίμοις ἐκείνοις
συνεχέστερον τῷ μειρακίῳ συνερχόμενος καὶ συμποσιαζόμενος,
οὐδὲ τῆς διατριβῆς ἐκείνων καὶ καταφρονήσεως μακρὰν ἦν·
μέριμνα δὲ αὐτῷ καὶ πολλὴ σφόδρα περὶ τοῦ Ἰγνατίου ἐνέκειτο
φροντὶς καὶ ἐγλίχετο κατ᾽ αὐτοῦ ἀκούειν καὶ ἐκνήθετο τὴν ἀκοήν·
20 καὶ εἴ τινα διαλοιδορούμενον εἰκῇ ἑώρα ἤ τινα ψιλὴν κατ᾽ ἐκείνου
καὶ ματαίαν κατηγορίαν ἐνιστάμενον, φίλον τοῦτον ἐτίθετο πιστὸν
καὶ ἤκουεν ἡδονῇ πολλῇ· καὶ γὰρ οὐδὲν οὕτως ἥδύνει ψυχὴν ἔχθρᾳ
κακῇ καὶ μίσει προκατειλημμένην ὡς ἡ κατὰ τοῦ μισουμένου λαλιά.
Ἀεὶ οὖν ἐκ τῶν τοῦ πατριάρχου συνήθων καὶ ὑπηκόων ὅσους
25 ἐδύνατο δώροις καὶ ἀξιώμασι κλέπτων καὶ ὑποποιούμενος δι᾽ αὐτῶν ἐξιχνίαζε καὶ ἐπὶ τὴν τοῦ δικαίου ἐθήρευε ψυχήν.

47. Τούτων εἷς καὶ Ἰγνάτιος ἦν ἐκεῖνος ὁ τοῦ ἁγίου μαθητὴς ὃς
κατὰ Δημᾶν | ἐκεῖνον τὸν πάλαι τὸν νῦν ἠγαπηκὼς αἰῶνα Φωτίῳ 19ᵛ
προσφεύγει· καὶ ἄρχων μὲν τέως τῶν μοναστηρίων τῶν κατὰ τὴν
30 Προποντίδα, ἔπειτα καὶ μητροπολίτης ὑπ᾽ αὐτοῦ τῆς Ἱεραπόλεως

2–3 cf.? Nah. 2.11   19–20 cf. 2 Tim. 4.3   28 2 Tim. 4.10

3 ὅτε δὴ B: τότε δὴ v   8 διδακτικῶς B: διδασκαλικῶς v   12 καὶ Xv: om. B | νῶτον Xv:
νότον B   13 ταῖς v: τοῖς B   14 ἔμελε v: ἔμελλε B   23 προκατειλημμένην v:
προκατηλημμένην X: προκατειλημμένη B   24 ὅσους v: ὅσοις B   25 ἐδύνατο B: ἠδύνατο
Xv

violently from both land and sea, paralyzing and shattering the hearts of the whole populace. And when indeed the statue of Justin was severed at the knee and dashed to pieces, then that Basilius, who had formerly been bishop of Crete but had been transferred to Thessalonica because of the invasion of the Hagarenes,[123] himself had the courage (and this, too, was to the shame of Photius, the presiding patriarch of Constantinople) to approach Michael, and he exhorted him by way of advice and with a teacher's authority to desist from his shameful and impious aping of the sacerdotal forms. For he maintained that by so acting Michael was incurring the wrath of God. Michael, however, was deeply hurt by this reproach and with violent blows he knocked out the venerable old man's teeth and abused his back so badly that he very nearly died under the torture.

46. That mercenary creature Photius showed not the least concern at this. In fact he himself was gradually growing to relish the sacrilege and he began to fraternize with the young lad and join in his revels more often in association with those vile performers. He was never far from their company or their contemptuous attitudes, but the main concern which weighed on his mind was Ignatius. He longed to hear adverse criticism of the latter—in fact his ears itched for it. And whenever he chanced upon someone fulminating against Ignatius and initiating empty accusations unsupported by evidence against him, he would make that man a trusted friend and listen to him with great pleasure. For nothing delights a heart preoccupied with wicked enmity and hatred more than to hear gossip directed against the hated person. And so he was forever trying to spirit away as many of Ignatius's friends and followers as he could, winning them over by offers of gifts and preferment, and through them he kept on the good man's trail and chased after him for the kill.

47. Now one of these was the disciple of holy Ignatius who was also called by the same name, and he, like Demas of old, was over-fond of the world in which he lived and now fled for refuge to Photius.[124] The latter made him archon of the monasteries in the Propontis for a while, then after that metropolitan of Hierapolis,

καθίσταται. Οὗτος τῆς τιμῆς αὐτὸν ἀμειβόμενος· "Ὦ δέσποτα" ἔφη "θαυμάζω πῶς τηλικοῦτόν σε τοῦ Ἰγνατίου διέλαθεν ἀτόπημα καὶ ἀδιόρθωτον παρημελήθη· μέσον γὰρ Πλατείας τῆς νήσου ναὸς τοῖς τεσσαράκοντα μάρτυσιν ἐνίδρυται, αὐτοῦ δὲ ἐχόμενα τῆς Θεομή-
5 τορος εὐκτήριον. Τούτου τὴν τράπεζαν πρώην οἱ Ῥῶς τὴν νῆσον πορθοῦντες κατέβαλον εἰς γῆν, ὁ Ἰγνάτιος δὲ ταύτην αὖθις ἀνεθρό-νισε." Τί οὖν ἐκεῖνος; ἆρα μικρὸν τοῦτο ἢ οὐδὲν ἄτοπον ἡγησάμε-νος παρεσιώπησεν ἢ μικρὰν ὑπὲρ τούτου ταραχὴν ἀνῆψεν; Οὐμεν-οῦν· ἀλλὰ καὶ τοῖς κρατοῦσιν ὡς μέγα τι καὶ δεινὸν οἷον ἀνέθετο.
10 Καὶ τῇ κατ᾽ αὐτὸν ἐκκλησίᾳ κοινωσάμενος Ἀμφιλόχιόν τε Κυζίκου καὶ Θεόδωρον τῶν Πατρῶν μητροπολίτας οὐ μόνον δέ, ἀλλὰ καὶ Παντολέοντα συγκλητικὸν τὸν ἐπικαλούμενον Βόθρον εἰς τὴν εἰρημένην ἀποστείλας νῆσον βεβήλων χερσὶ τὸ ἱερὸν ἐκεῖνο τραπέ-ζιον καθεῖλεν. Ἐνετείλατο δὲ πρὸς τῷ αἰγιαλῷ τῆς θαλάσσης κατ-
15 αγαγεῖν καὶ τεσσαράκοντα πλύσεις δοῦναι καὶ οὕτως ἀναγαγεῖν καὶ καθιδρῦσαι.

48. Τί σου θαυμάσαιμεν, ἄνθρωπε (προάγει γάρ με λοιδορεῖσ-θαί σοι μὴ βουλόμενον ἡ τῆς κακίας ὑπερβολή); μᾶλλον δὲ τί σου πρῶτον ἢ τί ὕστατον ἐπιμυκτηρίσαιμεν; τὴν ματαιότητα τῶν λο-
20 γισμῶν ἢ τὴν τῆς διανοίας δυστροπίαν; τὴν τῆς μνησικακίας ὑπερ-βολὴν ἢ τῆς ἀδικίας τὴν φιλοτιμίαν; Ταῦτα ἡ μακρὰ μελέτη καὶ νύκτες ἄϋπνοι καὶ ὁ δυσαρίθμητος τῶν βιβλίων ἑσμὸς καὶ τῶν ἀμοιβαίων ἀναγνωστῶν καὶ συνομιλητῶν, αἱ ποικίλαι περὶ τοὺς λό-γους φιλοτιμίαι καὶ διαπαρατριβαί; τοιαῦτά σε καρποφορεῖν αἱ
25 Παλαιαὶ Διαθῆκαι καὶ Καιναί, αἱ τῶν ἔξωθεν σοφῶν γνῶμαι | καὶ 20 τῶν ἁγίων οἱ νόμοι καὶ λόγοι παροτρύνουσιν ὥστε καταδιώκειν ἄνθρωπον πένητα καὶ πτωχὸν τῷ | πνεύματι καὶ κατανενυγμένον 533 τῇ καρδίᾳ τοῦ θανατῶσαι; Οὐκ ἤρκεσέ σου τὸν ἄμετρον ἀποπλῆ-σαι θυμὸν ἡ βιαία τοῦ θρόνου ῥῖψις, αἱ ἀθεσμόταται καθαιρέσεις, αἱ
30 ἀδικώταται ὑπερορίαι, αἱ κατὰ τῶν ποδῶν ἀλύσεις, αἱ μυρίαι φυγαὶ καὶ θλίψεις καὶ συκοφαντίαι καὶ διαβολαὶ αἷς αὐτὸν ἐσκαμμάτισας;

---

12 παντολέοντα Β: Πανταλέοντα v   15 τεσσαράκοντα...ἀναγαγεῖν Βv¹: om. Xv²
16 καθιδρῦσαι Βv¹: ἄλλην καθυδρῦσαι Χ: ἄλλην καθιδρῦσαι v²   30 φυγαὶ Χv: φημὶ Β
31 ἐσκαμμάτισας Β: ἔπληνας Χ: ἔπλυνας v

and it was in repayment for this office that he spoke to Photius in the following manner: "My lord, I am surprised that you have over-looked such a serious offence on Ignatius's part and have done nothing to correct it. For in the middle of the island of Plate[125] stands a shrine to the forty martyrs and, adjoining it, a chapel of the Mother of God. And recently when the Russians ravaged the island, they cast the altar of this chapel to the ground and it was Ignatius who reconsecrated it."[126] And what do you think Photius's reaction was? Did he think it of little consequence, nothing out of the ordinary, and pass over it in silence or make only a small fuss about it? Certainly not. On the contrary, he actually presented it to the ruling powers as a serious and most dreadful matter. And after consulting with his church, he despatched to the island Amphilo-chius, metropolitan of Cyzicus, and Theodorus, metropolitan of Patras, as well as Pantoleon, also called Bothrus, a man of senatorial rank, and had them seize that sacred altar with profane hands.[127] Their orders were to carry it down to the seashore, wash it forty times, then carry it back and set it up again in its place.

48. Which of your qualities, man, should we be astonished by? (It is your excessive wickedness that leads me to reproach you now, even though I've no wish to do so.) Rather, which thing should we hold up to ridicule first and which last? Your worthless powers of reasoning or the surliness of your disposition? Your excessive vengefulness or your zeal for injustice? Was this the result of those long hours of study, the sleepless nights, the inexhaustible supply of books and readers and contributors to the discussions, the subtle rivalries and heated contentions in argument? Was it the Old and New Testament, the advice of pagan sages, or the laws and precepts of the saints that incited in you the goal of persecuting a man who was penniless, poor in spirit and meek in disposition, with a view to putting him to death? Was it not enough to satisfy your immod-erate passion that he was violently ejected from his patriarchal seat and most unlawfully deposed; and that he suffered at your hands his unjust banishment, the fettering of his feet, the countless exiles and afflictions, the oppression and false accusations to which you subjected him? For in truth you washed him clean, as much as you

καὶ γὰρ ἔπλυνας ἀληθῶς τοσοῦτον ὅσον ἐρρύπανας σαυτόν. Οὐκ
ἤρκεσε ταῦτα, ἀλλὰ καὶ ἔτι βιάζῃ ῥοῦν ποταμοῦ μάτην ἀπολέσαι
φιλονεικῶν καὶ τὸν ὑπὸ τοῦ Θεοῦ δικαιούμενον κατακρίνειν καὶ
ἀδικώτατα καταδικάζειν ἐπιτιθέμενος καὶ ταύτῃ τὸν ἔλεγχον τῶν
5 ἰδίων ἀνομημάτων διαδρᾶναι λίαν ἀνοήτως διανοούμενος, ὥσπερ
οὐκ ἐφεστώσης Θεοῦ προνοίας τοῖς πράγμασιν, ἢ καιροῖς ἰδίοις
ἑκάστῳ πάντως τὴν ἰδίαν ἀποδώσει πρᾶξιν; Ἐγὼ λογίζομαι ὅτι καὶ
αὐτὸς ἐν ἡμέρᾳ ἐπισκοπῆς πρὸς τοῦ λέγοντος ἀκούσῃ Θεοῦ· "Ἵνα
τί σὺ ἐκδιηγῇ τὰ δικαιώματά μου καὶ ἀναλαμβάνεις τὴν διαθήκην
10 μου διὰ στόματός σου;" καὶ ὅσα τῆς ἱερολογίας ἑξῆς. Κρεῖττον γὰρ
οἶμαι ἀνδρὶ ἀναλφαβήτῳ πάντῃ καὶ ἀμαθεῖ μετὰ συνειδήσεως
ἀγαθῆς ἀνεπιλήπτως βιοῦντι ἢ πάντας θείους καὶ ἀνθρωπίνους
λόγους σοφίας ἀνελίττοντι διὰ γλώσσης καὶ μακροῖς λόγων συν-
τάγμασιν ἐπαινουμένῳ ἀναρριπίζειν κατὰ τοῦ πλησίον βουλὴν
15 φονικήν. Πῶς οὐδὲ τοῦ μεγάλου Βασιλείου τῶν λόγων κατακούων
ἠὐλαβήθης ἐν ἐκπλήξει περί τινος εἰπόντος ὅτι πλειόνων ἀκμασάν-
των αἱρεσιαρχῶν κατὰ τὴν οἰκουμένην ἅπασαν οὐδεὶς ἀναθρονιασμοὺς τελέσαι ἐθάρρησεν εἰ μὴ ὁ Ἀγκυρογαλάτης Εὐστάθιος,
οὗτινος τὴν μυσαρότητα ἡ ἐν Γάγγραις ἁγία παρίστησι σύνοδος;
20 Ἀλλὰ τούτοις ὁ σοφώτατος οὐ μόνον οὐκ ἐνεκαλύπτετο, ἀλλὰ
τοὐναντίον καὶ ἐνελαμπρύνετο δόξαν μᾶλλον τὰ ἔργα τῆς αἰσχύ-
νης καὶ ἰδίαν τιμὴν ἡγούμενος, | εἴγε καινοπρεπῆ καὶ τῆς ἐκκλησια- 20ᵛ
στικῆς παραδόσεως ἀλλότρια τεχνάζοιτο. Ἀλλ' ὁ μὲν οὕτως.

49. Οὐ κατασιγήσω δὲ ἐγὼ τὸν τοῦ καίσαρος ὄνειρον· οὐδὲ
25 δίκαιον. Εἰ γὰρ καὶ οἱ πολλοὶ μὲν αὐτῶν ἐκ τῶν μεθημερινῶν φρον-
τίδων καὶ ἐνθυμημάτων ἔχουσι τὰς ἀρχάς, πολλοὶ δὲ καὶ ὑπὸ
δαιμόνων καθεύδουσιν ὑποτυποῦνται, ἀλλὰ καὶ ὑπὸ ἀγγέλων Θεοῦ
ἔστιν ὅτε προστάγματι σχηματίζονται Θεοῦ. Καὶ ἐν τοῖς ἄρχουσι δὲ
μάλιστα καὶ βασιλεῦσιν, εἰ καὶ μὴ εὐσεβεῖς εἶεν, ἀλλ' οὖν τὸ πνεῦμα
30 τῆς προφητείας εἴτε πρὸς τὸ αὐτοῖς ἐκείνοις εἴτε καὶ πρὸς <τὸ> τοῖς
ὑπηκόοις λυσιτελοῦν πολλάκις ἐνεργεῖν οἶδεν· ὡς ἐπὶ τοῦ Φαραὼ

---

2 cf. Sirac. 4.26 6–7 Matth. 16.27 8 cf. Is. 10.3 8–10 Ps. 49.16 15–19 Bas., *Ep.* 130,
PG 32, 564 B9–C3 31–72.1 cf. Gen. 41; Dan. 2; 4

12 βιοῦντι B: βιοῦν Xv 14–15 ἀναρριπίζειν…φονικὴν B: φιλικὴν ἀνερριπίζειν κατὰ τοῦ
πλησίον βουλ. X: φονικὴν ἀναρριπ. κατὰ τοῦ πλησίον βουλ. v 22 ἡγούμενος Xv:
εἰσηγούμενος B 28 ἐν B: ἐπὶ Xv 30 καὶ πρὸς B: om. Xv | τὸ² suppl. Westerink

defiled yourself. As if this were not enough, you would still out of contentiousness make every effort to stem the flow of that river (all in vain), to condemn the man who has been vindicated by God, and to inflict upon him by your attacks a most unjust judgment. And all too stupidly you thought that by acting this way you would escape reproof for your own transgressions, as if the affairs of men were not presided over by God's Providence, which in its own time will repay each in full for his own conduct. And on the day of your visitation I think that you too will hear God say: "What hast thou to do to declare my statutes, or that thou shouldest take my covenant in thy mouth?" and the rest of that passage from the Holy Scriptures. For I think it better for a man to be completely illiterate and unlearned and to live a blameless life with good conscience rather than be capable of explaining in words all the precepts of divine and human wisdom and be praised for it by others in long treatises, but at the same time be fomenting murder plots against his neighbor.[128] How is it that you did not even listen to and heed the words of Saint Basil when he spoke in alarm about another? Namely, that of all the many heresiarchs who have flourished throughout the world, none has ventured to perform re-consecrations except for Eustathius from Ancyra in Galatia, whose abominations were exposed by the holy synod held at Gangrae.[129] But our most wise Photius not only felt no shame for this conduct, but the very opposite—he prided himself on it, thinking rather that his shameful deeds would be a source of personal glory and honor if only he could devise something novel and foreign to the tradition of the Church. So much for Photius.

49. Nor shall I pass over in silence Bardas the caesar's dream— that wouldn't be right. For although most dreams have their origins in the cares and thoughts of the day, while many others are formed in sleepers' minds by evil spirits, nevertheless it sometimes happens that they are fashioned by God's angels upon God's command. And particularly in the case of magistrates and rulers, even if they are not men of piety, the spirit of prophecy often knows how to make itself felt, whether it is for the advantage of the rulers themselves or their subjects, just as we learned in the case of Pharaoh and

καὶ τοῦ Ναβουχοδονόσορ μεμαθήκαμεν. Οὕτω καὶ Βάρδας ὁ
καῖσαρ αὐτὸς Φιλόθεον ἐκεῖνον γενικῶν ποτε λογοθέτην καὶ φίλον
αὐτῷ πιστὸν ὄντα προσκαλεσάμενος λίαν ἐῴκει τεθορυβημένῳ καὶ
ἄσθματι πυκνῷ συνεχόμενος· "Ὦ Φιλόθεε" ἔφη "ὅραμα εἶδον καὶ
5 πάντα μου συνέτριψε τὰ ὀστᾶ καὶ τοὺς ἀρμοὺς τῆς ὀσφύος μου
διέλυσεν. Ὤιμην γὰρ κατὰ ταύτην τὴν νύκτα ὡς δῆθεν προελεύ-
σεως οὔσης εἰς τὴν Μεγάλην Ἐκκλησίαν μετὰ τοῦ βασιλέως
εἰσιέναι· | κατὰ πάσας δὲ θυρίδας τὰς ἄνω καὶ τὰς κάτω εἰκόνας 536
ὁρᾶν ἐδόκουν ἀρχαγγελικὰς πρὸς τὸν ναὸν βλεπούσας· καὶ ὅτε
10 πλησίον ἦμεν τοῦ ἄμβωνος ὤφθησαν ὥσπερ κουβικουλάριοι δύο
ἀπότομοι καὶ ἐμβριθεῖς· ὧν ὁ μὲν δέσμιον τὸν βασιλέα λαβὼν καὶ
ἐπὶ τὰ δεξιὰ κατασύρων ἐξωθεῖτο τῆς σολέας κατακρίνων ὡς ὑπεύ-
θυνον· ἐμὲ δὲ ὁ ἕτερος ὁμοιοτρόπως διὰ τῶν ἀριστερῶν ἀπῆγεν.
Ἄφνω δὲ περιβλεψάμενος ὁρῶ ἐν τῷ συνθρόνῳ τοῦ ἀδύτου καθή-
15 μενον ἄνδρα γηραλέον ἀπαραλλάκτως ἐοικότα τῇ εἰκόνι τοῦ κορυ-
φαίου τῶν ἀποστόλων Πέτρου καὶ αὐτῷ | δύο τινὲς παρειστήκεισαν 21
φοβεροὶ πραιποσίτων τάξιν ἐπιφαίνοντες. Ὁρῶ δὲ πρὸς τοῖς γόνασι
τοῦ καθημένου τὸν Ἰγνάτιον ἱκετεύοντα καὶ πολλοῖς δάκρυσι
περιρραινόμενον οὕτως ὥστε κἀκεῖνον αὐτῷ συλλυπούμενον
20 στενάξαι. Καὶ αὐτὸς ἐβόα· Κλειδοῦχε τῆς βασιλείας τῶν οὐρανῶν
καὶ πέτρα ἐν ᾗ Χριστὸς ὁ Θεὸς τὴν αὐτοῦ Ἐκκλησίαν ἐστηρίξατο, εἰ
οἶδας ὅτι ἠδικήθην, παραμύθησόν μου τὸ πολύθλιπτον γῆρας.' Ὁ δὲ
πρὸς αὐτόν· 'Δεῖξον' ἔφη 'τὸν ἀδικήσαντά σε καὶ ὁ Θεὸς σὺν τῷ
πειρασμῷ ποιήσει καὶ τὴν ἔκβασιν.' Καὶ στραφεὶς ὁ Ἰγνάτιος τῇ
25 δεξιᾷ χειρὶ ἐπέδειξεν ἐμὲ λέγων· Οὗτος περισσότερον πάντων
ἐλυμήνατό με καὶ κόρον τῆς κατ' ἐμοῦ ὕβρεως οὐκ ἔσχεν.' Νεύσας
οὖν ὁ ἐπὶ τοῦ θρόνου πρὸς τὸν ἐκ δεξιῶν αὐτοῦ καθεστηκότα καὶ
μικρὰν πάνυ μάχαιραν ἐκβαλὼν εἰς ἐπήκοον πάντων ἀπεφήνατο·
'Τὸν θεόργιστον Βάρδαν παράλαβε καὶ πρὸ τοῦ νάρθηκος ἔξω
30 κατάκοψον μεληδόν.' Αὐτίκα τοίνυν ἑλκόμενος δῆθεν πρὸς θάνατον εἶδον ὅτι καὶ τῷ βασιλεῖ τὴν χεῖρα ἐπισείων, ''Εκδέξαι' ἔφη

20–21 Matth. 16.18–19   23–24 cf. 1 Cor. 10.13

---

2 αὐτὸς B: οὗτος Xv   3 προσκαλεσάμενος Xv: προσκαλούμενος B   6 διέλυσεν B: ἔλυσεν
Xv   13 δὲ B: om. v   17 φοβεροὶ B: σοβαροὶ v   29 πρὸ Xv: πρὸς B

Nebuchadnezzar. And so the caesar Bardas summoned his faithful friend the well-known Philotheus, who was once *logothetes genikon*,[130] and he was in a state of great confusion, his breathing short and sharply drawn, as he said: "I had a dream, Philotheus, which wore out all my bones and left my backbone weak. I dreamed tonight that I went with the emperor in full procession to Saint Sophia and at all the windows, high and low, I could see images of the archangels looking into the church. When we came close to the pulpit, two chamberlains, grim and severe, came into view, one of whom put the emperor in chains and dragged him off to the right, then ejected him from the solea, as if passing judgment upon him as a sinner. The other one dragged me off to the left in a similar fashion. Suddenly looking around, I saw seated on the patriarchal throne in the inner sanctuary an old man who looked exactly like the icon of Peter, leader of the apostles, and beside him stood two awesome individuals who displayed the rank of *praepositi*. And at the knees of the seated figure I saw Ignatius, beseeching him as a suppliant and so thoroughly soaked from all his crying that Peter too was joining in his grief and groaning aloud. Then Ignatius cried out: 'You who hold the keys of the Kingdom of Heaven and are the rock on which Christ the Lord established His Church, if you know how I have been wronged, soothe my hard-pressed old age.' And Peter replied: 'Point out the one who has wronged you and God will make the outcome of the affair fit the trials which you have suffered.' Then Ignatius turned around and, pointing at me with his right hand, he said: 'He was the one who maltreated me worst of all and could not get enough of acting with wanton violence against me.'[131] At this the figure on the throne nodded to the one standing on his right and, brandishing a tiny dagger, he pronounced his decision in everyone's hearing: 'Seize Bardas who is hateful to God and outside in the forecourt cut him to pieces.' And immediately I was dragged off to my death and, as I went, I saw him shake his hand at the emperor too and say: 'Await

ἀσεβότεκνον.' Καὶ οὕτως ἐμαυτὸν εἶδον ὡς ὕπαρ καταμελιζόμενον."

50. Ταῦτα μὲν ὁ καῖσαρ θαμβούμενος ἅμα καὶ κλαίων ἐξηγεῖτο. Πρὸς ὃν ἐκεῖνος· "Φεῖσαι, ὦ δέσποτα, τοῦ παναθλίου γέροντος" εἶπε "καὶ πρὸς τὸ τοῦ Θεοῦ κριτήριον ἀφορῶν μήτε δικαίως μήτ' οὖν ἀδίκως ἔτι πονηρεύου κατ' αὐτοῦ." Ἀλλ' ὅμως ἐκεῖνος οὐδ' οὕτως ἠβουλήθη συνιέναι τοῦ ἀγαθῦναι· ἀμνηστίᾳ δὲ τὴν φρικώδη ταύτην παραδοὺς ἀπειλὴν ἔσπευδε τὰς οἰκείας ἀναπληρῶσαι ἁμαρτίας, ἵν' ἔνδικον ἄνωθεν ἐφ' ἑαυτὸν ἐπισπάσηται τὴν ὀργήν.

51. Εὐθὺς γὰρ πρὸς αὐταῖς τῶν νηστειῶν ταῖς εἰσβάσεσι Λέοντα ἐκεῖνον τὸν Πτυολαίμην ἐπονομαζόμενον συγγενῆ Φωτίου τυγχάνοντα μετὰ στρατιωτῶν εἰς τὴν νῆσον ἀποστέλλει καὶ παραγγέλλει οὕτω τηρεῖσθαι τὸν Ἰγνάτιον ὡς μὴ ἐξεῖναι αὐτῷ | παντάπασι τὴν ἱερὰν ἀναφέρειν λειτουργίαν μήτ' οὖν εἰσιέναι τινὰ πρὸς αὐτὸν μήτ' ἐξιέναι συγχωρεῖσθαι. Ἐπὶ τρεῖς δὲ μῆνας ἡ τοιαύτη περὶ αὐτὸν ἐστερεοῦτο φυλακὴ καὶ οὕτως ἡ τοῦ ὀνείρατος ἔφθασεν ἀπόφασις. Ἐπειγομένῳ γὰρ κατὰ τῆς Κρήτης τῷ Μιχαὴλ καὶ αὐτὸς ὁ Βάρδας ἄχρι τῶν λεγομένων Κήπων συστρατεύων ἐκεῖ δὴ τὴν ἐσχάτην ἔτισε δίκην. Πρόφασιν γὰρ ὡς ἐπιβουλεύοντα τῷ βασιλεῖ ἡ θεήλατος αὐτὸν μετῆλθεν ὀργὴ καὶ ξίφεσι μεληδὸν ἀθλίως κατακοπτόμενος οὕτω δυσκλεὲς τέλος ἀπηνέγκατο ὥστε καὶ ὑπ' αὐτοῦ στηλιτευθῆναι τοῦ φιλτάτου. Ὁ γὰρ τὰ μεγάλα εὐεργετηθεὶς καὶ τὴν πατριαρχικὴν ὑπ' ἐκείνου τιμὴν κληρωθεὶς ζῶντα μὲν ὑπερετίμα | καὶ προστάτην εἶχε τοῦ βίου παντοίαις εὐφημίαις ὑπερεπαινῶν· ἀποθανόντι δὲ παλινῳδίας ᾖσε καὶ ὡς ἀλιτήριον τοῦτον καὶ τρισκατάρατον ἄξιον τοιαύτης ἀπεφήνατο τελευτῆς. Τοιοῦτος ὁ δεινὸς ἐκεῖνος ἦν σοφιστὴς ἀεὶ πρὸς τοὺς καιροὺς μεταβαλλόμενος καὶ τὰ πράγματα καὶ τοῖς τῶν κρατούντων συμπεριαγόμενος θελήμασιν. Ὁ γὰρ τῆς θεαρχικῆς βουλῆς καὶ ῥοπῆς δι' ἔλλειψιν πίστεως διαμαρτὼν καὶ τοῖς ἀνθρώποις ἐπηλπικώς, ἐπειδὴ σαθρῷ θεμελίῳ τὸν νοῦν ἐπερείδεται, ἄπιστός τε πρὸς πάντας καὶ ἀβέ-

21ᵛ

537

6–7 Ps. 35.4   9 cf. 1 Thess. 2.16

---

8 ἀναπληρῶσαι Xv: ἀναπληρώσειν B   9 ἵν Xv: om. B   11 πτυολαίμην B: Πταολήμην Xv
18 συστρατεύων Xv: συνστρατεύων B   25 ᾖσε B: εἶδε Χ: ᾔδε v

your turn, impious son.' And so I imagined that I was in reality being cut to pieces."[132]

50. Bardas the caesar recounted this in a terrified and tearful state and Philotheus replied as follows: "Spare that utterly wretched old man, my lord. Take heed of God's tribunal and do not keep up your acts of wickedness against him, no matter whether your motives are just or unjust." But all the same, Bardas refused to accept that he should do the right thing. He put this awful threat out of his mind and hastened to complete the course of his own sins, so as to bring down upon himself righteous indignation from above.

51. It was the very beginning of Lent, and straightaway he sent off to the island with a group of soldiers Photius's kinsman, that Leo, the one called Ptyolaemes.[133] And he gave orders that Ignatius be guarded so closely as to make it altogether impossible for him to celebrate the holy liturgy, and that no one be allowed to go in and out to visit him. This close guard had been kept on him for a period of three months when the assertion of the dream was brought to fruition in the following manner. Michael was making an expedition against Crete and Bardas himself joined in the campaign as far as the place called Kepoi, which is where he paid the ultimate penalty. On the grounds that he was plotting against the emperor, he was pursued by divinely inspired anger and wretchedly cut to pieces by the sword.[134] And he won for himself such an inglorious end that he was even denounced by his closest friend. For the man who had received great benefits from Bardas and had been assigned the office of patriarch by him, who had honored him exceedingly while he was alive and praised him beyond measure with all kinds of acclamations, since he regarded him as the protector of his life— this man, Photius, changed his tune now that Bardas was dead and declared him to be wicked, accursed and deserving of such a death. That is the sort of clever sophist he was, always changing his affairs to fit the occasion and going along with the wishes of the ruling powers. He strayed from God's good counsel and influence through lack of faith and pinned his hopes upon men, but since he based his intentions upon an unsound foundation, he was exposed as being

βαιος ἐλέγχεται· ὑψουμένοις μὲν συνήγορος, κατήγορος δὲ γινόμενος ταπεινουμένοις· καὶ πρὸς ἓν μόνον ὁρῶν ἀρέσαι τοῖς δυνατοῖς,
τοῦ μὴ τῆς κατ' αὐτὸν ἀρχῆς ἐκπεσεῖν.

52. Τότε μὲν οὖν ὁ αὐτοκράτωρ παρευθὺς πρὸς τὴν βασιλεύ-
5 ουσαν παλινοστεῖ. Πεντηκοστὴ δ' ἄρ' ἦν καὶ Βασίλειον πατρίκιον
ὄντα καὶ παρακοιμώμενον στέμματι κατακοσμήσας ἀναγορεύει
βασιλέα. Ὁ πολύφρων δὲ Φώτιος πάμπολλα κατὰ Νικολάου τοῦ
πάπα μηχανορραφῶν, ἐπειδὴ οὐδὲν εἶχεν ἄλλο δρᾶν κατ' αὐτοῦ,
πείθει πολλαῖς παραινέσεσι τὸν βασιλέα συναινέσαι σύνοδον
10 συγ|κροτῆσαι καὶ τοῦτον καθαιρῆσαι καὶ τοῖς αὐτῷ κοινωνοῦσιν   22
ἀφορισμὸν ἀντισηκοῦντα τῷ παρ' ἐκείνου πρώην πεμφθέντι δια-
πέμψασθαι. Συναγαγὼν οὖν πάντας τοὺς ὑπ' αὐτὸν ἐπισκόπους ὁ
γεννάδας καί τινας μιαροὺς ἀνθρωπίσκους καὶ ἀσήμους ἐκ τῶν
ἀνατολικῶν δῆθεν πατριαρχείων τοποτηρητὰς ἐπαγόμενος καὶ
15 ψευδοσύλλογον ποιούμενος καθαίρεσιν, ὡς ἐνόμιζε, καὶ ἀναθεματισμὸν ἐπ' οὐδενὶ λόγῳ εὐλόγῳ ποιεῖται Νικολάου. Δώροις γὰρ
λαμπροῖς ὅτι μάλιστα τὸν ῥῆγα Φραγγίας Λοδόηχον καὶ Ἠγγιβέρ-
γαν δὲ τὴν αὐτοῦ γαμετὴν ὑποποιούμενος βασιλεῖς τούτους ἀνευ-
φημεῖν ἐν Κωνσταντινουπόλει ἐπηγγέλλετο, εἴγε συνεργήσαιεν
20 αὐτῷ πρὸς τὴν ἄτοπον ταύτην καὶ ἄθεσμον ἐπιθυμίαν καὶ τὸν
δίκαιον ἄνδρα τῆς κατ' αὐτὸν Ἐκκλησίας βιαίως ἐξωθήσαιεν.
Τούτων δὲ ὑπισχνουμένων λόγου θᾶττον ἀλόγως ὁ μάταιος μάτην
ἀπεφαίνετο. Ἐντεῦθεν ὑπογραφαὶ καὶ φωναὶ κανονικῶν τε προσώπων καὶ πολιτικῶν, μητροπολιτῶν καὶ πατρικίων· πάντα κενά,
25 πάντα τῶν ἐπὶ σκηνῆς θρυλλουμένων ματαιότερα καὶ καταγελα-
στότερα· ἡ γὰρ ἐκ παιδὸς αὐτῷ παρεπομένη τῆς ψυχῆς οἴησις εἰς
ὑπερηφανίαν τε τοῦτον ἐσχάτην καὶ ἀπόνοιαν μετεωρίσασα ἀδεῶς
τε καὶ ἀναιδῶς ἀνέπειθε τὰ τοιαῦτα τολμᾶν. Ὁ μὲν οὖν ταῦτα κατα-
σκευασάμενος διὰ χειρὸς Ζαχαρίου τοῦ Κωφοῦ ὃς ὑπ' αὐτοῦ τῆς
30 Χαλκηδόνος κεχειροτόνητο μητροπολίτης καὶ Θεοδώρου τοῦ ἀπὸ
Καρίας εἰς Λαοδίκειαν μετατεθέντος τὰς παραλόγους αὐτοῦ καὶ
ἐναγεῖς πράξεις πρὸς τὴν Ἰταλίαν ἐξαπέστειλεν. Αὐτὸς δὲ τῆς ἐμφύ-
του κατὰ τῆς τοῦ ἁγίου μήνιδος εἴχετο καὶ τῶν γνησίων αὐτοῦ

---

4 παρευθὺς ν: παρευθῦ B   10 συγκροτῆσαι Χν: τε κροτῆσαι B   16 εὐλόγῳ B: om. Χν
17 Λοδόηχον ν: δολόηχον B   22 ἀλόγως BΧν: ἄλογος C   24 κενά B: καινά ν   32 τὴν
B: om. ν | ἐξαπέστειλεν ν: ἐξαπέστειλαν Χ: ἐξαπέστελλεν B   33 τῆς B: om. Χν

fickle and faithless to all. Supporter of men when they were exalted, betrayer of them when they were humbled, he was interested in only one thing—being obsequious to the powerful, so as not to lose his own sphere of influence.

52. And so the emperor then immediately returned to Constantinople. It was Pentecost, and he garlanded Basil, patrician and *parakoimomenos*, with a wreath and proclaimed him *imperator*.[135] As for that ingenious fellow Photius, he was forming all kinds of crafty schemes against Pope Nicolaus, and when there was nothing left for him to try, he persuaded the emperor with many exhortations to agree to convoke a synod, to have the pope deposed and to send notices of excommunication (to match those sent earlier by the pope) to those communicating with him. And so this excellent fellow convened all his bishops and called in some foul creatures of no significance to act as legates from the eastern patriarchates, and he held a fake synod at which, as he believed, he had Nicolaus deposed and excommunicated—all for no good reason.[136] And he actually won over Ludovicus, king of France, and his wife, Ingelberga, with the most splendid of gifts and promised to recognize them as emperors at Constantinople if they would assist him in achieving this outrageous and unholy desire and forcibly drive out just Nicolaus from his Church.[137] After they speedily agreed, he, the vain fellow, foolishly made a show of himself to no avail. Out of this meeting came signed statements and oral anathemas from persons both religious and secular, metropolitans and patricians alike, but it was all in vain, all more empty and ridiculous than words spoken in a theatrical production. It was in fact the self-conceit in his heart which had been with him since early childhood that now buoyed him up to carry through his final piece of arrogance and dementia and persuaded him to dare such things without any shame or fear. And so the author of these machinations despatched to Italy the miscalculated and abominable acts of his synod through the agency of Zacharias the Deaf, whom he had appointed metropolitan of Chalcedon, and Theodorus, who had been transferred from Caria to Laodicea.[138] Meanwhile, he himself clung to his innate wrath against holy Ignatius and by spiriting

θεραπευτῶν, μᾶλλον δὲ νόθων ὅσους ἠδύνατο κλέπτων καὶ ταῖς
ματαιότησι τῶν ἀξιωμάτων δελεάζων δι᾽ αὐτῶν τὴν πτέρναν τοῦ
ἀναιτίου ἐπετήρει· ἥμάρτανε δὲ τῶν ἐλπίδων· πάσης γὰρ ὑψηλότε-
ρος κατηγορίας ὁ | μακάριος ἦν· ἐν τοῖς ἔργοις δὲ τῶν αὐτοῦ χειρῶν   22ᵛ
5 κακουργῶν συνελαμβάνετο.

53. Ἀγνοῶν δὲ ἀληθῶς εἰς τίνα τὸ κράτος τῆς βασιλείας περι-
ΐσταται ποτὲ μὲν πρὸς τὸν Μιχαὴλ διέβαλλε Βασίλειον, αὖθις δὲ
τοῦτον πρὸς ἐκεῖνον ἀμφοῖν, ὡς ἐνόμιζε, φιλίαν καταπραττόμενος,
ὁ ἀμφοτέρων τὴν φιλίαν οὐκ ἐν ἀληθείᾳ | ὑποκρινόμενος καὶ   540
10 οἰόμενος ὡς ὁποῖος ἂν τούτων μονοκράτωρ ἀναδειχθῇ τοῦτον εἰς
οἰκειότητα προσήσεται. Οὐκ ἤρεσκε δὲ τῷ Βασιλείῳ ταῦτα, πάνυ
δὲ ταῖς πανουργίαις προσώχθισε τοῦ σοφοῦ. Μικρὸν τὸ ἐν μέσῳ
καὶ αὐτὸς ὁ Μιχαὴλ πρὸς τῷ τεμένει τοῦ Μάρτυρος Μάμαντος
δολοφονεῖται ἀξίαν τῆς ἀνοίας εἴτουν ἀδικίας αὐτοῦ καὶ ἀσεβείας
15 δεξάμενος τελευτήν· χρόνους μὲν πεντεκαίδεκα καὶ μῆνας ὀκτὼ
συμβεβασιλευκὼς τῇ μητρί, ἐννέα δὲ παρὰ βραχὺ μόνος ἔτη κεκρατηκὼς καὶ τὸ πονηρὸν ἐνώπιον τῆς Ἐκκλησίας Κυρίου πεποιηκὼς
τελευτᾷ. Πρώτη μὲν ἰνδικτιῶν εἶχεν ἀρχήν, εἰκάδα δὲ καὶ τετάρτην
ὁ Σεπτέμβριος καὶ ὁ Βασίλειος πρὸς τὰ βασίλεια κατευθυνόμενος
20 αὐτοκράτωρ ἀνηγορεύετο. Παρευθὺς δὲ πέμψας εἰς καταδρομὴν
τοὺς περὶ τὸν Ζαχαρίαν Χαλκηδόνος ἐκ μέσης ἀπέστρεψε τῆς ὁδοῦ.
Τῇ ἐξῆς δὲ μετὰ τὴν ἀναγόρευσιν τοῦ πατριαρχικοῦ θρόνου τὸν
Φώτιον καταβιβάζει καὶ ἐν μοναστηρίῳ τινὶ καλουμένῳ Σκέπῃ
τοῦτον εὐθὺς ὑπερορίζει· καὶ τῇ ἐπαύριον Ἠλίαν τὸν περιφανέστα-
25 τον τοῦ βασιλικοῦ στόλου δρουγγάριον σὺν τῷ βασιλικῷ δρόμωνι
πρὸς τὸν ἁγιώτατον ἀποστέλλει πατριάρχην, ὅπως αὐτὸν ἐκ τῆς
νήσου πρὸς τὴν βασιλεύουσαν μετὰ τῆς πρεπούσης ἀνενέγκῃ
τιμῆς· καὶ τέως μὲν ἐν τοῖς γονικοῖς αὐτοῦ παλατίοις τοῖς καλουμέ-
νοις Μαγγάνοις ἀποκαθίστησιν αὐτόν.
30 54. Ἵνα δὲ πᾶσα ἡ κατὰ τοῦ ἁγίου γένηται πονηρία καταφανής,
ὁ δρασσόμενος τοὺς σοφοὺς ἐν τῇ πανουργίᾳ αὐτῶν, πολυπλόκων
δὲ βουλὰς ἐξιστῶν αὐτὸς ἐμβάλλει καὶ τῷ αὐτοκράτορι Βασιλείῳ

2–3 cf. Gen. 3.15   4–5 cf. Ps. 9.17   17 cf. Iud. 2.11   31 1 Cor. 3.19   31–32 Iob 5.13

4 αὐτοῦ χειρῶν Β: χειρῶν αὐτοῦ Χν   7 διέβαλλε Χν: διέβαλε Β   11 προσήσεται Β:
προστήσεται ν   12 τὸ Χν: τῷ Β   18 Πρώτη Χν: πρώτην Β   20 ἀνηγορεύετο Χν:
ἀνηγόρευται Β | παρευθὺς Ε: παρευθὺ ΒΧν   21 χαλκηδόνος Β: Καλχηδόνος ν

away as many as possible of his true (or, I should say, his supposed) followers, enticing them with empty offers of preferment, he tried by this means to stay on the heels of the guiltless patriarch.[139] But he failed to realize his hopes, because blessed Ignatius was above every accusation, and in fact he was caught out by wicked deeds of his own making.

53. Since he could not be sure upon whom the imperial power would devolve, Photius would sometimes run down Basil in the presence of Michael, then again Michael in the presence of Basil. By so doing, he reasoned that he would gain the friendship of both (though friendship from his side was feigned in an underhand manner), thinking that whichever of the two was proclaimed sole ruler would admit him to his intimate circle. But in this he incurred the displeasure of Basil, who was heartily sick of that shrewd character's villainy. Shortly afterwards, Michael himself met with an end that befitted his own folly (or rather, I should say, his injustice and impiety) when he was murdered at the shrine of the holy martyr Mamas.[140] He had shared the imperial power with his mother for fifteen years and eight months, then ruled alone for almost nine years, and he had acted wickedly in the eyes of the Church of the Lord. Thus was Basil guided towards the imperial power and on September 24th, at the beginning of the first indiction [i.e., 867], he was proclaimed emperor. And immediately he sent off men in quick pursuit and turned aside from their path Zacharias of Chalcedon and those with him.[141] On the day after his appointment he expelled Photius from the patriarchal throne and banished him immediately to a monastery called Skepe.[142] And on the next day he despatched Elias, most distinguished *drungarius* of the imperial fleet, with the imperial *dromon* to the most holy patriarch Ignatius, in order that he might bring him back from his island to the capital with all due honor.[143] And for the time being he reinstated him in his ancestral residence which was called Mangana.[144]

54. In order that all the wickedness practiced against holy Ignatius might be exposed, the Almighty Himself, Who apprehends the shrewd in the midst of their villainy and confounds the plots of

λογισμόν. Καὶ ἀποστέλλει πρὸς Φώτιον τὰ ἰδιόχειρα | πάντα ὅσα 23
ἀπὸ τοῦ πατριαρχείου κατιὼν ἔλαβεν ἀνυπερθέτως αὐτῷ πέμψαι
παρακελευόμενος. Ὁ δὲ ὅρκοις ἐψεύδετο μηδὲν τοιοῦτον ἐκεῖθεν
λαβεῖν τῷ κατεπείγεσθαι πρὸς τὴν κατάβασιν. Ὡς οὖν ταῦτα παρ᾽
5 αὐτοῦ πρὸς τὸν πραιπόσιτον Βαάνην ἐλέγετο, οἱ αὐτοῦ θορυβού-
μενοι θεραπευταὶ ἑπτὰ σάκκους πλήρεις ἐσφραγισμένους μολίβδῳ
εἰς τὸν πλησίον ἐνίεσαν καλαμῶνα κατακρύβοντες· οὓς οἱ περὶ τὸν
πραιπόσιτον ἰδόντες καὶ τῆς χειρὸς ἀφαρπάσαντες πρὸς τὸν
βασιλέα ἀπεκόμισαν. Ἀνοίξαντες δὲ τούτους δύο εὑρίσκουσι βιβλία
10 χρυσῷ καὶ ἀργύρῳ σὺν ὀξέσιν ἐνδύμασιν ἔξωθεν κεκοσμημένα,
ἔσωθεν δὲ φιλοκάλως καὶ ἐπιμελῶς γράμμασι γεγραμμένα τερπ-
νοῖς. Περιεῖχε δὲ τὸ ἓν πράξεις ἑπτὰ συνοδικὰς τὰς μηδέποτε οὔσας
ἢ γενομένας κατὰ τοῦ Ἰγνατίου, μάτην δὲ κακοδαίμονι μόνον
ἀναπεπλασμένας διανοίᾳ. Ἐν ταῖς ἀρχαῖς δὲ τούτων ἐφ᾽ ἑκάστης
15 πράξεως αὐτουργίᾳ τοῦ Συρακουσίου Ἀσβεστᾶ (ἦν γὰρ καὶ
ζωγράφος ὁ γεννάδας εἰς προσθήκην τῶν αὐτοῦ, οἶμαι, κακῶν) διὰ
χρωματικῆς ζωγραφίας ἐνεγέγραπτο Ἰγνάτιος. Καί (ὦ τῆς ἀκαθ-
έκτου λύσσης! ὦ μανίας οὐδεμίαν ὑπερβολὴν ἀπολειπούσης!) κατὰ
τὴν πρώτην μὲν πρᾶξιν συρόμενόν τε αὐτὸν καὶ ῥαβδιζόμενον
20 ἐμόρφωσεν, ἄνωθεν δὲ τῆς κεφαλῆς ἐπέγραψεν· "Ὁ διάβολος." Ἆρ᾽
οὐκ ἐφρίξατε τὴν ὑπερβολὴν τῆς βλασφημίας; Ἀλλὰ μὴ θαυμάσητε.
Εἰ γὰρ τὸν οἰκοδεσπότην Βεελζεβοὺλ ἐκάλεσαν, τί πρὸς τοὺς οἰκει-
ακοὺς αὐτοῦ; Κατὰ τὴν δευτέραν δὲ ἐμπτυόμενον καὶ βιαίως
ἑλκόμενον αὐτὸν καὶ ἡ ἐπιγραφή· "Ἀρχὴ τῆς ἁμαρτίας." Κατὰ τὴν
25 τρίτην δὲ καθαιρούμενον καί· "Ὁ υἱὸς τῆς | ἀπωλείας" ἐπιγραφόμε- 541
νον. Δεσμούμενον δὲ καὶ ἐξοριζόμενον κατὰ τὴν τετάρτην πρᾶξιν
εἰκόνισεν αὐτὸν καί· "Πλεονεξίαν τοῦ μάγου Σίμωνος" ἐπέγραψε.
Κατὰ τὴν ἀρχὴν δὲ τῆς πέμπτης κλοιοὺς αὐτὸν σχηματίζει περικεί-
μενον καὶ ἡ λοιδορία· "Ὁ ὑπεραιρόμενος ἐπὶ πάντα θεὸν καὶ | σέ- 23ᵛ
30 βασμα." Κατὰ τὴν ἕκτην δὲ εἰς καταδίκην αὐτὸν ἐμβαλλόμενον
εἰκόνισεν· ἡ δὲ κατ᾽ αὐτοῦ ἀργολογία· "Βδέλυγμα τῆς ἐρημώσεως."

---

22 Matth. 10.25 **24** cf. Sirac. 25.24 **25** 2 Thess. 2.3 **27** cf. Acta 8.9–24 **29–30** 2 Thess.
2.4 **31** Matth. 24.15; Marc. 13.14; cf. Dan. 9.27

---

2 πατριαρχείου v: πατριαρχίου Χ: πατριάρχου Β **9** τούτους Χv: ταῦτα Β **10** σὺν ὀξέσιν
Β: σηρικοῖς v **13** τοῦ v: om. Β **16** οἶμαι κακῶν Β: κακῶν οἶμαι Χv **31** ἀργολογία
ΒΧv¹ : ἀπολογία v²

the cunning, actually suggested an idea to the emperor Basil. He in turn sent to Photius and ordered him to return immediately all the documents written in his hand which he had taken with him when he left the patriarchal seat. Photius for his part perjured himself by saying that in his haste to get started on his journey into banishment he had not taken any such documents with him. But while he was telling this to the *praepositus* Baanes, his attendants in their confusion threw seven full sacks sealed with lead into the straw-stack nearby in an attempt to conceal them.[145] And they were seen by the *praepositus's* men, who snatched them from their hands and conveyed them to the emperor. When they opened them up, they found two books decorated on the outside with gold and silver on bright cloth and on the inside with delightful lettering beautifully and painstakingly written.[146] One of them contained seven Acts of a synod against Ignatius which didn't exist and had never been held—they had been fabricated, all in vain, by that ill-starred genius. And at the beginning of each of the Acts Ignatius had been depicted in colour by the hand of the Syracusan Asbestas (for this fine gent, just to add to his own afflictions, I think, was also a painter).[147] What unbridled madness! What a matchless piece of insanity! For beside the first Act he represented Ignatius being dragged off and beaten, and above his head he wrote the words: "The Devil." Doesn't his excessive blasphemy make you shudder? And yet you should not be too surprised, for if they call the head of the house Beelzebub, what words must they use to describe his household? Beside the second Act Ignatius was shown being spat upon and violently dragged along under the caption: "Source of sin." The third Act had Ignatius being deposed under the heading: "Child of perdition," and beside the fourth Act he was shown in chains and being sent into exile with the inscription: "The covetousness of Simon the Magian."[148] At the beginning of the fifth Act Ignatius was depicted wearing a prisoner's collar under the insulting caption: "The man who exalts himself above every god and object of worship." The sixth Act saw him being given up to condemnation, and the idle words used against him read: "Abomi-

Κατὰ τὴν ἑβδόμην δὲ καὶ τελευταίαν πρᾶξιν συρόμενον αὐτὸν καὶ καρατομούμενον διεζωγράφησε· καὶ ἡ ἐπιγραφὴ αὐτοῦ ἦν ἔγραψεν ἥν· "Ἀντίχριστος."

55. Ταῦτα ἐγὼ μὲν αἰσχύνομαι, νὴ τὴν ἀλήθειαν, ἐπὶ γλώσσης
5 ἄγων καὶ εἰς μνήμην τούτων ἰών· καὶ διὰ τοῦτο παντάπασιν, εὖ ἴστε, κατεσίγησα ἄν, εἰ μὴ ἑώρων τοὺς ταῦτα καταπραξαμένους καὶ τοὺς αὐτῶν οἰκείους οὐ μόνον ἐν τούτοις οὐκ ἐγκαλυπτομένους, ἀλλὰ καὶ ἐγκαλλωπιζομένους καὶ δόξαν ἁγιωσύνης ἐπιψευδομένους ἑαυτοῖς· ἀψευδὴς γὰρ ὁ εἰπών· "Ὅταν ἔλθη ἀσεβὴς εἰς βάθος κα-
10 κῶν, καταφρονεῖ· ἐπέρχεται δὲ αὐτῷ ἀτιμία καὶ ὄνειδος."

56. Ὤμοσαν κατὰ τοῦ φόβου Κυρίου καὶ κατὰ τῆς δόξης τῆς ἰσχύος αὐτοῦ οἱ ἐπὶ τῇ ἀναγνώσει τῶν ἐναγῶν πράξεων ἐκείνων εὑρεθέντες πεντήκοντα καὶ δύο ἀναμφίβολα καὶ πᾶσιν ὡμολογη- μένα ψευδῆ κεφάλαια γεγράφθαι ἐξ ἀσεβοῦς μᾶλλον ἢ μανικῆς
15 διανοίας εἰς κατηγορίαν τοῦ μάκαρος Ἰγνατίου προφερόμενα. Ἑκάστης δὲ κατηγορίας πρὸς τῷ τέλει ἄγραφον στίχον κατελίμπα- νον, εἴ τινά ποτε τῶν ἀξίων ἀγχόνης δώροις ἢ ἀξιώμασιν ἀπατῆσαι δυνηθεῖεν, ἵν' ἔχοιεν τόπον ἐγγράψασθαι τῷ ψεύδει.

57. Καὶ ταῦτα μὲν ἡ μία τοῦ διαβόλου περιεῖχε βίβλος· ἡ ἑτέρα
20 δὲ συνοδικὴ κατὰ Νικολάου τοῦ πάπα Ῥώμης κατεσκεύαστο πᾶσαν συκοφαντίαν καὶ βλασφημίαν ἄτοπον εἰς καθαίρεσιν ἀνδρὸς ἁγίου καὶ ἀναθεματισμὸν ἀθέως καὶ πονηρῶς δραματουργοῦσα, ἀξία καὶ αὐτὴ τῆς τε τοῦ πονηροῦ δαίμονος ὑπαγορίας καὶ τῆς τοῦ Φωτίου ὑπουργίας. Ἀπαραλλάκτως δὲ ταύτας ὁ τολμητίας δὶς ἀναγραψά-
25 μενος τὰς δύο μὲν Ζαχαρίᾳ παρέσχετο καὶ Θεοδώρῳ τοῖς προειρη- μένοις μετὰ εὐφημιῶν καὶ δώρων πολλῶν καὶ λαμπρῶν πρὸς τοὺς | 24 τῆς Φραγγίας βασιλεῖς ἀπενεγκεῖν, τοῦ τὸν πάπαν Νικόλαον ὡς καθηρημένον ἐξώσασθαι τοῦ θρόνου· τὰς δύο δὲ παρ' ἑαυτῷ κατεῖ- χεν. Τότε δὲ τῶν τεσσάρων τούτων βιβλίων δραξάμενος ὁ βασιλεὺς
30 καὶ τῇ συγκλήτῳ πρότερον καὶ τῇ Ἐκκλησίᾳ ποιήσας καταφανεῖς τὴν ὅλην οὕτω Φωτίου σκευωρίαν καὶ κακίστην συνείδησιν ὑπ'

3 1 Ioann. 2.18; 22 et cett. 9–10 Prov. 18.3 11–12 cf. Is. 2.10; 19; 21

2 καρατομούμενον B: παρατομούμενον v 3 ἦν v: om. B 9 ἑαυτοῖς Duffy : ἑαυτοὺς B: αὐτῷ Xv: 15 προφερόμενα X: προσφερόμενα Bv 18 ἔχοιεν B: ἔχῃ Xv 20 κατεσκεύαστο Xv: κατεσκεύασται B 26 πολλῶν καὶ Xv: om. B 29 τότε δὲ B: om. Xv | τῶν…τούτων B: τούτων τῶν τεσσ. Xv

nation of desolation." And beside the seventh and final Act he was shown being dragged off and beheaded, and the caption that Asbestas gave to this picture was: "Antichrist."

55. I am, in truth, ashamed to speak of such things and even to mention them. In fact, I assure you that I would not have breathed a word about it if I had not seen that those responsible and their familiars are so far from hiding their faces in shame as to be actually taking pride in their actions and falsely giving Photius credit for sanctity. For the man spoke with unerring truth who said: "When an impious man plumbs the depths of wickedness, he is filled with contempt and he brings upon himself ignominy and reproach."

56. Those who had been present at the reading of those accursed actions swore by their fear of the Lord and His reputation for might that fifty-two points had been written down that were without a doubt falsehoods, as all agreed, but were alleged in accusation against blessed Ignatius by a disposition more impious than unbalanced. And at the end of each accusation they left a line free so that, if they managed to deceive by offering bribes or preferment any of those who deserved no better than the gallows, they might have room to include them in the deception.

57. This was what the first book of the Devil contained. The second of the two was made out to be a synod against Nicolaus, the Roman pope, and in wicked and impious fashion it invented every kind of misrepresentation and monstrous slander with a view to deposing and anathematizing that holy man. It was, in itself, a worthy product of the Devil's counsel and Photius's assistance. And reckless Photius had an exact copy made of each of these two books and gave one copy of them to Zacharias and Theodorus (whom I mentioned above) to take to the rulers of France,[149] along with praises and many splendid gifts, in the hope that they might drive Pope Nicolaus from his papal seat on the grounds that he had been deposed. The other copy of the books Photius himself kept. These four books now came into the emperor's possession and, to begin with, he made them known to the Senate and to the Church, thereby bringing before the eyes of the whole state the extent of

84

ὄψιν ἁπάσῃ τῇ πολιτείᾳ κατεστήσατο. Ἐξέστη πᾶς ἄνθρωπος ὁρῶν
καὶ ἀκούων ταῦτα οὐ μόνον ἐπὶ τῇ κακονοίᾳ καὶ παντορρημοσύνῃ
τοῦ σοφιστοῦ, ἀλλὰ καὶ τῇ ὑπερβολῇ τῆς μακροθυμίας καὶ ἀνοχῆς
τοῦ Θεοῦ. Ἀλλὰ ταύτας μὲν τὰς βίβλους ὕστερον ἐνεγκόντες ἐπὶ
5 τῆς συνόδου καὶ κατὰ πρόσωπον τῷ αὐτουργῷ αὐτῶν παραστή-
σαντες καὶ παραδειγματίσαντες οὕτω παρέδοσαν τῷ πυρί.

58. Τότε δὲ καὶ ὁ αὐτοκράτωρ Βασίλειος σελέντιον ἐπὶ τῷ
παλατίῳ Μαγναύρας ποιούμενος καὶ τὸν πατριάρχην ἀγαγὼν καὶ
πολλοῖς τοῦτον ἐπαίνοις κατέστεψε. Κυριακὴ μὲν τῶν ἡμερῶν ἦν,
10 εἰκάδα δὲ καὶ τρίτην εἶχε Νοέμβριος, ὥσπερ καὶ ὅτε πρῶτον | ἐξωρί-   544
ζετο· καὶ αὐτὸς ὑπερασπισμῷ καὶ χρηστότητι τοῦ Θεοῦ δι' ἐννέα
τελείων χρόνων τελείαν ἄθλησιν ὑπὲρ ἀρετῆς ἐπιδειξάμενος ἀπο-
καθίσταται τῇ Ἐκκλησίᾳ· καὶ ὁ λύχνος λαμπρότερον ἀναφθεὶς
περιφανέστερον ἢ πρῴην τῇ λυχνίᾳ ἐπιτίθεται καὶ ὁ ποιμὴν ἐπέγνω
15 τὰ πρόβατα καὶ αὐτὸς τοῖς προβάτοις σαφέστερον ἐπέγνωσται.

59. Πάσης οὖν σχεδὸν φάναι τῆς πόλεως ἐπευφραινομένης
αὐτοῦ τῇ ἀναβάσει προαγούσης τε καὶ ἑπομένης ἐν ἀγαλλιάσει
αὐτὸς μὲν διὰ τοῦ Ἁγίου Φρέατος ἀνάγεται· πρὸς τοῖς ὑπερῴοις δὲ
τοῦ μεγάλου Ναοῦ διὰ τῆς δεξιᾶς πύλης εἰσιόντι προσυπαντᾷ αὐτῷ
20 τῶν πατρικίων ἡ τάξις προσκυνοῦσα καὶ δεξιουμένη· ἡ ἱερὰ δὲ τότε
λειτουργία κατὰ τὸ ἔθος ἐτελεῖτο. Ἄξιον δὲ μηδὲ τὴν ἐπὶ τῇ εἰσόδῳ
συμπεσοῦσαν ἱερὰν κληδόνα παραλιπεῖν· | ὁ μὲν γὰρ ἐσῄει, οἱ δὲ   24ᵛ
προσεκύνουν· ὁ ἱερεὺς δέ· "Εὐχαριστήσωμεν τῷ Κυρίῳ" τὴν ἀνα-
φορὰν ἐν τοῖς ἀδύτοις ποιούμενος ἀνέκραγεν· ὁ λαὸς δέ· "Ἄξιον
25 καὶ δίκαιον" ἀπεκρίνατο.

60. Οὕτως ὁ ἱερὸς Ἰγνάτιος ὑπ' ἀγαθοῖς συμβόλοις τὸν οἰκεῖον
θρόνον ἀπειληφὼς καὶ τοὺς οἴακας αὖθις τῆς Ἐκκλησίας ἐγχειρισ-
θεὶς εἴργει μὲν τῆς ἱερᾶς λειτουργίας οὐ Φώτιον μόνον καὶ τοὺς
χειροτονηθέντας ὑπ' αὐτοῦ, ἀλλὰ καὶ πάντας τοὺς κεκοινωνηκότας
30 αὐτῷ· ἐκλιπαρεῖ δὲ τὸν βασιλέα οἰκουμενικὴν σύνοδον κροτῆσαι,

---

3–4 cf. Rom. 2.4 13–14 cf. Matth. 5.15; Marc. 4.21; Luc. 8.16; 11.33 14–15 cf. Ioann.
10.15; 27 16–17 cf. Marc. 11.9 23–25 e.g. Bas. *Liturg.*, PG 31, 1636

2 παντορρημοσύνῃ B: κακορρημοσύνῃ v   3 ἀλλὰ καὶ v: ἀλλὰ καὶ ἐν X: ἢ B | ἀνοχῆς Xv:
ἀνοχῇ B   6 παρέδοσαν B: παρέδωκαν Xv   7 καὶ Xv: om. B | σελέντιον B: σιλέντιος X:
σιλέντιον v   8 καὶ² B: [καὶ] v, fortasse recte   9 κατέστεψε v: καταστέψας B

Photius's knavery and his most evil disposition. Everyone was dumbfounded when they saw and heard these things, not only at the malice and unrestrained tongue of that sophist, but also at the extreme forbearance and patience of God. Then at a later date they brought these books before the synod, confronted their author with them, and made a spectacle of them before finally consigning them to the fire.

58. It was at that same time too that the emperor Basil granted Ignatius an audience at the palace of Magnaura, and when he received the patriarch, he showered him with praises. It was Sunday the twenty-third of November, the very same day on which Ignatius was first sent into exile; and it was thanks to the protection and goodness of God that he was now restored to his position in the Church after displaying over a period of nine full years a full and perfect struggle in the interests of virtue. The lamp was more brilliantly lit, as it were, and set more prominently than before upon its stand, and the shepherd knew his flock again and was himself more clearly recognized by them.[150]

59. And so virtually all the populace rejoiced at Ignatius's return, going before him and following after him in their great joy, as he was led up through the Holy Well to the upper level of the great church.[151] And as he came in through the doorway on the right, he was met by the members of the patrician order venerating and paying honor to him. It was just the time when the holy liturgy was being celebrated in the customary manner, and it would not be right to leave out the sacred omen which accompanied his entrance. For as he came in and the patricians venerated him, the priest was making the oblation in the sanctuary and he called out: "Let us give thanks to the Lord." And the congregation replied: "It is meet and right so to do."

60. In this way holy Ignatius regained his patriarchal throne and was again entrusted with the helm of the Church. And he excluded from the holy liturgy not only Photius himself and his appointees, but also all those who had been communicating with him. Moreover, he urged the emperor to hold an ecumenical council, thinking that by this means all the lapses into sin might be

δι' ἧς ἔσεσθαι τῶν σκανδάλων πάντων ὑπελάμβανε τὴν ἴασιν.
Εὐθέως τοίνυν Ἰωάννης μὲν ὁ τῆς Πέργης ὡς ἐν πάσαις ταῖς θλίψεσιν Ἰγνατίῳ συγκακοπαθῶν ἐκ τοῦ μέρους τοῦ κατ' αὐτόν, ἐκ τοῦ
κατὰ τὸν Φώτιον δὲ Πέτρος ὁ τῶν Σάρδεων πρὸς τὸν πάπαν Νικό-
5 λαον ἀποκρισιάριοι προεχειρίζοντο· σὺν αὐτοῖς δὲ καὶ Βασίλειος ὁ
καλούμενος Πινακᾶς ἀπῄει σπαθάριος τὴν ἀξίαν καθεστώς· καὶ
ἀπῇεσαν ἐν δυσὶ δρόμωσι στελλόμενοι τὸν πλοῦν. Ἀλλὰ Πέτρος
μὲν ὁ καλούμενος Δείλαιος ἐν τῷ κόλπῳ Δαλματίας κινδύνῳ περιπεσὼν δείλαιος ὤλετο· ὁ Ἰωάννης δὲ σὺν τῷ Βασιλείῳ διασωθεὶς
10 Ἀδριανὸν εὗρε πάπαν τοῦ Νικολάου ἤδη τὴν ἐν σώματι καταλιπόν-
τος ζωήν.

61. Οὐ πολὺς οὖν ἐν τῷ μέσῳ χρόνος καὶ παρῆσαν τοποτηρη-
ταί, Στέφανος μὲν καὶ Δονᾶτος ἐπίσκοποι τοῦ πάπα Ῥώμης καὶ
Μαρῖνος εἷς τῶν ἑπτὰ διακόνων σὺν αὐτοῖς· ἐκ δὲ τῶν τῆς Ἀνατο-
15 λῆς πατριαρχείων τοῦ αὐτοκράτορος δώροις καὶ γράμμασι τὸν τῆς
Συρίας ἄρχοντα παρακαλέσαντος Ἰωσὴφ μέν, ἀρχιδιάκονος καὶ
σύγκελλος, τοποτηρητὴς Μιχαὴλ ἦλθε τοῦ πάπα τῆς κατ' Αἴγυπτον
Ἀλεξανδρείας· Θωμᾶς δὲ μητροπολίτης Τύρου τόπον Μιχαὴλ ἐπλή-
ρου τοῦ τῆς Ἀντιοχείας τῆς κατὰ Συρίαν πατριάρχου· Ἠλίας δὲ
20 πρεσβύτερος καὶ σύγκελλος εἰς τόπον Θεοδοσίου | πατριάρχου τῶν ²⁵
Ἱεροσολύμων παρῆν. Οὗτοι πάντες ἅμα Ἰγνατίῳ τῷ ἁγιωτάτῳ
πατριάρχῃ Κωνσταντινουπόλεως καὶ τοῖς σὺν αὐτῷ δώδεκα τὸν
ἀριθμὸν ἐπισκόποις τοῖς συγκεκοπιακόσι καὶ ἀπ' ἀρχῆς μέχρι
τέλους συνηθληκόσιν αὐτῷ ἐν τοῖς δεξιοῖς μέρεσι τῶν κατηχουμε-
25 νείων τοῦ περιωνύμου ναοῦ τῆς τοῦ Θεοῦ Σοφίας μετὰ τοῦ αὐτοκράτορος Βασιλείου προεκάθισαν. Τῶν τιμίων δὲ καὶ ζωοποιῶν
ξύλων τῶν τε ἱερῶν Εὐαγγελίων προκειμένων, συμπαρούσης δὲ καὶ
τῆς ἱερᾶς συγκλήτου πρῶτον μὲν αἱ πεμφθεῖσαι παρὰ τοῦ πάπα τῆς
πρεσβυτέρας Ῥώμης Ἀδριανοῦ ἐπιστολαὶ καὶ αἱ παρὰ τῶν ἀνατο-
30 λικῶν δὲ πατριαρχῶν | κατὰ τάξιν ἀναγινωσκόμεναι πᾶσαν καὶ ⁵⁴⁵
ἱερὰν εὐθημοσύνην τό τε πιστὸν καὶ ἄμωμον καὶ ἀνεπίληπτον τῶν
ἀπεσταλμένων τοποτηρητῶν τό τε κανονικὸν καὶ ἔνθεσμον τῶν
ἀποστειλάντων αὐτοὺς ἐνώπιον πάντων ἀπεδείκνυσαν.

---

1 ὑπελάμβανε ν: ὑπελάμβανεν Χ: ὑπέλαβε Β   8 Δείλαιος Χν: δίκαιος Β   9 ὁ Β: om. Χν |
τῷ Β: om. Χν   10 πάπαν ν: πάπ( ) Χ: πάπα Β   30 δὲ Β: om. Χν

remedied.[152] And so straightaway legates were chosen to go to Pope Nicolaus: John, bishop of Perge, from Ignatius's party (since he had shared with Ignatius all the tribulations), and Peter, metropolitan of Sardis, from Photius's side. They were accompanied by Basil, known as Pinacas, who held the office of *spatharius*, and they left on their journey sailing in two *dromons*.[153] But Peter, also called the Pitiful, ran into danger in the Dalmatian gulf and came to a pitiful end. John, however, and Basil came through safely and found Hadrian to be pope, since Nicolaus had already departed this life.[154]

61. And so it was that soon afterwards delegates arrived at Constantinople: Stephanus and Donatus, bishops in the Roman Church, accompanied by Marinus, one of the seven deacons.[155] And as a result of the emperor's interceding with the ruler of Syria by sending gifts and letters, there came from the patriarchates of the East Joseph, archdeacon and syncellus, legate of Michael the bishop of Egyptian Alexandria; Thomas, metropolitan of Tyre, representing Michael the patriarch of Syrian Antioch; and Elias, presbyter and syncellus, in place of Theodosius, patriarch of Jerusalem.[156] In the far-famed church of Saint Sophia, in the right-hand part of the *catechumenia*, in the presence of the emperor Basil, they all presided over the council together with Ignatius, most holy patriarch of Constantinople, and the twelve bishops who had throughout everything from first to last been his allies and supporters.[157] The precious, life-giving Cross and the Holy Gospels were given pride of place, and in the presence too of the sacred senate the letters sent by Hadrian, the pope of Old Rome, and those from the patriarchs of the East were read first, with all due order and holy regard for precedence. These letters demonstrated to all not only the faith, sincerity and unimpeachable behavior of the legates who were sent, but also the correctness in terms of ecclesiastical canons and regulations of those who sent them.

62. Ἔπειτα τῇ ἑξῆς ἱερεῖς τε καὶ ἀρχιερεῖς πάντες ὅσοι Μεθο-
δίου μὲν καὶ Ἰγνατίου χειροτονίᾳ τῶν ἁγιωτάτων ἐτύγχανον πατρι-
αρχῶν, πανουργίαις δὲ παντοδαπαῖς καὶ ποικίλαις κολάσεσι καὶ
ἐπινοίαις Φωτίου τῇ κοινωνίᾳ συναπήχθησαν, οὗτοι πάντες λιβέλ-
5 λους μετανοίας ἐπιδεδωκότες καὶ μετὰ δακρύων τῇ ἁγίᾳ συνόδῳ
προσπίπτοντες καὶ ἐξομολογούμενοι καὶ μέντοι καὶ συγγνώμης,
κατὰ τὴν ὑπὲρ αὐτῶν τοῦ βασιλέως παράκλησιν καὶ τὴν τῶν Ῥωμαίων ψῆφον, ὡς βιασθέντες ἀξιούμενοι, ναὶ δὴ καὶ τῷ διωρισμένῳ
θέμενοι ἐπιτιμίῳ οὕτω τῆς τῶν ἐπισκόπων καθέδρας τοῖς ἀνεγκλή-
10 τοις ὁμοίως καὶ αὐτοὶ κατηξιοῦντο.
63. Ἐντεῦθεν εἰς ἑκατὸν δύο τὸν ἀριθμὸν ἐπισκόπους ἡ σύνοδος ἐκείνη συγκροτουμένη καὶ πάντα εὐσχημόνως καὶ κατὰ τάξιν
καὶ πάντα σὺν λόγῳ καιρίῳ καὶ κανονικαῖς διατάξεσι λέγειν καὶ
πράττειν διαλογιζόμενοι τὸν ὑπεύθυνον Φώτιον παράγουσι καὶ μὴ
15 βουλόμενον· καὶ δὴ | ἐλέγχουσι μὲν ἀποτόμως τῆς φονικῆς κατὰ   25ᵛ
Ἰγνατίου τοῦ ἱεράρχου προαιρέσεως καὶ τῆς παραλόγου καὶ μανιώ-
δους καθαιρέσεως· ἐλέγχουσι δὲ καὶ τὰς ψευδοεπείας αὐτοῦ καὶ
δυσφημίας καὶ ὅσα κατὰ Νικολάου τοῦ πάπα πεφώραται δεδρακώς.
Εἶτα πυνθάνονται παρ’ αὐτοῦ εἴ τι ἔχει δικαίωμα πρὸς τὴν κατ’
20 αὐτοῦ πάλαι γενομένην παρὰ τῶν Ῥωμαίων κατάκρισιν ἀνθυπενεγ-
κεῖν. Αὐτοῦ δὲ σιωπῶντος τῷ μηδεμίαν εὔλογον ἔχειν ἀπολογίαν
πρὸς τὰ ἐγκαλούμενα, ἐπειδὴ ὑπό τε τῶν τοποτηρητῶν αὐτῶν ὑπό
τε τοῦ βασιλέως αὐτοῦ καὶ τῆς συγκλήτου παραινούμενος συγ-
γνώμην αἰτῆσαι ὥστε κἂν τῆς τῶν πιστῶν κοινωνίας ὡς λαϊκὸς
25 ἀξιωθῆναι παντάπασιν ἐξ αὐθαδείας ἀπεσείσατο τὴν συμβουλίαν,
κοινῇ λοιπὸν ψήφῳ καὶ δικαιοτάτῃ κατακρίνουσι καθαιροῦσί τε
τοῦτον καὶ ἀναθεματίζουσιν ὡς ἐπιβήτορα καὶ μοιχὸν καὶ διωγμῶν
χαλεπωτάτων καὶ σκανδάλων μυρίων ταῖς τοῦ Θεοῦ Ἐκκλησίαις
αἴτιον γενόμενον. Καὶ ἀποφαίνονται συνῳδὰ τῇ Νικολάου τοῦ
30 πάπα καθαιρετικῇ ψήφῳ τῇ μετὰ πολλῆς ἀκριβείας πρῶτον καὶ
κανονικῆς ἤτοι συνοδικῆς κρίσεως ἀποφανθείσῃ κατ’ αὐτοῦ. Ὑπο-

---

12 συγκροτουμένη Xv: συγκεκρατημένη B   13 σὺν λόγῳ v: συλλόγῳ B   14 καὶ B: om. v
15 δὴ ἐλέγχουσι B: διελέγχουσι Xv   21 σιωπῶντος Bvⁱ : διειπόντος X: εἰπόντος v² | τῷ vⁱ:
τὸ BXv²   23 αὐτοῦ B: om. Xv   29 συνῳδὰ coni. Westerink: συνοδᾶ B: σὺν ἅμα Xv²:
συνοδικῶς vⁱ | τῇ Bv²: om. Xvⁱ

62. Then, on the following day, all the priests and bishops who were appointees of the most holy patriarchs Methodius and Ignatius, but had been seduced into communicating with Photius by every kind of trickery and by devices and chastisements many and various—they now offered petitions of repentance, fell down in tears before the holy synod and made public confessions. And indeed, in accordance with the emperor's entreaties on their behalf and with the vote of the Romans, they were judged worthy of absolution on the grounds that they had been forced to act as they did. And so it was that after having submitted to the prescribed penalty, they too were deemed worthy of sitting as bishops just like those who had been above reproach.

63. Thus that synod came to consist of one hundred and two bishops, and calculating how they might by their words and actions arrange everything in a decent and orderly manner and in accordance with appropriate reasoning and ecclesiastical regulations, they next introduced the guilty party, Photius, though against his will. And they reproved him severely for his murderous designs against the patriarch Ignatius and for deposing him in such mad and unreasonable fashion; likewise for his lies and slanders and for all the actions against Pope Nicolaus in which he had been detected. Then they asked if he could offer any plea in his defence against the condemnation which had been made against him long before by the Romans. He in turn remained silent, since he had no legitimate answer to the charges, but when he was advised by the (Roman) legates themselves, by the emperor himself and by the senate to ask for mercy, so that he might at least be thought worthy of sharing in the communion of the faithful as a layman, he completely repudiated the advice out of wilfulness. And so it was, then, that by a unanimous and most just vote they condemned, deposed and anathematized him for being a violator and adulterer[158] and for being responsible for the harshest of persecutions and countless offences against the churches of God. And their decision was in agreement with the vote of condemnation which had originally been made against him with great accuracy and canonical, i.e. conciliar, judgment by Nicolaus the pope. Moreover,

γράφουσι δὲ τῇ καθαιρέσει οὐ ψιλῷ τῷ μέλανι τὰ χειρόγραφα
ποιούμενοι, ἀλλά (τὸ φρικωδέστατον), ὡς τῶν εἰδότων ἀκήκοα
διαβεβαιουμένων, καὶ ἐν αὐτῷ τοῦ Σωτῆρος τῷ αἵματι βάπτοντες
τὸν κάλαμον οὕτως ἐξεκήρυξαν Φώτιον, οὕτως αὐτὸν κατεδίκασαν
5 καὶ πάντας τοὺς κεχειροτονημένους ὑπ' αὐτοῦ.

64. Ἐνταῦθα γενόμενος κατηγορήσειν μοι δοκῶ τῆς συνόδου·
μέμψομαι δὲ καὶ τὴν κρίσιν ταύτην, εἰ καὶ τολμηρόν. Πάσας γὰρ τὰς
πράξεις καὶ τοὺς διωρισμένους ἐν αὐτῇ κανόνας ὁμοίως τοῖς ἐν
ταῖς προλαβούσαις ἑπτὰ συνόδοις οἰκουμενικαῖς καὶ τούτους ὡς | 548
10 θεοπνεύστους | λίαν προσιέμενός τε καὶ ἀποδεχόμενος τοῦτο 26
μόνον τῆς ὀγδόης συνόδου ταύτης ἐπιμέμφομαι, οὐχ ὅτι θυμῷ
βαρεῖ καὶ μνησικακίᾳ, ὥς τινες οἴονται, τῶν ὑπευθύνων ἀνηλεῶς
κατεψηφίσατο, μᾶλλον μὲν οὖν τοὐναντίον μεμπτέα τυχὸν αὕτη
παρά γε δικαίῳ τῶν τοιούτων κριτῇ, ὅτι φιλανθρωπότερον ἢ ἔδει
15 τὴν κρίσιν ποιουμένη οὐκ ἀπροσωπόληπτον οὐδὲ καθαρῶς ἀποστολικὴν ἐπήγαγε ψῆφον· δέον τῷ τριακοστῷ κεφαλαίῳ ᾧ πρῶτον
τὸν ἄμεμπτον ὁ συκοφάντης κατεδίκαζεν, ὡς διὰ κοσμικῆς δυναστείας ἐγκρατῆ γενόμενον τῆς Ἐκκλησίας, τούτῳ μᾶλλον ἰσχυρί-
σασθαι νῦν κατ' ἐκείνου, ὡς οὐ ψήφῳ Θεοῦ καὶ ἱερέων, ἀλλ' ὑπερ-
20 βολῇ φιλαρχίας καὶ δοξομανίας διὰ κοσμικῆς δυναστείας τυραννή-
σαντος τῆς Ἐκκλησίας. Αὐτόν τε διὰ ταῦτα καθαιρεῖν ἔδει καὶ ὅτι
παρὰ καθηρημένου χειροτονεῖσθαι κατηξίου καὶ τοὺς κεκοινωνηκότας δὲ αὐτῷ κατὰ τὴν ἀποστολικὴν ἀπόφασιν πάντας· καὶ μὴ
φιλανθρωποτέρους Θεοῦ καὶ Θεοῦ γινομένους κρίσεως τὴν ἀπό-
25 φασιν τοῦ παναγίου Πνεύματος ἀκυροῦν. Τοῦτο τὰ ἄνω κάτω
πεποίηκε· τοῦτο τὸ κρῖμα οὐκ ἔστιν ὅσων εἰπεῖν κακῶν αἴτιον καὶ
σκανδάλων ἐχρημάτισεν. Οἶμαι γὰρ ὡς εἰ ἀποστολικῶς τότε καὶ
κανονικῶς κατὰ πάντων ἀπεφήναντο οὐ τὸν αἴτιον μόνον τῆς
διχοστασίας τε καὶ τῶν σκανδάλων, ἀλλὰ καὶ τοὺς κοινωνήσαντας

16–19 Can. apost. 29   21–23 an ad 2 Ioann. 9–11 spectat?

---

1 ψιλῷ Xv: ψιλὰ B   5 κεχειροτονημένους Xv: χειροτονουμένους B   18 γενόμενον B:
γενάμενον v | τούτῳ v: τοῦτο B   26 ὅσων v: ὅσον B

when they put their signatures on the decree of deposition, they did not merely sign in ink, but—horror of horrors (and I have heard this confirmed by those who do know)—they actually dipped the pen in the very blood of the Savior.[159] This was the way in which they excommunicated and condemned Photius and all those who had been ordained by him.

64. Having arrived at this point, I think I must now be critical of the synod, and this is the judgment with which I must find fault, if I might be so bold. For while I approve only too readily of all the actions and canons declared at the synod and accept them as being on an equal footing with those of the previous seven ecumenical councils and as being inspired by God, on this one point alone I find fault with the eighth council—not because, as some think, it condemned the guilty in an oppressive and malicious spirit and showed no mercy, but rather, on the contrary, would a fair judge criticize it for just the opposite reason, that it reached a judgment that was more humane than was required and brought down a vote that was not impartial nor strictly in accordance with apostolic doctrine. It should have relied on the thirtieth canon, by which the slanderer had in the first place condemned blameless Ignatius, on the grounds that he had gained mastery over the Church by means of secular influence, and it should now have turned it against Photius, for the reason that *he* had by means of secular influence gained despotic control of the Church—not by vote of God and the clergy, but thanks to his own lust for power and mad thirst for fame.[160] Not only Photius himself should have been deposed (both for this reason and because he thought it right to be ordained by someone who had himself been deposed), but also, according to apostolic decree, all those who had communicated with him.[161] And those attending the synod should not have shown themselves more merciful than God and His judgment in setting aside the sentence of the All-Holy Spirit. This is what confused the issue, and it is impossible to say how many evils and how much divisiveness this decision caused. For I think that if they had pronounced judgment upon all of them at that time in accordance with apostolic doctrine and ecclesiastical canons and excommunicated not only the one

αὐτῷ πάντας ἐκκηρύξαντες, οὐδεμίαν ἂν ἔτι κατὰ τῆς Ἐκκλησίας
εἶχε παρείσδυσιν ἡ ἀδικία. Ὥσπερ δὲ πρῶτον κατὰ τὴν ἐπὶ Ταρασίου
τοῦ θείου σύνοδον κατὰ τῶν Εἰκονομάχων γενομένην, ἐπειδὴ
συμπαθέστερον μᾶλλον ἢ δικαιότερον ἐχρήσαντο τοῖς αἱρετικοῖς,
5 καιροῦ πάλιν ἐκεῖνοι δραξάμενοι τὴν οἰκείαν δυσσέβειαν χαλεπώ-
τερον ἀνενεώσαντο· οὕτω καὶ νῦν τῆς συνόδου ταύτης πεφεισμέ-
νως ἀλλ' οὐκ ἀπροσπαθῶς καὶ κανονικῶς τὴν κρίσιν ἀποφηναμέ-
νης εὗρεν αὖθις ἡ πονηρία κατὰ τῆς Ἐκκλησίας χώραν. Καὶ διὰ τῶν
προσειλημμένων ὁ ἀπόβλητος καὶ διὰ τῶν ὑποκριτῶν ὁ καθηρημέ-
10 νος ὡς κοινωνικῶν ὄντων αὐτοῦ καταδραμὼν καὶ αὖθις τὸν ἱεραρ-
χικὸν θρόνον τυραννήσας καὶ τῶν ἱερῶν καταπαίξας θεσμῶν καὶ
πάντα μὲν ἀποστολικὸν κανόνα, πᾶσαν δὲ παράδοσιν ἐκκλησιαστικὴν καταπεπατηκὼς καὶ πάντας μὲν τῶν οἰκείων ὁμολογιῶν καὶ
χειρογράφων ἀθετητάς, πάντας δὲ σταυροπάτας οἷος ἐκεῖνος
15 γίνεσθαι | καταναγκάζων καὶ τῶν πρώτων τὰ ἔσχατα χείρω διαθέ-   26ᵛ
μενος τὰς ἁπάντων συνειδήσεις ἐβεβήλωσε καὶ κατέχρανε.

65. Τοῦτο μέν, ὡς ὁ ἐμὸς λόγος, τῆς συνόδου ταύτης τὸ ἐλάτ-
τωμα, διὰ τῆς καταδοχῆς καὶ κοινωνίας τῶν παραπεσόντων καὶ τὸν
λύκον, ὡς οὐ προσεδόκα, τοῖς προβάτοις ἐπεισαγούσης. Τοῦτο δέ
20 τινες καὶ ἀπὸ τῶν παρηκολουθηκότων τοῖς τότε χρόνοις τεκμηρίων
ἐμφρόνως ἐστοχάσαντο. Καὶ γὰρ μήπω ταυτησὶ τῆς συνόδου συγ-
κεκροτημένης, ἔτι δὲ ἐλπιζομένης βούβαλοι ἔξωθέν ποτε ἐλαυνό-
μενοι κατὰ μέσης διήγοντο τῆς πόλεως· ἀθρόως | δὲ θροηθέντες   549
ὧδε κἀκεῖσε διεσκορπίζοντο. Εἷς δὲ αὐτῶν κατὰ τῆς Μεγάλης
25 εὐθυδρομήσας Ἐκκλησίας καὶ ἔνδον τοῦ ἱεροῦ γεγονὼς ἄχρις
αὐτοῦ τρέχων τοῦ ἄμβωνος κατήντησεν. Ὥρα δὲ ἦν ἐνάτη τῆς
ἡμέρας καὶ αὐτὸς οὐκ ἀγαθὸς ἄγγελος τοῖς τὰ τοιαῦτα κρίνειν
εἰδόσι κατεφαίνετο. Τούτου δὲ μείζων ἀπόδειξις ὁ φρικωδέστατος
σεισμὸς ὃς κατ' ἐκεῖνον συνέβη τὸν καιρόν. Ἐνάτην εἶχεν Ἰαννου-
30 άριος καὶ πολλαὶ μὲν ἐκκλησίαι, ἔμβολοι δὲ πλεῖστοι καὶ οἶκοι
ἠδαφίσθησαν κτηνῶν τε καὶ ἀνθρώπων ἀμύθητος γέγονε πανωλε-

15–16 cf. Matth. 12.45; Luc. 11.26; 2 Petr. 2.20

6–7 πεφεισμένως v: -μένος Β   **9** προσειλημμένων Βν²: προειλημμένην Xv¹ | ὁ¹ ΒΧν¹: om.
ν² | ὑποκριτῶν ΒΧν²: ἀποκρίτων ν¹   **13** καὶ² ΒΧ: om. ν   **14** ἀθετητάς Χν: ἀ[..]τητάς Β
28–94.11 τούτου…πεσόν deest X

responsible for the dissension and divisiveness, but all those too who had communicated with him, then injustice would no longer have had any avenue by which to attack the Church. But just as once before at the time of the synod held against the iconoclasts, when Tarasius the holy was patriarch, they treated the heretics with more sympathy than justice dictated and the latter seized another opportunity and renewed their impious acts with even greater ferocity;[162] so now when this synod pronounced judgment in an indulgent rather than an unemotional manner and not strictly in accordance with ecclesiastical canons, the wickedness once again found a foothold against the Church. Photius, the excommunicated, Photius, the deposed, hurried back from exile with the aid of those hypocrites who had been readmitted by the synod, since they were in communion with him, and he once again gained absolute sway over the patriarchal seat. He mocked at the holy ordinances, riding roughshod over all the apostolic canons and ecclesiastical traditions, and he forced everyone to set aside their own vows and written undertakings and to follow his example in trampling under foot the holy Cross.[163] Making the last worse than the first, he defiled and befouled the consciences of all.

65. This then, as I see it, is the shortcoming of the synod, that by receiving back and renewing association with those who had fallen into sin, it actually, against its own expectation, let the wolf in among the sheep. And there were some who wisely divined this from the signs that attended those times. For this synod had not yet been convoked and was still being awaited, when some buffalo, which were being driven in from outside and led through the middle of the city, were suddenly startled and they scattered in all directions. One of them went directly to the great church, entered the sanctuary and ran right up as far as the very pulpit. It was the ninth hour of the day, and it did not seem in itself to bear good tidings to those who knew how to interpret such things.[164] But a greater proof than this came in the form of the most awful earthquake which took place at that time. It was the ninth of January, and many churches as well as countless colonnades and houses were dashed to the ground. There was untold destruction of beasts

θρία καὶ αὐτὸς δὲ ὁ μέγας τῆς τοῦ Θεοῦ Σοφίας οἶκος κατὰ πολλὰ μέρη διεκινδυνεύετο ῥηγνύμενος, εἰ μὴ τῆς ἀξίας πρὸς τῶν κρατούντων ἐτύγχανεν ἐπιμελείας.

66. Ταῦτα μὲν πρὸ τῆς συνόδου· καὶ μετ᾽ αὐτὴν ἐξαίφνης
5 ἐπῆλθε πνεύματος σφοδρὰ καταιγίς. Ὀκτώβριος ἐνίστατο μὴν καὶ οὕτω βιαίως ἐπέθετο τὸ πνεῦμα ὡς πολλῶν μὲν ἐκκλησιῶν, πολλῶν δὲ παλατίων καὶ τοῦ πατριαρχικοῦ δὲ οἴκου τὸν μόλιβδον οἷα μεμβράνας συνελίσσειν καὶ εἰς τοὔδαφος κατασπᾶν· οὐ μόνον δέ, ἀλλὰ καὶ τοῦ τετραπλεύρου μονολίθου κίονος ἐν τῷ ἱπποδρομίῳ τὸ ἐπὶ
10 τῆς κορυφῆς ἐστηλωμένον χαλκοῦν στροβίλιον βαρύτατον ὂν ὡς πορρωτάτω συνετρίβη πεσόν. Οὐκ εἰκῆ δὲ ταῦτα παρηκολούθηκε τὰ σημεῖα, ἀλλὰ τῆς μελλούσης αὖθις ἀκαταστασίας καὶ ταραχῆς διὰ τοῦ ταραχοποιοῦ δαίμονος ἐπὶ τῆς Ἐκκλησίας ἀνίστασθαι τεκμήρια σαφῆ· ἅπερ ἴσως οὐκ ἂν συνέπεσεν, εἰ κατὰ τὸν ἀποστολικόν,
15 ὡς εἴρηται, | τὰ κατ᾽ αὐτὸν ἐκρίθη θεσμόν.   27

67. Ἀλλ᾽ ὅμως οὐ ῥυπαίνει ταῦτα τὴν τοῦ πατριάρχου δόξαν, ὅτι μὴ αὐθεντικῶς εἶχε πᾶν ὃ ἐβούλετο δρᾶν· μᾶλλον δὲ τοῖς Ῥωμαίοις κατὰ τὴν ἄνωθεν ἐκκλησιαστικὴν παράδοσιν τὴν τῆς κρίσεως ἐξουσίαν παρεχώρει. Ἀλλ᾽ οὐδ᾽ ἡ σύνοδος ἐκείνη τοῖς κεκοι-
20 νωνηκόσι Φωτίῳ, εἰ καὶ τὰ μάλιστα βιασθεῖσι, τοσοῦτον ἤθελε συμπαθεῖν ὅσον ἡ τοῦ βασιλέως ἁπλότης, ἵνα μὴ λέγω κουφότης, προσώπων ἡττωμένη παρακλήσεσί τε καὶ τῶν ἀνθρώπων ἐπαίνοις ὑποχαυνουμένη καὶ φιλανθρωπίας ὀνόματι τῆς ἀκριβοῦς τοῦ Θεοῦ δικαιοσύνης ὡς ἐπίπαν ἀποπίπτουσα. Πλὴν ταῦτα μὲν τοῦτον
25 γέγονε τὸν τρόπον.

68. Αὐτὸς δὲ ὁ μέγας Ἰγνάτιος τῶν τῆς Ἐκκλησίας οἰάκων τὸ δεύτερον ἐπιλαβόμενος ἔδειξε καὶ τοῖς τυφλώττειν ἑκουσίως ἐθέλουσιν ὡς μάτην ὁ ἐχθρὸς ἐνεκαυχήσατο κατ᾽ αὐτοῦ. Ἐπιστημονικώτερον γὰρ καὶ μᾶλλον θειότερόν πως καὶ ἀσφαλέστερον ἢ
30 πρῴην τὴν Ἐκκλησίαν ἐκυβέρνα ἅτε δὴ ταῖς μακραῖς ταλαιπωρίαις καὶ ποικίλαις θλίψεσιν ἱκανὴν ἐμπειρίαν ἑαυτῷ συνειλοχώς· ἀδέκαστος μὲν πάντῃ καὶ ἀπροσωπόληπτος ἐν ταῖς κρίσεσι δεικνύμενος,

---

7 μόλιβδον v: μόλιβον B   11 παρηκολούθηκε v: παρηκολουθηκέναι B   13 ἀνίστασθαι B: ἐνίστατο v   14 κατὰ B: μετὰ v   17–19 ση(μείωσαι) ὅπως ἐκρίνοντο πάντες οἱ π(ατ)ριάρχ(αι) ὑπὸ τοῦ ῥώμης add. mg. al. m. B   18 κατὰ B: μετὰ v   22 τε B: om. v | τῶν ἀνθρώπων B: τοῖς παρὰ τούτων Xv

and of human life, and God's great church of Saint Sophia was itself in danger by reason of cracks in many places and would have collapsed, were it not for the proper care it received from the emperors.

66. All this took place before the synod. And after the synod a violent squall suddenly sprang up. It was the beginning of October, and the wind attacked with such force that it rolled up like parchment and dragged to the ground the roofing lead of many churches and palaces, including even the patriarch's residence; and not only that, but the very heavy bronze pine cone finial set on top of the four-sided monolith column in the hippodrome came down and was shattered a long way off. It was no accident that these signs occurred—they were clear indications of the chaos and confusion that was about to be set in motion once again in the Church by the Devil, maker of mischief.[165] And it might never have happened if, as I have said, Photius's case had been judged according to apostolic ordinance.

67. All the same, these matters do not taint the honor of the patriarch, because he did not have the authority to do all that he desired. Instead, he yielded to the Romans the right to pass judgment in accordance with longstanding ecclesiastical tradition. But not even that synod desired to show to those who had been in communication with Photius (even if it had been for the most part under duress) as much sympathy as the emperor in his naivety— not to say shallowness. Overcome by men's entreaties and puffed up by people's praises, he completely missed the mark of God's perfect justice, all in the name of clemency. Anyway, this was the way in which these matters turned out.

68. As for great Ignatius himself, when he took the helm of the Church for the second time, he showed even to those who wished of their own accord to remain blind to it how pointless the fiend's vaunting against him had been. For he guided the Church more skillfully, with more sanctity, too, and in greater security than before, since he had indeed gained sufficient experience from his great tribulations and many and various afflictions. He showed himself completely incorruptible and impartial in his judgments

λίαν δὲ ἀκριβὴς ἐν ταῖς χειροτονίαις, τοῖς ἀδικουμένοις ἐπικουρῶν,
τοῖς λυπουμένοις συλλυπούμενος, τοῖς πενομένοις ἐπαρκῶν καὶ
τὴν ἔνδειαν τούτοις ὅση δύναμις ἱλαρῶς παραμυθούμενος· καὶ
τοὺς ἀσθενοῦντας μὲν τῇ πίστει ἢ καὶ τῷ σώματι παρακαλῶν καὶ
5 ψυχαγωγῶν, τοὺς ὀλιγοψύχους δὲ τῇ χάριτι τῆς τοῦ Πνεύματος
ἀνακτώμενος διδασκαλίας· καὶ πᾶσι πάντα γινόμενος ἔσπευδε
κερδαίνειν, ὅσον ἐπ' αὐτῷ, πάντας ἐν σπλάγχνοις Ἰησοῦ.

69. Δύο μὲν αὐτῷ διὰ σπουδῆς ἦσαν ὁδοί· ἡ μὲν πρὸς Θεὸν
ἰθυτενῶς ὁρῶσα διὰ καθαρᾶς τε καὶ ἀνεκλείπτου προσευχῆς, ἡ δὲ
10 πρὸς τὴν τῆς Ἐκκλησίας οἰκοδομὴν καὶ περιποίησιν. | Διὰ τῆς αὐτῆς 552
δὲ σπουδῆς ἀμφότερα κατώρθου· οὐ κατὰ πάρεργον γὰρ οὐδὲ
ῥαθύμως ὥσπερ τινές, ἀλλὰ καὶ λίαν ἐπιμελῶς καὶ συντόνως ἐκ
νεότητος ἕως γήρους καὶ πρεσβείου βάθεος ταῖς ἱεραῖς λειτουρ-
γίαις εὐηρέστει καὶ κατὰ πάντα σεβάσμιον οἶκον τῇ τε πανυμνήτῳ
15 Μητρὶ τοῦ Θεοῦ τοῖς τε θείοις ἀποστόλοις καὶ μάρτυσιν ἐν ἀγαλλιάσει καρδίας θεοπρεπῶς ἐπανηγύριζεν. Οὕτω δὲ θεοφιλῶς καὶ
πνευματοκινήτως ἀνῆγε τὴν προσφορὰν ὡς ἐπ' αὐτῆς ὁρᾶν τῆς
θείας τραπέζης ἐναργῆ τῆς τοῦ Πνεύματος παρουσίας τὰ τεκμήρια.
Ὡρᾶτο γὰρ ὁ θεῖος ἄρτος ὅλος ἠλλοιωμένος, ὅλος ὥσπερ ἄνθραξ
20 οὐράνιος χάριν ἀποστίλβων τοῦ οὐρανίου πυρός. Ὤπταί ποτε
κραδαινόμενος καὶ ὁ ὑπεράνω τῆς ἁγίας τραπέζης ἀπαιωρούμενος
σταυρός· | ἠρέμα μὲν πολλάκις σειόμενος ὑψουμένου τοῦ ἄρτου 27ᵛ
καθωρᾶτο τὴν τοῦ ἁγίου δηλαδὴ Πνεύματος ἐπισκίασιν ὑποσημαί-
νων. Ἐν ἡμέρᾳ δέ ποτε τοῦ Πάσχα μάλιστα οὕτω διεκινήθη σφο-
25 δρῶς ὡς πάντας ἱερεῖς καὶ ἀρχιερεῖς καὶ μάλιστα τοὺς ἐκ τῶν
ἄλλων πατριαρχικῶν θρόνων τὸ μυστήριον ἐκπεπληγμένους
μεγάλῃ φωνῇ δοξάζειν ἐπὶ πολὺ τὸν Θεόν.

70. Οὕτως ὁ μέγας ἱεράρχης ἀχράντους θυσίας ἐν τελειότητι
πίστεως γνησίως ἀναφέρων καὶ ταύταις ἱλασκόμενος τὸν Θεὸν ἱεροπρε-
30 πῶς ἱερούργει τὴν σωτηρίαν τοῦ λαοῦ. Ἀεὶ δὲ τοὺς ἐγγίζοντας αὐτῷ
τοιαύταις κατεφώτιζε διδαχαῖς·

---

4 cf. Rom. 14.1   6–7 cf. 1 Cor. 9.19–22   7 Phil. 1.8

8 σπουδῆς Xv: παντὸς Β   11 κατὰ Β: μετὰ v | γὰρ Β: om. Xv   13 γήρους Β: γήρως v |
βαθέος Xv: βαθέως Β   14 κατὰ Β: μετὰ v   18 τὰ Β: om. v   29 ταύταις Xv: τούτοις Β

and most painstaking in his ordinations; he helped those who were wronged, shared the grief of the distressed, gave assistance to the poor and cheerfully relieved their lack of means as far as he was able; and he encouraged and refreshed those who were weak in faith or in body and revived the faint-hearted with the grace of the Holy Spirit's teaching. He became all things to all men and, as far as it lay in his power, he strove to win them all in the love of Christ.

69. His exertions lay in two directions—looking unerringly towards God with pure and unfailing prayer on the one hand and towards the edification and safekeeping of His Church on the other. Both of these tasks he performed with the same zeal and not in a halfhearted or sluggish fashion, as some did. Instead, he fulfilled the holy rites with the greatest of care and zeal from tender youth to profound old age, and in every church he made fitting celebration with joyful heart of the holy festivals in honor of the Mother of God, to whom all praise is due, and of the holy apostles and martyrs. And he celebrated the eucharist with such devotion to God and inspiration from the Holy Spirit that it was possible to see on the very altar clear signs of the presence of the Holy Spirit. For the holy bread was seen to be completely transformed, altogether like a heavenly coal shining brightly with the grace of heavenly fire. On one occasion even the cross which hangs above the holy altar was seen to be quivering, and it was observed to be gently agitated many times over while the bread was raised on high, clearly indicating the shadow of the Holy Spirit.[166] And on the day of the Easter in particular it was shaken with such violence that all the priests and bishops, especially those from the other patriarchal sees, were astonished at the symbolic event and for a long time glorified God with loud voices.

70. Thus did the great patriarch in true and perfect faith offer up sacrifices pure and undefiled, and by propitiating God with these, he ministered to the salvation of the people as a priest should. And he was forever enlightening those who approached him with teachings such as the following:[167]

71. "Προσέχετε" λέγων "έαυτοῖς, ἀδελφοί, καὶ βλέπετε πῶς ἀκριβῶς τοῦ βίου περιπατεῖτε τὴν ὁδὸν μὴ ὡς ἄσοφοι, ἀλλ' ὡς σοφοί. Καὶ μὴ γίνεσθε ἄφρονες, ἀλλὰ συνιέντες τὰ ἀρεστὰ τῷ Θεῷ." Καί· "Μὴ σχηματίζεσθε τῷ αἰῶνι τούτῳ, ἀλλὰ μεταμορ-
5 φοῦσθε" κατὰ τὸν θεῖον ἀπόστολον "τῇ ἀνακαινώσει τοῦ νοὸς ὑμῶν εἰς τὸ δοκιμάζειν ὑμᾶς καὶ εἰδέναι ὅ τι τὸ θέλημα τοῦ Θεοῦ τὸ ἀγαθὸν καὶ εὐάρεστον καὶ τέλειον· καὶ τίς ἡ κλῆσις τῆς πίστεως ὑμῶν καὶ τῆς ἐλπίδος ἐν Χριστῷ Ἰησοῦ τῷ Κυρίῳ ἡμῶν." Ἤτω ὁ λύχνος τῆς καρδίας ὑμῶν τῷ Κυρίῳ Πνεύματι ἀεὶ καιόμενος καθα-
10 ρός, εἰλικρινής, ἁπλοῦς, ὅλος διαυγὴς καὶ φωτοφανής, ἵν' ὅλη δι' αὐτοῦ καταυγάζηται ὑμῖν ἡ ψυχή. Ἔστω ὁ νοῦς ὑμῖν ἀνατεταμένος ἀεὶ πρὸς Θεόν, μονότροπος μονόλογιστος ἓν ἔργον καὶ μίαν σπου-δὴν καὶ μίαν προηγουμένως ἔχων ἐνέργειαν, τὴν θεωρίαν τοῦ ἀγαθοῦ, πρὸς μόνον τὸ φύσει καὶ κυρίως ὂν ἀγαθὸν ἐπεστραμ-
15 μένος ἀεὶ καὶ ἐν αὐτῷ ζῶν καὶ κινούμενος καὶ ὢν καὶ ἐν αὐτῷ λαμ-πρυνόμενος καὶ ἀγαθυνόμενος καὶ κατὰ τὸ ἐφικτὸν ὁμοιούμενος καὶ θεούμενος. Οὕτω γὰρ ὑψοῦ τὸν λογισμὸν αἴροντες καὶ πάντων μὲν αἰσθητῶν, πάντων δὲ νοητῶν κτισμάτων ὑπεραναβαίνοντες, μόνῃ δὲ τῇ τριαδικῇ θεαρχίᾳ, μόνῃ τῇ ἐν ἀπορρήτοις ἑστώσῃ κρυ-
20 φιότητι καὶ ὑπερουσιότητι τὸν οἰκεῖον ἱδρυσάμενοι νοῦν· καὶ μίαν μὲν Πατρὸς καὶ Υἱοῦ καὶ ἁγίου Πνεύματος ὥσπερ φύσιν θεότητος οὕτω καὶ δύναμιν καὶ ἐνέργειαν καὶ δόξαν καὶ μεγαλοπρέπειαν ὁμολογοῦντες καὶ πιστεύοντες· τὸν ἕνα δὲ τῆς τρισυποστάτου θεαρχίας τὸν ἄναρχον καὶ συνάναρχον τῷ Πατρὶ Λόγον τὸν ἀόρα-
25 τον τὸν ἀσώματον τὸν ὁμοφυᾶ τῷ Γεννήτορι καὶ | ὁμοδύναμον 553 τοῦτον Υἱὸν ἀνθρώπου καθ' ἡμᾶς ἐκ τῆς ὑπεραμώμου γενόμενον Θεομήτορος εἰδότες· καὶ ἕνα μὲν τῷ προσώπῳ, διπλοῦν δὲ ταῖς φύσεσι καὶ ἐνεργείαις καὶ θελήσεσι κηρύσσοντες· καὶ ταύτῃ σχολά-ζοντες ἐπιμελέστερον τῇ θεωρίᾳ τῶν θείων καὶ θεολογίᾳ καὶ διὰ
30 τῆς ἱερᾶς τῶν Γραφῶν μελέτης ἀνακαθαιρόμενοι καὶ δι' ἀενάου προσευχῆς ἁγνιζόμενοι ὑπεροράσει τῶν ματαίων ὑπερίδωμεν μεριμνῶν καὶ τοῖς τῆς ἀτιμίας μὴ ὑποκύπτωμεν πάθεσιν καὶ πρὸς

1–4 Ephes. 5.15–17   4–7 Rom. 12.2   7–8 cf.? Ephes. 1.18   15 Acta 17.28

1–104.15 προσέχετε...κεχρημένος deest X   11 ὑμῖν¹ v: ἡμῖν B | ὑμῖν² v: ἡμῖν B
12–13 σπουδὴν...μίαν B: om. v   15 καὶ ἐν² B: om. v

71. Look to yourselves, brothers, and see to it that you tread the path of life scrupulously, not as fools but as wise men; and do not be senseless, but be aware of what is pleasing to God. And, in the words of the holy apostle, do not be conformed to this world, but transform yourselves by the renewing of your minds, that you may put to the proof and know what is the good, acceptable and perfect will of God, and also what is the vocation of your faith and hope in Jesus Christ Our Lord. Let the light of your hearts be forever kindled by the Lord, the Holy Spirit, and be pure, upright, sincere, completely radiant and brilliant, so that your souls might be fully illuminated by it. Let your minds be forever reaching up towards God, constant, unwavering, and primarily concerned with a single function, goal and activity—the contemplation of the Good. And let them be ever attentive to that which alone is naturally and properly Good, and live, be moved and exist in It, be illuminated and exalted in It, and as far as possible become like It and be deified by It. Let us elevate our powers of reason in this way, rise above all visible and invisible creatures, and establish our own minds solely on the foundation of the supreme Trinity, Its mystery and Its supersubstantiality grounded in the ineffable. Let us acknowledge and believe in the one divine nature of Father, Son and Holy Spirit and equally in its power, activity, glory, and majesty. Let us recognize that the one Word of the Godhead in three persons, Which is eternal and coeternal with the Father, invisible, incorporeal, and of like nature and power with the Father, was born of the immaculate Mother of God in our nature as the Son of man. And let us proclaim Him as one in person but twofold in nature, activity and will. And by devoting ourselves with greater diligence to this contemplation of things divine and to theology, by purifying ourselves through study of the Holy Scriptures and by cleansing ourselves through continual prayer, let us look with contempt and disdain upon empty cares and avoid submitting to disgraceful

ἀνονήτους | φροντίδας μὴ καταπίπτωμεν. Καὶ πᾶς θυμὸς θηριώδης 28
καὶ πᾶσα παράλογος ἐπιθυμία ἀρθήτω ἀφ' ἡμῶν· μᾶλλον δὲ ὁ μὲν
θυμὸς ὅπλον ἡμῖν κατὰ τῆς ἁμαρτίας καὶ τοῦ τῆς ἁμαρτίας ἔστω
πατρός, ἡ ἐπιθυμία δὲ πρὸς τὸ κυρίως καὶ ἀληθῶς ἐπιθυμητὸν
5 μετασκευαζομένη πᾶσα συνεργὸς ἡμῖν γινέσθω πρὸς τήρησιν τῆς
Δεσποτικῆς ἐντολῆς.

72. Τοιαύτας οὖν ἔχοντες παραγγελίας, ἀγαπητοί, διὰ προφη-
τῶν μὲν πρῶτον, ἔπειτα διὰ τῶν ὑψηλῶν τοῦ Χριστοῦ μαθητῶν καὶ
εὐαγγελιστῶν καὶ διὰ τῶν πατέρων δὲ μετὰ ταῦτα καὶ ἱερῶν διδα-
10 σκάλων γινομένας εἰς ἡμᾶς, μᾶλλον δὲ δι' ἑνὸς καὶ τοῦ αὐτοῦ
Πνεύματος λαλουμένας ἀεὶ καὶ πολυτρόπως κηρυσσομένας ἐν ἡμῖν
μὴ καταφρονῶμεν, μηδὲ ῥαθύμως καὶ ἐκμελῶς, ἐπιμελῶς δὲ τὴν
πρᾶξιν καὶ σπουδαίως μετίωμεν τῆς ἀρετῆς, ἐλεημοσύναις μὲν καὶ
πίστει πάσης ἁμαρτίας ἀποκαθαιρόμενοι, ἀγάπῃ δὲ τελείᾳ καὶ
15 ταπεινοφροσύνῃ ἀληθεῖ παντὸς μολυσμοῦ σαρκὸς καὶ πνεύματος
ἀποδιυλιζόμενοι· ἵνα κατὰ πᾶν τὸ θέλημα τοῦ Θεοῦ περιπατήσαν-
τες ἄξιοι τῆς τοῦ ἐπουρανίου Πατρὸς βασιλείας ἐν Χριστῷ Ἰησοῦ
ἀναφανῶμεν. Ἀποθώμεθα τοιγαροῦν πᾶν πάθος καὶ πάντα πονη-
ρίας ἀποτριψώμεθα λογισμόν, ἵνα καθαροὶ τῷ καθαρωτάτῳ προσ-
20 ενεχθῆναι δυνηθῶμεν. Ἀπορριψώμεθα γαστριμαργίας πάθος ὀλέθριον ὡς πάσης ἀλλότριον ἀρετῆς καὶ παντοίας γεννητικὸν κακίας·
ἀντ' αὐτῆς δὲ τὴν κοσμιωτάτην ἐγκράτειαν ὡς διπλοΐδα περιθώ-
μεθα, τὴν τῶν ἀγγέλων σύντροφον, τὴν τῶν ἁγίων σύσκηνον, τὴν
τῆς ἄνω τερπνότητος πρόξενον καὶ τρυφῆς. Πορνεία δὲ μηδὲ ὀνο-
25 μαζέσθω ἐν ἡμῖν, οὐ μόνον ἡ κατ' ἐνέργειαν καὶ πρᾶξιν, ἀλλὰ μηδὲ
πορνικαῖς φαντασίαις ῥυπαινώμεθα. Πάσῃ δὲ μηχανῇ καὶ σπουδῇ,
πάσῃ ταπεινοφροσύνῃ καὶ προσευχῇ τὴν κακὴν ῥίζαν προθέλυμνον
ἐκτίλωμεν, τὴν θολερὰν πηγήν, τὸ τῆς ἡδονῆς ἐμπύρευμα, τὸ τῆς
ἀκολασίας ζώπυρον, τὸ πορνικὸν τῆς καρδίας εἴδωλον πρῶτον
30 ἐξανέλωμεν ἢ μειώσωμεν. Οὕτω γὰρ ἡμῖν τὸ ἱερὸν τῆς σωφροσύνης
ἐπανθήσει κάλλος, οὕτω καὶ τὸν νοητὸν Νυμφίον καὶ ἅγιον ἁγιο-
πρεπῶς ἑαυτοῖς ἐπισπασόμεθα. Φιλαργυρίαν δὲ καὶ πλεονεξίαν
πᾶσαν ὡς εἰδωλολατρίαν ἀποφύγωμεν. Ταὐτὸν γὰρ κατὰ τὸν τοῦ

---

15 2 Cor. 7.1   24-25 Ephes. 5.3   32-33 Col. 3.5; Ephes. 5.5

---

2 ἡμῶν ν: ὑμῶν Β   14 πίστει ν: πίστεσιν Β   28 ἐκτίλωμεν Β: ἐκτίλλωμεν ν

passions and falling into unprofitable anxieties. And let all our wild aggression and every irrational desire be taken away from us. Instead, let aggression be our weapon against sin and against the father of sin; and let desire be completely transformed in the direction of what is truly and properly to be desired and be a help to us in keeping the Lord's commandments.

72. And so, dearly beloved, since we have such precepts as these which have come down to us in the first place through the prophets, then through the sublime disciples of Christ and the evangelists, and after that through the Church fathers and holy teachers (or rather they are forever spoken of and proclaimed among us in many and various ways through one and the same Holy Spirit), let us not treat them with disdain nor pursue the practice of virtue sluggishly and carelessly, but rather with zeal and careful attention, purified of all sin by almsgiving and faith and strained clear, as it were, of every taint of flesh and of spirit by perfect love and true humility; so that by walking the path of life in accordance with the full will of God we might appear to be worthy in Jesus Christ of the kingdom of the Heavenly Father. So then, let us put all passion aside and reject all thought of wickedness, in order that we might in purity be able to approach Him Who is most pure. Let us cast out the ruinous passion of gluttony as something foreign to every virtue and producing every kind of evil. In its place let us assume the mantle of that most modest abstinence which is the comrade of the angels, companion of the saints, and bringer of delight and joy in the world above. Let there be no mention even of fornication among us—not only the act and practice of it, but let us not defile ourselves either by lewd imaginings. And by every effort and contrivance, with all humility and prayer, let us pluck out the evil by the roots; let us first of all destroy or diminish its foul source, the spark of lust, the hot ember of licentiousness, the lewd fancy of the heart. For in this way the sacred beauty of chastity will blossom forth in us and we shall win for ourselves in all holiness our spiritual and holy Bridegroom. And let us shun all avarice and greed as a form of idolatry. For according to the apostle's rule the

102

ἀποστόλου πέφυκε νόμον, εἴπερ οἱ ταύτης ὀρεγόμενοι ἀπεπλανή-
θησαν ἀπὸ τῆς πίστεως· οὐ μόνον δέ, ἀλλὰ καὶ ἑαυτοὺς περιέπει-
ραν ὀδύναις πολλαῖς. Εἴπερ οὖν καὶ τῆς σωτηρίου πίστεως ἀλλο-
τριοῖ καὶ πολυώδυνον ἡμῖν καθίστησι τὴν ζωήν, πῶς οὐχὶ φευκτέα
5 μᾶλλον ἁπάντων καὶ βδελυκτὴ τῷ γε μὴ πάντη καπηλικῷ τὴν
ψυχήν; Οἱ γοῦν τὸ | πολίτευμα ἐν οὐρανοῖς ἀποτιθέμενοι καὶ πρὸς   556
τὸν ἐκεῖ βίον καὶ τὴν ζωὴν τὴν αἰώνιον μετατασσόμενοι ἔχοντες
διατροφὰς καὶ σκεπάσματα τούτοις ἀρκώμεθα. Καὶ γὰρ οὕτω
κούφως ἡμᾶς καὶ εὐστάλως τῶν ἀρετῶν ἀνιέναι τὴν κλίμακα δεῖ
10 εἰδότας ὅτι ὥσπερ ἀμήχανον ὄρνιν ἐπὶ γῆς δεδεμένην ἀναπτῆναι
πρὸς οὐρανόν, οὕτως ἀνένδεκτον εἶναι τὸν γηΐνοις κτήμασι καὶ
χρήμασιν ἐν προσπαθείᾳ καταδεδεμένον τὴν πρὸς Θεὸν ὑψοῦσαν
εὐθυβόλως οἶμον δραμεῖν. Ὀργὴν δὲ ὡς ἐκστάσεως οὖσαν | παρά-   28ᵛ
φυσιν, ὡς ἀσχημοσύνης μητέρα καὶ ὡς τοῦ πονηροῦ τυγχάνουσαν
15 ἔξαλμα φυγῇ φύγωμεν, μήποτε τῇ ταύτης ἐξαναλωθῶμεν φλογί.
Ἀναλάβωμεν δὲ πραΰτητα ἐπιείκειαν μακροθυμίαν. Ταῦτα γὰρ τῆς
τοῦ Ἰησοῦ γνωρίσματα φιλανθρωπίας καὶ ταῦτα ὑπερουσίως
ἐκεῖνος ὢν ταῦτα νομοθετεῖ. Σχεδὸν γὰρ αἱ ἐντολαὶ πᾶσαι τοῦ
Κυριακοῦ στόματος πραΰτητος διδασκαλία καὶ ἀνεξικακίας εἰσί, δι᾽
20 ὧν καὶ ἡ κορυφαία τῶν ἀρετῶν ἀγάπη συνίσταται καὶ κατορθοῦται.
Λύπην δὲ καὶ ἀκηδίαν ἐκτρεπώμεθα ὡς ἐμπόδιά τε καὶ σκῶλα καθ-
εστώσας τῆς ὁδοῦ. Ῥίψωμεν λύπην τὴν δι᾽ ἀποτυχίαν ἢ ἔλλειψιν
γεηροῦ πράγματος ἐγγινομένην καταβαρύνουσάν τε καὶ πυροῦσαν
ἡμῶν τὴν ψυχὴν καὶ οὕτω σκληρῶς ἐκθλίβουσαν καὶ ἐκπιέζουσαν
25 ὥστε μὴ δύνασθαι πρὸς τὸν δοτῆρα τῆς ἀληθινῆς ἀτενίσαι χαρᾶς
καὶ πρὸς αὐτὸν ἐν ἀγγαλιάσει Πνεύματος ἁγίου δραμεῖν. Ῥίψωμεν
ἀκηδίαν τῆς κακῆς λύπης ἔγγονον, τὴν ῥαθυμίας μητέρα τὴν ἀπο-
γνώσεως φίλην, τὴν ἐκλελυμένην τὴν πάρετον καὶ πρὸς πᾶσαν
ἐντολὴν θείαν καὶ πρὸς πᾶν ἔργον ἀγαθὸν ἀδόκιμον. Ἐνδυσώμεθα
30 δὲ μᾶλλον τὴν κατὰ Θεὸν λύπην τὴν μητέρα τῆς μετανοίας, τὴν
κατανύξεως γέμουσαν, τὴν χαρᾶς πλήρη πνευματικῆς. Ἐνδυσώμεθα
προθυμίαν σπουδὴν εὐσέβειαν πᾶσαν καὶ ἀρετήν. Καὶ τῷ πνεύματι

1-2 1 Tim. 6.10   6 Phil. 3.20   7-8 1 Tim. 6.8   10 cf.? Bas. *Ep.* 293.17–20 (ed. Courtonne)
29 Tit. 1.16   30 cf. 2 Cor. 7.10   32–104.2 Rom. 12.11–12

---

9 κούφως Β: κούφους v | εὐστάλως Β: εὐσταλεῖς v   13 ἐκστάσεως v: ἔκστασιν Β
13–14 παράφυσιν Βv: παρὰ φύσιν EJ   22 δι᾽ v: δ᾽ Β

two are the same, seeing that those who strive after greed are straying from the faith. And not only that, but such sinners also pierce themselves with much painful distress. And so if greed actually estranges us from faith that brings deliverance, and makes our lives very painful, is it not surely to be avoided above all else and abominable at least to anyone who is not an out-and-out peddler in his soul? We, therefore, who regard our citizenship as being in Heaven and are passing over to existence there and to eternal life, should be satisfied if we merely have means of subsistence and clothing to cover our bodies. For we should be likewise lightly equipped and attired when we ascend the ladder of virtues, being aware that as impossible as it is for a bird to fly up to the heavens when it is bound upon the ground, it is equally impossible for the man who is tied in passionate attachment to earthly possessions and wealth to run a straight course along the path which elevates us to God. And let us flee from anger as being an offshoot of derangement, mother of disgrace, and an outburst of the Devil, lest we be consumed by its flames. Let us on the contrary adopt gentleness, forbearance and patience. For these are the marks of Jesus's clemency and these are the things He prescribes, since in His supra-essentiality He *is* these things. Indeed, almost all the injunctions from the mouth of Our Lord are teachings of gentleness and forbearance, and it is through these qualities too that the chief virtue, charity, is created and brought to a successful issue. But let us avoid grief and listlessness as obstacles and stumbling blocks in our path. Let us cast aside grief, which comes from failure in, or falling short of, an earthly pursuit; it burdens and inflames our souls, it afflicts and distresses us with such harshness that we are unable to focus our eyes on the giver of true joy and to run to Him in the exultation of the Holy Spirit. Let us cast aside listlessness, the child of evil grief, the mother of inertia, the ally of despair; it is feeble, enervated, and worthless in relation to all God's injunctions and all good deeds. Instead, let us assume that sorrow which belongs to God and is the mother of repentance, full of compunction and spiritual joy. Let us adopt eagerness, zeal, and all piety and virtue. Then, by being

104

ζέοντες, τῷ Κυρίῳ δουλεύοντες, τῇ ἐλπίδι χαίροντες, τῇ θλίψει
ὑπομένοντες, τῇ προσευχῇ προσκαρτεροῦντες δυνηθείημεν ἂν
οὕτω καὶ τῆς ἀνοσίας κενοδοξίας καὶ τῆς ἀνοσιωτέρας ὑπερηφα-
νίας, τῶν ἀκροτάτων παθῶν, τῶν πρωτογόνων τοῦ διαβόλου θυγα-
5 τέρων ὑπέρτεροι γενέσθαι ἐν Χριστῷ Ἰησοῦ· καὶ δι᾽ ἄκρας μὲν
ταπεινώσεως τὸν πολύπλοκον δαίμονα τῆς κενοδοξίας ἐκκρουόμενοι καὶ συμπατοῦντες, τὸν κολοφῶνα δὲ τῶν κακῶν τὴν ὑπερηφανίαν ἐν πίστει καὶ δυνάμει Θεοῦ τέλεον ἀνατρέποντες καὶ κατ-
αργοῦντες. Καὶ οὕτως ὅλον τὸ σμῆνος τῶν πονηρῶν τῆς ψυχῆς
10 ἀναιροῦντες παθῶν τὴν ἱερὰν ἀπάθειαν καὶ τὸν τῆς ἀπαθείας Θεὸν
καθαρῶς ἐπενδυσώμεθα. Καὶ οὕτως ἡμᾶς διὰ πάσης κατηρτισμέ-
νους ἀρετῆς ὁ Μονογενὴς καὶ ἀγαπητὸς ἠγαπηκὼς ἐλεύσεται μετὰ
τοῦ Πατρός, ὡς ὑπέσχετο, καὶ μονὴν ποιήσει παρ᾽ ἡμῖν.

73. Τοιαύταις ἀεὶ παραγγελίαις ὁ θεῖος Ἰγνάτιος, τοιαύταις
15 νουθεσίαις καὶ διδασκαλίαις κεχρημένος καὶ ἰδίᾳ μὲν τοὺς μοναχι-
κοὺς καὶ ἐρημικοὺς ὡς πρακτικώτατος ταῖς ἐμπράκτοις ὁμιλίαις
ψυχαγωγῶν καὶ τὸν πόθον αὐτοῖς τῆς ἀσκήσεως ἐπιτείνων, ἰδίᾳ δὲ
τοῖς πλουσίοις παραγγέλλων μὴ ὑψηλοφρονεῖν μηδ᾽ ἐπ᾽ ἀδηλότητι
πλούτου πεποιθέναι· | τοῖς ἄρχουσι μὴ φυσιοῦσθαι μηδὲ κατεπαί- 29
20 ρεσθαι τῶν | πενήτων παραινῶν, ἰδίᾳ δὲ πάλιν ἱερεῖς τε καὶ ἀρχ- 557
ιερεῖς ὡς ἱεραρχικώτατος καὶ γραφικώτατος καὶ ταῖς κανονικαῖς
θεσμοθεσίαις ἐπανορθούμενος· καὶ πᾶσι, συνόλως εἰπεῖν, δι᾽ ὧν
ἐποίει καὶ ἐδίδασκε, τὸν τοῦ Θεοῦ νόμον καὶ τὴν ἐντολὴν ὑποτιθέ-
μενος εἰς λιπαρὸν ἤδη καὶ πῖον ἐληλάκει γῆρας, ἐπεθύμει δὲ τὴν
25 ἀνάλυσιν καὶ τῶν χρονίων κόπων καὶ νόσων καὶ θλίψεων ἐπεπόθει
τὴν ἀπαλλαγήν. Καὶ μέντοι καὶ τυγχάνει ταύτης καὶ ἐπ᾽ ἀγαθαῖς
ἄγαν ἐλπίσι τοῦ μέλλοντος ἀποτίθεται τὴν παροῦσαν ζωήν. Ἐξίστα-
ται θορύβων καὶ ταραχῆς καὶ φθόνου μίσους τε καὶ ἀντιλογίας τῶν
ἀτόπων ἀνθρώπων καὶ μοχθηρῶν, ἐν εἰρήνῃ δὲ ἐπὶ τὸ αὐτὸ ἐκοι-
30 μήθη καὶ ὕπνωσε· καὶ εἰς χεῖρας Κυρίου τὸ πνεῦμα παραθέμενος
προστίθεται τοῖς ὁσίοις ὁ ὅσιος, τοῖς ἱεράρχαις ὁ μέγας ἱεράρχης,

---

12-13 cf. Ioann. 14.21; 23 18-19 1 Tim. 6.17 29-30 Ps. 4.8 30 Luc. 23.46

6-7 ἐκκρουόμενοι B: ἐκκρινόμενοι v 11 ἐπενδυσώμεθα B: ἐπενδυσόμεθα v 12 καὶ
ἀγαπητὸς trsp. v 16 πρακτικώτατος B: πρακτικότερους X: πρακτικωτέρους v 21 καὶ² B:
om. Xv 22 συνόλως Bv: συντόμως X 25 ἐπεπόθει B: ἐπόθει v

fervent in spirit, by serving the Lord, by rejoicing in His hope, by patiently enduring afflictions, and by persevering in prayer, we might be capable of triumphing in Jesus Christ over the supreme passions that are the firstborn of the Devil's daughters—impious vainglory and, what is worse still, arrogance. And by practicing extreme humility we could drive back and trample under foot the intriguing demon of vainglory, whilst completely overthrowing and rendering ineffective the crowning evil, arrogance, in God's faith and might. And by destroying in this fashion all the tribe of the soul's wicked passions, let us in all purity adopt the holy state of freedom from passion and the God of that holy state. And once we are equipped in this way with every virtue, God's only begotten Son, Who is beloved and also loves us, will come to us with the Father, as he promised, and make his abode with us.

73. Such were the precepts, admonitions and teachings that holy Ignatius was forever employing. In the case of monks and solitary figures, he would take the most practical approach and try to win them over by sermons of a practical nature and incite in them the desire for asceticism. As for the rich, he would exhort them not to be haughty, nor to put their trust in the uncertainty of wealth. The ruling powers he advised not to puff themselves up or be arrogant towards the poor. Then again, in the case of priests and bishops, since he was the highest-ranking member of the clergy and best versed in the Scriptures, he would actually give them further instruction in canon law. And to all, to speak generally, by his actions and teachings he provided instruction in the law and commandments of God. By this stage he had advanced to a bounteous and plentiful old age and was desirous of death, longing for relief from his long-continued toils and illnesses and afflictions. And indeed his wish was granted and he left the present life with very high hopes for the future. He left behind the clamor and confusion, the jealousy and hatred, the disputing of wicked and evil men, and he peacefully went to his rest and fell asleep. He commended his soul into the hands of the Lord and he was added to the number of holy men as Ignatius the holy, to the bishops as the great bishop, to the confessors of the faith as confessor, and to

τοῖς ὁμολογηταῖς ὁ ὁμολογητὴς καὶ μεγάλοις πατράσιν ὁ ὑπὲρ
δικαιοσύνης Θεοῦ καὶ ἀληθείας οὐδενὸς ἔλαττον ἐκείνων κεκοπια-
κώς.

74. Ἄξιον δὲ μηδὲ τὸν τρόπον τῆς αὐτοῦ παραδραμεῖν μετα-
5 στάσεως. Ἔκειτο μὲν τὰ τελευταῖα πνέων ὁ ἅγιος καὶ αὐτὸς κατὰ
τὸν μέγαν ἐκεῖνον ὑπὸ τῆς ἄνω χοροστασίας ἐπιζητούμενος· καὶ τὰ
τῆς φωνῆς ὄργανα τούτῳ ἤδη παρείθη καὶ ἡ ζωτικὴ δύναμις ἔσβη
καὶ τὰ μέλη νεκρὰ πάντα καὶ ὅλη τῆς ἐκδημίας ἦν ἡ ψυχή. Καὶ ἰδοὺ
ὁ ὑπηρέτης κατὰ τὸν τῆς Ἐκκλησίας τύπον (μέσαι δὲ νύκτες ἦσαν)
10 καὶ μεγάλῃ φωνῇ τὸ "Εὐλόγησον, Δέσποτα" βοῶν ἀνακέκραγεν.
Καὶ ὁ μακάριος ἠρέμα τῇ χειρὶ τὸ στόμα σφραγίσας καὶ τὰ τίμια
χείλη βραχὺ κεκινηκὼς μόλις διακουομένῃ τοῖς ἔγγιστα παρ-
εστῶσιν ἐπύθετο τῇ φωνῇ· "Τίνος ἁγίου σήμερον μνήμη;" Οἱ δέ·
"Ἰακώβου" φασὶ "τοῦ ἀδελφοθέου, τοῦ φίλου σου, ὦ δέσποτα." Ὁ
15 δὲ μακάριος πρὸς αὐτούς· "Τοῦ δεσπότου μου" κατανυκτικῶς ἔφη·
"λοιπὸν σώζεσθε." Εἶτα λέγει· "Εὐλογητὸς ὁ Θεὸς ἡμῶν πάντοτε,
νῦν καὶ ἀεὶ καὶ εἰς τοὺς αἰῶνας τῶν αἰώνων. Ἀμήν." Καὶ ἅμα τῇ
δοξολογίᾳ συναπῆλθε καὶ τῇ εὐχαριστίᾳ συγκατέληξε τὴν ζωήν.

75. Εὐθὺς οὖν κηδεύουσι τὴν ζωήν, ὡς ἄν τις εἴπῃ αὐτόν· ζωὴ
20 γάρ, ἐπεὶ μετέστη πρὸς τὴν ζωήν, καὶ ἔστι καὶ γέγονε· καὶ τὴν
ἱεραρχικὴν οἱ οἰκεῖοι, | ὡς ἔθος, ἀμφιεννύντες στολὴν ἐπ᾽ αὐτῇ καὶ   **29ᵛ**
τὴν σεβασμίαν αὐτῷ ἐπωμίδα τοῦ ἀδελφοθέου σεβασμίως ἐπιβάλ-
λουσιν, ἣν πρὸ χρόνων τινῶν ἐξ Ἱεροσολύμων ἀποσταλεῖσαν αὐτῷ
οὕτως ἐτίμα καὶ πανευλαβῶς ἐσέβετο ὡς αὐτὸν ἐκεῖνον Ἰάκωβον
25 τὸν μέγαν ἀπόστολον καὶ πρῶτον ἱεράρχην ἐν αὐτῇ καθορῶν·
ταύτην αὐτῷ διὰ τοῦτο καὶ συνταφῆναι κατεδέξατο. Καὶ μέντοι
κατὰ τὴν ἐκείνου μνήμην—εἰκάδι γὰρ τρίτῃ Ὀκτωβρίου—καὶ αὐτὸς
ἀπῆρε πρὸς Κύριον. Ἔνδειγμα τοῦτο σαφὲς τῆς πρὸς τὸν ἀδελφὸν
τοῦ Κυρίου οἰκειώσεώς τε αὐτοῦ καὶ μεταστάσεως. Οὕτω μὲν οὖν
30 τότε τὸ τίμιον ἐκεῖνο δέμας καὶ ἱερὸν ἱερῶς καὶ τιμίως ἐνταφιαζό-
μενον γλωσσοκόμῳ ξυλίνῳ κατακρύπτεται καὶ πρὸς τῷ ναῷ τῆς

5–6 Greg. Naz., *Or. fun. in Bas.*, cap. 79

---

1 ὁ¹ v: om. B | ὁμολογητὴς Xv: om. B   **7–114.7** φωνῆς…μέλλων deest X   **18** συν-
απῆλθε B: περιαπῆλθε v   **20** ἔστι v: ἔστη B   **21** καὶ v: δὲ καὶ B   **22** τὴν B: om. v
27 εἰκάδι… τρίτῃ v: εἰκάδα γὰρ τρίτην B

the great Fathers of the Church as the one who had striven no less than any of them on behalf of God's justice and truth.

74. Nor would it be right to overlook the way in which he died. The saint lay there breathing his last and he too, like the great one [i.e., Basil], was "sought by the heavenly choir." His voice box was already paralyzed, his life force was spent, all his limbs were lifeless, and his soul was wholly given over to dying. It was the middle of the night, and in accordance with the prescribed forms of the Church the minister cried out in a loud voice and said: "Lord, give us Your blessing." And blessed Ignatius, slowly touching his mouth in making the sign of the cross, scarcely moved his venerable lips as he inquired in a voice that was barely audible to those standing nearest to him: "Which saint's day is being celebrated today?" And they replied: "That of James, Christ's brother and your dear friend, master."[168] And he said in all humility: "That of my master. And so farewell." His final words were: "Blessed is Our God for all time, now and for always and forever and ever, amen." And he departed this life and gave up the ghost with these words from the doxology and the eucharist.

75. Straightaway then they made the final arrangements—not for his death, one might say, but for his new life. (For even though one life was over, he continues to exist, since he passed on to the next life.) His servants dressed him in the patriarchal garments, as custom requires, and over them they reverently put on the venerable stole of Christ's brother, James. It had been sent to Ignatius some years earlier from Jerusalem, and he used to hold it in as much honor and pious reverence as if he could see in it James himself, the great apostle and first hierarch. It was for this reason that he permitted the stole to be buried with him. Moreover, it was on James's name day, the twenty-third of October, that Ignatius too departed to join the Lord—clear proof of his affinity with the Lord's brother and of his departure to join him. And so it was that his venerable and holy body was now prepared for burial with holiness and reverence and enclosed in a wooden coffin. And it was placed

τοῦ Θεοῦ μεγάλης Σοφίας πρῶτον κατατεθὲν τῆς προσηκούσης
δοξολογίας τε καὶ προσκυνήσεως καταξιοῦται. | 560

76. Ἐπὶ τοσοῦτον δὲ τὸ εἰς αὐτὸν σέβας ἀνῆπται τοῖς λαοῖς
ὥστε καὶ τὰ ἐπὶ τοῦ σκίμποδος, ἐν ᾧ κατέκειτο, θράνη ἀντὶ λειψά-
5 νων διηρπάσθαι καὶ τὸ ἐπ' αὐτοῦ δὲ κείμενον πέπλον μυρίοις κατα-
διαιρούμενον τμήμασιν εἰς ἁγιασμοῦ δῶρον καταμεμερίσθαι τοῖς
πιστοῖς· μόγις οὖν τότε τὸ σῶμα τοὺς κρατοῦντας διαφυγὸν καὶ
πρὸς τῷ μεγάλῳ ναῷ τοῦ Μεγαλομάρτυρος καταντῆσαν Μηνᾶ
ἐκεῖ δὴ πάλιν κατατίθεταί τε βραχὺ καὶ τῆς ἐκ τῶν ὕμνων, ὡς θέμις,
10 τυγχάνει δεξιώσεως. Ὅπου καὶ δύο γυναῖκες ὁμοῦ πονηροῖς πνεύ-
μασιν ὀχλούμεναι καὶ δεινῶς ἀναβρασσόμεναι, ὡς μόνον ἔψαυσαν
τῇ τοῦ ἁγίου σορῷ, ἐνώπιον παντὸς τοῦ λαοῦ κατέστησαν ὑγιεῖς
ἀναντιρρήτου τυχοῦσαι τῆς ἰάσεως καὶ μεγάλη φωνῇ δοξολογοῦ-
σαι τὸν Θεόν. Ἐντεῦθεν τῶν περὶ αὐτὸν ἐν πλοίῳ καταθεμένων τὸν
15 πολύτιμον θησαυρὸν τῆς θαλάσσης μὲν τότε κορυφουμένης, ἐν
ἀνέμῳ δὲ νότῳ βιαίῳ τῶν κυμάτων εἰς ὕψος αἰρομένων καὶ ἀπρόσ-
ιτον ὑποδεικνύντων τὸν πλοῦν, ὡς μόνον ἡ θεία σορὸς ἐκείνη
ἐπιβέβηκε τῆς νηός, ἣν ὁρᾶν παραυτὰ γινομένην Δεσποτικὴν θαυματουργίαν. Ἀοράτως γὰρ ὑπὸ τοῦ μεγάλου ἀρχιερέως τῆς καταιγί-
20 δος ἐπιτιμωμένης ἵστατο μὲν εἰς αὔραν ἡ θάλασσα, τῶν κυμάτων δὲ
κατασιγαζομένων οἱ τοῦ ἁγίου θεραπευταὶ ἐν γαλήνῃ διαπεραιού-
μενοι καὶ δοξάζοντες καὶ πρὸς τῷ ἱερῷ καὶ παγκάλῳ τοῦ ἀρχιστρα-
τήγου | ναῷ τὸν πιστότατον οἰκοδόμον ἐκείνου καὶ λάτριν ἀγαγόν-   30
τες πρὸς τοῖς δεξιοῖς σεβασμίως ἐν μαρμαρίνῃ κατατιθέασι σορῷ,
25 νόσων τε παντοδαπῶν ἰατήριον καὶ πνευμάτων πονηρῶν ἐλατή-
ριον καί, συνόλως εἰπεῖν, παντοίων παθῶν ψυχῆς τε καὶ σώματος
τοῖς ἐγγίζουσιν ἀλεξητήριον.

77. Οὕτως ὁ ἱερὸς τοῦ Θεοῦ ἄνθρωπος διὰ πολλῶν θλίψεων
ἐν γῇ πειρασθεὶς καὶ ὡς χρυσὸς ἐν χωνευτηρίῳ δοκιμασθεὶς καὶ
30 ἄξιος οὕτως ἀποδειχθεὶς τοῦ Θεοῦ τῆς οὐρανίας μακαριότητος καὶ
τῆς ἐν ὑψηλοῖς τῶν ἁγίων κατηξιώθη τιμῆς. Ἐματαιώθη δὲ ἡ σκοτία

11–12 cf. Luc. 7.14–15   **19–21** cf. Matth. 8.26; Marc. 4.39   **29** Sap. 3.6; cf. 1 Petr. 1.7
31–110.1 cf. Ioann. 1.5

---

2 τε v: om. B   **3** ἐπὶ B: ἐπεὶ v   **4** τὰ…θράνη v: τὰς…νάνους B   **26** συνόλως B:
συντόμως v   **30** οὕτως v: ὄντως B | οὐρανίας B: οὐρανίου v   **31** ὑψηλοῖς v: ὑψιλῆς B

first of all in God's church of Saint Sophia, where it was honored with fitting praise and veneration.

76. The adoration for him excited among the people was so great that even the wooden framework of the funeral bier on which he was lying had pieces broken off for relics and the sheet that was placed over him was torn into a thousand pieces, which were divided up among the faithful as consecrated offerings. And so it was with some difficulty that his body then escaped the hands of those who were laying hold of it and passed on to the great church of the mighty martyr Menas, where it was once again set down for a little while and, in accordance with established custom, was welcomed with songs of praise.[169] It was there too that two women, both possessed by evil spirits and frothing horribly at the mouth, when they did no more than touch the saint's coffin, they were made whole in the presence of all the people. They were undeniably cured and they gave glory to God with loud voices. Next, Ignatius's attendants put their much-revered treasure on board ship, and though the sea was heaving at the time, its waves whipped high by a violent south wind which made sailing impossible, nevertheless as soon as that holy coffin came aboard the ship, then straightaway it was possible to see a miracle of the Lord being worked. For the squall was invisibly rebuked by the great patriarch, and as a result the sea stood still, ruffled only by a light breeze, the waves were calmed, and the saint's attendants sailed across on a tranquil sea and praised the Lord. And they brought to the holy and beautiful church of Saint Michael, leader of the heavenly host, its architect and most faithful servant and they buried him there reverently on the right-hand side of the church in a marble coffin—to be a cure for all kinds of ills, to drive away evil spirits, and in general to provide protection against every kind of suffering of body and of soul for those who approached him.[170]

77. Thus was the holy man of God put to the test on earth by many afflictions, and once he had been proven like gold in a furnace and shown by this means to be worthy of God, he was deemed worthy of heavenly bliss and of a place of honor in the lofty realms of the saints. And so darkness, having pursued the light

διώξασα μὲν τὸ φῶς, οὐ καταλαβοῦσα δέ. Τοσούτῳ δὲ μᾶλλον εὐηργέτησεν, ὅσῳ πλέον ᾠήθη λυπεῖν· διώκουσα γὰρ ἵνα πατήσῃ καὶ κατακαυχήσηται ἑαυτῆς μὲν τὸ φεῦγον ἐμάκρυνε, προσεγγίσαι δὲ παρεσκεύαζε καὶ μὴ βουλομένη τῷ ἀγαθῷ τοσοῦτον, ὅσον
5 ἑαυτὴν τῷ κακῷ διὰ τῆς πολυμηχάνου στραγγαλιᾶς προσῳκειώσατο.

78. Δέκα μὲν οὖν ἔτη τὸ δεύτερον, τὰ πάντα δὲ τριάκοντα καὶ μικρόν τι πρὸς ὁ μέγας ἀρχιερατεύσας Ἰγνάτιος, ὀγδοηκοστὸν δὲ ἤδη γεγονὼς ἔτος ἐν εἰρήνῃ πρὸς τὸν Ἀρχιερέα τὸν μέγαν ἀνελή-
10 φθη Χριστόν.

79. Ὅσοις μὲν οὖν καὶ ἡλίκοις αὐτὸν τεραστίοις ὁ ἐν αὐτῷ δοξαζόμενος ἐδόξασε Κύριος καὶ ἔτι δὲ δοξάζων οὐ διαλιμπάνει ἱστορίας ἔργον καὶ οὐ τοῦ παρόντος ἂν εἴη διηγεῖσθαι καιροῦ. Ὀλίγα δὲ ἐκ πολλῶν καὶ ὅσα τὴν αὐτοῦ μὲν πίστιν, τὴν τοῦ Θεοῦ δὲ
15 ἐν αὐτῷ χάριν μετρίως ὑποδείκνυσιν ἐπιτόμως ὑπομνήσαντες τὰ κατὰ μέρος ὡς ἀριθμὸν ὑπερβαίνοντα παρήσομεν.

80. Παῖς γὰρ ὡς ὀκτὼ ἢ καὶ ἐννέα καθεστὼς χρόνων | πνεύ- 561 ματι ἀσθενείας πληγεὶς καὶ ἀθρόως παρεθεὶς ὅλος οὐ μόνον ἄναυδος πάντη καὶ ἀνήκοος, ἀλλὰ δὴ καὶ ἀκίνητος ὁλοτελῶς γεγονὼς
20 καὶ ὑπὸ τῶν ἰδίων αὐτοῦ βασταζόμενος τῷ κοινῷ τῶν πιστῶν ἰατρείῳ τῷ ἱερῷ τοῦ θεοφόρου πατρὸς προσρίπτεται τάφῳ. Δι᾽ ἡμερῶν δὲ τεσσάρων τῆς τοῦ ἁγίου καταξιωθεὶς ἐπισκέψεως ἐξαπίνης ἰδίοις ἐξανέστη ποσὶ καὶ δι᾽ ἑαυτοῦ τὴν τοῦ ναοῦ πύλην ἀνοίξας καὶ ὑγιὴς ὅλος ἐξελθὼν ἔξω ἐλάλει τοῖς παροῦσι καὶ ἤκουεν εὐ-
25 λογῶν τὸν Θεὸν καὶ τὰ θαυμάσια ἀναγγέλλων τοῦ ἁγίου.

81. Ἄλλος πάλιν (ἐξ ἐπηρείας, οἶμαι, καὶ τοῦτο τοῦ πονηροῦ) ἐπιληψίας ἑαλωκὼς πάθει | δεινῶς ἐξανέστραπτο μὲν τὸ στόμα, 30ᵛ παρήρητο δὲ καὶ τοῦ κατὰ φύσιν φθέγματος τὴν φωνήν, ὡς ἐλεεινόν τε αὐτὸν καὶ δυσέντευκτον θέαμα προκεῖσθαι. Οὗτος ἐπειδὴ
30 ἀδιστάκτῳ πίστει ἐπεκαλεῖτο τὸν ἅγιον, ὁρᾷ μὲν αὐτὸν ὄναρ ὥσπερ

---

9 cf. Hebr. 4.14   17–18 cf. Luc. 13.11

---

2 εὐηργέτησεν v: εὐεργέτησεν B   4 παρεσκεύαζε B: παρεσκεύασε v   9–10 ἀνελήφθη v: ἀνελείφθη B   17 α´ add. mg. B   26 β´ add. mg. B | πάλιν B: πλὴν v   29 ἐπειδὴ B: ἐπεὶ v

without catching him, was set at naught, and however much it thought it was causing him distress, by so much the more was it bringing him benefit. For by pursuing him in order to trample upon and exult over him, it was distancing the fugitive from itself, and as much as it linked itself with what is evil by a tightly drawn and subtly worked knot, in an equal amount did it make him approach what is good, even though that was not at all its wish.[171]

78. And so for ten years the second time around, and in all for a little more than thirty years was great Ignatius patriarch, and when he was eighty years old he was taken up peacefully into the hands of Christ, the great High Priest above.

79. Well now, to relate all the many great portents with which the Lord, Himself honored in Ignatius, paid the latter honor (and has not ceased paying him still further honor) would be the task for a history and not for the present occasion. And so we shall pass over the details of all the individual cases, since they are infinite in number, and make brief mention of only a few of them—cases which give an adequate indication of his faith and of the grace of God inherent in him.[172]

80. For instance, there was a boy of about eight or nine who was smitten by a spirit of infirmity and was suddenly left completely paralyzed.[173] Not only did he lose altogether his powers of speech and hearing, but he was also completely unable to move. And he was carried along by his own people and deposited beside the sacred tomb (the faithful's common place of treatment) of holy father Ignatius, inspired of God. After four days he was deemed worthy of the saint's visitation and he suddenly stood up, opened the door of the church by himself, and came out completely cured. He was able to speak to those who were there and to hear them, and he praised God and proclaimed the miracles of the saint.

81. Then again there was another who was overtaken by epilepsy—and this too, I think, as a result of the Devil's ill treatment. His mouth was terribly distorted and he was even deprived of the natural sound of his voice, which resulted in his appearance being both pitiable and physically repulsive. And when this man appealed to the saint with unwavering faith, he had a

112

τινὰ κλεῖδα κατέχοντα τῇ χειρὶ καὶ ταύτην τῷ στόματι αὐτοῦ
ἐπεμβαλόντα καὶ ὡς δῆθεν θύραν ἀνοίγοντα συστρέψαι καὶ πρὸς
αὐτὸν εἰπεῖν· "Εἰ οἶδας, τίς εἰμι ἐγώ;" Τὸν δὲ μὴ εἰδέναι φάμενον
ἀκοῦσαι πρὸς αὐτοῦ ὡς αὐτὸς εἴη Ἰγνάτιος ὁ πατριάρχης· "Καὶ
5 ἰδού" φησὶν "ἀπὸ τοῦ νῦν καθέστηκας ὑγιής." Ἔξυπνον δὲ τοῦτον
γενόμενον ὑγιῆ παντελῶς ἑαυτὸν εὑρεῖν ὡς μηδεπώποτε ἴχνος
τοιαύτης ἑωρακότα κακώσεως.

82. Ἄλλος πάλιν νόσῳ κοιλιακῇ περιπεσὼν καὶ πρὸς ταῖς
ἐσχάταις ἠγγικὼς δι᾽ αὐτὴν ὥραις τῆς μὲν ἀπὸ τῶν ἰατρῶν βοηθείας
10 λοιπὸν ἀπέγνω, τὸν ἅγιον δὲ πόρρωθεν ἐξ ὁλοκλήρου πίστεως
ἀνακαλούμενος ὁρᾷ μὲν τοῦτον ὄναρ αὐτῷ παρεστῶτα καὶ εὐθυ-
μεῖν ἐπαγγελλόμενον. Αὐτίκα δὲ τῆς ῥύσεως ἀναξηρανθείσης τῆς
γαστρὸς εἰς τροφῆς ἔφεσιν ὁ κάμνων καὶ τελείαν ὑγείαν ἀποκαθ-
ίσταται.

15 83. Πάλιν γυνή τις ἀνδρὶ νομίμως συνοικοῦσα καὶ παίδων
μήτηρ γεγονυῖα τριῶν ξηρὰν πάντη καὶ ἄνικμον προέβαλλε τὴν
θηλήν, ὥστε τὰ ὑπ᾽ αὐτῆς τικτόμενα βρέφη παραυτὰ ξέναις ἐκδί-
δοσθαι τιθηνεῖσθαι τροφοῖς, ἕως ἐπὶ νοῦν ἦλθε τοῖς οἰκείοις αὐτῆς
τῷ ἁγίῳ προσδραμεῖν. Καὶ δὴ τῶν ἁγίων αὐτοῦ τριχῶν ἀπομυρισ-
20 θεισῶν καὶ τῇ ἀρτιτόκῳ πιεῖν δεδωρημένων ἐπὶ τοσοῦτον εὐθὺς
γαλοῦχος ἀπεφάνθη ὡς καὶ πολὺ πλέον τῆς χρείας τὸ γάλα τῶν
μαζῶν καταρρεῖν. Καὶ τοῦτο οὐκ εἰς μίαν μόνην φασὶ γυναῖκα γεγο-
νέναι, ἀλλὰ καὶ εἰς ἑτέραν πάλιν τῷ αὐτῷ κάμνουσαν ἀρρωστήματι
τῆς φύσεως διὰ τῆς ὁμοίας τῶν ἁγίων τριχῶν ἀπομυρίσεως τῆς
25 ὁμοίας ἰάσεως τυχεῖν.

84. Ἄλλη δὲ πάλιν γυνὴ τῶν εὐγενῶν καὶ περιφανῶν καὶ αὐτὴ
νομίμως ἀνδρὶ ἐπιδόξῳ συνοικοῦσα ἐν ἔτεσι πλείοσι στεῖρα καὶ
ἄπαις ἐγνωρίζετο. Τοῦ ἀνδρὸς δὲ πίστει τῷ τάφῳ προσπεπτωκότος
τοῦ ἁγίου καὶ ἔλαιον ἅγιον ἐκεῖθεν εἰληφότος τῇ γυναικὶ κἀκείνης
30 ἐκ πίστεως ἀλειψαμένης καὶ τὴν τοῦ μεγάλου ἀρχιερέως εὐχὴν

---

1 τινὰ B: τὴν v   4 ὁ B: om. V   6 μηδεπώποτε B: μηδέποτε v   8 γ´ add. mg. B   15 δ´
add. mg. B   16 προέβαλλε v: προέβαλε B   26 ε´ add. mg. B

dream in which he saw Ignatius holding a key in his hand. And the latter inserted this key into his mouth and turned it, as if indeed he were opening a door, and said to him: "Do you know who I am?" And when the man replied that he did not know him, he was told that it was Ignatius himself, the patriarch. "Behold," said the latter, "from this moment on you are cured." And when the man awoke, he found that he was completely cured, just as if he had never seen any trace of such an affliction.

82. In another case a man who had fallen victim to dysentery and had been brought close to death by it finally despaired of receiving help from the doctors and appealed to the saint from afar in complete faith. And he had a dream in which he saw Ignatius standing beside him and bidding him be of good cheer. And straightaway the outpouring from his bowels dried up and the sick man regained his appetite for food and was restored to full health.

83. Then again there was a woman who was lawfully wedded to a man and mother of three children but always found when she offered her breasts that they were dry and without milk. As a result, the babies she produced had to be handed over straightaway to outside nurses to be suckled, until one day it occurred to her relatives to approach Ignatius. And having procured liquid made holy by contact with the saint's hair,[174] it was given to the woman to drink just after she had given birth. Then indeed she was straight-away shown to have so much milk that her breasts flowed with much more than she actually needed. And they say that this happened not just to one woman but to another also who was suffering from the same affliction of nature and who obtained a similar cure by means of liquid likewise sanctified by the saint's hair.

84. In another case a woman of high and noble birth, and she too lawfully married to a distinguished husband, was for several years recognized to be barren and childless. Her husband, however, prostrated himself in faith at the saint's tomb and from there took holy oil to his wife. And when she had in faith anointed herself with the oil and called upon the intercession of the great patriarch,

114

ἐπικαλεσαμένης παραυτίκα τῶν τῆς στειρώσεως ἀπελύθη δεσμῶν
καὶ λοιπὸν τέκνων πλειόνων ἀναδείκνυται μήτηρ.

85. Ἀλλ' οὐ μόνον τοῖς τῷ ἱερῷ τάφῳ πελάζουσιν αἱ θαυματ-
ουργίαι τοῦ ἱεράρχου πηγάζουσιν, ἀλλ' ἤδη | καὶ τοῖς ἐπ' ἀλλοδα- 564
5 πῆς γῆς καὶ τὰ ἄκρα τῆς οἰκουμένης οἰκοῦσιν ἐπικαλουμένοις ὁ
θεόληπτος πατὴρ ἐπιφαίνεται. Καὶ τούτου μάρτυς ἡμῖν ἀψευδὴς ὁ
τῆς Σικελίας στρατηγὸς φρικτοῖς | ὅρκοις πληροφορῶν, ὡς μέλλων 31
εἰς πόλεμον συμβαλεῖν ἐν Σικελίᾳ τοῖς Ἀγαρηνοῖς καὶ ἀγῶνι πολλῷ
συνεχόμενος καὶ τὸν μέγαν Ἰγνάτιον εἰς συμμαχίαν θερμῶς ἐπικα-
10 λούμενος. "Εἶδον" φησὶν "αὐτὸν ὀφθαλμοφανῶς ἐπὶ τοῦ ἀέρος
ὥσπερ ἐφ' ἵππου λευκοῦ καθήμενον καὶ παρεγγυώμενον πρὸς τοῖς
δεξιοῖς μέρεσιν ὁδηγεῖν τὸν στρατὸν καὶ τὴν δόξαν εὐθὺς καθορᾶν
τοῦ Θεοῦ." Ὃ καὶ πεποιηκότα τὸν στρατοπεδάρχην (Μουσιλίκης δὲ
ὄνομα τῷ ἀνδρί) κατακράτος τοὺς ὑπεναντίους ἑλεῖν.

15 86. Πῶς δὲ τὸ τῆς γυναικὸς ἐκείνης θαυμάσιον πάθος καὶ τὴν
θαυμασιωτέραν ἐπ' αὐτῇ τοῦ ἁγίου παραδοξοποιΐαν σιωπήσαιμεν;
Ἥτις ἄρρεν ἐγκυμονοῦσα καὶ ὠδίνουσα ἤδη πρὸς τὸ τεκεῖν, ἐπειδὴ
ἐπὶ πόδας τὸ βρέφος κατηνέχθη, οὔτ' αὐτὸ προελθεῖν ἔτι δυνατὸν
ἦν καὶ τῇ τικτούσῃ ὀξυτάτας καὶ ἀνυποίστους τὰς ἀλγηδόνας
20 προσετίθη. Καὶ ἐπεὶ εἰς ἀμηχανίαν περιέστη τὸ πρᾶγμα, ἵνα μὴ καὶ ἡ
γυνὴ συναπόληται, παρῆσαν μὲν ἰατροὶ χειρουργεῖν τὸ ἔμβρυον καὶ
ἐξέλκειν τεμνόμενον μεληδόν, προνοίᾳ δὲ θειοτέρᾳ τοῦ καθ' ἡμᾶς
ὑπεμνήσθησαν μεγάλου θαυματουργοῦ. Καί τις ἐκ τῶν παρόντων
λείψανον ἔχων τοῦ πέπλου βραχύτατον τοῦ κατὰ τὴν ἡμέραν τῆς
25 αὐτοῦ κηδείας ἐκ πίστεως καταμεμερισμένου τοῖς λαοῖς καὶ τοῦτο
προαγαγὼν καὶ τὸν ἅγιον ἐπικαλεσάμενος, ἐπειδὴ μόνον τῇ ὀσφύϊ
περιῆψε τῆς γυναικός, περιέστραπται μὲν τὸ βρέφος εὐθὺς ἐπὶ
κεφαλήν, ἀκινδύνως δὲ λοιπὸν γεννηθὲν Ἰγνάτιος πρὸς τῶν γεννη-
τόρων κατωνόμασται εἰς ὑπόμνησιν ἥκων διὰ τοῦ ὀνόματος τῆς ἐπ'
30 αὐτῷ γενομένης διὰ τοῦ πατριάρχου θαυματοποιΐας. Τοῦτο τί τῶν
ἀποστολικῶν τεράτων ἀπολείπεται; Τοῦτο τί τῆς ἐν Πέτρῳ καὶ
Παύλῳ δυνάμεως ἐνδεῖ; Ἡ γὰρ ἐν ἐκείνοις ἐνεργοῦσα χάρις τοῦ

31–32 cf. Acta 5.12; 15–16 et cett.

4 πηγάζουσιν v: προσπελάζουσιν Β   15–116.7 πῶς…πιστῶν deest Χ   20 περιέστη v:
περίεστι Β   21 συναπόληται v: συναπόλλυται Β | χειρουργεῖν τὸ v: χειρ. μὲν τὸ Β

she was immediately freed from the bonds of infertility and showed herself thereafter to be the mother of several children.

85. But it is not only for the benefit of those who approach Ignatius's sacred tomb that the miracles gush forth. Indeed, the holy father, inspired of God, appears even to men in foreign lands and to those inhabiting the ends of the earth when they call upon him. And we have as an impeccable witness of this fact the governor of Sicily, who gave assurances of it with awful-sounding oaths. It was when he was on the point of engaging in a war in Sicily with the Hagarenes, and being troubled by great anxiety, he made an ardent appeal to great Ignatius for assistance. "I saw him in full view in the air," he said. "He was sitting on a white horse and exhorted me to lead my force over to the right flank and straightaway see the glory of God." And when the commander, whose name was Musilices,[175] had done this, he said that he took the enemy by storm.

86. And how could we pass over in silence the marvelous experience of that other woman and the even more marvelous miracle worked by the saint in her case? She was pregnant with a male child, and when she was in the throes of childbirth, the baby offered itself feet first, thus making it impossible for the birth to proceed further as well as inflicting most sharp and intolerable pains upon the laboring mother. And when the situation became desperate, in order to prevent the woman too from perishing with her child, doctors attended her to operate on the baby and draw it out by cutting off its limbs.[176] However, by the agency of a more divinely inspired Providence they called to mind our great worker of miracles. And one of those present had a tiny remnant of the sheet which had been distributed in faith to the people on the day of his funeral. Producing this, he appealed to the saint, and just as soon as he put it upon the woman's loins, the baby was turned around onto its head and was born then without danger to the mother. And the parents called the child Ignatius, so that the name would remind them of the miracle worked upon him by the patriarch. In what respect does this fall short of the wonders performed by the apostles? How is it inferior to the mighty works done in the name of Peter and Paul? For the same grace of the Holy Spirit

116

Πνεύματος, ὡς καὶ διὰ τῶν σουδαρίων καὶ σιμικινθίων ἐκείνων τὰ θαυμασιώτατα δρᾶν, αὕτη καὶ νῦν διὰ τοῦ ἀποστολικοῦ τούτου ἀνδρὸς καὶ νέου ὡς ἀληθῶς θεοφόρου καὶ διὰ τῶν ἐπὶ τοῦ σκίμπο- δος ἱματίων τῶν τῷ ἱερῷ λειψάνῳ ἐγγισάντων καὶ διὰ τῶν σιδηρῶν 5 κλοιῶν οἷς τοὺς ἱεροὺς πόδας ἄνδρες κατέκλεισαν ἀσεβεῖς τὰ ὅμοια πιστεύεται δρᾶν εἰς τὴν | τοῦ Θεοῦ δόξαν καὶ σωτηρίαν τῶν 31ᵛ πιστῶν.

87. Ἐῶ λέγειν ὅσους νεφρικῷ τετρυχωμένους νοσήματι καὶ ἐκτενῶς ἐπικαλεσαμένους ἐθεράπευσεν· ὅσους λεπροὺς καὶ ἐλε- 10 φαντιῶντας ἐκαθάρισε καὶ τυφλοὺς ἐφώτισε καὶ παρειμένους ἀνώρθωσε καὶ ξηρὰς χεῖρας καὶ πόδας ἔχοντας ἰάσατο. Ἀφίημι καὶ ὅσους ὑπὸ πυρετοῦ καὶ ῥίγους τρυχομένους καὶ ὅσους ὑπὸ πνευμά- των πονηρῶν ἐταζομένους ἄχρι καὶ τήμερον ἰᾶται καὶ διὰ τῆς τιμίας ὡς ἐπίπαν ἁλύσεως πᾶσαν, ὡς εἰπεῖν, νόσον καὶ πᾶσαν μαλα- 15 κίαν ἀποκαθαίρων τῶν ἐν ἀληθείᾳ καὶ πίστει προσφευγόντων τῇ ἁγίᾳ θεραπεύει σορῷ. Οὐδὲ γὰρ εἰ βουληθείημεν ταῦτα τῷ λόγῳ δυνατὸν ἐξαριθμεῖσθαι. Ἑνὸς δὲ ἔτι μνημονεύσαντες τῶν θαυμα- σίων ὀλίγα τῶν μετὰ τὴν τοῦ ἁγίου κοίμησιν ἱστορουμένων ἔτι τῷ λόγῳ | συνάψωμεν. Πῶς γὰρ τοῦ Λυδοῦ σακελλαρίου σιωπῇ τὸ πρᾶγμα 565 20 παραπέμψομεν; ὃς ὑποβολῇ Φωτίου τοῦ ἀναιδοῦς εἰς τὸ μοναστή- ριον εἰσελθὼν ὥστε πάντας τοὺς τῷ ἁγίῳ τάφῳ προσλιπαροῦντας ἀσθενεῖς μετὰ μαστίγων ἐξῶσαι καὶ ὕβρεων· καὶ τοῦτο δεδρακὼς προστίθησι κακὸν τῷ κακῷ καὶ προστάσσει πλησιαίτατα τοῦ ἱεροῦ τάφου κατορύσσειν καὶ εἰς βάθος ἀνασκάπτειν τὴν γῆν, πρόφασιν 25 μὲν ὡς ἐν αὐτῷ τῷ τόπῳ πρῴην ὑπὸ τοῦ πατριάρχου χρυσίου κατα- κρυβέντος πολλοῦ, τὸ δ᾽ ἀληθὲς ὡς ἂν ἀτιμίαν τῷ τιμίῳ λειψάνῳ προστρίψαιτο. Οὕτως αὐτῷ ὁ φθόνος πάντη κατακεκυριευκὼς τῆς μανιώδους ψυχῆς οὐδὲ μετὰ τὸν θάνατον ἠρεμεῖν εἴα. Ἅμα δὲ τῷ λόγῳ τοῦ ἀθεμίτου ἐκείνου προστάγματος καὶ θελήματος τὸν ἀσεβῆ 30 μετῆλθεν ὀργή, ἐνταῦθα μόνον οὐκ ἀνασχομένης ἐπ᾽ αὐτῷ τῆς τοῦ Θεοῦ μακροθυμίας, ἀλλ᾽ ὀξυτάτην ἐνδίκως ὑπενεγκούσης τὴν

1 Acta 19.11–12   14–15 cf. Matth. 4.23; 9.35; 10.1

1 τὰ B: om. v   3 καὶ¹ B: om. v   8 νεφρικῷ B: νεφριτικῷ v | τετρυχωμένους v: τετρυχομένους B   12 ὅσους¹ Xv: τοὺς B   14 ὡς ἐπίπαν B: om. Xv   19 συνάψωμεν B: συνάψομεν v   20 παραπέμψομεν v: παραπέμψαιμεν v   21 εἰσελθὼν Xv: ἐξελθὼν B   27 αὐτῷ v: αὐτὸν B

which operated in them to the extent that the most miraculous acts were performed even by means of their handkerchiefs and aprons —this same grace is now also believed to be performing similar acts, for the glory of God and salvation of the faithful, through the agency of Ignatius, a man worthy of the apostles, in truth a new inspired Father,[177] and by means of the clothing which was next to his holy remains on the bier and the iron fetters in which impious men had confined his holy feet.

87. I leave out of my account all the many people wasted by kidney disease whom he healed when they earnestly invoked him; all those suffering from leprosy and elephantiasis whom he cleansed; all the blind to whom he restored sight; all the paralyzed whom he restored to health; and all those with withered hands and feet whom he cured. I likewise omit all those consumed by fever or shivering fits and all those afflicted by evil spirits whom he cured— and continues to cure right up to the present day, purging of virtually every disease and sickness and healing (for the most part by his venerable fetters) those who seek refuge in true faith at his holy tomb. For it would be impossible to count them all, even if we wanted to. But let me make mention of one further miracle and then add to the account just a few of all the occurrences recorded after the saint's death. For how can we pass over in silence the case of the Lydian *sacellarius*? At the instigation of that shameless Photius he entered Ignatius's monastery and drove out with whips and violent blows all the sick who were suppliants at the saint's tomb. And when he had done this, he piled evil upon evil by giving orders to excavate very close to the holy tomb and to dig down deep into the ground, on the pretext that a large amount of gold had earlier been buried in that very spot by the patriarch, but in reality so that he might inflict indignity upon the venerable remains.[178] So completely had jealousy gained mastery over his frenzied soul that he did not allow Ignatius to rest even after his death. But at the same time as that wicked order was spoken, the impious man was visited by heaven-sent anger and on this one occasion the patience of God did not suffer his action to go unpunished, but with justice brought down upon him the sharpest of cutting blows. Immedi-

118

τομήν. Εὐθὺς | οὖν μεγάλα βοῶν ὁ σοβαρὸς οἷα σφαγιαζόμενος 32
ἄνωθέν τε καὶ κάτωθεν τῷ οἰκείῳ αἵματι κρουνηδὸν περιρραινόμενος καὶ φοράδην οἴκαδε ἀναγόμενος ἄφωνος ἐν ἡμέραις τέσσαρσιν
ἀπέψυξε τιμωρούμενος.

5   88. Τοιαῦτα τοῦ ἡμετέρου πατρὸς τὰ διηγήματα, τοιαῦτα τοῦ
καλοῦ ποιμένος τὰ προτερήματα. Οὕτως ὁ μακαριώτατος καὶ ζῶν
ἐπὶ γῆς ἐννομώτατός τε ἦν καὶ χριστοφιλέστατος πάντα λέγων καὶ
πράττων εἰς δόξαν Θεοῦ καὶ τῆς Ἐκκλησίας οἰκοδομήν· καὶ πρὸς
Θεὸν μεταστὰς ὠφελιμώτατος καὶ σωτήριος ὡς ἀμέσως ἐντυγχά-
10 νων ὑπὲρ ἡμῶν τῷ Θεῷ.

         89. Τί δὲ ὁ λεγόμενος Φώτιος; ἆρα τὴν ἐπ' αὐτῷ γενομένην
κρίσιν ὡς ἔνδικον καταδεξάμενος τῶν πολυπλόκων ἀπέσχετο
διαβουλίων; ἢ ὑπὸ τὴν κραταιὰν τοῦ Θεοῦ χεῖρα τατεινωθεὶς τῆς
θείας ἑαυτὸν ῥοπῆς ἐξῆψε λοιπόν; ἢ τέλεον μὲν τῆς αὐτοῦ κακομη-
15 χανίας οὐκ ἐξέστη, μετριώτερος δὲ ἑαυτοῦ καὶ ἐπιεικέστερος διὰ
τῆς κατακρίσεως κατέστη; Οὐδαμῶς. Πάντα δὲ τὸν δεκαετῆ
χρόνον τῆς ὑπερορίας μυρίας κατὰ τοῦ ἁγίου κακονοίας κινῶν,
ἐπειδὴ πανταχόθεν ἀνάλωτον αὐτὸν ἑώρα καὶ ἄληπτον, τοῦ βασιλέως ἐφ' ἑαυτὸν τὴν εὔνοιαν ἐπισπᾶσθαι μηχανᾶται· καὶ πᾶσαν μὲν
20 βουλήν, πᾶσαν δὲ τριβὴν λογισμῶν πρὸς τοῦτο κινῶν εὗρεν ὁδὸν
λοιπὸν δι' ἧς τῆς ἁπλότητος ἤτοι κουφότητος κατωρχήσατο τῆς
βασιλικῆς. Καὶ σκοπεῖτε ὡς πιθανὴν καὶ τί γὰρ ἢ τῆς ἐκείνου ψυχῆς
ἀξίαν· τῶν ὀνομάτων γὰρ ἕκαστον περισκεψάμενος (αὐτοῦ τε,
φημί, Βασιλείου τοῦ βασιλέως Εὐδοκίας τε τῆς αὐτοῦ γαμετῆς καὶ
25 τῶν παίδων Κωνσταντίνου Λέοντος Ἀλεξάνδρου καὶ Στεφάνου), ἐξ
ἑκάστου δὲ τὸ πρῶτον γράμμα λαβὼν καὶ συντιθεὶς ἐντεῦθεν | 32ᵛ
λαμβάνει τῆς ἀπάτης τὴν ἀφορμήν. Ἱστορίαν γὰρ ἤτοι γενεαλογίαν
τὴν μήτ' οὖσαν μήτ' οὖν ποτε γενομένην ἀναπλάσας Τηριδάτην
μὲν ἐκεῖνον τὸν μέγαν τῶν Ἀρμενίων βασιλέα, τὸν ἐπὶ τοῦ ἱερομάρ-
30 τυρος λέγω Γρηγορίου, προπάτορα τίθεται τῷ λόγῳ, ἐξ ἐκείνου δὲ
τὴν γενεαλογίαν ὀνόμασιν οἷς ἠθέλησεν ἐπισυνείρων καὶ ἄλλους ἐξ
ἄλλων τῇ πλασματώδει κατάγων ἱστορίᾳ, ἡνίκα δὴ πρὸς τὸν

5-6 Ioann. 10.11; 14 7-8 cf. 1 Cor. 10.31 et cett. 8 cf. 1 Cor. 14.12 9-10 Rom. 8.34;
Hebr. 7.25 13 1 Petr. 5.6

---

14 ἑαυτὸν v: ἑαυτοῦ B 19 ἐπισπᾶσθαι B: ἐπισπάσασθαι Xv 22 τί…ἢ E: τί γὰρ εἰ B:
om. v 25 παίδων Xv: παιδίων B 29 τῶν B: om. v

ately the arrogant one let out a loud cry, like a victim at the slaughter, as he spattered himself all over with his own gushing blood. And he was carried off home where, unable to utter a sound, he died within four days and thus received his punishment.

88. Such is the story of our father Ignatius and such the success of that good shepherd. So very righteous and loving of Christ was the most blessed patriarch even when he was alive on earth, saying and doing all things for the glory of God and edification of the Church, and having gone to join God he has become most beneficial and salutary, since he intercedes with Him on our behalf.

89. And what of the one called Photius? Did he accept the judgment made against him as legitimate and desist from his crafty plotting? Was he so humbled beneath the mighty hand of God that he surrendered thereafter to His overriding will? Or did he, without abandoning completely his evil scheming, yet become more humble and modest than he was before as a result of the condemnation? Not at all! In fact for the whole ten-year period of his banishment he formed countless malicious intentions against holy Ignatius, and when he saw that the latter was completely unassailable and irreproachable, he contrived to win for himself the emperor's favor. To this end he turned all his deliberation and all the attention of his thoughts, until finally he found a way to charm the emperor's naivety—or his empty-headedness, I should say. And just look how plausible it was and how completely worthy of Photius's genius. For he examined each of their names—those of the emperor Basil himself, I mean, and of Eudokia, his wife, and of their children, Constantinus, Leo, Alexander and Stephanus—and taking the first letter of each and putting them together, he drew from it the starting point of his deception.[179] He made up a history, or rather a pedigree, which did not exist and never had existed, and by his account reckoned the first of the line to be that famous Tiridates, the great king of Armenia, who lived in the time of Saint Gregory the martyr.[180] After Tiridates he strung together the family tree in arbitrary fashion, making up different ancestors for different

120

πατέρα κατῆλθε Βασιλείου, τοῦτον ἔγραψεν ὡς ἄνδρα γεννήσει
τοιοῦτον οἷος αὐτὸς Βασίλειος | ἦν· τὸ δὲ ὄνομα εἶναι Βεκλᾶς· ὃν 568
εὐτυχέστατα καὶ πολυχρονιώτατα τῶν ἐξ αἰῶνος βεβασιλευκότων
βασιλεύσοντα προφητεύει. Μυρίοις δὲ ψεύδεσιν, οἷς ᾔδει γάννυ-
5 σθαι τοῦτον ἀκούοντα, τὸ σύγγραμμα καταρτισάμενος ἐπὶ παλαιο-
τάτων μὲν τοῦτο χαρτίων γράμμασιν Ἀλεξανδρίνοις τὴν ἀρχαϊκὴν
ὅτι μάλιστα χειροθεσίαν μιμησάμενος γράφει· ἀμφιέννυσι δὲ καὶ
πτύχαις παλαιοτάταις ἐκ παλαιοτάτου βιβλίου ἀφαιρούμενος κἀν-
τεῦθεν τῇ μεγάλῃ τοῦτο τοῦ παλατίου ἀποτίθεται βιβλιοθήκῃ.
10   90. Ὁ κατὰ ταῦτα δὲ πιστῶς ὑπηρετούμενος καὶ τὴν ἀπάτην
αὐτῷ τοῦ δράματος συγκατασκευαζόμενος Θεοφάνης ἐκεῖνος ἦν,
κληρικὸς μὲν τότε βασιλικὸς καὶ δόξαν σοφίας ἱκανῶς ἔχειν παρὰ
τῷ βασιλεῖ νομιζόμενος, ὕστερον δὲ καὶ Καισαρείας Καππαδοκίας
ἐπίσκοπος γεγονὼς ἆθλον δηλαδὴ τοῦτο τῆς κακοτεχνίας ταύτης
15 λαβών. Λαβὼν γὰρ τὸ πλασματῶδες ἐκεῖνο βιβλιδάριον καὶ τῇ
βιβλιοθήκῃ, καθὼς εἶπον, ἀποθέμενος εἶτα ὥρας εὐθέτου δραξάμε-
νος ἐπιδείκνυσι τῷ βασιλεῖ ὡς πάντων βιβλίων θαυμασιώτατον καὶ
μυστικώτατον ὄν. Σκήπτεται ἀπορεῖν, οὐκ αὐτὸς μόνος, ἀλλ᾽ οὐδ᾽
ἄλλος τις, φησίν, ἀνθρώπων ἢ Φώτιος τοῦτο διαγνῶναι δύναιτ᾽ ἄν.
20 Τοίνυν εὐθὺς ἀποστέλλεται πρὸς αὐτόν. Σχηματίζεται ἐκεῖνος μὴ
δύνασθαι πρὸς ἄλλον εἰπεῖν τὸ μυστήριον ἢ πρὸς αὐτόν, ὑπὲρ οὗ
καὶ γέγραπται, τοῦ βασιλέως. Τί οὖν; ἡττᾶται λοιπὸν τῆς ῥαδιουρ-
γίας ταύτης ὁ Βασίλειος, ἀποτίθεται τὴν δυσμένειαν καὶ εἰς καταλ-
λαγὰς ἐντεῦθεν | χωρεῖ. Οἶδε γὰρ ἡ ἀγαθὴ πρόρρησις, κἂν ὅτι 33
25 μάλιστα ψευδὴς ᾖ, καταχαυνοῦν καὶ ἐκλύειν καὶ ὅλην ἑαυτῆς ποιεῖσθαι τὴν μεγαλόφρονα καὶ φιλοδοξοτάτην ψυχήν.
     91. Τοῦτο πρὸς Βασίλειον τῆς τοῦ Φωτίου φιλίας ἀρχή, τοῦτο
τῆς ἐκκλησιαστικῆς εἰρήνης κατάλυσις καὶ τῆς πρώτης ἀκαταστασίας ἀνανέωσις. Ἐντεῦθεν συνεχῶς τοῖς βασιλείοις ὁ πολυμήχανος
30 ἐπεχωρίαζε κλέπτων μὲν τὴν εὔνοιαν τοῦ κρατοῦντος, ὅλον δὲ
πρὸς ἑαυτὸν τὸν ἄνδρα ταῖς γοητείαις τῶν λόγων καὶ αἱμυλίαις τῶν

---

4 βασιλεύσοντα ν: βασιλεύσαντα Χ: βασιλεῦσαι Β   5 καταρτισάμενος ν: καταρτυσάμενος Β
10 πιστῶς ν: πιστὸς Β   13 καὶ Β: om. Χν   15 βιβλιδάριον Β: βιβλίον Χν   17 πάντων Β:
πάντων καὶ ν

persons in his fictitious narrative, and when indeed he came down to the father of Basil, he wrote that he would father such a man as Basil himself and his name would be Beclas. And he predicted that the latter would be the most successful and long-lasting emperor of all time. He then finished off his composition with countless falsehoods, which he knew would delight the ears of the emperor, and wrote it on very old sheets of papyrus in Alexandrine letters, imitating as far as possible the ancient style of writing.[181] And he also put it inside very old cover plates, which he took from a very old book, before depositing it in the great library of the imperial palace.

90. His faithful servant in all this and helper in organizing the deception of the piece was the famous Theophanes, who at that time was a cleric at the imperial court and was considered by the emperor to have a sufficient reputation for wisdom.[182] Later, in fact, he became bishop of Caesarea in Cappadocia and that, of course, was the reward he received for this wicked scheming. For he took the forged book and deposited it in the library, as I have said, then at a convenient time took it out and showed it to the emperor, claiming it to be the most wonderful and mystical of all books. He pretended to be puzzled and said that not only was he himself unable to make it out, but no one other than Photius could do so. And so it was straightaway despatched to Photius and he pretended that he could not reveal the mystery to anyone other than the emperor, about whom it had in fact been written. So what happened then? Basil was taken in by this fraud and setting aside his enmity was reconciled with Photius from that point on. For a favorable prediction, even if it is an outright lie, has the power to soften and weaken the arrogant spirit that craves for glory, and make it completely its own.

91. This marked the beginning of Photius's friendship with Basil and signaled the breaking of peace in the Church and a renewal of the original anarchy. From this point on the resourceful Photius got into the habit of making frequent visits to the palace, during which he stole away the emperor's favor and altogether won him over to his side by his beguiling words and wheedling ways.

122

τρόπων κατασκευαζόμενος. Ἐπεγένετο δὲ καὶ εὐθὺς ἄλλη τις οἰκει-
ώσεως ἀφορμή· Θεόδωρον γὰρ ἐκεῖνον ἄχρι τοῦ σχήματος τῶν
ἱματίων ἀββᾶν, πάντων δὲ δεινῶν ὄντα δεινότατον καὶ πανούργων
πανουργότατον, τὸν Σανταβαρηνὸν οἶδ᾽ ὅτι πάντες ἀκούετε·
5 τοῦτον οὐκ οἶδ᾽ ὅπως ὁ Φώτιος εὑρηκώς (καὶ γὰρ τῷ ὁμοίῳ αὐτοῦ,
κατὰ τὴν παροιμίαν, προσκολληθήσεται ἀνήρ) ὡς ἄνδρα ἅγιον καὶ
διορατικώτατον καὶ προφητικώτατον—ταῦτα μὲν οὐκ ὄντα, πόθεν;
πολλοῦγε καὶ δεῖ· μαντικῆς δέ, μᾶλλον δὲ μαγικῆς, φασί, καὶ ὀνει-
ροκριτικῆς ἤτοι δαιμονιώδους σοφίας καὶ ψυχικῆς μετεσχηκότα—
10 τῷ αὐτοκράτορι προσάγει καὶ μυρίοις ἐπαίνοις προσοικειοῖ· καὶ
ἐγκόλπιον αὐτῷ ποιησάμενος τῷ πατριάρχῃ μὲν ἐπεβούλευε καὶ
τὴν ἀπὸ τοῦ πατριαρχείου ῥῖψιν δι᾽ αὐτοῦ βαθέως ἐπάγειν ἐπειρᾶτο,
ἑαυτῷ δὲ αὖθις ἀνόμως τὴν ἀνάβασιν ἐμνᾶτο. Ἐπεὶ δὲ τοῦτο
συνεῖδε σκληρὸν ὄν, φανερῶς εἰς ἱερωσύνην παρὰ τοῦ ἁγίου
15 δεχθῆναι πᾶσαν ἐμηχανᾶτο μηχανή. Ἀλλ᾽ ὁ πατριάρχης κανόσι
Θεοῦ καὶ θεσμοῖς ἐκκλησιαστικοῖς ἀκολουθῶν, καίτοι γε πολλὰ
παρενοχληθείς, οὐ κατεδέξατο οὐδὲ τῷ φονίῳ λύκῳ κατὰ τοῦ
ποιμνίου πάροδον παρέσχεν, ἵνα μὴ αὐτὸς ἑαυτῷ περιπεσών καὶ | 569
ταῖς ἰδίαις ἐναντιωθεὶς ὁμολογίαις ἐνδίκως ἀποστερηθῇ τῆς τιμῆς.
20 Τὸν γὰρ ὑπὸ συνόδου κανονικῶς καθῃρημένον οὐ μερικῆς μόνον,
ἀλλὰ καὶ οἰκουμενικῆς, μᾶλλον δὲ ὡς μηδὲ τὴν ἀρχὴν ἐνθέσμως
τῆς ἱεραρχίας ἁψάμενον | †πλέον αὐτὸν† ἀποκεκηρυγμένον ἀμήχα- 33ᵛ
νον εἶναι διετείνετο ἄνευ συνόδου μείζονος καὶ κυριωτέρας ἀθῳ-
οῦσθαι. Ἀλλ᾽ ἐκεῖνος οὐδενὸς λόγον κανόνος ἢ νόμου ποιούμενος
25 ἑαυτῷ τὰ τῆς ἱερωσύνης ἐπέτρεψε· καὶ ἤδη πρὸς τοῖς βασιλείοις ἐπὶ
τῇ καλουμένῃ Μαγναύρᾳ καταμένων ἐξάρχους τε προεβάλλετο καὶ
χειροτονίας ἐπετέλει καὶ ὅσα πρὸς ὕβριν μὲν τῆς Ἐκκλησίας τοῦ
Θεοῦ, θλῖψιν δὲ τοῦ πατριάρχου, ἀπώλειαν δὲ τῆς ἰδίας ψυχῆς
ἀνοσίως ὁ ἀνοσιώτατος εἰργάζετο. Οὕτω τῆς βασιλικῆς εὐηθείας

5-6 Sirac. 13.16   17-18 cf. Ioann. 10.12

1 εὐθὺς… τις B: ἄλλη τις εὐθὺς Xv   8 δεῖ v: δή B   14 συνεῖδε Xv: συνοῖδε B   22 cruces
posuit Smithies   29 εὐηθείας B: εὐθείας v

Furthermore, there arose immediately another basis for their affinity. I'm sure you've all heard of the famous Theodorus, who was an abbot to judge by the appearance of his robes, but in reality was the most terrible of all terrors and the most wicked of all villains— Santabarenus, I mean.[183] Well, I don't know how Photius found him ("birds of a feather flock together," as the proverb says), but he introduced him to the emperor as a holy man of the clearest perception and prophetic insight. None of this was true, of course —how could it be? No, far from it, since he possessed a devilish and material-minded sort of wisdom that took the form of divination, or rather (so they say) magic and the interpreting of dreams. Anyway Photius associated him with countless praises for the bene- fit of the emperor, and when he had brought him into intimacy with the latter, he began plotting against the patriarch and made a profound effort to bring about Ignatius's expulsion from the patri- archal palace with Theodorus's aid, as he once again impiously solicited for himself advancement to the position. But when he realized that this was a difficult thing to do, he contrived by every means to have himself openly accepted into the priesthood by the holy patriarch. The latter, however, followed the canons of God and the ordinances of the Church and refused to receive him back, even though he was very much pestered about it.[184] He did not provide an opening for the murderous wolf to get in among the flock for fear that he might himself be caught in his own snare and be with justice deprived of his office for contradicting his own vows. For he earnestly maintained that without a higher and more authoritative synod it was impossible to absolve a man who had been condemned by a synod in accordance with ecclesiastical canons— and an ecumenical synod at that, not just a local synod—and who had furthermore been publicly renounced for not even having taken up his priesthood in the beginning in a lawful manner. Photius, however, paying no heed to any canon or law, simply arrogated to himself the rights of the priesthood. He was already residing at court in the palace known as Magnaura and now the monster of impiety began to propose exarchs for election, hold ordinations and perform every impious act that would outrage the

124

κατεφρόνει, μᾶλλον δὲ τῆς ἀνοχῆς τοῦ Θεοῦ καὶ μακροθυμίας ὁ
δοξοχαρὴς ἐκεῖνος καὶ σκανδαλοποιὸς ἄνθρωπος ὑπερφρονῶν καὶ
πᾶν τὸ περὶ τὸν βασιλέα θεραπευτικὸν καὶ οἰκίδιον ὑποποιούμενος
καὶ τὴν ἐνδομυχοῦσαν αὐτῷ κακίαν καὶ πονηρίαν πολὺ μᾶλλον ἢ
5 πρῴην ἐντονωτέραν ἐπιδεικνύμενος καὶ τὴν ἀπὸ τῆς κοσμικῆς
δυναστείας πολλῷ πλέον προσλαμβανόμενος ῥοπήν· οὔπω τρίτη
μετὰ τὴν τοῦ ἁγίου παρῆλθε μετάστασιν ἡμέρα καὶ τὸν πατριαρχικὸν ἐπικαταλαμβάνει θρόνον καὶ τὴν πάλαι ληστρικὴν αὐτοῦ καὶ
τυραννικὴν γνώμην καὶ τὴν κατὰ τοῦ ἀθῴου λύτταν ἀνανεούμενος
10 πάντας μὲν τοὺς οἰκείους ἐκείνου θεραπευτὰς φυλακαῖς καὶ πλη-
γαῖς καὶ ἐξορίαις καὶ θλίψεσιν ἀνηκέστοις περιέβαλλεν· πάντας δὲ
τοὺς ἀντιλέγοντας αὐτοῦ τῇ ἀνόδῳ ὡς οὐ κανονικῶς, ἀλλ᾽ ἀθέσμως καὶ παρανόμως γενομένῃ μυρίαις ἐπινοίαις κατεστρατήγει· οὓς
μὲν δώροις καὶ ἀξιώμασι καὶ θρόνων μεταθέσεσι πρὸς τὴν μετ᾽
15 αὐτοῦ κοινωνίαν ἐπαγόμενος, οὓς δὲ συκοφαντῶν καὶ ἐπ᾽ αἰσ-
χρουργίαις ἀρρήτοις διασύρων τὸ πρῶτον καὶ πικρῶς διαλοιδορούμενος, εἴ τις αὐτῶν αὐτῷ μετὰ ταῦτα κοινωνεῖν ἀνωμολόγησεν,
αὔραις φέρειν ἐξαπίνης ἐκεῖνα πάντα παρεχώρει. Καὶ συλλειτουρ-
γὸς αὐτῷ σήμερον ὁ ἱερόσυλος χθές· καὶ ἱεροφάντης μέγας καὶ
20 τίμιος ὁ κλέπτης καὶ πόρνος καὶ βέβηλος πρῴην ὑπ᾽ αὐτοῦ μεθ᾽
ὅρκων ἀποδεικνύμενος. Οὓς δὲ πρὸς τὴν αὐτοῦ κοινωνίαν ἑώρα
στερρῶς ἀνθισταμένους (ἐνίσταντο δὲ πάντες ὅσοι ἀληθῶς τῆς
Χριστιανικῆς πίστεως ἀντείχοντο τῷ ὑπὸ ἁγίας καὶ οἰκουμενικῆς | 34
συνόδου κανονικῶς ἀνατεθεματισμένῳ καὶ καθῃρημένῳ ἐπικινδυ-
25 νότατον λογιζόμενοι καὶ ὀλέθριον κοινωνεῖν καὶ εἰς ἓν σῶμα τούτῳ
συγκεκρᾶσθαι τῷ μυριάκις τὸν τίμιον τοῦ Χρίστου καταπεπατηκότι
σταυρὸν καὶ πάντας καταπατεῖν διὰ τῆς τῶν χειρογράφων ἀπαιτή-
σεως καταβιαζομένῳ), τούτων οὖν ὅσους φυλακαῖς καὶ μάστιξι
πείθειν οὐκ εἶχε, τῷ ὠμοτάτῳ πάντων ἀνθρώπων καὶ ἀπηνεστάτῳ
30 παρέπεμπε γαμβρῷ· Λέων δὲ οὗτος ἦν ὁ καλούμενος Κατάκοιλας
τῆς βίγλης δρουγγάριος ὑπ᾽ αὐτοῦ προβιβασθείς, ὃς τῆς τιμῆς

1 cf. Rom. 2.4

9 ἀθῴου Β: ἁγίου Χν   11 περιέβαλλεν Β: περιέβαλεν ν   13 παρανόμως Χν: παραλόγως Β
14 μετ᾽ ν: κατ᾽ Β   15 ἐπ᾽ ν: ἐν Β   21 τὴν...κοινωνίαν Χν: τὴν ἀξίαν τῆς αὐτοῦ κοινωνίας
Β   28 τούτων Χν: τούτους Β   30 κατάκοιλας Β: κατακάλλος Χ: Κατάκαλος ν
31 βίγλης Β: βίγλας Χν

Church of God, oppress the patriarch and bring his own soul to perdition.[185] That craver of glory and schismatic was so disdainful of the emperor's naivety, or rather so despised the patience and forbearance of God, that he tried to win over by intrigue all the emperor's attendants and domestic staff, showing his latent evil and wickedness much more strongly than before and accepting far more help from secular power. And not three days after the saint had passed on, he took over the patriarchal seat and, reviving his piratical and tyrannical disposition of old and his fury against guiltless Ignatius, he dealt out to all his household servants periods of detention, beatings, banishments, and pernicious afflictions. Moreover, by countless designs he outwitted all those who were disputing his rise to power on the grounds that it was carried out illegally and not in accordance with ecclesiastical canons and ordinances. He won over some of them to his side by offering gifts and preferment and by shuffling of bishoprics, whilst against others he made false accusations—charging them in the first place with unspeakable obscenities and bitterly reviling them, but if any of them agreed to join him after that, he would suddenly cast all the charges to the winds. Yesterday's desecrator was today's colleague in the ministry, and the man whom Photius under oath had earlier demonstrated to be a thief, adulterer, and profaner was now a great and venerable teacher of sacred truths. As for those whom he saw to be obstinate in their resistance to joining him (and he was opposed by all those who were true adherents of the Christian faith, since they thought it most dangerous and destructive either to associate with one who had been condemned and deposed by a holy ecumenical synod in accordance with ecclesiastical canons or to be intimately united in the one body of Christ with a man who had trampled underfoot the venerable Cross of Christ on countless occasions and was constraining everyone else to follow suit by demanding their signatures)[186]—as many of these, then, as he was unable to persuade by imprisonment and the lash he handed over to his brother-in-law, the cruelest and most savage of all men. This man Leo, surnamed Katakoilas, had been advanced by Photius to the position of *drungarius* of the Guard[187] and—to sum up the

αὐτὸν ἀμειβόμενος πάντας τοὺς πρὸς αὐτὸν πεμπομένους, ἵνα
μικρῷ λόγῳ τὴν μιαιφονίαν παραστήσω, ἴσα Λικινίῳ τῷ πάλαι τῇ
κατὰ τῶν ἁγίων ὠμότητι ἐχρῆτο. Καὶ πολλοὺς μὲν ἀνεῖλεν ἄχρι
τέλους τὴν ὑπὲρ τῆς ἀληθείας ἔνστασιν ἐνδειξαμένους, πλείους δὲ
5 τῶν ἀνυποίστων βασάνων ἡτ|τωμένους ὡς δῶρα τίμια πρὸς τὸν   572
πέμποντα τούτους ἀνταπέστελλεν.

92. Τίς ἱκανῶς τοῦ τότε καιροῦ τὴν κακίαν, μᾶλλον δὲ τίς τοῦ
σκολιοῦ δράκοντος ἐκείνου τὰς ἐνέδρας ἐξείποι καὶ μηχανάς;
Πολλοὺς πολλάκις ὁ δόλιος δολίᾳ γλώσσῃ συκοφαντῶν ἢ ἐπ’
10 ἐγκλήμασι δῆθεν καθαιρῶν, εἰ συνέθεντο μετὰ ταῦτα κοινωνεῖν,
τούτους αὖθις ἀποκαθίστη συνιστῶν καὶ ἐπὶ μείζους ἐνίοτε θρό-
νους μεθιστῶν. Καὶ μετὰ ταῦτα δὲ πάλιν εἴ τις αὐτοῦ προσοχθικῶς
ταῖς ἀπονοίαις ἀπέσχετο τῆς κοινωνίας, αὖθις καθήρει τοῦτον καὶ
ὑποκύπτοντα προσίετο πάλιν. Οὕτως ἔτρεχεν ἐν δίψει πάντα
15 κανόνα θεῖον καὶ πᾶσαν θεσμοθεσίαν ἱερὰν διὰ τῆς αὐτοῦ φιλαρχίας συγχέαι καὶ δοξομανίας. Πρὸ τούτων δὲ πάντων πειρᾶται τὴν
τοῦ πατριάρχου προχείρισιν μεθιστᾶν καὶ τοὺς κατ’ αὐτὸν καθηρη-
μένους ταῖς ἐκκλησίαις ἀντικαθιστᾶν. Ἐπεὶ δὲ οὐκ ἤρεσκεν οὕτως
τῷ βασιλεῖ, ὁρᾶτε οἷον ἐτόλμα. Τοὺς ὑπὸ τοῦ ἁγίου τετελεσμένους
20 ἐπειρᾶτο ἀναχειροτονεῖν. Ἐπεὶ δὲ καὶ τοῦτο τῶν ἀτοπωτάτων ἔδοξε
καὶ ἀπευκτῶν, οὐδ’ οὕτως ἠπό|ρησεν ἡ πονηρία· ὠμοφόρια δὲ καὶ   34ᵛ
ὀράρια ὠνούμενος καὶ ὅσα τῆς ἱερατικῆς σύμβολα χρηματίζει
τελειώσεως καὶ τούτοις ἐν μυστηρίῳ οἰκείας ἐπιλέγων εὐχάς (εἴγε
ταύτας εὐχάς, ἀλλ’ οὐ δυσφημίας ἐναγεῖς ὀνομάζειν χρεών) οὕτως
25 ἑκάστῳ λόγῳ φιλοτιμίας ἐδίδου καὶ χαρίσματος. Ἵνα δὲ καθ’ ὑπερ-
βολὴν ἁμαρτωλὸς γένηται ἡ ἁμαρτία, πανταχοῦ ὅρκος, πανταχοῦ
τῶν χειρογράφων ἀπαίτησις, ἐν χειροτονίαις ἐν ἀξιώμασιν ἐν μετα-
θέσεσιν· ἐν πᾶσιν οἷς εὐεργετεῖν ἐνομίζετο, κατεδεῖτό τε καὶ ἰδιοχεί-
ροις ἰσχυροτάτοις ἠσφαλίζετο πανταχόθεν τὴν ἰδίαν δόξαν ζητῶν

7–8 cf. Is. 27.1   25–26 Rom. 7.13

9 γλώσσῃ Xv: γλώσσει B   12 προσοχθικῶς Duffy: προσωχθικῶς B: προσωχθηκὼς v
18 οὕτως B: οὕτω Xv   22 ὀράρια B: ὠράρια v

man's bloodthirstiness in just a few words—he repaid him for the honor by treating all those sent to him with the same savagery as Licinius of old once used against men of God.[188] He did away with many of them, since they displayed to the end an unshakable resolve in the interests of truth, and still more of them he returned as worthy gifts to the sender once they had given way beneath intolerable tortures.

92. Who could give an adequate account of the iniquity of that time, or rather of the treachery and wiles of that writhing serpent? On many different occasions the treacherous one made false accusations with his treacherous tongue against many individuals, or indeed deposed them upon false charges, but if after that they agreed to join him, he recommended and restored them once again, sometimes transferring them to sees of greater importance.[189] And then again if anyone after that was angered by his acts of madness and ceased to associate with him, Photius deposed him once again, only to readmit him to his association if that man subsequently submitted to his will. Such was his feverish desire to confound every divine canon and every sacred law by his lust for power and mad thirst for fame. And above all he tried to overturn the selections made by the patriarch and to restore to their churches those who had been deposed by him. When the emperor did not find this to his liking, just look what Photius had the audacity to do next—he tried to re-ordain those who had already been ordained by holy Ignatius. And when this too was thought to be most improper and abominable, not even then did his wickedness fail him. He purchased bishops' pallia, deacons' stoles and all the insignia which belong to initiation into the priesthood, and pronouncing prayers of his own over them in secret (if indeed they should be called prayers and not foul blasphemies), he gave them out to each man by way of a gift and a bestowal of favor. And in order to make the sin sinful in the extreme, there were in all his dealings oaths and demands for signatures, whether he was performing ordinations, offering preferments, or shuffling bishoprics. In all cases where he was thought to be doing men service he was binding them to himself and making sure of them

128

καὶ χαίρων ταῖς καινοτομίαις· καὶ οὐ διὰ τοῦ Θεοῦ οὐδὲ διὰ τῆς
ἐκείνου συστῆναι πώποτε προνοίας ἢ πιστεύων ἢ προσδοκῶν, διὰ
δὲ τῆς οἰκείας πολυτεχνίας ἢ κακοτεχνίας ἑαυτὸν ἐπιχειρῶν συν-
ιστᾶν καὶ πᾶσαν οὕτω συγχέων ἐκκλησίαν καὶ πᾶσαν οὕτω σκανδα-
5 λίζων ψυχὴν καὶ τὸ ὄνομα τοῦ Χριστοῦ βλασφημεῖσθαι διὰ τῆς
αὐτοῦ κακομηχανίας παρασκευαζόμενος.

93. Μετὰ γοῦν τὸ τὸν θρόνον τὸ δεύτερον κατασχεῖν Θεόδωρον ἐκεῖνον (ὃν ἐν ἐξορίᾳ καθήμενος αὐτὸς μὲν εἰς τὰς Πάτρας
ἐχειροτόνησε μητροπολίτην, Ἀφαντοπόλεως δὲ τοῦτον ἀστείως οἱ
10 παρ᾽ ἐκείνῳ κατωνόμαζον), τοῦτον πρὸς Ἰωάννην τὸν πάπαν ἀπο-
κρισιάριον προεχειρίσατο γράψας ὅτι βίᾳ πολλῇ τῆς Ἐκκλησίας
ὅλης καὶ τῆς πολιτείας ἀναγκασθεὶς ἐπὶ τὸν θρόνον ἀνῆλθε καὶ μὴ
βουλόμενος· ἵνα δὲ βεβαιώσηται τὸ ψεῦδος τῶν ἐπιστολῶν, διὰ τοῦ
μυστογράφου Πέτρου, ὃς καὶ τὰς Σάρδεις ὕστερον ἔπαθλον τῶν
15 πλασμάτων ἠνέγκατο, δι᾽ αὐτοῦ κλέπτει μὲν τὰς σφραγῖδας τῶν
βουλωτηρίων τῶν ὅλων μητροπολιτῶν, συναρπάζει δὲ καὶ αὐτοὺς
μὴ εἰδότας ὑπογράψαι τῷ λιβέλλῳ πρόφασιν ὡς ἐπὶ μυστικῇ ἀγροῦ
ἀγορασίᾳ. Τοσοῦτος τὴν πανουργίαν ἐκεῖνος καὶ τηλικοῦτος
ὑπῆρχε τὴν δεινότητα. Πῶς δὲ καὶ τὰ κατὰ τὸν Εὐφημιανὸν ἐκεῖνον
20 παρέλθωμεν σιωπῇ; ὃς Εὐχαΐτων μὲν ἐπίσκοπος ἦν, ἐπειδὴ δὲ ὁ
Σανταβαρηνὸς τῆς ἐπισκοπῆς ἐκείνης ὡς γείτονος ὠρέγετο, τὸν
μὲν βίᾳ | σχολάζειν ἀναγκάζει, τὸν δὲ ἀντ᾽ αὐτοῦ χει|ροτονεῖ. Οὐ ⟨35⟩
μόνον δέ, ἀλλὰ καὶ ἐπισκοπὰς ἐκ τῶν γειτνιαζουσῶν μητροπόλεων ⟨|573⟩
ὅσας ἐκεῖνος ἤθελεν ἀφαιρεῖται καὶ δίδωσιν αὐτῷ. Καὶ οὐ ταῦτα
25 μόνον, ἀλλὰ καὶ παρ᾽ ἑαυτῷ καθίζων πρωτόθρονον τοῦτον κατωνόμα-
ζεν· καὶ Νικηφόρον μὲν Νικαίας μητροπολίτην ὄντα βιάζεται παραιτησάμενον ὀρφανοτρόφον εἶναι, Ἀμφιλόχιον δὲ τὸν Κυζίκου
πρὸς τὴν Νίκαιαν μεθίστησι. Καὶ ταχὺ θανόντος αὐτοῦ τὸν Συρα-
κούσιον ἀντικαθίστησι Γρηγόριον· ὃν καὶ αὐτὸν μετ᾽ οὐ πολὺ θα-
30 νόντα οἵοις ἐσέμνυνεν ἐπιταφίοις ὡς τῶν μεγάλων Πατέρων ἐφ-

---

2 πώποτε Β: ποτε v   3 δὲ...οἰκείας Β: τῆς...δὲ Xv   6 κακομηχανίας v: μηχανίας Β
10 ἐκείνῳ Xv: ἐκείνου Β   12 ἀνῆλθε v: ἀνῆλθεν X: ἀνῆλθον Β   17 ἀγροῦ Β: om. Xv
20 παρέλθωμεν Xv: παρέλθοιμεν Β | εὐχαΐτων Β: Εὐχαΐτων v   21 Σανταβαρηνὸς v:
σανταβαρινὸς X: σανδαβαρηνὸς Β | γείτονος Β: γείτων Xv

with the firmest signed undertakings, everywhere seeking his own glory and delighting in new schemes. And he did not believe or expect ever to have the support of God or His Providence, but endeavored instead to support himself by his own versatility or artifice, thereby confounding every church, leading every soul into sin and causing the name of Christ to be blasphemed through his evil scheming.

93. Well now, after seizing the patriarchal throne for the second time, Photius appointed the well-known Theodorus (whom he himself while still residing in exile had appointed metropolitan to Patras, while Theodorus's own household had wittily dubbed him metropolitan of Aphantopolis or "No-such-city")—he appointed Theodorus ambassador to Pope John and wrote to the latter that under great pressure from the whole Church and the state he had returned to the patriarchal throne against his will.[190] And in order to put the lies of his letter on a sound footing, he stole the sealings[191] of all the metropolitans with the help of Peter the *mystographus*, who later in fact received Sardis as the reward for his fabrications.[192] Furthermore, without their knowledge, he trapped them into subscribing to the document, on the pretext that it was for a confidential purchase of land—such a mighty initiator of wickedness was he and such a fertile source of iniquity! And how can we also pass over in silence the case of the famous Euphemianus?[193] He was bishop of Euchaita, but when Santabarenus hankered after his bishopric because it bordered on his own, Photius forced Euphemianus to give up his see and appointed Santabarenus in his place. And not only that, but he robbed the neighboring metropolitans of any bishoprics to which Santabarenus took a fancy and handed them over to him. And as if that wasn't enough, Photius had him sit by his side and named him chief bishop. Furthermore, he forced Nicephorus,[194] metropolitan of Nicea, to abdicate and become *orphanotrophus* and transferred to Nicea Amphilochius, metropolitan of Cyzicus. And when the latter died soon afterwards, he replaced him with Gregorius of Syracuse, who died himself only a short time thereafter.[195] And how Photius extolled him in the funeral speech, pretending that his life had

130

ἄμιλλον βεβιωκότα βίον δι᾽ οὐδὲν ἄλλο τοσοῦτον, ὅσον ὅτι κατὰ τοῦ ἁγίου καθώσπερ ξυρὸν ἄχρι τέλους τὴν γλῶσσαν ὁ δύστηνος παρέθηξε.

94. Διὰ ταῦτα καὶ ἔτι πλείω τούτων ἀτοπώτερα ἦλθεν ἡ ὀργὴ
5 τοῦ Θεοῦ ἐπὶ τοὺς υἱοὺς τῆς ἀπειθείας· καὶ εὐθὺς μὲν τότε τῷ Βασιλείῳ τέθνηκε Κωνσταντῖνος ὁ τριπόθητος καὶ πρωτότοκος υἱός, ὃν
καὶ ἅγιον ὁ τολμητίας οὗτος εἰς τὴν τοῦ πατρὸς χάριν ἐξ ἑαυτοῦ
χειροτονῶν μοναστηρίοις τε καὶ ναοῖς ἀνθρωπαρεσκίᾳ τιμῶν οὐκ
ἠὐλαβεῖτο.

10 95. Αὐτίκα δὲ καὶ ἡ μεγάλη πόλις Συράκουσαι τὴν φρικτὴν
ὤλετο πανωλεθρίαν· καὶ πᾶσα νῆσος καὶ πᾶσα πόλις καὶ χώρα
προνομεύεται καὶ καταφθείρεται μέχρι καὶ τήμερον τοῖς ἐχθροῖς
οὐδεμιᾶς ἐκ τῶν ἱερᾶσθαι δοκούντων ἱλεουμένης τὸν Θεὸν προσ-
ευχῆς· ἀλλὰ κατὰ τὸ γεγραμμένον· "Ἐγενόμεθα ὄντως ὡς πρόβατα
15 οἷς οὐκ ἔστι ποιμήν." Χρονίσασα γὰρ ἡ κακία καὶ πολλοῖς ὑποδείγ-
μασι παγιωθεῖσα νόμος νενόμισται τοῖς ἀνομοῦσι καὶ τὸ | ἄθεσμον 35ᵛ
ἔθος εἰς φύσιν τρόπον τινὰ τοῖς καταφρονηταῖς καταστὰν ὅλην
ἐπισπᾶται τοῦ Θεοῦ τὴν ὀργήν.

96. Ἀλλὰ τὸ μὲν καθέκαστον ἐπεξιέναι τὰς καινοτομίας καὶ
20 παρανομίας αὐτοῦ τε Φωτίου τοῦ πρωτοστάτου τῶν ὑποκριτῶν καὶ
σταυρομάχων καὶ πάντων μὲν καθεξῆς τῶν αὐτοῦ διαδόχων καὶ τῆς
φιλαρχίας κοινωνῶν ἱστορίας ἔργον καὶ οὐ τοῦ παρόντος τῷ λόγῳ
σκοποῦ.

97. Ἡμεῖς δὲ τὴν ὑπεράπειρον μακροθυμίαν καὶ ἀνοχὴν ὑμ-
25 νοῦντες τοῦ τῶν ὅλων Θεοῦ εὐχώμεθα τῆς μερίδος ἐξαιρεθῆναι
τῶν τὰ σκάνδαλα καὶ τὰς διχοστασίας διὰ τῆς κακίστης αὐτῶν
ἐπιθυμίας κατεργαζομένων, κοινωνοὶ δὲ γενέσθαι τοῦ τῶν ἁγίων
κλήρου τῶν διὰ πίστεως καὶ ἀγάπης Θεοῦ ταπεινοφροσύνης τε καὶ
πραΰτητος τῆς ἐπουρανίου βασιλείας καὶ ἱεραρχίας ἁγίας τοῦ ὑπερ-
30 αγίου καταξιουμένων, | πρεσβείαις τῆς ὑπεράγνου καὶ παναμώμου 36
Θεομήτορος καὶ τῶν ἐκλεκτῶν καὶ ἱερῶν ἀγγέλων καὶ τῶν πανευ-
φήμων ἀποστόλων καὶ τῶν πανενδόξων ἀθλοφόρων καὶ τῶν ὅλων

4–5 Ephes. 5.6; Col. 3.6 14–15 cf. Matth. 9.36; Marc. 6.34 24–25 cf. Rom. 2.4 26 cf. Rom. 16.17

5–6 βασιλείῳ B: βασιλεῖ v 14 ὡς B: om. v 16 νόμος Xv: νόμοις B 21 μὲν B: om. v 32 τῶν ὅλων B: ὅλων τῶν v

rivaled those of the great Fathers of the Church, for the one and only reason that the wretch had right to the end sharpened his tongue like a razor against holy Ignatius![196]

94. Because of these and other things even more outrageous the anger of God came down upon the sons of disobedience. Straightaway Constantinus, Basil's much-longed-for and firstborn son, died, and that reckless Photius did not fear either to consecrate him as a saint on his own initiative in order to win his father's favor or to honor him with monasteries and shrines in order to be sycophantic.[197]

95. It was at this time too that the great city of Syracuse was laid waste in awful destruction. And all the islands, every city and region continue to be ravaged and devastated by our enemies right up to the present day, since no prayer from those who are supposed to carry out the holy rites can appease God. But, as the Holy Scriptures say, "we have become in truth sheep without a shepherd." For the iniquity has become habitual and, reinforced by so many examples, has become law to the lawless. Wicked habits have become virtually second nature to the disdainful and now bring down upon them the full anger of God.

96. Well, to give a full account of all the new schemes and individual transgressions of Photius himself, leader of the hypocrites and enemies of the Cross, and of all his successors and partners in ambition, would be the job of a history and it falls outside the scope of my present account.

97. But let us praise the supremely infinite forbearance and patience of the God of all things and pray that we may be exempted from the lot of those who perpetrate sinful deeds and dissension by reason of their most wicked passions. Let us share instead in the lot of the saints, who by reason of their faith and love of God, their humility and gentleness, are deemed worthy of the Kingdom of Heaven and of the holy priesthood of the Supreme Deity, thanks to the advocacy of the most pure and wholly blameless Mother of God and to the suitable and holy petitions of God's chosen and holy angels, the blessed apostles, the most glorious martyrs and all the

ἁγίων ταῖς εὐπροσδέκτοις καὶ ἱεραῖς ἱκετηρίαις. Πρὸς τούτοις πᾶσι δὲ καὶ τοῦ ἐν ἁγίοις πατρὸς ἡμῶν Ἰγνατίου ἀρχιεπισκόπου Κωνσταντινουπόλεως τοῦ νέου ἀληθῶς ὁμολογητοῦ καὶ θεοφόρου, ἐν Χριστῷ Ἰησοῦ τῷ Κυρίῳ ἡμῶν, ᾧ ἡ δόξα καὶ ἡ τιμὴ
5 καὶ ἡ προσκύνησις ἅμα τῷ ἀνάρχῳ Πατρὶ καὶ τῷ συνανάρχῳ καὶ ζωοποιῷ αὐτοῦ Πνεύματι, νῦν καὶ ἀεὶ καὶ εἰς τοὺς αἰῶνας τῶν αἰώνων. Ἀμήν.

---

1 τούτοις Xv: τοῖς B

saints. And to all these I add the name of Ignatius, patriarch of Constantinople, our own holy father and saint, who is in truth the new confessor of the faith and bearer of God's message, in the name of Jesus Christ Our Lord, to Whom together with the eternal Father and His equally eternal and life-giving Spirit all glory and honor and reverence is due, now and always and forever and ever. Amen.

NOTES TO THE TEXT

1   The use of the word ἄθλησις in the title rings the bell of "martyrdom," and it is a leitmotif of the work that Patriarch Ignatius suffered persecution on behalf of orthodoxy. The biography finishes on the same note, when Nicetas calls Ignatius "the new confessor of the faith" (τοῦ νέου . . . ὁμολογητοῦ, 132.3). Strictly speaking the phrase τοῦ καὶ . . . Παφλαγόνος should not be printed as part of the title, being a later addition in ms. B, the main witness for the text.

2   Apart from the devil, there is more than one villain in the *Life of Ignatius*, from the point of view of the author, but the main focus of the attacks throughout is Photius (*ODB* 3:1669–70; *PmbZ* #6253). It is therefore legitimate to think that Nicetas is anticipating his prime target, when he uses the words πικρὸς διώκτης, as he certainly is when he refers to the αὐτουργὸς τῆς κακίας καὶ τῆς ἀδικίας at 4.16.

3   The contrast between holy lives of the remote past and those nearer in time to the era of the author is a common topic in Byzantine hagiography. See, for example, the prologue to the *Life of John the Almsgiver* by Leontius of Neapolis (ed. A.-J. Festugière [Paris, 1974]) and the comments of Festugière (ibid., 529–31); the biographers in question, like Nicetas David, are at pains to offer a kind of *apologia* for writing about near-contemporaries.

4   In Rader's edition (reproduced by Migne in PG, vol. 105) there is a good suggestion (489A) that σκοπὸς should be added to the text after νῦν; perhaps it would be even better placed after μοι in the same line.

5   It is unfortunate that some chronological indications given here and elsewhere (e.g. 4.11–12 χρόνοις ἱκανοῖς) are so vague; otherwise scholars would not have had such an intractable problem in trying to pin down the date at which the *Life of Ignatius* was written. See n. 9 to Introduction, above, p. xxxi.

6   Apart from this general remark, Nicetas provides no other details about his written sources. On the side of documents, and for restricted portions of the *Life*, the evidence is somewhat indirect. I. Tamarkina in her article, "The Date of the Life of the Patriarch Ignatius Reconsidered," *BZ* 99 (2006): 626 ff., has shown that Nicetas has copied from the same document as the compiler of the treatise *De stauropatis*, that is to say, they both use the unabridged version of the Greek acts of the Council of 869–870; P. Karlin-Hayter (ed., *Vita Euthymii patriarchae CP* [Brussels, 1970]) has demonstrated that the *Life of Ignatius* and the letter of Stylianos of Neocaesarea draw on a common source,

and I have argued along similar lines for parts of the *Synodicon Vetus* (ed. J. Duffy and J. Parker [Washington, D.C., 1979], xv). S. A. Paschalides, "From Hagiography to Historiography: The Case of the *Vita Ignatii*," in *Les Vies des saints à Byzance,* ed. P. Odorico and P. Agapitos (Paris, 2004), 161–73, has made a convincing case for Nicetas's authorship of a (now lost) *History*, the second book of which contained a later elaboration of the *Vita Ignatii.* We are no closer, however, with that important news, to knowing more about the works that Nicetas used for his information.

As for oral informants, we have no way of ascertaining how much may have come to him by this route; he does remark at one point (90.2) ὡς τῶν εἰδότων ἀκήκοα, but as the information "received" (if not fabricated) amounts to a most unlikely story, the author's statement is hardly good evidence for anything.

7 Nicetas is already setting the tone for the stark, white and black, contrast between Ignatius and Photius that permeates the work. A. Kazhdan, in the second volume of *A History of Byzantine Literature* (Athens, 2006) provides a fresh literary appreciation of how the hero and anti-hero are presented by the author of this *Life* (97–102).

8 The author stresses not only the distinction and piety of all related to Ignatius, but also the legitimacy of his father's reign (4.29–30: ψήφῳ μὲν Θεοῦ, ψήφῳ δὲ τῆς συγκλήτου πάσης). Legitimacy and virtue will characterize the patriarchate of Ignatius, while Photius will be consistently depicted as an adulterous intruder on the throne and a murderous persecutor.

9 Michael I Rangabe (*ODB* 2:1362; *PmbZ* #4989) reigned for two years, 811–813, before he abdicated and entered the monastic life, along with his family. His wife Procopia (*PmbZ* #6351) was the daughter of Emperor Nicephorus I, and sister of Stauracius who likewise had abdicated and taken the monastic habit, after a reign of only a few months in the year 811.

10 The rank of *curopalates* (*ODB* 2:1157) was a very distinguished one at this period, being conferred primarily on members of the imperial family.

11 For a brief discussion of Nicetas's apparent reluctance to qualify his work as "history" see Paschalides, "From Hagiography" (n. 6 above), 164 ff.

12 Leo V the Armenian (*ODB* 2:1209–10; *PmbZ* #4244) was acclaimed emperor in 813 and ruled for some seven years. Previously he had been military governor of the Anatolikon theme (*ODB* 1:89–90) in Asia Minor.

It suits Nicetas's dramatic purposes very well to say that Ignatius's father, Michael "the blessed," willingly abdicated when "faced with the man who attacked him as a usurper" (cf. also 6.32). In that sense Leo is a "forerunner" of Photius, who later will be described as having seized the patriarchal throne τυραννικῶς (48.31–50.1). See also n. 17 below.

13   The Princes' Islands (*ODB* 3:1720), a group of nine islands in the Sea of Marmara (Propontis), were a favorite site for banishment and also had many monasteries.

14   Some limited information on the family members is provided in the *PmbZ*, under Michael I #4989. See also J. B. Bury, *A History of the Eastern Roman Empire: From the Fall of Irene to the Accession of Basil I, A.D. 802–867* (London, 1912), 29–30.

15   For this office see the article on *domestikos ton Hikanaton* in *ODB* 1:647.

16   In this way the possibility of a future attempt on the throne by Michael's sons was removed. See Bury, *History*, 29, and the article on eunuchs in *ODB* 2:746–47.

17   In the Greek there is some play on the word ἀρχή, but Nicetas is more likely to have intended "he won for himself an end worthy of the beginning," i.e., wicked and violent.

There was already the violent overthrow of Michael I, then the wicked reintroduction of iconoclasm, followed by the violent removal of patriarch Nicephorus, and finally the "worthy" violent end that Leo (813–820) himself met, all described in 6.31–10.9. Significantly, almost the identical thing is said of Photius at 34.30 ff.

18   The first period of Iconoclasm (*ODB* 2:975–77) may be dated from 726, in the reign of Leo III (717–741), through the reign of his son Constantine V (741–775), and beyond. Nicetas passes over the years of Leo IV in which the movement was on the wane, wishing to highlight only the two main proponents, and cites the end that was officially introduced by the Second Council of Nicaea in 787.

19   Nicephorus I (*ODB* 3:1477), a major figure in the struggles on behalf of icon veneration, was patriarch from 806 to 815, the nine years that Nicetas mentions. For details of his banishment see Bury, *History*, 67–68, where it is specified that the monastery in question was that of St. Theodore, on the Asiatic side of the Bosphorus.

20   Theodotus I Kassiteras (*ODB* 3:2054; *PmbZ* #7954) was made patriarch in 815 and his installment may be said to mark the start of the second period of iconoclasm (815–843). The appointment of nonclerics to the patriarchal throne is a hugely sore point with Nicetas and those who shared his very conservative views. When he comes to Photius he will make the most of that man's elevation from the status of layman.

21   There is some uncertainty about which palace church is in question. See Bury, *History*, 52–53 and the final portion of Mango's article on the Nea Ekklesia in *ODB* 2:1446.

22   Michael II (*ODB* 2:1363; *PmbZ* #4990), the founder of the Amorian dynasty, ruled from 820 to 829. He had been appointed by Leo the Armenian to command a corps of the imperial guard; for the office see *Domestikos ton*

Exkoubiton in *ODB* 1:646–47. While this text assigns him the Greek nickname of Ψελλός, most other sources give it as Τραυλός.

23   One of the Princes' Islands.

24   The Byzantines of all periods had a great love of nicknames and other derogatory terms, especially for those whose religious views clashed with their own. Some of these labels, even as blunt weapons, may have meant something fairly concrete in their day, but for us no longer "in the know" they are often obscure and imprecise. Some sources, in imputing heretical views to Michael, mention a connection to Judaism (see *PmbZ* #4990, p. 254 and nn. 14–16 there), but Σαββατιανός seems to be confined to our text. For a possible clue to its general meaning we may cite the *Synodicon Vetus*, chap. 70, where it is reported that, at a fourth-century synod held in Phrygia, a group of heretics "issued a decree to allow the celebration of Easter according to Jewish practice. By supporting this decision, Sabbatius drew many adherents from among the Byzantines, and these people to this very day are called Sabbatians after him." If we take the compiler of the *SV* at his word, the term still had its uses into the ninth or tenth century. Whatever else Nicetas might say in criticism of Michael II he is happy to note that he did not use violence against the iconodule Orthodox (unlike his successor Theophilus).

25   Antony I (*ODB* 1:124–25; *PmbZ* #550), a former iconodule, became patriarch in 821. His usual nickname is Kassymatas ("shoemaker"), though in our text the term is "tanner"; both of these could be an indication of low social origin, which would be accurate in the case of Antony. However, the possibility should be left open that the name has further implications; e.g. while Theodotus was given a similar sobriquet ("tinker"), we know that he came from a distinguished family. For Perge see *ODB* 3:1980 (s.v. *Syllaion*).

26   Theophilus (*ODB* 3:2066; *PmbZ* #8167) succeeded his father Michael II in 829 and occupied the throne until 842. From the point of view of ecclesiastical policy he was a much more active and determined iconoclast than his father.

27   This is John VII the Grammarian (*ODB* 2:1052; *PmbZ* #3199) to whom Nicetas will return after an interlude (20.8 ff.). Like his predecessor Antony, he was iconodule in an earlier phase of his life, but was recruited by Emperor Leo V to work on a florilegium of texts in support of iconoclasm, in preparation for the local council of 815, which condemned images. He was the recipient of a series of derogatory names of which Nicetas (20.9) cites two. At one time he was a tutor of the future emperor Theophilus. The date of his accession to the patriarchal throne is not known for sure (837?), but he was deposed in 843, after Empress Theodora assumed control of the empire and the official attacks on sacred images came to an end. See S. Gero, "John the Grammarian, the Last Iconoclastic Patriarch of Constantinople: The Man and the Legend," *Byzantina* [*Nordisk tidskrift för bysantinologi*] 2 (1973): 25–35.

28   Having just provided an overview of the period from roughly 813 (the castration and tonsure of Ignatius) to 843 (the end of the reign of Theophilus), Nicetas now turns his attention to his hero and fills in the details of the career and activities of Ignatius during those thirty years. What he evokes is a picture of an exemplary life spent as a monk, priest, and friend of those persecuted under the tyrannical enemies of image veneration. Appropriately for the genre of hagiography, the whole high-powered description is brought to a close by the scene in which the famous Theophanes the Confessor lays a blessing hand on Ignatius and recognizes him (presumably in the presence of others) as a future patriarch. The idea is commonplace in saints' lives.

29   Unlike Photius (the hagiographer would like us to understand; cf. 68.21 ff.), Ignatius confined himself to the careful study of Scripture and the writings of the Church Fathers; on that basis he pursued the practice and theory of a holy and virtuous life (12.13 ff.).

30   Most of these practices would constitute the classic virtues of the monastic life. It is particularly intriguing that Ignatius is said to have withstood the physical and spiritual "abuse" of a monastic superior who was an ardent iconoclast. Whether true or not, the description certainly makes Ignatius out to be a "martyr" even as a novice and well prepared for "persecutions" to come during his patriarchal years. Some wide-eyed comments on this section are to be found in P. Karlin-Hayter, "Gregory of Syracuse, Ignatios and Photios," in *Iconoclasm*, ed. A. Bryer and J. Herrin (Birmingham, 1975), 142.

31   Nicetas is reminding us that his hero is on a spiritual journey and striving for perfection. He is being initiated in stages, and after the first is successfully completed (12.26 κάλλιστα προτελούμενος) he proceeds to the higher levels (12.28 τὰ τελεώτερα).

32   In addition to the passage in 1 Cor. 13.13 we should have in mind as well the 30th and final step in the *Heavenly Ladder* of John Climacus, the account *par excellence* of monastic striving for perfection through a series of virtues gained and vices avoided. In the heading for step 30 the author calls these three the ἐνάρετος τριὰς ἐν ἀρεταῖς. The idea of the ladder occurs explicitly later at 42.8–11 and 102.8 ff. It is relevant to mention also that Nicetas David himself composed an extant encomium on John Climacus; it is item no. 6 in the collection of texts edited by F. Lebrun, *Nicétas le Paphlagonien: Sept homélies inédites* (Leuven, 1997).

33   The "impious" (οἱ ἀσεβοῦντες) are of course the iconoclasts. Even if during his early monastic life Ignatius might not have yet come into much direct contact with the persecutions and the victims, we have seen already (n. 30) the suggestion of the hagiographer that he confronted the evil in the person of his superior.

34 The former emperor Michael Rangabe (see n. 9 above) died as a monk on the island of Plate in 844. This would mean that Ignatius (born ca. 799) was in his mid-forties when he became head of his community.

The unnamed καθηγητής must be the same as the καθηγεμών mentioned earlier (12.21). The transmitted text reads Καὶ γὰρ τοῦ πατρὸς αὐτῷ καὶ τοῦ καθηγητοῦ τὸν ἀνθρώπινον μετηλλαχότων, but one should accept without hesitation the excellent emendation suggested in passing by P. Karlin-Hayter, "Gregory" (n. 30 above), 142 and 145.

35 Later we are given an extended sample of Ignatius's preaching and teaching from the time of his second patriarchate (98.1–104.13).

36 As we learn below (14.24 ff.), Ignatius founded a monastery on each of three Princes' Islands (Plate, Hyatrus, and Terebinthus), but in what order or when exactly we have no way of knowing. The fourth foundation was situated on the Asiatic side of the Bosphorus at a place called Satyros and was built in 873/74, dedicated to the Archangel Michael; see *ODB* 3:1847, s.v. *Satyr*, and Bury, *History* (n. 14 above), 30. Recent excavations by A. Ricci seem to have identified the remains of the Satyros monastery at a site known as the Küçükyaly Archeological Park in the Maltepe district of the modern city. For Terebinthus see R. Janin, *La géographie ecclésiastique de l'empire byzantin*, vol. 1, *Le siège de Constantinople et le patriarcat oecuménique*, pt. 3, *Les églises et les monastères*, 2nd ed. (Paris, 1969), 61–63.

37 Ἐν τούτοις picks up again the story of the 30-year period begun at 12.3 (Ἐν τούτοις) and now moves to the time of Ignatius's priesthood. Nicetas does not choose his words without a purpose. His use here of the formulaic ψήφῳ μέν . . . ψήφῳ δέ (cf. n. 8 above) is meant to signal clearly that at every stage of his career Ignatius both deserved advancement and achieved it in a fully legitimate way. Most crucially, it will apply to his elevation to the patriarchal throne, when in Nicetas's version there will be no mention of imperial involvement (22.6–7 ἐνεργείᾳ μὲν Θεοῦ Πνεύματος, συνεργίᾳ δὲ καὶ ψήφῳ ἀρχιερέων Θεοῦ). A point much stressed later by Nicetas is how starkly different the appointment of Photius was.

38 Even the procession of Ignatius through the lower ranks of the clergy (in contrast to that of Photius, as the author will assure us) is orderly and legal. Not only does the presiding bishop (Basil, *PmbZ* #935) have impeccably Orthodox credentials—he suffered persecution on behalf of the holy icons—but more importantly, the whole process is directly inspired by the Holy Spirit (16.9 αὐτουργίᾳ τοῦ παναγίου Πνεύματος).

39 The wording of the Greek text here (18.9–10) is quite similar to a passage in the *Synodicon Vetus* (154.11) dealing with the iconoclastic synod of 815 and the hardships inflicted on the supporters of icons; it reads δημεύσει, ἐξορίαις, λιμῷ, καὶ φυλακαῖς.

40   There is some disagreement in the sources as to whether, after the abdication of her husband Michael I Rangabe, Procopia stayed at her own convent in Constantinople or shared banishment with her offspring on the Princes' Islands; see *PmbZ* #6351. This passage of the *Life of Ignatius* would tend to support the latter scenario. The two sisters of Ignatius were Georgo (*PmbZ* #2290) and Theophano (*PmbZ* #8164); it is not possible to say which of the two is in question here.

41   This is the famous Theophanes the Confessor (*ODB* 3:2063; *PmbZ* #8107), who composed one of the most important Byzantine chronicles. He died ca. 817 and was revered by the Orthodox for his stand against iconoclasm (hence his designation as Ὁμολογητής, i.e., Confessor). The monastery that he founded, Megas Agros, was situated at Mt. Sigriane on the southern shore of the Propontis. See also n. 28 above.

42   For Theophilus, see n. 26. Theodora (*ODB* 3:2037–38; *PmbZ* #7286), empress wife of Theophilus, following the death of her husband assumed the role of regent for her infant son Michael and acted in that capacity from 842 to 856. Despite some initial hesitation (see Bury, *History,* 145–49), Theodora consented to the restoration of the cult of icon veneration. Perhaps in order to get around the considerable confusion in the sources about the sequence of events of the year 843 (including the deposition of John the Grammarian and the selection of Methodius) the author of the *Life of Ignatius* does not even mention the synod of 843, which officially brought an end to iconoclasm.

See *Synodicon Vetus,* chap. 156 and notes to that chapter.

43   For John see n. 27 above. The large number of unflattering nicknames he received reflects the level of animosity against him amongst the Orthodox. Of the two cited in this text, Ἰαννῆς is a play on his name that connects him with one of the two Egyptian magicians who confronted Moses, according to St. Paul (2 Tim. 3.8). In the apocryphal tradition they are said to have misled the Pharaoh, which would be very appropriate in this context, seeing that John in our text is assigned the blame for leading the emperor Theophilus astray on the matter of images. Bury (*History,* 148, n. 1), in his discussion of efforts to save the reputation of the emperor, cites this passage of the *Life of Ignatius* and comments, "One way of mitigating the guilt of Theophilus was to shift the responsibility to the evil counsels of the Patriarch John."

44   Methodius I (*ODB* 2:1355; *PmbZ* #4977) was patriarch from 843 to 847.

45   It is hard to say for sure whether there is a slight criticism of Methodius's appointment in the phrase τῆς βασιλίδος συνεργίᾳ. Despite the otherwise very laudatory words in Methodius's favor, it should not be ruled out that the hardliner Nicetas David, who normally bristles at any imperial involvement in patriarchal appointments, wishes to record a small note of displeasure here. On the other hand, since the imperial figure involved is the

τιμιωτάτη τῶν γυναικῶν καὶ πιστοτάτη, he may be feeling more lenient and accommodating. See also n. 37 above.

46 It could be regarded as curious that Nicetas is completely silent on the staunch opposition encountered by Methodius from the side of extremist elements in the Church, and presents him (contrary to all the evidence) as a rigorist in his treatment of former iconoclast bishops and clergy. This is all the more surprising given that, as Dvornik (*Photian Schism*, 13) comments, the new patriarch "was selected, not from the Extremists, . . . but from the partisans of a more liberal policy." He notes in another passage (ibid., 14) his suspicion that the campaign against Methodius originated from the circle that bred the enemies of Photius, in other words, forerunners of Ignatian diehards like Nicetas himself. Perhaps an empress and a patriarch who restore icons to their place in the Orthodox Church are beyond all reproach.

47 Patriarch Tarasius (*ODB* 3:2011; *PmbZ* #7235) and Empress Irene (*ODB* 2:1008–9; *PmbZ* #1439) convened the Second Council of Nicaea in 787, which decreed the restoration of icons after First Iconoclasm.

48 The monk, and former soldier, Ioannicius of Mt. Olympus (*ODB* 2:1005–6; *PmbZ* #3389) was a staunch supporter of icons and a highly influential spiritual figure throughout the first half of the 9th century.

49 It is a commonplace of hagiography that the advancement and success of holy figures is part of a divinely ordained plan. Dvornik (*Photian Schism*, 8–17) gives a clear account of the background to the struggles between the rival church parties putting forward candidates to succeed Methodius. See also Bury, *History*, 180–84.

50 The pious reluctance of Ignatius to accept the patriarchal throne is in stark and deliberate contrast to the behavior of Photius, as presented later by Nicetas (36.2–9).

51 This interesting passage has been astutely analyzed by Dvornik (*Photian Schism*, 17–18). As he points out, Ioannicius died in November of the previous year and nobody at that time could have foreseen the death of Methodius; nor was it possible for Theodora to be contemplating a possible successor then. Dvornik comments, "Nicetas only meant to show by this deliberate fabrication how groundless were the criticisms of Ignatius's adversaries about his alleged hostility to Methodius's religious policy." It is equally, if not more, likely that Nicetas wanted to provide a spiritual cover and excuse for the actions of Theodora. It looks very probable, as Dvornik goes on to suggest, that the Empress dispensed with the formalities of a synod and proceeded to the appointment of Ignatius after consulting some influential bishops. Other sources are short of precise information on the process, though the *Synodicon Vetus* (a text strongly biased in favor of Ignatius) goes out of its way to state baldly: κανονικῶς ἐπὶ τὸν θρόνον ἀναβιβάζεται (chap. 157). It is of interest to note that another hagiographical text associates Ioannicius with the choice of Ignatius's

predecessor. According to the anonymous *Life of Michael the Synkellos* (ed. M. B. Cunningham [Belfast, 1991], 102–4), following the deposition of John the Grammarian, the synod of bishops and Empress Theodora sent a delegation of two clerics and an imperial *spatharios* to consult the holy man at Mt. Olympus. After spending seven days alone in prayer Ioannicius emerged to announce that the man to be chosen as patriarch was the monk and presbyter Methodius.

52   The long litany of Ignatius's Christ-like virtues and noble qualities is meant not only to put him on a pedestal, but also to highlight the contrast with his enemies, among whom Nicetas has Photius foremost in mind. At the same time he makes little attempt to gloss over the frequent critical reactions to Ignatius's spirit of no compromise in dealing with ecclesiastical matters. His "boldness of speech" (παρρησία, 24.19), especially to the face of imperial figures, landed him in very serious trouble and cost him the patriarchal throne.

53   Bardas (*ODB* 1:255–56; *PmbZ* #791) was the brother of Empress Theodora, but reached a role of real power only after 856, when her son Michael III (*PmbZ* #4991) took over the throne. Some years later, in 862, Bardas was crowned Caesar by Michael.

54   The rumor (and Nicetas does not insist that it was more than that) was to the effect that Bardas, following the death of his son, began an illicit relationship with his widowed daughter-in-law, Eudokia Ingerina (*ODB* 2:739; *PmbZ* #1632). Dvornik (*Photian Schism*, 37) puts a very charitable and not unreasonable interpretation on the rumor, but the actual facts of the matter are lost forever. Bury, *History* (n. 14 above), 188, is less sympathetic to Bardas. Dvornik provided a later and more detailed account of the affair in "Patriarch Ignatius and Caesar Bardas," *Byzantinoslavica* 27, no. 1 (1966): 7–22, esp. 12 ff.

55   The feast of the Epiphany (τὰ Θεοφάνια) was celebrated in the capital by the patriarch, with the Emperor present, on the 6th of January in Hagia Sophia. See *ODB* 1.715, s.v. Epiphany. The episode will have taken place between 856 and 858, though Bury (*History*, 188) does not hesitate to assign it to 858. For a sense of the difficulties in dating events in this short period see app. 7 in Bury, *History*, 465–71.

56   The Domestic of the Schools was an important military rank and designated the commander of a regiment of troops.

57   Dvornik (*Photian Schism*, 37) comments on the reaction of Ignatius: "It was not so much his religious temperament and his rectitude that caused him to demur, but the fact that he owed the Empress everything: she had selected him for the patriarchal dignity and he meant to remain loyal." Bury, on the other hand (*History*, 188–89), cites in addition the evidence of the so-called *Libellus Ignatii*; according to this source the grounds for Ignatius's refusal were that Theodora and her daughters were unwilling to undergo tonsure. For

a similar explanation reported by Anastasius the papal librarian see the text quoted by Dvornik, *Photian Schism*, 55.

58 Our text is the sole source for the story about this Gebo (*PmbZ* #1942).

59 Located in the Propontis; most westerly of the Princes' Islands.

60 There are differences of understanding in the various sources and it is not at all clear whether τὰ Καριανοῦ refers to the palace of that name or to a monastic foundation. The matter is discussed by Bury, *History*, 160, n. 3, and Janin, *Les églises* (n. 36 above), 278; see also A. Berger, *Untersuchungen zu den Patria Konstantinupoleos* (Bonn, 1988), 476–77. Our text seems to indicate a monastery.

61 The episode of Ignatius's banishment, and the events leading up to it, are well presented by Bury, *History*, 188–89.

62 The passage (32.3–16) highlights the pivotal role of the Devil in the troubles of the era. In the phrase ὁ ἀπ' ἀρχῆς ἀνθρωποκτόνος there is a clear echo of John 8.44: ὑμεῖς ἐκ τοῦ πατρὸς τοῦ διαβόλου ἐστὲ καὶ τὰς ἐπιθυμίας τοῦ πατρὸς ὑμῶν θέλετε ποιεῖν. ἐκεῖνος ἀνθρωποκτόνος ἦν ἀπ' ἀρχῆς.

There is an interesting parallel in a fragment of Nicetas's commentary on the Psalms, where the target of the remarks is Photius: Τούτων ἀρχὴ τῶν σκανδάλων, μετὰ τὸν Σατάν, εὐθὺς ὁ κακῶς δι' αὐτοῦ ταῖς ἱεραῖς ἐκκλησίαις παρεισφθαρείς. . . . The fragment is quoted by Tamarkina, "Date of the Life" (n. 6 above), 621, from an unpublished French thesis.

63 For a thorough treatment of the resignation of Ignatius and the election of Photius see Dvornik, *Photian Schism* (n. 46 above), chap. 2.

64 *Protospatharios* was a high imperial dignity and it usually conferred membership of the senate (see *ODB* 3:1748). The "chief secretary" (πρωτασηκρῆτις) was head of the imperial chancery (*ODB* 3:1742).

65 Nicetas David, in a tour de force of descriptive writing, first presents a realistic picture of Photius's many intellectual accomplishments, but then quickly turns around to catalogue his major failings and to assure the reader that he lacked all of the virtues that should characterize the holder of the patriarchal office (virtues, it goes without saying, that his hero Ignatius had in abundance).

66 The verb used by Nicetas, μυσταγωγεῖται, is possibly a scoffing reference to the title of one of Photius's major writings, the Περὶ τῆς τοῦ ἁγίου πνεύματος μυσταγωγίας, though we cannot be sure that it was meant to cast aspersions on the Eastern view of the procession of the Holy Spirit. Henry Chadwick, in a chapter devoted to this issue and the treatise of Photius (*East and West: The Making of a Rift in the Church; From Apostolic Times until the Council of Florence* [Oxford, 2003], chap. 25), makes the comment that "No extant text from the Ignatian milieu discloses whether their leaders at any time expressed a view about the *Filioque*" (156) and he goes on to add (157) that "long after both Ignatius and Photius had passed from the scene there was to remain a

critical tradition at Constantinople which frankly regretted what Photius had said and done," i.e., in attacking the Latin doctrine of the *Filioque*.

67 The actual words of the church canon forbidding this type of appointment are quoted later at 48.14 ff.

68 For his part Photius, in a letter to Bardas (*Photii Epistulae et Amphilochia*, ed. Laourdas and Westerink, vol. 1, ep. 6), insists that he only very reluctantly and under pressure accepted the patriarchal throne. On the rival parties and the background to the election Dvornik (*Photian Schism*, 49–50) provides this account: "For fear of a schism, it was then agreed to eliminate all the bishops, whether Ignatians or anti-Ignatians, and to look for a capable candidate among the higher officials. This tradition had for a time proved popular in Byzantium, when troubles were many, and the practice had been resorted to with excellent results, as in the case of Tarasius and Nicephorus. So the synod presented to the government, besides an Ignatian and an anti-Ignatian, a neutral candidate, the *protasecretis* Photius, the very man whom the Emperor and Bardas had in mind from the beginning."

69 Again it will be useful to cite Dvornik's matter-of-fact comments (*Photian Schism*, 50): "The new Patriarch's consecration was a hurried affair, for he received all the degrees of the priesthood within the space of a week, a procedure that was of course against the rules of canon law, but under such exceptional circumstances the Byzantines considered themselves exempt from habitual practice. Nor was it an isolated case in Byzantium. Had not the consecration of the Patriarchs Paul III in 687, Tarasius in 784, and Nicephorus in 806, all laymen at the time of their elections, been conferred in total disregard of canonical rules?"

70 Gregory Asbestas (*ODB* 1:202–3; *PmbZ* #2480) was archbishop of Syracuse and an ally of Patriarch Methodius who had appointed him to the Sicilian position in 843/44. Whatever the "criminal charges" were, it would appear that the deposition took place only some years after the incident at Ignatius's consecration (847) recorded here, i.e., in ca. 853. For the "schism" that ensued as a result of the treatment meted out to Gregory in 847, see Bury, *History* (n. 14 above), 185. Much later, after Photius's installment for the second time as patriarch, Asbestas was given and occupied for a short time the bishopric of Nicaea (128.28–29).

71 Nicetas seems to recognize that, however well justified it might be, the reaction of Ignatius was a political blunder and not a wise start to his patriarchate.

72 For Peter of Sardis and Eulampius of Apameia see *PmbZ* #6088 and #1672.

73 The author's phrase "unable to quench" (οὐχ οἷος . . . κατασβέσαι) contains a word play on Gregory's second name (Ἀσβεστᾶς).

74   Here and elsewhere Nicetas insists on speaking of the "murderous" intentions of Photius against Ignatius. See 62.18–19 (ἀποστερῆσαι τὸν Ἰγνάτιον, εἰ δυνατόν, τῆς ζωῆς), 38.29 (πρόφασιν ἀπώλειας ἐζήτει κατ᾽ αὐτοῦ), 50.29 and 68.28 (θανατῶσαι), 62.21–22 and 88.15–16 (φονικὴ προαίρεσις), 70.14–15 (φονικὴ βουλή), 122.17 (τῷ φονίῳ λύκῳ); cf. 56.16 (ἀναιρεῖσθαι τοῦτον).

75   In fact, in a series of letters from Photius to Bardas (most notably the one cited earlier in n. 68) the patriarch passionately objects to the persecution initiated by the government. See Dvornik, *Photian Schism* (n. 46 above), 54 and Bury, *History*, 192.

76   Hieria was a suburb of the capital, situated on the Asiatic side of the Bosphorus to the south of Chalcedon. See Janin, *Les églises* (n. 36 above), 35–36.

77   Promotus was another suburb of Constantinople, across the Golden Horn in Galata. The reference may be to a monastery there known as τὰ Προμότου; see Janin, *Les églises*, 444–45. Leo Lalaco(n) (*PmbZ* #4508) held the title of Domesticus of the Numeri, among whose duties was supervision of the city prison of the Noumera (see *ODB* 1:647).

78   The prison of the Noumera was near the imperial palace; see previous note.

79   In his letter to Bardas (see n. 68) Photius explicitly refers to the case of Blasius (*PmbZ* #1015), mentioning, among other acts of violence against him, the cutting out of his tongue; he also notes sadly his own failed attempts to intervene on behalf of this cleric. For the office of *chartophylax*, which Blasius held, see *ODB* 1:416–17.

80   There is a detailed discussion of this "meeting" or synod, and the differences between the various sources that refer to it, in Dvornik, *Photian Schism*, 57–62; see also Bury, *History*, 191, n. 2.

81   For the idea of "ladder of virtues" see n. 32 above.

82   Nicolaus I (*ODB* 2:1466) became pope in April 858 and the embassy was sent in the first part of 860. The patriarch's letter to the pope is extant (*Photii Epistulae et Amphilochia*, ed. Laourdas and Westerink, vol. 3, ep. 288) and Bury (*History*, 193) characterizes it as "a masterpiece of diplomacy." The issue of Photius's connection with the end of iconoclasm has been dealt with in typically crisp and enlightening fashion by Cyril Mango in his contribution to the volume *Iconoclasm* (see n. 30 above), 133–40, entitled "The Liquidation of Iconoclasm and the Patriarch Photios." However, it is worth pointing out that, with regard to the view that after 843 iconoclasm was no longer a live issue, Henry Chadwick in *East and West* (n. 66 above), 145, n. 13, makes the following important remark on Mango's position: "This judgement is more likely to be true in political than in religious terms." There certainly has to be some good reason why Photius and the church at Constantinople were still so exercised about iconoclasm in the 850s and 860s.

83   Nicetas singles out for mention only two metropolitans, Theophilus of Amorium (*PmbZ* #8228) and Samuel of Chonae (*PmbZ* #6503). Dvornik, *Photian Schism* (n. 46 above), 71 ff. puts together a more detailed account of the delegation and its full membership (representing both Emperor Michael and the patriarch).

84   The wording of the Greek text here is very similar to what is reported in another pro-Ignatian document, the *Synodicon Vetus* (n. 6 above), chap. 159: παραιτησάμενον διὰ γῆρας λιπαρὸν καὶ ἀσθένειαν σώματος Φώτιος ἀνεδίδασκε τὸν Ἰγνάτιον. In actual fact, as Bury (*History*, 193) points out, Photius in his letter to the pope "abstained from saying anything against his predecessor." The termination of Ignatius's patriarchate will have been addressed in the letter from the emperor; see ibid., n. 2.

85   Zacharias (*PmbZ* #8636) was bishop of Anagni in central Italy and his colleague Rodoaldus (*PmbZ* #6404) had his episcopal see in Porto, near Rome.

86   Nicetas Ooryphas (*PmbZ* #5503) was commander of the imperial fleet at a particular point in his career, though not necessarily at the time in question (860). Bury, *History*, 143, n. 7, has clarifying remarks on the likely career and identity of this man.

87   The attack of the Russians in the summer of 860 is described in some detail by Bury, *History*, 419 ff.

88   Even the *Synodicon Vetus*, which is pro-Ignatian and purports to be a complete record of all synods, has no mention of these plural συνέδρια. It does of course cover the synod of 861 (chap. 159), which Nicetas is about to mention.

89   Both Bury (*History*, 196, n. 1) and Dvornik (*Photian Schism*, 80) understand this to be a palace at Poseus that belonged to his mother, the former Empress Procopia (cf. 54.1). On the other hand Janin, *Les églises* (n. 36 above), 80, takes τὰ Πόσεως to indicate merely a region of the city.

90   Dvornik provides a detailed account of the synod of 861, held in the Church of the Holy Apostles, in chapter 3 of *Photian Schism*. The main points are discussed by Bury, *History*, 195–97.

91   Baanes Angoures (*PmbZ* #719) was a palace official who held a number of positions of high rank in the course of his career. At the time of the council of 861, according to our text, he was a *praepositus* (*ODB* 3:1709). Later he had an active role in the council of 869–70, as described by Dvornik (*Photian Schism*, 147–50). See also 80.6 ff.

92   For the Church of St. Gregory of Nazianzus and its possible location see Janin, *Les églises*, 80–81. John Coxes (*PmbZ* #3315, perhaps the same person as #3310 and #3308) is here designated as a patrician; if he is identical with #3310 he will have also held the titles of *protospatharius* and *strategus*. *ODB* has articles on each of these dignities (3:1748, 1935–36).

93   Chadwick (*East and West* [n. 66 above], 142) nicely explains why the witnesses numbered precisely 72. It was part of the effort by the Greeks to be

accommodating to Roman conciliar customs and procedures; in the so-called "canons of Pope Sylvester" there is a stipulation that 72 witnesses are required in cases against prelates.

For the two patricians there are brief entries in *PmbZ* (#4455 and #7896); our text is the sole source of information. *Magistros* was a high-ranking dignity, and the entry in the *ODB* (2:1267) strangely omits this relatively early attestation for the office.

94 The obscure term "dibaptist" is attested only in this text; Du Cange, in his *Glossarium ad Scriptores Mediae et Infimae Graecitatis* (Lyon, 1688), already noted it from the *Vita Ignatii*, but did not hazard a suggestion as to its meaning.

95 The full text of canon 30, as quoted here, can be found in the edition of G. A. Rhalles and M. Potles, *Σύνταγμα τῶν θείων καὶ ἱερῶν κανόνων*, vol. 2 (Athens, 1852), 37. In the letter of Pope Nicolaus I to Emperor Michael, as quoted by Dvornik (*Photian Schism,* 75), we read, "For this purpose the legates will make a careful inquiry into his (i.e., Ignatius's) deposition and censure, with a view to discovering whether the canons have been observed or not."

It is possible that the "foolish judges" citing the canon is meant to include the papal legates, Zacharias and Rodoaldus. The words of the psalm quoted just before this ("their right hands are filled with gifts") can be easily taken to refer to the gifts that were presented to the two emissaries upon their arrival at the port of Rhadestus on their way to Constantinople. Nicetas returns to the explicit charge later (58.22, describing the two envoys as ὑπὸ Φωτίου δωροδοκηθέντες), and Pope Nicolaus came to the same conclusion some time after their return to Rome. See Chadwick, *East and West,* 146. Dvornik (*Photian Schism,* 77–78) discusses this episode and argues for a more innocent interpretation of the "presents" offered and accepted.

96 With this paragraph the writer puts in a nutshell the core of his argument in favor of Ignatius and against Photius.

97 The cleric Procopius (*PmbZ* #6376) is known only from the context of the council of 861.

98 In the case of Zacharias and Rodoaldus the reference is to their eventual condemnation by Pope Nicolaus at two Roman synods of 863 and 864; see Bury, *History,* 199 and Dvornik, *Photian Schism,* 101–2.

99 See n. 74 above.

100 Dvornik (*Photian Schism,* 87) is probably right to say that Nicetas David's account of the alleged suffering of Ignatius at the hands of his jailers "is undoubtedly exaggerated."

101 Presumably the tomb of Constantine V "Copronymus" (*ODB* 1:501; *PmbZ* #3703) would have been appropriate, as that of an ardent iconoclast, if the point of the mocking were to associate Ignatius with iconoclasm.

Karlin-Hayter (n. 30 above) argues plausibly for such an association dating from the patriarch's days in monastic life.

Does the word ἕδραν (52.10) refer rather to the "rump" of Ignatius? If so, then the meaning of the text would be somewhat different.

102 For these three men see *PmbZ* #7725 (Theodorus), #3306 (John), and #5604 (Nicolaus, son of Theodulus #7991).

103 On his mother's residence see n. 89 above.

104 On this episode and the subsequent flight of Ignatius Dvornik (*Photian Schism,* 87) comments, "This is just another story to be taken with caution, for the 'hagiographer' is certainly not saying everything."

105 The disciple of Ignatius, Cyprianus (*PmbZ* #4181), is not otherwise attested. There is no other extant instance of the word Συκαΐτικον, but it is most likely to indicate the place from which boats crossed over the Golden Horn to Sykae. This conjecture has been endorsed by Albrecht Berger, one of the leading experts on the historical topography of the capital. He writes (in a personal communication) that at the lower end of the portico in question (see below), "there was a gate in the sea wall, and outside was the jetty which is called *scala sycena* in the *Notitia urbis Constantinopolitanae,* and simply *Perama* by most later Byzantine sources. There is no doubt that this is also the *Sykaitikon*." He also specifies that the portico in this passage will have been the best known of all those in the city, namely, the "Great Portico" (Μακρὸς Ἔμβολος) which ran down from the central avenue or main street (the *Mese*) to the Golden Horn.

106 Blachernai (*ODB* 1:293) is in the northwest sector of the city, and the area included a famous church of the Virgin as well as an imperial palace. Just the words "dressed in white" by themselves would be enough to tell us that the "man" that Ignatius encountered was a divine apparition; it is a typical element of hagiographic stories. Further to his comments in the previous note A. Berger adds, "the usual way of processions from the Great Palace or the Hagia Sophia to the Blachernai went along the *Mese,* then down the *Makros Embolos* and along the Golden Horn to the northwest. It is quite natural, therefore, that Ignatios meets on his way a man who was just going to the Blachernai."

107 Referring to the main island groups within the Sea of Marmara (*ODB* 2:1303).

108 For (Nicetas) Ooryphas see n. 86 above. A *dromon* (*ODB* 1:662) was a swift warship employed by the Byzantine navy. For a full recent account the reader is referred to J. H. Pryor and E. M. Jeffreys, *The Age of the Dromon: The Byzantine Navy ca. 500–1204* (Leiden and Boston, 2006).

109 It is a common element of Byzantine mentality to believe that God's anger against mankind (ὀργὴ θεοῦ or, frequently, θεομηνία) manifests itself in the form of earthquakes and other natural disasters. Chronicles, from the time of Malalas in the 6th cent., provide many examples. The idea is also

encapsulated in a section of the *Histories* of Agathias from the same period (bk. 5, chap. 10), where he describes the plague that struck Constantinople in the year 558. He cites the explanations that Egyptians and Persians give for such phenomena and contrasts them with those of "others" (meaning the Byzantines): ἕτεροι δὲ ὀργὴν τοῦ κρείττονος αἰτίαν εἶναί φασι τῆς φθορᾶς, μετιοῦσαν ἀξίως τὰ τοῦ ἀνθρωπείου γένους ἀδικήματα καὶ τὸ πλῆθος ὑποτεμνομένην.

110 This will have been in the year 862.

111 Petronas (*ODB* 3:1644–45; *PmbZ* #5929), brother of the Empress Theodora and of Bardas, held a number of important positions, mostly military, during his career. An encolpion (*ODB* 1:700) was an object (usually of precious metal and decorated) hung around the neck to bring protection to the wearer. Here the encolpion, belonging to the emperor, is given to the fugitive Ignatius as a guarantee of security and safe passage.

112 The author confidently puts forward the conclusion that fair treatment meted out to his saintly hero was responsible (after God) not only for bringing the earthquake to a sudden halt, but also for leading the Bulgarians to baptism. It is meant of course as a direct and positive reflection on Ignatius and not at all on Bardas, who is elsewhere depicted as the chief enemy and tormentor of the patriarch (72.23 ff.).

113 On the "gifts" or "bribes" see n. 95 above.

114 See n. 98 above and the additional literature cited there.

115 The Lateran Synod of 863, whose acts have not survived. It is described in a letter of Pope Nicolaus, the one he sent three years later to the Eastern Patriarchs and which is mentioned in our text at 60.6–7. See Dvornik, *Photian Schism* (n. 46 above), 97–98. In the first canon of the synod Photius is referred to as *adulter et pervasor*, a phrase that is the exact match for ἐπιβήτορα καὶ μοιχόν cited by Nicetas (58.28) and as reported by the *Synodicon Vetus*, chap. 160: Φώτιον ὡς μοιχὸν ἀναθεματίζει καὶ ἐπιβήτορα. As Dvornik (*Photian Schism*, 99) intimates, these and similar derogatory names for Photius may well have been supplied by the supporters of Ignatius in Rome.

The idea of "adultery" in this context reflects the notion that a patriarch receives the Church as his "bride." Earlier (36.2–5), Nicetas had remarked about Photius, "For he did not refuse his appointment to the Church on the grounds that it was handed over to him in a lawless and unbecoming manner by the secular authorities, nor did he feel any qualms about the fact that after being united with another man it was now being betrothed to him in an adulterous union."

116 In 381 Maximus the Cynic was a rival contender for the patriarchal throne of Constantinople, having been consecrated by some Alexandrian bishops to replace Gregory of Nazianzus. The episode is discussed by Chadwick, *East and West*, 23–24.

117 Emperor Michael III had crowned his uncle as *Caesar* in 862. For the office of *curopalates* see n. 10 above.

118 There is considerable uncertainty about the exact identity of this Theophilus, and the best summation of the evidence will be found in *PmbZ* under the name of Theophilus Gryllus (#8222).

The *Vita Basilii*, composed by his grandson Constantine VII Porphyrogenitus, also contains a detailed and vivid account of young Michael's scandalous behavior, including two episodes involving Patriarch Ignatius; the text is in Theophanes Continuatus, 243B–246B. Worth reading also are the comments of Bury, *History* (n. 14 above), 162–63.

119 It is impossible to decide whether the man at the center of this strange episode, Eustratius (*PmbZ* #1829), was a real monk or an imposter. In any event the whole thing may be a fiction made for the purpose of showing how the cleverness of Photius turned back on itself and misfired.

120 For Cyprianus, from the entourage of Ignatius, see n. 105 above.

121 It is hard to know what precisely this means. If Photius had the man appointed to any kind of police force, he is not likely to have been a monk. Perhaps Nicetas simply wants to say that Photius made him head of a group of men who were pursuing and "persecuting" Ignatius on his behalf. A little later it is said of Photius that he was "hunting down" his rival (66.26: ἐπὶ τὴν τοῦ δικαίου ἐθήρευε ψυχήν).

122 And God, as the following paragraph reveals, was one of the parties angered by the behavior of Photius; He unleashed another earthquake (cf. 56.28–29), which also toppled the statue of Justin II, a bad omen. Cyril Mango devotes a few lines with customary precision to this event in "Épigrammes honorifiques, statues et portraits à Byzance," in Ἀφιέρωμα στὸν Νίκο Σβορῶνο, vol. 1 (Rethymno, 1986), 23–35 (here 32). This reference was gratefully received from Ivan Drpić. Though Nicetas mentions a precise day, the Feast of the Ascension (celebrated on the fortieth day after Easter), he provides no indication of the year in question. It may have been 863; Mango suggests around 865, perhaps on the basis of the chronicle accounts that he cites.

123 This bishop Basilius (*PmbZ* #941) was clearly a supporter of Ignatius.

124 The career and side-changing of Ignatius, the patriarch's namesake, is discussed in *PmbZ* (#2676). Demas was a trusted follower of St. Paul who abandoned the apostle when he was imprisoned in Rome. In assigning a reason, Paul was moved to say of him (2 Tim. 4.10) that he "loved this present world" (ἀγαπήσας τὸν νῦν αἰῶνα), an accusation echoed here in the wording of Nicetas.

125 It will be recalled that Ignatius had active connections with three of the Princes' Islands, including Plate; see n. 36 above.

126 This is the Russian attack of 860 described earlier in the text, 44.10 ff.

127 The "ritual purification" was entrusted to two bishops and a senator. Amphilochius (*PmbZ* #223) was appointed by Photius ca. 859 to the see of Cyzicus as a replacement for the deposed Ignatian bishop Antony. He was also active at the council of 861 (see Dvornik, *Photian Schism* [n. 46 above], 82). Theodorus (*PmbZ* #7728) is hardly known apart from this source; the possibility, as suggested by *PmbZ* (loc. cit.), that he may be identical with Theodore Santabarenus (#7729), seems rather slight. Pantoleon (*PmbZ* #5707), designated as "senator" (συγκλητικός) by our text, may be the same man as the Pantoleon addressed by Photius as πρωτοσπαθάριος in two letters (*Photii Epistulae et Amphilochia*, ed. Laourdas and Westerink, vol. 1, *ep.* 22 and vol. 2, *ep.* 168). But this is by no means certain; see the introductory remarks of Westerink to the first of those letters.

The condemnatory "with profane hands" is part of the rich vein of tit for tat that runs through the *Vita Ignatii*.

128 Prominent in this extended outburst (68.17–70.23) is the attack on the learning, vast library, and wide reading of Photius, and not even his theological and exegetical writings are spared by the inventive and vicious tongue of Nicetas.

129 The citation refers to the passage in *Letter* 130 of St. Basil (PG 32:562–64), where the main topic is Eustathius of Sebasteia and his doctrinal fickleness. The term ἀναθρονιασμός is peculiar to Nicetas (cf. his use of the equally rare verb ἀναθρονίζω at 68.6) and the phrase ἀναθρονιασμοὺς τελέσαι ἐθάρρησεν would seem to correspond to Basil's words (564C) ἀναχειροτονῆσαί τινας ἐτόλμησεν. The issue of ordinations by Photius was an important element in the controversies of the era. In view of the episode of the rededication of the altar on Plate (66.27 ff.) and the use of the term ἀναθρονίζω there, it is possible that Nicetas means to include that incident as well among the "abominable" acts carried out by Photius.

It is puzzling why our author connects Eustathius with Ancyra. The synod of Gangra (*ODB* 2:821–22) condemned some of the radical ideas and doctrines associated with Eustathius and his followers.

130 Philotheus (*PmbZ* #6191), the friend of Caesar Bardas, was a fiscal official of high rank. The wording in our text, γενικῶν λογοθέτην, could easily be a mistake in transmission for γενικὸν λ., as the more usual title for the holder of this office is γενικὸς λογοθέτης. See *ODB* 2:829–30, s.v. *genikon*.

131 Dvornik, *Photian Schism*, 88, n. 1, comments on this passage, which makes Bardas the main culprit in the persecution of Ignatius. A similar tone, with regard to Bardas and the emperor, is adopted in the so-called *Libellus* addressed to Pope Nicolaus by Theognostus, in the name (and voice) of Ignatius. The text is in PG 105:856–61 and Mansi 16:296–301.

132 The "prophetic" dream was literally fulfilled some three months later; see 74.15–22.

133 Ignatius at this time was in the Princes' Islands, but on which one is not known for sure; the episode described at 68.1 ff. might be an indication that he was stationed on Plate. The Leo Ptyolaemes (*PmbZ* #4510) named here as a kinsman of Photius is not otherwise attested.

134 The violent death of Bardas seems to have caught the Byzantine imagination. It took place during an expedition against the Saracens of Crete, when the forces were assembling in the theme of Thrakesion at a place called Kepoi, near the Maeander River in Asia Minor. Chronicle accounts speak of several ominous signs that forecast the event. The "History of Emperors" that goes under the name of Genesius has no fewer than three different episodes, including the dream, that gave forewarnings to the Caesar (Michael III, chaps. 20–22). Skylitzes (Emperor Michael, chap. 22), after noting "appearances of comets and portentous apparitions," goes on to describe two of the three occurrences featured by Genesius. In the illustrated version of the chronicle, the Madrid Skylitzes (Bibl. Nac. vitr. 26–2), both the dream (fol. 79r) and the assassination scene (fol. 80r) are depicted.

135 Basil ("the Macedonian") (*PmbZ* #832; *ODB* 1:260), of peasant origin, had been the emperor's chamberlain (*parakoimomenos)* and was crowned co-emperor in 866 following the removal of Bardas.

136 This was the Synod of Constantinople, held in 867. Our author styles it a ψευδοσύλλογος, which is matched by the *Synodicon Vetus*, where it is called a ψευδοσύνοδος (chap. 161). The two sources are also in complete agreement on the wording of the synod's outcome; both of them state that the pope was subjected to condemnation (καθαίρεσις), and anathema was declared against him (ἀναθεματισμός).

137 For the likely secret negotiations between Photius and Louis II of France (equally at odds with the papacy), see Bury, *History* (n. 14 above), 201; further details on the politico-religious background in Chadwick, *East and West*, 158 ff. Dvornik, *Photian Schism,* 121 ff., is more skeptical about "negotiations" between Constantinople and the court of Louis prior to the council of 867.

138 Zacharias (*PmbZ* #8635), bishop of Chalcedon, was a staunch supporter of Photius and later played a prominent part on the Photian side at the councils of 869–870 and 879–880. Theodore (*PmbZ* #7726), bishop of Laodicea (and formerly of Caria), was likewise a faithful follower of Photius throughout the latter's career as patriarch. As we are soon informed by Nicetas (78.20–21), this embassy to the Franks was recalled by Emperor Basil in September 867; see also *PmbZ* (*loc. cit.*), Dvornik *Photian Schism*, 124, and Bury, *History*, 203.

139 For this sentiment, and the language in which it is couched, cf. 66.24–25; 82.17–18.

140 Nicetas David does not recall here the dream of Bardas (72.11–12 and 30 ff.), which he might have done to good effect. The fate of Michael III is

unmistakably predicted there. While chronicle sources say that Michael was murdered in the "palace" of St. Mamas (i.e., in the suburbs, across the Golden Horn), our text seems to place the scene at the monastery of St. Mamas. The location of that institution was long a matter of dispute, but Janin, *Les églises*, 318–19, accepts the view of Pargoire that it was in the city proper and not beside the palace across the Golden Horn.

141 See n. 138 above.

142 The site of this rarely mentioned monastery was probably, according to Janin (*Les églises*, 455), not far from the city, on the European side of the Bosphorus.

143 It would appear (from some letters of Photius addressed to Elias) that this man held the title of *protospatharios* before being appointed a "commander of the imperial fleet"; see *PmbZ*, Elias #1503. For the latter office see *ODB* 1:663–64, *Droungarios tou Ploimou*.

144 The family of Michael I Rangabe (the father of Ignatius) owned a mansion in the Mangana region of the capital; it was converted into an imperial domain by this same Emperor Basil I. See *ODB* 2:1283–84, s.v. Mangana.

145 For Baanes see n. 91 above.

146 The whole episode of the illustrated acts of the synod (80.1–82.3) has been translated by C. Mango in *The Art of the Byzantine Empire* (Englewood Cliffs, NJ, 1972), 191–92. See also the useful remarks in L. Brubaker and J. Haldon, *Byzantium in the Iconoclast Era: The Sources* (Aldershot etc., 2001), 52–53, and in T. Papamastorakis, "Tampering with History: From Michael III to Michael VIII," *BZ* 96 (2003): 193–209 (in particular 200–1). One can only agree with Brubaker and Haldon (53) that the story is suspect. But even if it were not true, it would still be a marvelous piece of invention by a master of invective.

The physical description of these books is remarkably similar to that of a volume presented early in the following century to the patriarch Euthymius by Emperor Leo VI: βίβλον τε πάντερπνον ἐξ ἐνδύματος ὀξέου καὶ διαργύρου καὶ διαχρύσου περικεκοσμημένην (*Vita Euthymii*, 50.16–17), which the editor Karlin-Hayter translates as "and a delightful book in a purple binding embellished with silver and gold." Mango renders the Nicetas passage as "two volumes adorned on the outside with gold, silver and silken cloth." This reflects the reading of the Raderus (and PG) edition, where σὺν ὀξέσιν is replaced by σηρικοῖς.

147 For Asbestas see n. 70 above.

148 Whatever the precise nature of the criticism aimed at Ignatius in the inscription, the "covetousness" of Simon Magus will refer to the episode in Acts 8.9–24, where money is offered to buy power or office in the Church (the original act of simony). There may also be a suggestion of "iconoclasm"; see Papamastorakis, "Tampering," 201, as well as n. 82 above.

149 See above, 76.26 ff. and n. 138. By the "rulers of France" the author means Emperor Louis II and his wife Ingelberga.

150 For the immediate background to the restoration of Ignatius and the dethronement of Photius in November 867, see Dvornik, *Photian Schism* (n. 46 above), 132–37.

151 The Ἅγιον Φρέαρ was a building situated at the southeast corner of Hagia Sophia. It is mentioned with some frequency in the *De cerimoniis* of Constantine Porphyrogenitus and is briefly described in the Διήγησις περὶ τῆς Ἁγίας Σοφίας, section 22, in the edition of T. Preger, *Scriptores originum Constantinopolitanarum*, pt. 1 (Leipzig, 1901; repr. 1975).

152 This was to be the council of 869–870. It was later annulled by the synod of 879–80 and lost its ecumenical standing in both East and West until the eleventh century, when it became again the Eighth Ecumenical Council in the eyes of the Roman Church. See Dvornik, *Photian Schism*, 309–30.

153 For John the bishop of Perge-Syllaion in Pamphylia, see Dvornik, *Photian Schism*, 140 and 175. Peter of Sardis is fully covered in *PmbZ* #6088. Basil the *spatharios* does not seem to have an entry in *PmbZ*, but is noted by Dvornik, *Photian Schism*, 140–41.

154 Hadrian II (*ODB* 2:892), the successor of Nicolaus I, was consecrated pope on 14 Dec. 867. If Dvornik's hunch is correct, the delegates from Byzantium will have arrived in Rome at the end of winter 869 or slightly later (*Photian Schism*, 139–40).

155 Further information on the legates Donatus and Marinus will be found in *PmbZ*, #1390 and #4819.

156 A brief discussion of the Eastern legates is provided by Chadwick, *East and West* (n. 66 above), 166. On the question of the Patriarch of Antioch at the period (here identified as Michael), the *Synodicon Vetus* (chap. 162) names him Nicolaus, while the acts of the council (Mansi 16:18A) indicate that the see was vacant during these years.

157 A detailed account of and commentary on this council will be found in chapter 5 of Dvornik's *Photian Schism*.

158 For the terms used here see n. 115 above.

159 Dvornik, *Photian Schism*, 149, n. 4, comments on the "tallness" of this anecdote.

160 On the canon in question see n. 95 above. In his tirade against this aspect of the council Nicetas shows his true colors as an arch-conservative and rigid interpreter of church canons. He was not a man to compromise and the same hard-line stance landed him in trouble during the tetragamy affair of Emperor Leo VI. See Dvornik, *Photian Schism*, 273 and *ODB* 3:1480 (Niketas David Paphlagon). From Nicetas's point of view it was the failure of the council to fully implement canon 30 that led directly to the second patriarchate

of Photius (878–886) or, as he colorfully puts it (92.8–19), that "let the wolf in among the sheep."

161 The reference here is to Gregory Asbestas in particular; see above 36.16 ff. and n. 70.

162 In 787 Empress Irene and Patriarch Tarasius convened the Seventh Ecumenical Council (the Second Council of Nicaea), which sought to bring iconoclasm to an end. A. Kazhdan comments in his *ODB* (3:2011) entry on the patriarch, "Tarasios, however, in his desire for pacification, assumed a mild position with regard to former Iconoclasts as well as repentant clergymen condemned for simony. The patriarch's moderate attitude inspired criticism by Theodore of Stoudios and his partisans." He goes on to remark that the dispute between the two factions of iconophiles became especially acute during the troubles associated with the fourth marriage of Emperor Leo VI, an illustration of which we have here in the criticisms of Nicetas. See also n. 160.

163 The Greek term is σταυροπάται ("those who trample on the Cross") and Dvornik (*Photian Schism*, 216) explains as follows: "i.e. the Photianists who, by frequently violating their promises, had discredited the cross which by common usage preceded their signatures." See also n. 6 above.

164 In hindsight the lone buffalo who ran right up to the pulpit will have been Photius.

165 Just as an earthquake that occurred following Photius's first consecration (56.28 ff.) was taken by the supporters of Ignatius as a sign of God's anger, so here violent weather and other omens were understood to indicate the machinations of the Devil against their hero.

166 In this section of the *Vita* we find Nicetas in his most hagiographic mode. It was a tenet of Byzantine popular belief that the Holy Spirit descended and made its presence known at the celebration of the Eucharist (a phenomenon often designated by the term ἐπιφοίτησις), and this could occur only in the case of a worthy celebrant. The belief is reflected, for example, in several stories collected by John Moschus in his *Spiritual Meadow* (trans. J. Wortley [Kalamazoo, MI, 1992]), namely, nos. 25, 27, and 150. There is also an interesting episode revolving around the topic in the *Life of John the Almsgiver* by Leontius of Neapolis, ed. A.-J. Festugière (Paris, 1974), 387.

167 At 104.14 ff. Nicetas usefully lists the various distinct groups that were the audiences for the patriarch's preaching or instruction: monks and hermits, rich people, secular rulers, and members of the church hierarchy. It is not clear whether the whole section from 98.1 to 104.13 is an example taken from one sermon to one particular audience or represents words addressed to more than one of those groups. Certainly the part from 100.7 to the end sounds eminently suited for monastic ears, and the virtues and vices discussed there are the ones typically associated with solitaries. This impression is strengthened by the evocation of the "ladder of virtues" (τῶν ἀρετῶν ἀνιέναι τὴν κλίμακα,

102.9), which in turn may be a nod towards one of the best known works of monastic spirituality, the *Heavenly Ladder*, written by John Climacus (*ODB* 2:1060–61); see n. 32 above. The earlier part of Ignatius's "preaching" seems by contrast to have more of a theological or doctrinal bent and may reflect an address to members of the hierarchy. All of this is to assume (without proof) that these are in fact the actual words and thoughts of Ignatius and not a text made up by his biographer.

168 James "the brother of the Lord" is traditionally commemorated in the Orthodox Church on 23 Oct. (*ODB* 2:1030–31). Ignatius died on 23 Oct. (877), as is spelled out at 106.27–28. Further time and age specifications are provided at 110.7–9.

169 The church of the martyr Menas was situated due north of Hagia Sophia in the acropolis area of the city; see Janin, *Les Églises* (n. 36 above), 333–35. According to our hagiographer the miracles performed by the saintly patriarch already began to occur at this church during the brief layover of his corpse there.

170 The final resting place of the body was the church of St. Michael the Archangel, at the site of Ignatius's monastic foundation across the Bosphorus; see n. 36 above.

171 Presumably this is all another thinly veiled reference to the clever and unholy machinations of Photius and his supporters.

172 The writer subscribes to the stock ideas of hagiographers and professes to be able to provide only a few examples from a countless multitude of miracles worked by God through the agency of the holy man.

173 The account of the miracles contains all the typical elements of the genre: incubation at the tomb of the saint, visitations from the holy man by way of visions and dreams, healing effected by means of oil or fluid sanctified by contact with the relics, or cures by touching objects associated with him (in the case of Ignatius, cloth and chains); and cures produced (through faith) at a distance from the tomb.

174 There is no general consensus on what precisely the verb ἀπομυρίζω means in Byzantine hagiographic texts. None of the standard dictionaries of late antique or medieval Greek (including the *Lexikon zur byzantinisch-en Gräzität*) has a fully satisfactory definition: "to wipe off ἀπομύρισμα" (Sophocles); "? anoint with holy oil" (Lampe); "(Reliquien) mit Weihwasser besprengen" (*Lexikon*). The best explanation is almost certainly that of J. Pargoire in the entry "Apomyrisma" in *DACL* 1:2603–4, who understands the noun ἀπομύρισμα to refer to substances that were blessed or sanctified by contact with a saint's relics. For the case presented by our text, the drink that was given to the woman was, in the view of Pargoire, water that had been poured over the beard or the hair of the saint. It is conceivable too that the water had been blessed rather by the immersion of some of the saint's hair in it. In any

case, the passive of the verb here (τριχῶν ἀπομυρισθεισῶν) indicates that the hair was subjected to a certain process for the purpose of preparing blessed water. This same process (ἀπομύρισις) was employed for the second woman as well (112.23–24). The whole issue has been dealt with in considerable detail by V. Ruggieri in a valuable article, "ΑΠΟΜΥΡΙΖΩ (ΜΥΡΙΖΩ) ΤΑ ΛΕΙΨΑΝΑ, ovvero la genesi d'un rito," *JÖB* 43 (1993): 21–35, though he does not include the Nicetas text in his discussion and is probably off the mark on some points of his exposition. In the cure of the next woman (lines 26 ff.), the holy oil is likely to have been taken from a lamp burning over or beside the tomb of Ignatius.

175 This individual is otherwise unknown. It is noteworthy that in the present story Ignatius is given the role of a military saint.

176 In the seventh-century *Epitome of Medicine* by Paul of Aegina, for example, there is a full description of the surgical procedure of embryotomy (6.74), employed when the mother's life is in danger due to difficulties in childbirth.

177 The reference is to our hero's namesake, Ignatius the famous first-century bishop of Antioch, who is consistently labeled ὁ θεοφόρος in the headings to his letters.

178 The ecclesiastical *sakellarios* (*ODB* 3:1828–29) was a church treasury official, originally associated (as here too, presumably) with the Great Church in the capital. As such, he would have been an appropriate person to send in search of treasure (as alleged) in a monastery just across the Bosphorus.

179 The invented name Beclas (Βεκλᾶς) will turn out to be (120.2–4) a reference to Emperor Basil I himself.

180 According to tradition, Tiridates (Trdat) the Great (*ODB* 3:2110) became the first Christian king of Armenia early in the fourth century, after being converted by Gregory the Illuminator (*ODB* 2:883–84), whom he had previously persecuted. Among the mosaics in Hagia Sophia there was a group of thirteen bishops in the south and north tympana of the nave, two of which depicted Patriarch Ignatius (north) and Gregory the Illuminator (south). C. Mango, in *Materials for the Study of the Mosaics of St. Sophia at Istanbul* (Washington, D.C., 1962), 55–57, has some interesting comments on the somewhat unexpected presence of the portrait of Gregory and speculates on a possible connection with a cult of that saint promoted by Basil I "for political and dynastic reasons."

181 There is a full discussion (with earlier bibliography) of the script of the fake book in G. Cavallo, "ΓΡΑΜΜΑΤΑ ΑΛΕΞΑΝΔΡΙΝΑ," *JÖB* 24 (1975): 23–54, and especially 23–31.

182 Apart from what we are told here we know next to nothing about this imperial cleric who later, according to our text, became bishop of Caesarea in Cappadocia. It is intriguing that the author of the chronicle known as Pseudo-Symeon Magistros (*ODB* 3:1983) gives Theophanes the otherwise unattested

sobriquet Σφηνοδαίμων and has one or two other details different from the version of Nicetas. It is possible that they were drawing variously on the same source, or that Pseudo-Symeon was using another (historical) account of the times by Nicetas. See also n. 6 above.

183   On Theodore Santabarenus and his checkered career see *ODB* 3:1839 and *PmbZ* #7729.

184   For the conflicting reports on the issue of a supposed reconciliation between Photius and Ignatius, see Dvornik, *Photian Schism* (n. 46 above), 167–72.

185   Dvornik (ibid., 164–65) raises the possibility that Photius at this time may have resumed teaching at the so-called Magnaura "university," a school set up at the Magnaura palace during the reign of Emperor Michael III (842–867).

186   For the notion of "trampling on the Cross" see n. 163 above.

187   Leo Katakoilas is mentioned a few times in the anonymous *Vita Euythmii* of the tenth century (ed. P. Karlin-Hayter [Brussels, 1970]), where he is designated as δρογγάριος without additional specification (chap. 2, p. 11.16). It may be of significance that in the only other place in which that *Vita* mentions a δρογγάριος the title is distinguished as δ. τῶν πλοΐμων, "*drungarius* of the fleet" (chap. 17, p. 109.27). There is some further information on Leo available in *Byzantine Monastic Foundation Documents*, ed. J. P. Thomas et al. (Washington, D.C., 2000), 1:120. For the office "*drungarius* of the guard" (δρουγγάριος τῆς βίγλης), see *ODB* 1:663.

188   Licinius (*ODB* 2:1225–26), the fourth-century emperor and onetime colleague of Constantine I, became a persecutor of the Christians later in his career.

189   Even this last element is meant to be a criticism of Photius, as canon law forbade the transfer (μετάθεσις, cf. 124.14, 126.27–28) of bishops from one see to another, though this occasionally did happen.

190   We have little further information about Theodore of Patras. See the short article by V. Grumel, "Qui fut l'envoyé de Photius auprès de Jean VIII?" *Échos d'Orient* 32 (1933): 439–43. John VIII (*ODB* 2:1052–53) had become pope in 872, five years before the reinstatement of Photius as patriarch.

191   Literally, "the sealings of the sealing devices." The devices (βουλλωτήρια) were iron pliers, each head of which would have carried, engraved on it, the name of the metropolitan and his see. The sealing material was lead, and it was lead blanks squeezed between the heads that received the image contained in the *boulloterion*; the sealing so made served to authenticate the signature on a document. This information was gratefully received from John Nesbitt.

192   This Peter will have worked in the office of the patriarchal secretary, if he was not the secretary himself. For a brief discussion of the secular title see *ODB* 2:1431–32, s.v. *mystikos*.

193 Euphemianus, bishop of Euchaita, is not well known to history, but the *Catalogue of Byzantine Seals at Dumbarton Oaks and in the Fogg Museum of Art*, vol. 4 (Washington, D.C., 2001), 44, records a seal bearing his name.

194 For Nicephorus of Nicaea see *PmbZ* #5333 and for the office of *orphano-trophos*, *ODB* 3:1537–38; in the present instance the position is clearly given to a churchman, as opposed to a layman, though it is not specified that he held it in the capital.

195 For Amphilochius, see n. 127 above, and for Gregory, n. 70.

196 Among the extant works of Photius no funeral oration on Gregory is found.

197 Constantine (*ODB* 1:498), the eldest and favorite son of Emperor Basil I, was killed in a hunting accident in September or October of 879, shortly before the council of 879–880.

Italy, western Greece, and Anatolia

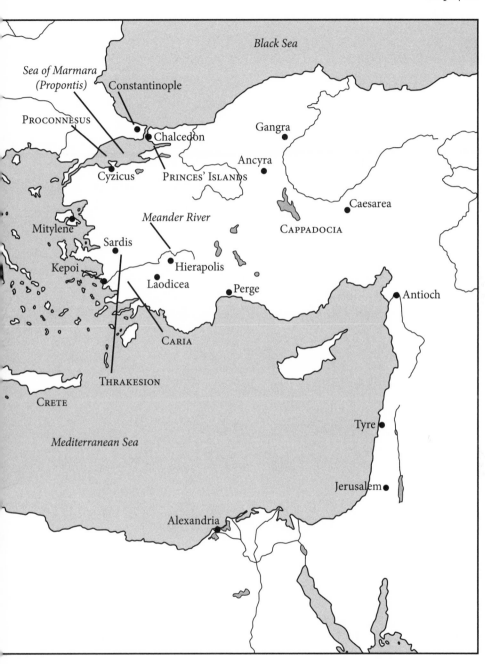

Black Sea

Sea of Marmara
(Propontis)   Constantinople

PROCONNESUS   Gangra

Chalcedon

Ancyra

Cyzicus   PRINCES' ISLANDS

Caesarea

Mitylene   Meander River   CAPPADOCIA

Sardis

Kepoi   Hierapolis

Laodicea

Perge   Antioch

CARIA

THRAKESION

CRETE

Mediterranean Sea

Tyre

Jerusalem

Alexandria

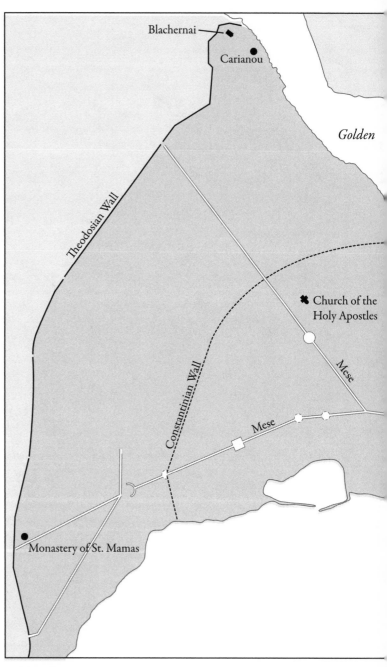

Constantinople

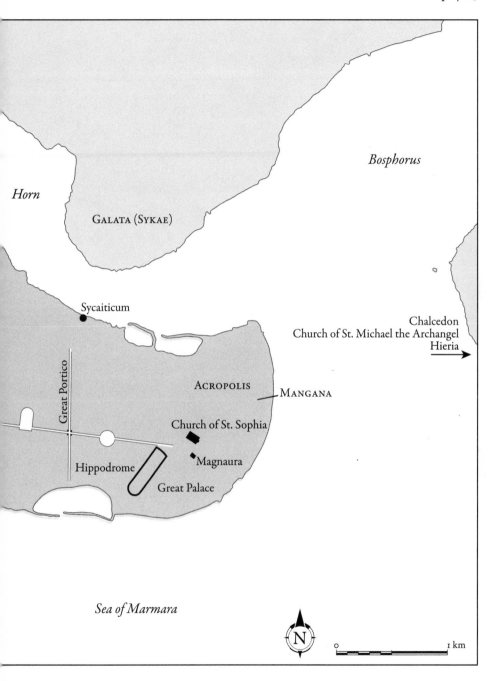

Bosphorus

Horn

GALATA (SYKAE)

Sycaiticum

Chalcedon
Church of St. Michael the Archangel
Hieria

Great Portico

ACROPOLIS

MANGANA

Church of St. Sophia

Magnaura

Hippodrome

Great Palace

Sea of Marmara

N

0   1 km

GREEK PROPER NAMES

GREEK TERMS AND VOCABULARY

ἀββᾶς 122.3
ἀβέβαιος 74.31
ἀγάπη 12.29, 31; 44.32; 64.2, 12; 100.14;
 102.20; 130.28
ἄγγελος 70.27; 100.23; 130.31;
 (messenger, harbinger) 92.27
ἅγιος 2.1, 6; 8.16; 16.5; 20.14; 36.10;
 70.19; 82.21; (Ignatius) 44.10; 54.14;
 66.27; 78.30; 108.12, 21; 112.10, 19, 29;
 114.26; 118.17; 126.19; 130.2; (Φρέαρ)
 84.18; (τὰ ἅ.) 12.6; (sup.) 78.26;
 86.21; 88.2
ἁγιωσύνη 82.8
ἁγνίζειν 24.1; 98.31
ἀγνωσία 4.12
ἄγραφος (στίχος) 82.16; -ως 4.8
ἀγρυπνία 12.19
ἀγών 2.23; 18.27; 40.15; 114.8
ἀγωνίζεσθαι 16.4, 12; 38.19; 48.18; 50.29
ἀγωνιστής 18.22
ἀδέκαστος 94.31
ἀδελφοκτόνος (μανία) 54.15
ἀδιαλείπτως 18.25
ἀδικία 4.16; 6.32; 10.18; 24.14; 30.2, 24;
 36.8; 40.5; 50.25; 58.2; 62.30; 68.21;
 78.14; 92.2 ἀδιόρθωτος 68.3
ἄδυτον, sanctuary of church 72.14; (pl.)
 10.5; 84.24
ἀείζωος 22.15
ἀειθαλής 22.15
ἀέναος 98.30
ἀθέμιτος (πρόσταγμα) 116.29
ἀθεσμία 30.28
ἄθεσμος 76.20; 130.16; (sup.) 68.29; -ως
 36.3; 124.12
ἀθετεῖν 28.23; 38.24
ἀθέτησις (εἰκόνων) 10.29

ἀθετητής 92.14
ἀθέως 82.22
ἄθλησις 2.1; 4.5; 84.12
ἀθλητής (of Ignatius) 42.32; 58.8
ἀθλίως 74.20
ἀθλοφόρος 130.32
ἀθῷος 30.25; (of Ignatius) 38.18; 46.4;
 54.3; 124.9; cf. 58.6
αἰκία 12.21
αἰκισμός 38.26
αἱμυλία 120.31
αἱρεσιάρχης 70.17
αἵρεσις 30.8, 9; (Iconoclasm) 8.14,
 30; 20.7, 17, 22; 42.19; (Sabbatianism)
 10.19, 24
αἱρεσιώτης 20.20, 27
αἱρετικός (ἀχλύς) 16.18; (λύμη καὶ
 ἀπώλεια) 22.14; (οἱ αἱρ.) 16.29;
 30.11; 92.4
αἰσχρός 66.9; (sup.) 48.7; 62.8
αἰσχρουργία 124.15
αἰσχύνη 36.7, 29; 66.6; 70.21
ἀκαθαρσία 24.3
ἀκάθαρτος 12.7
ἀκάθεκτος (ζῆλος) 2.10; (λύσσα) 80.17
ἀκανονίστως 48.31
ἀκαταίσχυντος (ἐλπίς) 12.31
ἀκαταστασία 26.8; 94.12; 120.28
ἀκηδία 102.21, 27
ἀκολασία 100.29
ἀκολουθία (πνευματική) 16.12
ἀκρασία 60.16, 19
ἀκρίβεια 4.7; 88.30
ἀκριβής 94.23; 96.1; -ῶς 98.2
ἀκρισία 42.5
ἀκυροῦν 90.25
ἀλαζονεία 6.8; 34.25

ζηλοῦν 4.16

ζηλωτής 8.30

ζημία 44.8; 46.30

ζωγραφία 80.17

ζωγράφος 80.16

ἦθος 6.1; (pl.) 8.28

θανατηφόρος 40.22

θαῦμα 18.31

θαυμάσιος 18.29; 114.15; (comp.) 114.16; (sup.) 116.2; 120.17; τὸ θαυμάσιον 110.25; 116.17

θαυματοποΐα 114.30

θαυματουργία 108.18; 114.3

θαυματουργός (of Ignatius) 114.23

θεανδρικός (παρουσία) 30.7

θεαρχία 98.19, 24

θεαρχικός 74.29

θεήλατος (ὀργή) 74.20; 116.29

θεῖος (ἐντολή) 102.29; (ἱεράρχης) 4.18; (λόγοι) 70.12; (ὄργια) 62.13; (σορός) 108.17; (τὰ θ.) 12.7; 60.19; (ὕδατα) 12.12

θεῖος (uncle) 26.12; 58.9

θεοβουλεύτως 20.25

θεόληπτος (of Ignatius) 114.6

θεολογικῶς (ref. Gregory of Nazianzus) 34.12

θεόργιστος 72.29

θεοφόρος 20.26; 110.21; 116.3; 132.3; (of bishops) 16.5

θεσμοθεσία 104.22; 126.15

θεσμός 92.11; 94.15; 122.16

θεωρία 12.16; (τοῦ ἀγαθοῦ) 98.13; (τῶν θείων) 98.29

θλῖψις 12.5; 16.8; 18.9, 24; 44.3, 5, 27; 56.23; 68.31; 86.2; 94.31; 104.1, 25; 108.28; 122.28; 124.11

θρόνος (episcopal) 128.7, 12; (papal) 82.28; (patriarchal) 8.22; 10.1; 12.2; 20.10; 22.7; 28.27; 36.14; 40.16; 50.1; 68.29; 78.22; 84.27; 92.11; 96.26; 124.8, 14; 126.11; sim. 72.27

ἴασις 86.1; 108.13; 112.25

ἰατήριος 108.25

ἰατρεῖον 110.21

ἰατρική 34.2

ἰατρός 112.9; 114.21

ἰδιόχειρον, autograph document 80.1; 126.28

ἱεράρχης, patriarch 2.25; 4.4, 18; 8.20; 26.5, 20; 88.16; 96.28; 104.31 bis; 114.4; bishop 16.5; 106.25

ἱεραρχία, episcopal/patriarchal office 2.9; 18.29; 22.7; 36.1; 38.7; 122.22; (of God 130.29)

ἱεραρχικός (θρόνος) 36.14; 92.10; (στολή) 50.8; 106.21; (sup., of Ignatius) 104.21

ἱερατικός (ἔργα) 66.8; (τελείωσις) 126.22; (ἡ ἱ., priesthood) 16.16; 18.14

ἱερεύς 16.11; 18.4; 20.18; 46.16; 60.24; 84.23; 88.1; 90.19; 96.25; 104.20

ἱεροκῆρυξ (of lector) 16.10

ἱερολογία, Holy Scripture 70.10

ἱερομάρτυς 118.29

ἱερόσυλος 124.19

ἱεροτελεστής 36.16

ἱερουργεῖν 96.30

ἱεροφάντης 124.19

ἱερωσύνη, priesthood 16.5; 20.10; 22.1; 122.14, 25

ἱκανάτοι 6.26

ἰνδικτιών 78.18

ἱπποδρόμιον (Constantinople) 94.9

ἱστορεῖν 4.32; (pass.) 116.18

ἱστορία 110.13; 118.27, 32; 130.22

ἰταμότης 58.4

καθαγιάζειν 14.30

καθαιρεῖν, condemn/depose 8.16; 20.11, 16; 36.20; 48.15, 21; 52.1; 58.29; 76.10; 80.25; 82.28; 88.26; 90.21, 22; 92.9; 122.20; 124.24; 126.10, 13

καθαίρεσις 20.24; 40.28; 42.20; 52.3; 54.5; 58.26; 68.29; 76.15; 82.21; 88.17; 90.1

καθαιρετικός (ψῆφος) 88.30

καθαρίζειν 116.10

καθέδρα (episcopal) 88.9; (patriarchal) 36.9

καθηγεμών 12.21; 14.20

καθηγητής 14.5, 8; 36.16

καθηγιάζειν 14.30

καθοσίωσις, high treason 28.1

παίδευμα 2.7
παιδοτριβεῖν 12.26
παλάτιον 4.28; 10.6; 94.7; (βιβλιοθήκη τοῦ π.) 120.9; (Magnaura) 84.8; (pl., Mangana) 78.28
παλινδρομεῖν 20.22
παλινοστεῖν 58.22
παλινῳδία 74.25
παμβασιλεύς (God) 6.14
παμβέβηλος 8.31
πανάγιος (Πνεῦμα) 16.9; 90.25
πανάθλιος 74.4
πανένδοξος 40.28; 130.32
πανευλαβῶς 22.5; 106.24
πανεύφημος 130.31
πανηγυρίζειν 96.16
πανίερος (of Ignatius) 54.32
πανουργία 78.12, 31; 88.3; 128.18
πανοῦργος 122.3; (sup.) 122.4
παντέφορος (ὀφθαλμός) 8.1
παντορρημοσύνη 84.2
πανύμνητος 96.14
πανωλεθρία 92.31; 130.11
πάπας, (patriarch of Alexandria) 86.17; Pope of Rome 42.16, 24, 29; 58.23; 62.29, 31; 64.12, 18; 76.8; 82.20, 27; 86.4, 10, 13, 17, 28; 88.18, 30; 128.10
παραγγελία 100.7; 104.14
παραδειγματίζειν 84.6
παραδοξοποιΐα 114.16
παράδοσις (ἐκκλησιαστική) 70.23; 92.12; 94.18
παραιτεῖσθαι request 36.2; abdicate, resign 28.27; 32.26; 128.26; cf. 42.25; refuse 22.5
παραίτησις 28.20
παράκλησις 2.7; 88.7; 94.22
παρακνίζειν 2.21
παρακοιμώμενος 76.6
παραλογιστής 8.17
παρανομεῖν 28.31
παρανομία 30.2, 28; 32.25; 58.2; 62.12; 130.20
παρανόμως 124.13
παραπικραίνειν 14.3
παρειμένος 116.10

παρείσδυσις 92.2
παρεισφθείρειν (of heresies) 30.8
παρθενικῶς 6.18
παροιμία 36.11; 56.22; 122.6
παροξυσμός 64.2
παρρησία 22.3; 24.19; 40.25; 62.2, 6
παρρησιάζεσθαι 24.16; 26.28
πατήρ (of monastic superior) 14.5, 20; parent, 4.20; 6.24; 16.32; 42.12; 60.20; 100.4; 120.1; 130.7; (of patriarch) 2.1; (pl., Holy Fathers) 12.15; sim. 106.1; 128.30; cf. 100.9; (of Ignatius) 2.1; 110.21; 114.6; 118.5; 132.2; (of God the Father) 30.3; 98.21, 24; 100.17; 104.13; 132.5
πατριαρχεῖον 28.13; 76.14; 80.2; 86.15; 122.12
πατριάρχης 20.1; 26.18; 28.9, 17; 36.23; 38.17, 26; 44.15; 48.25; 50.10; 58.1, 10, 23; 60.7, 27; 62.3; 66.24; 78.26; 84.8; 86.19, 20, 22, 30; 88.2; 94.16; 112.4; 114.30; 116.25; 122.11, 15, 28
πατριαρχικός (θρόνος) 12.2; 20.10; 78.22; 96.26; 124.7; (οἶκος) 62.25; 94.7; (τιμή) 74.23
πατρίκιος 4.22; 26.11; 28.25; 46.27; 48.2; 58.8; 76.5, 24; 84.20
πατρίς 4.18
πεζοπορεῖν 46.25
πέπλον 108.5; 114.24
περιβομβεῖσθαι 24.25
περιορίζειν 8.8
περιφανέστατος (of Constantinople) 4.20
πίστις 4.4; 12.28, 29, 30; 16.21, 28; 20.19; 22.3, 15; 34.22; 38.15; 74.30; 96.4, 29; 98.7; 100.14; 102.2, 3; 104.8; 110.14, 30; 112.10, 28, 30; 114.25; 116.15; 124.23; 130.28
πιστότατος (of imperial couple) 4.21; (empress) 20.5
πλάνη 20.9
πλάσμα 6.2; 30.19; 128.15
πλασματογραφία 62.25
πλασματώδης (βιβλιδάριον) 120.15; (ἱστορία) 118.32

πλάττεσθαι   36.10
πλεονεξία   80.27; 100.32
πληροφορεῖν   64.12; 114.7
πλοῖον   40.20; 44.19; 56.4; 108.14
πνεῦμα/Πνεῦμα, Holy Spirit   2.26; 12.13;
   14.9; 16.4, 9; 18.2; 22.6; 24.2; 54.17,
   31; 60.22; 90.25; 96.18, 23; 98.9, 21;
   100.11; 102.26; 132.6; (ἐναντίον) 60.23;
   (πονηρόν) 108.10, 25; 116.12; (sim.)
   110.17; (τῆς προφητείας) 70.29; spirit/
   soul 16.30; 68.27; 100.15; 102.32; 104.30;
   wind/storm 94.5, 6
πνευματικός (ἀκολουθία)   16.12;
   (διδασκαλία) 14.13; (ἡλικία) 12.27;
   (κολυμβήθρα) 8.5; (χαρά) 102.31
πνευματοκινήτως   96.17
ποίησις   34.1
ποιμαίνειν   20.29
ποιμήν, monastic superior   14.7; (of
   patriarch) 2.26; 20.12, 21; 22.12; 24.10;
   28.23; 38.3; 62.14; 84.14; 118.6; sim.
   130.15; (of Jesus) 50.19
ποίμνιον   14.14; 122.18
πόλεμος   6.8; 114.8
πόλις: ἡ π., Constantinople   6.11; 24.25;
   40.24; 42.28; 46.9; 56.11; 84.16; 92.23
πολιτεία, civil politics   32.32; state/
   government 60.5; 84.1; 128.12; way of
   life 4.2; 24.6; (μοναδική) 12.9
πολίτευμα (ἐν οὐρανοῖς)   102.6
πολιτικός, secular   76.24; (ἀξίωμα) 8.27;
   (πράγματα) 12.3; 24.23
πολύθλιπτος   72.22
πολυμήχανος   110.5; 120.29
πολύπλοκος   78.31; 104.6; 118.12
πολυτεχνία   128.3
πονηρία   42.12; 78.30; 92.8; 100.18;
   124.4; 126.21
πονηρός   8.11; 24.27; 42.7, 11; 52.13; 54.3;
   78.17; 104.9; (ὁ π., the Devil) 102.14;
   110.26; sim. 82.23; (πνεύματα) 108.10,
   25; 116.13; -ῶς 82.22
πορνεία   24.3; 100.24
πορνικός (εἴδωλον) 100.29; (φαντασία)
   100.26
πόρνος   124.20

πραιπόσιτος   72.17; (Baanes) 46.10;
   80.5, 8
πραιτώριος, city prefect   42.3
πρᾶξις, synodical act   80.12, 15, 19, 26;
   82.1, 12
πραΰτης   6.1; 12.23; 102.16, 19; 130.29
πρεσβευτής   42.15
πρεσβύτερος, presbyter   22.1;
   36.12; 46.24; 86.20; (γενεά) 2.19; ἡ
   πρεσβυτέρη Ῥώμη 46.20; 86.29
προαίρεσις (φονική)   62.22; 88.16
προαιώνιος   30.4
πρόεδρος (of patriarch)   20.16
προέλευσις   72.6
προθέλυμνον   100.27
προθυμία   16.14; 102.32
προκαθεζόμενος (of patriarch)   66.7
προκαθίζειν   86.26
προκατανοεῖν   30.6
προκαταρκτικός (αἰτία)   32.3
προκατηχεῖν   18.1
προκοπή   38.28
πρόληψις   2.25
πρόνοια (Θεοῦ)   8.16; 58.18; 70.6;
   128.2; sim. 54.26; 114.22; (of monastic
   superior) 14.25; (of rulers) 44.1
προνομεύεσθαι   130.12
προπάτωρ   118.30
πρόρρησις   120.24; (ἀποστολική) 60.12
προσευχή   12.20; 14.21; 18.25; 44.23;
   96.9; 98.31; 100.27; 104.2; 130.13
προσκυνεῖν   84.20, 23
προσκύνησις   108.2; 132.4
προσοχθίζειν   42.2; 64.28; 78.12; 126.12
πρόσταγμα (βασιλικόν)   56.13; (θεοῦ)
   70.28; (of church official) 116.29
προστασία (of patriarch)   20.31
προσφορά   60.30; 96.17
προφητεία   70.30
προφητεύειν   120.4
προφητικός (sup.)   122.7
προχειρίζεσθαι   6.5; 20.19, 31; 32.30;
   38.17; 46.12; 48.29; 60.27; 86.5; 128.11
προχείρισις   126.17
πρωτασηκρῆτις (Photius)   32.29
πρωτόθρονος   128.25

πρῶτος: τὰ π., highest rank   4.28
πρωτοσπαθάριος (Photius)   32.29;
   (Theophilus) 60.26
πρωτοστάτης (of Photius)   130.20
πρωτότοκος   6.21; 130.6
πρωτότυπον   18.5
πτύξ (pl.), book covers   120.8
πύλη (of Hagia Sophia)   84.19
πῦρ (οὐράνιον)   96.20
πύργος (τῆς ὀρθοδοξίας)   8.18
πυρετός   116.12
ῥαβδοῦχος, police constable   64.26
ῥᾳδιουργία   120.22
ῥαθυμία   102.27
ῥήξ (Φραγγίας)   76.17
ῥητορική   34.2
ῥῖγος   116.12
ῥομφαία   26.6
ῥυπαίνειν   94.16; 100.26
σακελλάριος   116.19
σεισμός   56.28; 58.1, 3, 18; 64.30; 92.29
σελέντιον   84.7
σεμνεῖον, monastery   8.24
σημεῖον, miraculous sign   18.31;
   ominous sign 94.12
σιδηροδέσμιος   40.19
σιμικίνθιον   116.1
σκαιότης   48.27
σκανδαλίζειν   128.4
σκάνδαλον   26.7; 30.6, 9, 12; 34.30; 60.1;
   86.1; 88.28; 90.27, 29; 130.26
σκανδαλοποιός   124.2
σκευώρημα   62.21
σκευωρία   46.5; 64.23; 82.31
σκῆπτρα   4.30; 10.20
σκίμπους   108.4; 116.3
σκοπός   20.33; 32.9; 40.31; 62.16; 130.23
σκοτόμαινα   36.25
σολέα   72.12
σορός   108.12, 17; 116.16; (μαρμαρινή)
   108.24
σουδάριον   116.1
σοφία   34.13, 23; 70.13; 120.12; (ἡ
   ἀληθής) 34.16; (δαιμονιώδης) 122.9;
   (κοσμική) 32.32; 34.25
σοφιστής   74.27; 84.3

σπαθάριος   86.6
σπυρίς   54.19
σταυροειδῶς   52.18
σταυρομάχος   130.21
σταυροπάτης   92.14
σταυροπατία   30.25
σταυρός   46.26; 96.22; (on document)
   52.25, 26; 124.27
στέμμα   76.6
στεφανοῦσθαι   6.22
στήλη (Ἰουστίνου)   66.3
στηλιτεύεσθαι   74.22
στίχος   82.16
στολή   12.11; (ἀρχιερατική) 46.23;
   (δουλική) 56.19; (ἱεραρχική) 50.8;
   106.21; (λαϊκή) 54.19; (λευκή) 54.28
στόλος (βασιλικός)   44.5; 78.25
στραγγαλιά   110.5
στρατεύεσθαι   6.6
στρατηγός   6.5; 114.7
στρατιώτης   40.1; 54.13; 74.12
στρατοπεδάρχης   114.13
στροβίλιον   94.10
σύγγραμμα   120.5
συγγραφή   30.14
συγγράφω   2.4
συγκακοπαθεῖν   86.3
συγκαταλήγειν   106.18
συγκατασκευάζεσθαι   120.11
σύγκελλος   86.17, 20
συγκλητικός, of senatorial rank   48.1;
   68.12
σύγκλητος, senate   4.29; 82.30; 86.28;
   88.23
συγκροτεῖν   76.10; 92.21
συκοφαντεῖν   64.8; 124.15; 126.9
συκοφάντης   64.14; 90.17
συκοφαντία   68.31; 82.21
συλλειτουργεῖν   42.1
συλλειτουργός   124.18
συμβασιλεύειν   78.16
σύμβολον   126.22; (ἀγαθά) 84.26
συμπεριάγεσθαι   74.28
συμποσιάζεσθαι   66.16
συνάγειν (ref. synod/bishops)   40.27;
   76.12

συναγωνίζεσθαι 18.23
συναθλεῖν 86.24
συναναιρεῖσθαι 44.29
συνάναρχος 98.24; 132.5
συναπάγειν 88.4
συναπέρχεσθαι 106.18
συνασπιστής 10.11
συνέδριον 46.3, 31
συνεπιψηφίζεσθαι 50.14
συνήγορος 76.1
σύνθρονον 72.14
συνοδικός (βίβλος) 82.20; (κρίσις)
  88.31; (πρᾶξις) 80.12
σύνοδος 8.16; 46.13, 22; 58.26, 28; 70.19;
  76.9; 84.5, 30; 88.5, 11; 90.6, 9, 11; 92.3,
  6, 17, 21; 94.4, 19; 122.20, 23; 124.24
σύνταγμα 70.13
συνωμότης 10.11
σφαγιάζεσθαι 118.1
σφραγίζειν, seal (μολίβδῳ) 80.6; make
  sign of cross 106.11 (cf. 16.17)
σφραγίς 128.15
σχῆμα monastic habit 6.13; 26.27;
  46.29; 62.24; 122.2; (δουλικόν) 56.3;
  (κληρικῶν) 10.12; sim. 28.5; semblance
  30.18
σχηματίζειν 70.28
σχολαί 26.11
σχολάζειν, to be without a see (of
  bp.) 10.25; 128.22; to study/devote
  time to 12.15; 34.9; 98.28
σωτηρία 20.11; 44.25, 31; 96.30; 116.6
σωτήριος 2.8; 102.3; 118.9
σωφροσύνη 16.32; 22.28, 32; 100.30
τάγμα 48.7; (τῶν ἱκανάτων) 6.27
ταλανισμός 30.10
ταξιάρχος/ταξιάρχης (ὁ μέγας τ.) 14.29
τάξις 86.30; 88.12; (μοναδική) 18.15;
  (πνευματικῆς ἀκολουθίας) 16.11;
  (πραιποσίτων) 72.17; (τῶν πατρικίων)
  84.20
ταπεινοφροσύνη 34.15; 100.15, 27;
  130.28
ταπεινόφρων 34.20
ταπείνωσις 12.24; 104.6
ταραχή 36.25; 68.8; 94.12; 104.28

ταραχοποιός 64.4; 94.13
τάφος (of Ignatius) 110.21; 112.28; 114.3;
  116.21, 24
τεκμήριον 92.20; 94.13; 96.18
τελειότης 14.4; 22.18; 96.28
τέμενος 40.28; 78.13
τέρας 114.31
τεράστιον 110.11
τετράπλευρος (κίων) 94.9
τολμητίας 82.24; 130.7
τοποτηρητής 42.16, 30; 46.7, 20; 58.21;
  76.14; 86.12, 17, 32; 88.22
τράπεζα 68.5; 96.18, 21
τραπέζιον 68.13
τριπόθητος 130.6
τρισκατάρατος 74.26
τρισυπόστατος (θεαρχία) 98.23
τροχαντήρ (πλοίου) 44.18
τύλος (γονάτων) 12.20
τυραννεῖν 52.29; 90.20; 92.11
τυραννικός (γνώμη) 124.9; (χείρ) 6.32;
  8.22; -ῶς 6.4; 48.31
τυραννίς 10.10; 16.19
τύραννος 10.13; 18.12
τυρεύειν 38.32
τυφλός 116.10
τυφλώττειν 94.27
ὕβρις 44.7; 72.26; 116.22; 122.27
ὑπαγορία 82.23
ὑπαίτιος 20.10
ὑπακοή 12.24
ὑπαναγινώσκειν (in a council) 48.13
ὕπαρ 74.1
ὑπεράγιος 54.32; 130.29
ὑπέραγνος 130.30
ὑπεράμωμος (Θεομήτωρ) 98.26
ὑπεραναβαίνειν 98.18
ὑπεράπειρος 130.24
ὑπερασπισμός 84.11
ὑπερηφανία 34.29; 76.27; 104.3, 7
ὑπεροπτικός (τὸ ὑ.) 24.13
ὑπερορία 18.9; 68.30; 118.17
ὑπερορίζειν 8.24; 28.14; 40.23; 78.24
ὑπερούσιος (Τριάς) 28.22; adv. 102.17
ὑπερουσιότης 98.20
ὑπερῷα (of Hagia Sophia) 84.18

ὑπεύθυνος 58.6; 72.12; 88.14; 90.12
ὑπογράφειν 40.32; 52.27; 88.31; 128.17
ὑπογραφή 52.29; 76.23
ὑποδιάκονος 16.11; 36.12; 50.9
ὑποκριτής 92.9; 130.20
ὑπομονή 2.11; 12.21
ὑποταγή 34.19
ὑποτυποῦσθαι 70.27
ὑπουργία 82.24
ὑποχώρησις 6.10
ὑφηγητής 4.1; 20.13
ὑψηλοφρονεῖν 104.18
φενακίζεσθαι 8.27
φθόνος 50.28 bis; 104.28; 116.27;
φιλανθρωπία 94.23; 102.17
φιλαργυρία 30.23; 50.2; 100.32
φιλαρχία 30.24; 90.20; 126.15; 130.22
φιλαυτία 30.23
φιληδονία 30.23
φιλονεικεῖν 70.3
φιλονεικία 36.26
φιλοσοφία 34.2
φιλοτιμία 38.9; 68.21, 24; 126.25
φιλοτίμως 10.7
φιλοφρόνως 58.21
φοινίσσειν 52.22
φονικός (βουλή) 70.15; (προαίρεσις)
    62.21; 88.15
φόνιος (λύκος) 122.17
φόνος 6.8
φοράδην 118.3
φρενοβλάβεια 16.29
φρουρά 8.9; 28.9; 40.13; 64.15
φυγάς 8.2; 58.5
φυλακή 18.9; 42.3; 124.10, 28; guard
    74.16

φύλαξ 54.21; 64.14
φυσιοῦσθαι 34.28; 104.19
φωτίζειν 116.10
φωτοφανής 98.10
χαρά 102.25, 31
χάρις 14.13; 16.13; 18.28; 34.16; 96.5, 20;
    110.15; 114.32; 130.7
χάρτη, document 52.25
χαρτίον 120.6
χαρτοφύλαξ 40.24
χειρόγραφον 38.20, 28; 90.1; 92.14;
    124.27; 126.27
χειροθεσία, handwriting style 120.7
χειροτονεῖν 36.21; 38.15; 48.10, 20; 60.2,
    25; 76.30; 84.29; 90.5, 22; 128.9; 130.8
χειροτονία 36.21, 29; 38.23; 88.2; 96.1;
    122.27; 126.27
χειρουργεῖν 114.21
χοροστασία 106.6
χριστοφιλής (sup.) 118.7
χρωματικός (ζωγραφία) 80.17
ψαλμῳδία 12.19
ψεύδεσθαι 80.3
ψευδής 42.23; 82.14; 120.25
ψευδοέπεια 88.17
ψευδομάρτυς 46.32
ψευδορκία 48.13
ψεῦδος 2.25; 24.14; 82.18; 120.4; 128.13
ψευδοσύλλογος 76.15
ψηφίζεσθαι 22.11
ψῆφος 4.29 bis; 16.4; 20.15; 22.7; 48.28;
    50.14; 58.29; 88.8, 26, 30; 90.16, 19
ψυχαγωγεῖν 96.5; 104.17
ψυχικός (σοφία),
    material-minded 122.9
ὠμοφόριον 50.12; 126.21

INDEX FONTIUM

ALII SCRIPTORES

Basilius Caesariensis
Ep. 130, PG 32:564 (B9–C3)   **70**.15–19
Ep. 293.17–20   **102**.10
Hom. in pr. prov., PG 31:421A   **22**.29–30
Liturg., PG 31:1636   **84**.23–25

Canones apostolorum
29   **48**.14–17, **90**.16–19

CPG
I 392   **28**.32
II 121   **56**.21
II 201   **26**.10

Demosthenes
De fals. leg. 81.4   **62**.20–21

Dionysius Halicarnassensis
Ant. Rom. X 13.4   **62**.20–21

Gregorius Nazianzenus
Or. II, PG 35:461B   **22**.29–30
Or. XXXII, PG 36:209A   **34**.20
Or. XL, PG 36:369A   **34**.20
In laud. Cypr., PG 35:1192B   **2**.10
Ad Julianum, PG 35:1049A   **2**.10
Contra Jul. I, PG 35:533A   **34**.12–13
Or. fun. in Bas., cap. 15   **32**.30–31
Or. fun. in Bas., cap. 26   **36**.10–11
Or. fun. in Bas., cap. 79   **106**.5–6

GENERAL INDEX